SPACES ON THE SPECTRUM

SPACES ON THE SPECTRUM

HOW AUTISM MOVEMENTS RESIST EXPERTS AND CREATE KNOWLEDGE

CATHERINE TAN

Columbia University Press *New York*

Columbia University Press
Publishers Since 1893
New York   Chichester, West Sussex
cup.columbia.edu

Library of Congress Cataloging-in-Publication Data
Names: Tan, Catherine, author.
Title: Spaces on the spectrum : how autism movements resist experts
and create knowledge / Catherine Tan.
Description: New York : Columbia University Press, [2024] |
Includes bibliographical references and index.
Identifiers: LCCN 2023027772 | ISBN 9780231206129 (hardback) |
ISBN 9780231206136 (trade paperback) |
ISBN 9780231556330 (ebook)
Subjects: LCSH: Autism spectrum disorders. | Autistic people—
Social conditions. | Sociology of disability.
Classification: LCC HV1570.23 .T36 2024 | DDC 616.85/882—
dc23/eng/20230728
LC record available at https://lccn.loc.gov/2023027772

Cover design: Noah Arlow

SPACES ON THE SPECTRUM

HOW AUTISM MOVEMENTS RESIST EXPERTS AND CREATE KNOWLEDGE

CATHERINE TAN

Columbia University Press   *New York*

Columbia University Press
Publishers Since 1893
New York   Chichester, West Sussex
cup.columbia.edu

Library of Congress Cataloging-in-Publication Data
Names: Tan, Catherine, author.
Title: Spaces on the spectrum : how autism movements resist experts
and create knowledge / Catherine Tan.
Description: New York : Columbia University Press, [2024] |
Includes bibliographical references and index.
Identifiers: LCCN 2023027772 | ISBN 9780231206129 (hardback) |
ISBN 9780231206136 (trade paperback) |
ISBN 9780231556330 (ebook)
Subjects: LCSH: Autism spectrum disorders. | Autistic people—
Social conditions. | Sociology of disability.
Classification: LCC HV1570.23 .T36 2024 | DDC 616.85/882—
dc23/eng/20230728
LC record available at https://lccn.loc.gov/2023027772

Cover design: Noah Arlow

For my parents,
Mão Tân and Bích Vân Đỗ

CONTENTS

PREFACE AND POSITION

I answered a Craigslist ad online in 2006. Stories that start this way usually have grisly endings; not in this case fortunately. The ad was posted by a couple in their early forties—Danuta and Allan—in urgent need of a babysitter for their autistic six-year-old son, Mickey (these are all pseudonyms). I was in my junior year of college and needed a flexible, part-time job. I met them at their stylish home located in Hillcrest, one of the most fashionable neighborhoods in San Diego at the time. It was decorated with French country decor. Danuta proudly shared that the light fixtures were alabaster, the paint on the walls was by Ralph Lauren, and the end table with floral inlay was an early-twentieth-century replication of a nineteenth-century design. They needed someone to start immediately because in a few days they were going to go to Poland. At that time, everything I knew about autism came from the movie *Rainman* and a *Time Magazine* article from 2002. But they judged me to be a nice and responsible enough stranger to trust with their only child, so I was promptly hired to stay with Mickey at night after the daytime nanny went home. To keep their minds at ease, I think they had a camera hidden somewhere in the house (I found the device's packaging a couple of weeks later). After

Danuta and Allan returned from their trip, I stayed on and continued babysitting Mickey for another two years, ten to fifteen hours each week.

Mickey had bright eyes and moppy brown hair. Allan affectionately called him Squiggles. Mickey would laugh uncontrollably when I pulled him around the spacious house on a blanket or swung him around by his arms in the backyard. He rarely cried or showed signs of discontent—except briefly once when I was pushing him on the swing and he flew off (he was fine). He had a sophisticated palate compared to the typical American child who only eats beige things. Mickey required a lot of support. I remember him cycling through different behavioral therapists; one of them rewarded him with gummy bears and another therapist pressed a clicker whenever he did something correctly. Danuta and Allan laughed uneasily, saying it was too much like animal training. Mickey did not have any verbal language and possessed limited sign language. He avoided eye contact and stared into the distance. If left alone, he could spin the wheels of his toy cars and the bobbles of his rattle for hours, rhythmically cooing to himself. Sometimes he would strain his face, furrow his brows, and shake his toys in frustration. When we lounged around with nothing to do, I sometimes sang to him Belle and Sebastian's "Judy and the Dream of Horses." I took him everywhere—diners, parks, the zoo, the annual pride parade, and my field site when I was working on my senior thesis. He was easy to manage, in the sense that he did not wander off or self-injure, but I had trouble interpreting the subtleties of his communication. I just knew he enjoyed eating and being swung around.

I also spent a lot of time with Danuta. She worked part-time as a piano teacher and was often at home doing chores and gardening as I watched Mickey. Danuta was always affectionate with him even though he rarely reciprocated, and she was patient even when he yanked fistfuls of her hair. Over time, Danuta and I became friends, socializing outside of my work hours. She wistfully said that Mickey verbally speaks to her when he appears in her dreams. She would get gloomy when thinking about how people felt sorry for her and her son. She could not help but speculate why Mickey is autistic. One evening, she confessed that before she knew she was pregnant, she went into a jacuzzi—*Could that have been the cause?* Another day, while she was putting away the laundry, she told me that they recently learned that Allan had an aunt who was intellectually disabled, suggesting Mickey's autism might have been inherited. To Danuta and Allan, Mickey represented so many unknowns about the past, present, and future. They worried a lot about what would happen to Mickey when he got older: Who will love him when they die? Later, some of their worries were put slightly at ease with the birth of another baby boy, the future conservator.

Micky was just one child. I never met another autistic child like him. I learned very little about autism, the condition, from working with him actually. However, being part of his and his parents' lives, I learned to appreciate the complicated relationship between autism and the non-autistic world. I cannot speak for Mickey or his experiences, but as his babysitter, I knew what made my job easier and what made it harder. My job felt easier when the people around us were patient and forgiving. My job felt harder when I could sense strangers pitying him. Of course, at the end of the day, I was able to just step away—this was my privilege. I am writing this book as a neurotypical person who was introduced to the world of autism through the kindness of autistic people, parents of autistic children, and practitioners. For years, they welcomed me into their lives and entrusted me with their stories. My intent (and hope) is that this book will honor the time my participants so generously shared.

ACKNOWLEDGMENTS

I would like to thank the participants of my study for sharing their stories and inviting me into their communities. Without them, there would be no book to write.

I cannot believe it took ten years to go from institutional review board approval to publisher approval. I really hope my next book does not take this long. Anyway, a lot of life happened over the last decade. During this time, so many people have supported me and this project.

Thank you to the team at Columbia University Press for making this book real. I especially want to thank Eric Schwartz for his support, feedback on chapters, and responsiveness—honestly, I do not know anyone who responds to emails as quickly as him. I am also especially thankful to my anonymous readers. Their suggestions and comments have made this book so much stronger and better. Readers, thank you for your time and invaluable insights.

Thank you to Allison Van Deventer for editing my book proposal and manuscript. I cannot wait to see your own book (coauthored with Katelyn E. Knox), *The Dissertation-to-Book-Workbook: Exercises for Developing and Revising Your Book Manuscript*, on the shelf soon! Also, thank you to Alana Dunn for organizing my bibliography.

I am beyond thankful to Jennifer Reich, who has carefully read this book more times than anyone else has or ever will. She has been there since this book was a mere proposal. I cannot thank you enough for your brilliant and incisive feedback. I have long admired your work and am so honored to have your guidance through this process. You should be getting a stained-glass squirrel lamp in the mail any day now—please accept this as a token of my appreciation.

Thank you, Miranda Waggoner, for your detailed and thoughtful comments on the full book manuscript. I was especially moved by your enthusiasm. Preparing a book for publication is a little scary, but your kind words inspired confidence.

I would have never pursued an academic career in sociology had it not been for the encouragement and advising I received from Christena Turner and Jeff Haydu at the University of California, San Diego, where I completed my bachelor's degree. I took my first sociological methods course with Christena in 2006 and knew then that this is what I wanted to do with my career. Afterward, I completed my senior thesis with Jeff, which allowed me to expand and develop the project I started in Christena's class. Since graduating from the University of California, San Diego in 2008, I get to see Christena and Jeff at least once a year. I feel so deeply fortunate to have the both of them in my life as mentors and friends.

I am thankful to my advisor and mentors at Brandeis University, where I completed my PhD. Peter Conrad, Sara Shostak, David Cunningham, and Laura Miller have each helped me become a stronger and more confident scholar. Peter Conrad, my advisor and dissertation chair, inspired this study after we coauthored a book chapter comparing the online presence of autism advocacy groups. Peter has been a source of inspiration and encouragement. Aside from teaching me how to think like a sociologist, Peter also modeled a healthy and balanced academic life. I am so honored to have been one of his advisees. From the Qualifying Portfolio to papers for journal submission, I turned to Sara for her sharp insights and critiques. When I could not see the forest for the trees, she was the one who pushed me to ask, "What is this a case of?" Throughout my graduate career, Laura offered constructive though brutal honesty on my work, provided extremely thorough remarks and edits on every piece of writing I sent her, and held me accountable—and for all that, I am so grateful to have had her as a mentor. On a more personal level, I consider Laura a very good friend. She is both wise and fun. I am sure that when this book comes out, we will celebrate over tiki cocktails.

I want to thank Gil Eyal, Thomas Mackie, and Laura Senier for providing opportunities for me grow as a sociologist. During my master's program at Columbia, I worked with Gil on a small study that examined an autism-only school; this resulted in my first published paper. I learned so much more about qualitative research from that project than from any methods course. Even though I have not been his student since 2010, Gil has always been so generous with his time and mentorship. He also gave me invaluable feedback on this manuscript at my book workshop. Since our time together at Brandeis, Tom has been both a friend and a role model. Toward the end of my graduate program, Tom brought me on as a research associate to work on the ABCD Project, a collaboration between multiple universities in Boston. That experience taught me how to work within a team and helped hone my academic writing skills. In my last year of graduate school, I got to work with Laura Senier. I eagerly welcomed this opportunity to explore a topic with which I was previously unfamiliar. I also appreciated Laura's mentorship style, which was full of enthusiasm and humor.

I would like to thank my community at Vassar College. I am so lucky to be part of this vibrant sociology department with John Andrews, Pinar Batur, Light Carruyo, Abby Coplin, Diane Harriford, Seungsook Moon, Leonard Nevarez, Erendira Rueda, and Gina La Fata—thank you for being wonderful, supportive colleagues. I am incredibly appreciative of Chris White, who participated in my book workshop and provided important feedback. Thank you, Marty, for occasionally popping into my office to ask how the book is coming along and cheer me on. Thank you to the dean of faculty, Bill Hoynes, and president, Elizabeth Bradley, for taking an interest in my research and reading my articles when they are published. It means so much to me. Across Vassar's campus, I am so grateful for the friendships I have made so far: Liz Lastra, Laura Haynes, Lee Kennedy-Shaffer, Katelyn Butler, Zach Cofran, Jess Beck, Louis Römer, Johanna Römer, April Beisaw, Jackie Villadsen, Payton Small, Jasmine Syedullah, Justin Patch, Osman Nemli, Anna Gommerstadt, Katie Gemmill, Amy Chin, Gretchen Lieb, Elizabeth Salmon, and so many others. They are not only colleagues but trivia teammates, boardgame opponents, hiking partners, writing buddies, stained glass classmates, and dates to the Raccoon Saloon.

I would like to thank the many other scholars who have supported me and my work over the last several years, including Phil Brown, Linda Blum, and Valerie Leiter.

I have dedicated this book to Mom and Ba. Both my parents, Mão Tân and Bích Vân Đỗ, worked incredibly hard and made many sacrifices to give my sister and me the educational opportunities that they did not have. Everything went into our education. In addition to school, I had private tutors, extra classes, and camps for almost every subject: math, English, French, creative writing, geometry with origami, SAT prep, guitar, piano, violin, typing, ballet, etc. They wanted me to go into medicine or pharmaceuticals, financially stable and reliable careers—and in a surprising turn, I went into sociology, which does not have any of the qualities that make health care seem so attractive to immigrant parents. It can be a tragedy to lose a child to social science—so, I thank you, Mom and Ba, for your unwavering and unconditional love and trust; for taking interest in my research; and for respecting how I used the opportunities you provided me, even if it was not what you had expected.

To my family, I am so lucky to have your love and support. Carol Tan (sister), Karter Harmon (sibling-in-law), Melissa Matusky (cousin-in-law), and Mark Graney (cousin-in-law) have all generously served as my nonsociologist readers, providing feedback on early drafts of the introduction and book proposal. Thank you to my grandmother, aunts, and uncles who, over the past three decades, have told me they are proud, celebrated my achievements, and showed up to my graduations. They also cared for me when I was a child, taking me to school, feeding me, and on a couple of occasions, volunteering at my kindergarten.

I would like to thank my husband, Josh Tan. Peter Conrad once said that, Josh, being an astronomer, is occupied with life up there and I, as a sociologist, am occupied with life down here. I took that to mean that our relationship is complementary and balanced, but I know that Josh puts in so much more work. Throughout my career, from the very beginning to now, Josh has provided encouragement and patience. This book exists because I am deeply cared for by him. I have more hours in a day than most people because Josh gives his time to me. He brings me coffee every morning, picks up the groceries, cooks dinner, does the laundry, cares for the dog, reads drafts, and the list goes on. It is impossible to fully express how much I appreciate everything he does each day to support my ambitions. My successes are afforded by the sacrifices he makes. Josh, I love you and thank you for loving me.

And thank you to my dog, Piscola, for being cute and chaotic. That said, she tried to undermine this project a number of times, destroying some books and articles I needed for the preparation of this manuscript. So reader, if you find my literature lacking and theory weak . . . it's the dog's fault.

I am endlessly grateful for my wonderful friends. I do not know how I managed to form so many meaningful relationships with such loving, brilliant, and intense people. There is the "Harlem Crew," which includes Josh, James Jones, Heba Gowayed, Janice Gallagher, Nick Occhiuto, and Efrain Guerrero. They make life rich, loud, ridiculous, and joyful. I met James, whom I call my other husband, at Columbia in 2009 and we became instant friends. He has read everything I have ever written, often before anyone else. He has given invaluable feedback on every paper, chapter, and outfit. I distinctly remember us, in the earliest days, dreaming of our futures while on the 2 train into Greenwich Village. Back then, all of now seemed so far away. But slowly and gradually, dissertations were defended, jobs were accepted, weddings were celebrated, homes were made, books were written. In a profession that is known to separate partners, friends, and family by distance, I feel so lucky to have not been separated from him—whom I consider to be all three. James introduced me to two other very important people: Janice and Heba. Janice and I spent hours writing our books next to each other. The best part, of course, was not the productivity but all the breaks we got to take together. Heba is a woman whose love and loyalty are so fierce you fear for the lives of your own enemies. She has more faith in me than I have in myself. Heba's encouragement and brilliant insights have pushed me across so many difficult finish lines (especially this one). Where would I be had she not showed up at my door years ago with a tray of chicken shawarma and bowl of hummus?

Thank you to Janani Umamaheswar, my dear friend and partner in research. I met her during the darkest time, in the bleakest place, Connecticut. At the new faculty orientation at Southern Connecticut State University, we looked into each other's eyes and knew we had made a huge mistake. Luckily, we have since moved on. Although it was a miserable two years, our marvelous friendship made it all worthwhile.

The friends I made in graduate school are lifelong friends. I might have finished my PhD sooner had they not made the process so much fun. Thank you, Alexis Mann, Jaleh Jalili, Kim Lucas, Sara Chaganti, Rachel Minkin, and Margaret Minkin, for the many study parties, accountability groups (that essentially turned into one long fundraiser for the pasta party), margaritas at Margaritas after pro-seminars, summers in Maine, ice cream cakes, tiki bars (this includes you, Laura Miller), annual apple-picking and Topsfield fair outings, vacations, and holiday parties. We had a lot of adventures those years, but what I appreciate most is finding a group of friends with whom to share the joys and frustrations of academic life, a group of friends who lift each other up. Even now, each week, I look forward to catching up with Alexis and Jaleh over Zoom. These scheduled conversations were especially important to me that first fall after graduation when we were finally adults but felt more unsettled than ever before. Although we have scattered across the country, when we find ourselves together, everything feels the same. Thank you for being my friends then and now.

Hold on, I have more friends to thank! Thank you, Anny Fenton, for your dark sense of humor, our Facetime work parties, and for letting me be your squatter roommate during my post-doc (I would have had to compromise my lifestyle if it were not for your and Neil's generosity that year). Thank you, Olivia Nicol, for your friendship and for inspiring me to be a better academic. I am not sure if you remember, but when I started the master's program, Columbia assigned you to be my grad buddy (or whatever it was called). Anyway, I am grateful they paired us together. Thank you, Becky Reimers, for being a fabulous friend since the third grade and for answering my many random medical questions as I was working on parts of this book (I am so glad you became a doctor).

Thank you, Guadalupe Castro and Paola Herrera, for keeping our house functioning. Guadalupe, you cared for Josh and I for so many years, giving us the gift of time to focus on our education and careers—we sincerely appreciate everything you have done for us.

Last but certainly not least, I want to express my appreciation to the teachers and other friends who have helped me find meaning in activities outside of academia. They brought balance to my life while I was writing this book (and the dissertation that came before it). Thank you to every person and horse at MLC Farm: Michelle Clopp for putting up with my stubbornness every Wednesday morning, Francisco and JB for keeping the farm running, and Capri, Glory, and Hank for being such good horses most of the time. Thank you to Jen Kola at Canton Equestrian, to Eduardo Macchino and Vale Hanel Gotelli at Centro Ecuestre Equilibre. Thank you, Gary and Natalie Dodge, for teaching me how to work with stained glass. Without the two of you, I would not have placed first at the Dutchess County Fair; granted, my entry was alone in its category.

I am truly lucky to have all these wonderful people in my life. Thank you.

SPACES ON THE SPECTRUM

1

WARRIORS AND ALIENS

Challenging Autism Experts

"**W**elcome to this warrior gang and we are bad motherfuckers!" exclaimed Jenny McCarthy to an audience of applauding parents. Many wore T-shirts proudly embellished with titles like "Mommy Warrior" or "Daddy Warrior." During an early autumn weekend in 2015, nearly seven hundred parents gathered at the InterContinental Hotel in Dallas, Texas, to learn and exchange combat strategies. McCarthy, a media personality who is infamous for her vaccine skepticism, exhorted her audience to remain stalwart in this fight: "If something doesn't work in your treatment along the way, you do *not* give up hope!" She admitted that it would be a very long war, possibly an endless one. Everyone in the room, including McCarthy, was fighting the same elusive enemy on their home turf: autism, a developmental disability that is highly diverse in its biology and behavioral presentation.

During McCarthy's talk, Melissa was sitting in the audience. As an active member of this community, she had heard variations of this talk before at other events and conferences. Like many other "warrior" parents in the room, she envisions autism as residing within her son, Logan—but distinctly separate from him. At one extreme, there was the "Tasmanian devil" who smeared feces on the walls and spat in her face; on the other, there was "my kid" who had "a very good sense of humor" and was "very loving and friendly." In the view of parents like Melissa, autism is not inherent to their children; rather, these parents insist that somewhere inside is a "typical," non-autistic person fighting to surface. Melissa remembered when it all started in July 2006: "He was developing fine and then he got his 15-month shots and—the MMR [measles-mumps-rubella], the DTaP [diphtheria, tetanus, and pertussis], and the Hib [Haemophilus influenzae type B]. And within three weeks Logan started losing different skills. He stopped responding to his name. He started hand-flapping, toe-walking. He became extremely afraid." Other parents told me similar stories about their children developing this complex developmental disability. They contended that autism is triggered by a variety of environmental exposures. Many blamed early childhood vaccines. Even though the idea of a link between vaccines and autism has been studied extensively and disproven definitively,[1] Melissa firmly maintained, "I know what happened to my child." Like the other warrior parents, she saw her child as tragically injured and sick, rather than born this way. Unsurprisingly, this belief has attracted criticism from medical professionals, scientists, and others outside this warrior parent community. As Melissa said, "We get all kinds of haters."

Vaccine hesitancy may be the main issue attracting "haters": it has contributed to the resurgence of vaccine-preventable diseases across the world.[2] But the public knows little about how some parents find hope in the darkness of vaccine fear. Warrior parents believe they can "recover" their children by reversing vaccine and other environmental injuries with alternative and experimental interventions, which I will refer to here as *alternative biomedicine* (parents and practitioners refer to it simply as "biomedical" or "biomed").[3] The basic narrative is this: if their children were at one point "typical" (not autistic) and later injured (made autistic), then they can be fixed and restored to their previous selves. After all, people can recover from all kinds of serious diseases and injuries—*so why not autism?* Though they are generally careful not to use the word "cure," the language of recovery assumes that there is a non-autistic child to bring back. Consequently, the goals of their experimental treatments are far more ambitious than those of popularly prescribed behavioral and educational therapies, which aim not to eradicate autism but rather to help autistic children develop adaptive skills. While popular interventions target *behavior*, alternative biomedical treatments locate autism within children's bodies and therefore target *biology*. Melissa, who is dedicated to Logan's recovery, has tried a number of these treatments, including special diets, vitamins, supplements, homeopathy, Flagyl (an antibiotic), Diflucan (an antifungal), hyperbaric oxygen therapy,[4] and chelation.[5] At one point, she even sought help from a magic buffalo. Aware of how these efforts may come across to an outsider, she humorously admitted to me, "We've done some crazy, crazy things."

Later that evening, just a couple of miles from the hotel, Melissa and the other warrior parents gathered at the Cavanaugh Flight Museum, which boasts a large collection of vintage aircraft dating from World War I to the Vietnam War. They passed through the gift shop and entered an enormous lot of parked fighter planes. In the distance, against a sunset backdrop, an open hangar emanated a soft glow and pop music. Inside the hangar, the parents socialized, drank, and danced. A few waiters floated around with underseasoned chicken satay. The event was sponsored by a holistic health practitioner who regularly attended these conferences. When the music stopped, the first openly autistic Miss America contestant, Alexis Wineman, was

welcomed to the stage. She had the classic all-American aesthetic, in the sense that she was white and from Montana. She
spoke of her many impressive achievements with a faint, charming lisp. Although Wineman seemed to require fewer supports
than many of the attendees' autistic children and did not discuss
any use of treatment, her presence reminded Melissa and the
other parents of what they were fighting for and represented the
promises of alternative biomedicine.

At this same time, in the rural Midwest, Codey was also
advocating for his fellow autistic people. However, his journey
was less glamorous than that of Miss Montana, and it had taken
him in an entirely different direction. It began when Codey
started asking questions about his fifteen daily pills. For as long
as he could remember, he had taken an assortment of drugs, not
knowing what they were for or what was wrong with him. He
knew he was not well because throughout his childhood he had
regularly traveled a long way with his parents to see a special
doctor and have his blood drawn. Over the years, his medical
treatment became so routine that his parents stopped supervis-
ing him and trusted him to adhere to the regimen. Then, when
he was fourteen years old, Codey investigated each medication
and discovered something peculiar: "The treatment didn't make
sense." He was taking a mélange of drugs that appeared entirely
unrelated—an antibiotic for strep throat, antidepressants, blood
pressure medication, vitamin supplements, an iron supplement,
acidophilus, and herpes medication. *What was his problem?*
Unable to interpret the combination of drugs, Codey looked up
his doctor: "The doctor ended up being like one of those doctors
that's like, alternative cures for autism." And that was how he
finally learned his diagnosis.

Like members of the warrior gang, Codey's parents had
placed him on alternative biomedical treatments for most of his

childhood. When he found out what the drugs were for, Codey started hiding the pills: "And like I didn't feel any different. Nothing happened." Because his autism diagnosis had been kept secret from him, Codey gathered that his parents did not see the condition as a positive trait: "I was taught that it wasn't something to be proud of. Like, they had kept it from me all this time." He struggled with mental illness and suicidal ideation in the few years following his discovery. Then, during college, he had an epiphany: "I didn't really feel like [college] was something that was realistic for me as someone who was autistic and had mental health conditions. And then, I think by being there, I sort of came to the realization that it wasn't because of my disabilities that it would be unrealistic, but because people wouldn't be accommodating to said disabilities." This shift in perspective motivated Codey to "work so that other people wouldn't have to be in that situation where they felt like they couldn't do something." During college, Codey became more involved in autistic communities and disability rights organizations. After graduation, he was hired as a program coordinator for the Autistic Self Advocacy Network (ASAN), whose mission is to empower autistic people and promote inclusion—not treatment.

Autistic rights activists like Codey do not see themselves as "warriors," nor do they see themselves as sick or injured people in need of recovery. An *autistic rights* approach conceptualizes autism as a human difference that should be respected and valued. Activists described themselves to me as "aliens" from another planet. In his famous "Don't Mourn for Us" address, Jim Sinclair, an early leader of autistic self-advocacy, argued that autism is a way of *being*—and certainly *not* a disorder in need of a cure. Sinclair depicted autistic people as metaphorical aliens from another world, placed in the care of a different species. Similarly, Temple Grandin, an autistic woman who has made a successful career as an animal scientist and public speaker, has described her experiences in the world as those of an "anthropologist on Mars."[6] Both Grandin and Sinclair use the alien metaphor to express their sense of being foreigners among non-autistics.[7] As autistic aliens, they are not lesser humans; instead, they have their own ways of being and are incomparable to non-autistics. Autistic rights activists use this metaphor to suggest that the difficulties of being autistic are not inherent to the individual person but rather emerge from social, structural, and institutional arrangements. They pose that autism and the person are inextricable. To them, there is no child waiting to be saved, and there will never be a cure because there is nothing to cure. Activists denounce popular therapies that aim to extinguish autistic behaviors. Instead, they demand acceptance of their differences. After all, a Martian will never be an Earthling, no matter how hard they try.

Both Melissa and Codey wanted a better life for autistic people, but they held radically different ideas about what a better life meant and how it could be achieved. Melissa's intimacy with autism as a parent and Codey's autistic embodiment guided this divergence. Melissa wanted to help her son fit into society by becoming more *neurotypical*—that is, having a cognitive profile that is considered normal or typical. Codey wanted society to make space for *neurodivergent* people like him—that is, individuals whose cognitive profiles are different from what is considered normal or typical.[8] Accordingly, Melissa and Codey occupied nearly polar opposite worlds of autism that rarely came into contact. Their communities held conflicting beliefs, objectives, and strategies. Despite these differences, they each saw themselves as struggling against the "mainstream" and against a set of actors who seemed to enjoy greater legitimacy—experts, professionals, and other parents of autistic children. Their struggles, then, are struggles to have their experiences legitimized. Studying the alternative biomedical and autistic rights movements, this book examines how people like Melissa and Codey reimagine autism, create knowledge, and locate their marginalized positions within the broader field of autism.

With these two communities, I show how members construct *contentious knowledge*, or knowledge that aims to challenge expert authority and orthodoxy. Contentious knowledge is transformed into lived realities within the alternative biomedical and autistic rights movements. Resisting dominant knowledge and ways of knowing involves a sophisticated, complex infrastructure. When challengers are united by a sense of shared identity, science and health movements can provide spaces where they can freely produce, practice, and protect ideas that may lack external support or legitimacy. Such spaces are demarcated by both physical locations (like meetings, conferences, retreats, and doctors' offices) and social networks (among members, affiliates, and allies). These socio-spatial environments—insulated from the intrusion of outsiders and perceived threats—help cultivate and enact ideas.

Contentious knowledge is more than an abstraction; it is something that is interacted into existence. It emerges from the mobilization of shared conceptual, material, and social resources. This means that such knowledge has signs, signals, and tangible artifacts. Challenging mainstream understandings of autism— what it is, who the experts are, who has the right to represent autistic interests, how it should be studied, how it should be treated—is a collective and coordinated effort. Furthermore, these beliefs about autism give rise to the development of shared tools and social norms. Beliefs about autism even spill over to change the way members think about their values and identities more generally.

The heterogeneity of autism and autistic experiences engenders competing ideas about what is best for autistic people. As I show, the alternative biomedical and autistic rights movements represent two voices of discontent, both resisting what they perceive to be the "mainstream" and "dominant" paradigm. Members of both movements visualize the field of autism as a space dominated by privileged actors—people who are *not* them. They argue that current understandings of autism oversimplify a complicated condition, as evidenced by the underrepresentation of their experiences in research, public health information, and policies. Although their beliefs about autism are not completely outside the mainstream, movement members differentiate themselves from other stakeholders. This boundary work sharpens each community's shared sense of solidarity, which plays an important supporting role as they collectively create their own knowledge about autism.

WHO GETS TO SPEAK FOR AUTISM?

When Leo Kanner, a psychiatrist at Johns Hopkins Hospital, first described autism in 1943, he observed an "*inability to relate themselves* in the ordinary way to people and situations from the beginning of life. . . . There is from the start an *extreme autistic aloneness* that, whenever possible, disregards, ignores, shuts out anything that comes to the child from the outside."[9] In 1980, autism was recognized as its own separate diagnosis in the *Diagnostic and Statistical Manual of Mental Disorders*. Since then, the diagnostic criteria have transformed through multiple iterations.

Today, autism spectrum disorder is described as a complex developmental disability characterized by atypical social communication and restricted and repetitive behaviors.[10] It was once considered to be a very rare condition, but as I write, autism is estimated to impact 1 in 36 children in the United States[11]—a steep increase from 4 in 10,000 children in 1989.[12] Why did the numbers spike in such a short period of time? Sociologists have proposed a number of explanations for the increase. A historical analysis traces this rise to deinstitutionalization, which picked up in the 1970s, and diagnostic substitution.[13] When children with disabilities were residents of institutions, they were not well differentiated by diagnostic label. It was not until they were moved into the care of families and treated in the community that it became advantageous to distinguish autism from the general label of "mental retardation," which is managed merely with custodial care.[14] By framing autism as a condition somewhere between an illness and mental retardation, families positioned themselves to advocate for habilitation care and special therapies. Looking at the increasing prevalence of autism today, scholars have also considered the role of social influence, finding that when an autism-diagnosed child moves into a new neighborhood, other neurodivergent children from that area are more likely to be diagnosed with autism than with a different diagnostic label (like mental retardation).[15] These studies suggest that being diagnosed with autism confers certain advantages, such as access to services.

The field of autism is a crowded and diverse place. For one thing, the autism diagnosis is applied to a wide range of people. Daniel Navon and Gil Eyal argued that geneticization broadened the diagnostic criteria for autism.[16] What was once a rare condition has stretched to include a much larger population. As the diagnostic criteria have expanded, people who would not have qualified for an autism diagnosis previously now qualify. This change has introduced new genetic mutations into the diagnosed population, including mutations that were previously unrelated. This looping effect contributes to autism's genetic heterogeneity, broader phenotype, and increased prevalence over time.[17] The autism spectrum, then, includes many very different people—from those who require full-time assistance to those who maintain independent lives (i.e., employed, living alone). But the diversity is not simply a gradient from high support needs to low support needs. Atypical sensory processing and social communication present in multiple ways. Some people have co-occurring and comorbid conditions.[18] The types of support and services that individuals require across their lifetime also vary. Popular discourses on autism, then, which refer to it as a single, cohesive entity, do not come close to capturing the diversity of autistic experiences.

The field of autism, moreover, is occupied by many actors who are not autistic themselves: parents, doctors, researchers, therapists, educators, advocates, donors, and so on. These stakeholders often have competing interests. Advocacy, in particular, is a contentious arena where autistic individuals and the parents of autistic children struggle to dominate public discourse and secure scarce resources.[19] One of the largest and most influential players in autism advocacy is Autism Speaks, a parent-oriented organization that frames autism as a global health crisis and prioritizes biomedical research to understand its cause, treatment, and prevention. In awareness campaigns, the organization popularized the blue puzzle piece to symbolize autism's complexity and unknowns. Autistic activists who compete against this behemoth organization perceive the parents as powerful and privileged. Yet the parents see themselves as being up against "massive bureaucracies, fiscal policies, laws, and professionals."[20] Despite their relative advantages, parents too are struggling to obtain appropriate supports and services for their children.[21]

Drawing from their lived experiences, both autistic activists and parents of autistic children claim to represent autistic people in good faith. Autistic activists mobilize their firsthand, embodied knowledge to push for acceptance and inclusion. Critics, however, question whether the experiences they politicize are truly representative of the full autism spectrum.[22] Most parents do not have embodied knowledge of autism because they are not autistic themselves. Instead, they can only *imagine* how their children experience autism.[23] Parents are intimately tied to their children, but most will never truly know what it is like to be autistic themselves.[24]

Given the heterogeneity of autism and its many stakeholders, who gets to speak for autism? It is a contentious condition in the sense that autistic people, parents of autistic children, and professionals have competing visions of how autism and autistic people should be.[25] Any given group can provide only partial representation, a phrase that refers to what happens when actors claim to represent an entire group but in fact engage with only a subset of the constituency.[26] Scholars warn that partial representation may "crowd out" marginalized groups, such as autistic people who are unable to express their desires.[27] This is one of the trickiest parts of autism advocacy: determining who is best equipped to speak on behalf of those who have limited communication skills, cognitive disabilities, and intellectual disabilities. Both the alternative biomedical and autistic rights movements want to speak for people with autism and feel overshadowed by more dominant actors and organizations. And both raise issues that they feel are underrepresented or misrepresented in public discourse.

The alternative biomedical and autistic rights movements challenge what Phil Brown terms the *dominant epidemiological paradigm* (DEP), which is "a set of beliefs and practices about a disease and its causation embedded within science, government, and public life. It includes established institutions entrusted with the diagnosis, treatment, and care of disease sufferers, as well as journals, media, universities, medical philanthropies, and government officials."[28] In other words, the DEP is the way most stakeholders talk about, think about, and manage a condition. The DEP emerges and evolves through social processes. It is neither neutral nor static. In this book, the DEP refers to the way mainstream experts and professionals conceptualize autism (see table 1.1).

The ways science and health movements challenge the DEP are related to the ways their members perceive it. Alternative biomedical and autistic rights movement members position themselves in opposition to the "mainstream," which they have separately constructed to highlight key aspects of their discontent. For alternative biomedical members, the "mainstream" represents a stubborn commitment to genetics research, which they believe forecloses opportunities to innovate treatment. To them, the promises of genetics research are too distant and cannot help their children right now. It is for these reasons that the parents of this movement rarely align with Autism Speaks. For autistic rights members, the "mainstream" represents ableism and a medicalized perspective, which they argue disempowers autistic people and prioritizes the interests of parents (specifically, the interest in reducing undesirable autistic traits) rather than the well-being of autistic people themselves. Although members of these two movements have their own critiques, they share a general understanding of what the dominant autism framework entails. In disputing the DEP, the two movements separately explain what autism is and what can be done for autistic people.

To reimagine autism is to participate in a collective struggle. Members recognize that their knowledge lacks external

TABLE 1.1 AUTISM FRAMEWORKS

	Beliefs about causation	Characteristics/ presentations of autism	Approaches
Dominant epidemiological paradigm (DEP)	No known single cause; many different environmental, biologic, and genetic risk factors	Deficits in social communication and social interaction; restricted, repetitive patterns of behavior, interests, or activities	Behavior, development, and education-based programs (e.g., applied behavior analysis)
Alternative biomedical movement	Genetic vulnerabilities "triggered" by environmental insults, causing immunologically related dysfunctions	Dysfunction of multiple physiological systems; neurological impacts and behavioral presentations as downstream effects	Dietary changes, supplements, and alternative/ experimental therapies
Autistic rights movement	Genetic; born autistic	Sensory processing and social communication differences; disabilities and challenges as outcomes of social barriers	Social and cultural acceptance; policies, services, and support programs to increase inclusion

legitimacy. As they fortify the boundary between themselves and others, movement members unite around their shared experiential and embodied knowledge. Their solidarity nurtures opportunities to understand autism in a way that is more hopeful, promising, and actionable. But challenging the dominant autism framework also makes it possible to reimagine the current arrangement of resources, relationships, and authority. When alternative biomedical advocates contend that autism is a form of environmental injury,[29] they perpetuate vaccine fear, undermine trust in knowledge institutions (e.g., government, science, medicine), and create new treatment markets. Similarly, when autistic rights activists argue that autism is a natural human variation and not a disorder, their demands extend to labor laws, health and mental health care, public accommodations, and social interaction norms.[30]

Across alternative biomedical organizations, parents and practitioners pursue more or less the same controversial goal: autism recovery. (To clarify, this goal is controversial because there is no known evidence-based medical treatment for the core symptoms.) Victoria, who worked for Generation Rescue, an organization that promoted alternative biomedical practices, emphasized this objective during our interview. Under her direction, Generation Rescue was rebranding its image to change its anti-vaccines reputation. As Victoria explained, she had been tasked with "moving the organization from this fringe movement to this actual organization who's providing regular health care for kids; that is what every parent wants for their kid and every person wants for themselves." This message would align more closely with that of other alternative biomedical organizations, emphasizing treatment, parent-to-parent mentorship, and advocacy. Victoria has a personal stake in autism advocacy because she manages much of her autistic brother's health care.

Unlike other health social movements that aim to bring about structural and policy changes—those that impact environmental regulation, health policies, and/or science research[31]—the alternative biomedical movement primarily aims to change individuals. While there is some cross-membership with organizations that oppose vaccine mandates, as whole, the alternative biomedical movement focuses on supporting strategic, individual consumer choices when it comes to autism prevention and treatment. As one mother explained, her goal was not to convince others but to treat her own children without outside interference: "I'm just going to handle my people. So as long as people just stay out of my way, I'm cool. I don't need to convince the masses. I just need them to not stop me." The prioritization of personal goals and lifestyle over policy has become more obvious as organizations like Generation Rescue and Talk About Curing Autism (TACA)[32] have started reducing their activism work around "vaccine safety" (that cast doubt on the safety of early childhood vaccines) and instead focused on treatments.[33] The alternative biomedical movement takes a neoliberal approach to autism advocacy, encouraging parents—mainly mothers—to protect their future children through the avoidance of potentially harmful chemicals and to recover autistic children through dedicated trial-and-error experimentation.[34] Thus, despite its concerns about toxic exposures, this movement operates less like an environmental health movement and more like self-help or self-improvement movements that share a collective identity but attend to individual projects, such as the women's postpartum support group movement and even the controversial pro-anorexia movements, which take place largely online.[35]

Over the years, Melissa has formed deep friendships and stepped into leadership roles within the movement, but in the beginning, she was desperately scouring the internet for a life-changing treatment: "Sleepless nights and sheer desperation on the internet and I found TACA and [Generation Rescue] and they were, like I said, they were the only thing I found that you saw 'my kid's getting better,' 'my kid got better,' 'my kid, you

know, stopped doing A, B, C, and D.' That was the only thing."
By joining this community, parents gain a network of peers,
specialized practitioners, functional laboratories, and treatment
opportunities that they think are instrumental to their children's
health and recovery. Although members are oriented toward
individual goals, many parents come to see themselves as advocates for both their own children and other families impacted
by autism. Melissa has volunteered as a parent mentor for both
Generation Rescue and TACA to help new members navigate
the serpentine world of alternative biomedicine. In addition, she
is a coordinator and chapter leader for TACA and started a support group for parents in her local area: "We would just go to a
restaurant, out to dinner, and talk. . . . It was just networking,
and you know, bawling at the table, talking about poop, whatever." Members form community around shared circumstances
and practices.

The autistic rights movement, which overlaps with and
stems from the disability rights movement, is typologically
situated somewhere between an embodied health and a civil
rights movement. It is partly an embodied health movement
because it politicizes collective experiences and challenges the
dominant autism framework, but its members are not asking
for an "illness" to be recognized;[36] rather, their objectives tend
to be about demedicalization. Concurrently, the autistic rights
movement is an identity-based civil rights movement because
of its demands for representation and inclusion. There is limited collaboration with medical professionals and scientists in
its members' activism. This is partly because activists disrupt the
taken-for-granted idea that autism is an issue under medical or
psychiatric jurisdiction. Instead, they adopt a social model of
disability to argue that autism-related disabilities largely stem
from *ableism*, which refers to the systemic devaluation of and

discrimination against bodies and brains that are perceived to be *less* perfect and "species-typical."[37] Thus, the autistic rights movement's mission and activities extend beyond matters of health care and medicine to address the structural and legal failures that have impeded their access to employment, education, housing, health care, and safety. In our interview, Lydia Brown, a disability justice activist and lawyer, described the wide scope of ASAN's mission as "[adhering] to the philosophy of the disability rights movement with respect to autism, so that means advocating policy change and working for the development of autistic community in the framework of rights, equality, inclusion, diversity and access." Autistic rights activists seek to effect institutional changes, but because they conceptualize autism as a civil rights issue (more than a health issue), they call upon a large and diversified population of allies: politicians, parents, employers, educators, and so on.

The autistic rights movement is a critical space for refining autistic culture. This aspect of participation has immediate value to activists, and for many, it is more personally meaningful than the activism work. Before Corey joined autistic rights organizations, his sense of self-worth had been diminished by destructive messages about his disability: "And I guess at a certain point, I was just like, I'm not going to get anywhere in my life feeling ashamed of everything all the time. And like, there has to be some other perspective out there that isn't telling me that I'm terrible because I'm disabled." His mother had given him a book on autism when he was younger, but from what he remembered, it was about a mother's journey to curing her child. This was not helpful. Corey searched the internet for a perspective on autism that was not "clinical" and did not center on parents' experiences. Yet, as he recalled, there were few autistic rights organizations at the time, and ASAN had only just formed. Although there were

limited resources, he found a community that valued his difference: "It's kind of morbid to think if like those sorts of resources
hadn't been out there I'd might have tried to kill myself again
or might be in a much worse place mental health-wise than
I am currently. And it's sort of gave my life a little bit more of a
purpose."

As I noted earlier, the field of autism is diverse because
the diagnosis is broad and because there are many voices trying to speak for autism. Within this field, one can imagine the
alternative biomedical movement on one end and the autistic
rights movement at the other end. Spread across the middle is
the "mainstream." Demographic differences largely account for
the two movements' disparate stances on autism and struggles
for representation. Alternative biomedical members are pre-
dominantly specialized practitioners and parents of autistic
children—and they are typically *not* autistic themselves. At the
time of research, most autistic children of this study's parent participants were under the age of eighteen, and all lived at home.
I met few of these children because they were rarely brought to
conferences and interviews. Based on parents' descriptions and
my observations at private practices, the alternative biomedical
movement is concerned with an autistic population that needs
relatively intensive forms of care and supervision. Parent participants also described their children as having many physiological
symptoms. In contrast, the autistic rights activists presented in
this book are autistic adults over the age of eighteen. Nearly all
participants have verbal communication skills and enough life
skills that they do not require safety supervision. Studies have
estimated that about 25 percent of autistic people are nonverbal or minimally verbal, and 30 percent are also diagnosed with
an intellectual disability.[38] Yet most autistic participants have
attained at least a college degree, some are employed, and most

live independently. Compared to the general autistic population, the participants are more independent.

The members of these two movements could not be any more different in their relationship to autism, the phenotype of the autistic population, and the age of the autistic population. These demographic differences structure access to experiential knowledge and concomitantly shape each group's priorities. Given the specific populations that make up these two movements, their mobilization empowers experiences and concerns that are underrepresented and, at times, invalidated. The parents, practitioners, and autistic individuals in this study recognize themselves as underdogs. From the margins, they find the freedom to enact and refine what they know about autism and autistic people.

A BRIEF HISTORY OF AUTISM AND ITS CONTROVERSIES

Since autism was identified, the emergence and passing of controversies and contestations have marked the different eras of its young history. In their resistances, the alternative biomedical and autistic rights movements pursue a paradigm shift that would dramatically redirect medical practice, research funding and priorities, policies, and public attitudes. Perceiving a mismatch between the DEP and their own experiences, movement members subscribe to a body of contentious knowledge about autism. Contentious knowledge is not created in a vacuum. The evolution of autism is propelled by uncertainty, discontent, and hope. Along this nonlinear trajectory, the movements arose, highlighting the instability and unsettled status of autism. In this section, I trace autism's controversies to briefly review its recent history and describe the epistemic landscape from which these two movements emerged.

Blaming "Refrigerator Mothers"

Early psychologists who studied autism suggested that the condition was psychogenic, brought on by unaffectionate, cold parenting—the fault of "refrigerator mothers." In his study of eleven autistic children, Leo Kanner noted that "they all come of highly intelligent families."[39] The children's fathers had achieved prestigious careers, and nine of the eleven mothers had graduated from college—at a time when only 4 percent of women over the age of twenty-five graduated from four-year colleges.[40] He described these educated parents (and family members) as intellectually engaged but socially withdrawn: "For the most part, the parents, grandparents, and collaterals are persons strongly preoccupied with abstractions of a scientific, literary, or artistic nature, and limited in genuine interest in people."[41] Kanner wondered if there was a relationship between a lack of parental affection and autism: "In the whole group, there are very few really warm-hearted fathers and mothers. . . . The question arises whether or to what extent this fact has contributed to the condition of the children."[42] However, unsure whether there was a causal relationship between withdrawn parenting and autism, Kanner cautiously defaulted to a less damning explanation, that autistic children simply "[came] into the world with innate inability to form the usual biologically provided affective contact with people."[43] He proposed that they were simply born this way.

However, from the 1940s to the mid-1960s, a psychoanalytic framework dominated autism discourse, and clinicians were eager to attribute the condition to the social environment.

Parents became convenient targets for blame.[44] The "refrigerator mother" hypothesis was popularized by Bruno Bettelheim, who elaborated the idea in his book *The Empty Fortress: Infantile Autism and the Birth of the Self* (1967). He rejected the hypothesis that autism is caused by an "organic defect," but argued that even *if* an "organic factor" predisposed certain children to autism, parents' negative responses to their babies contributed to the manifestation of autism. He proposed that autism is rooted in parents' rejection of their child, that it stems from parents' "wish that [their] child should not exist."[45] Explicitly blaming mothers, he said mothers' emotional responses to infants cause autism: "Maternal feelings, indifferent, negative, or ambivalent, are then made to explain infantile autism, while in my opinion only the extreme of negative feelings in the parents can set the autistic process in motion."[46]

Searching for the "Autism Gene"

Shortly before *The Empty Fortress*, Bernard Rimland, a psychologist and the father of an autistic boy, proposed an alternative to the refrigerator parent framework. In 1964, he published *Infantile Autism: The Syndrome and Its Implications for a Neural Theory of Behavior*, in which he disputed the psychogenic theory of causation and proposed a biological cause, thereby exculpating parents. Analyzing the literature, Rimland outlined the weaknesses of the psychogenic hypothesis, such as parents who do not fit the "refrigerator" stereotype, non-autistic siblings, the sex ratio (there are more autistic boys than girls), and autism in identical twins. In its place, he conceptualized autism as a neurological disorder with genetic risk factors. Rimland's publication shifted the autism paradigm, changing the way medical professionals and parents thought about the condition. Autism was no longer seen as something "caused" by the social environment, and mothers were no longer villains.

Today, research on autism's etiology is focused on genetics. During the mid-1990s, shortly after the Human Genome Project was initiated, parent advocacy groups actively steered autism research toward the search for biological and genetic causes.[47] Parent-led groups, such as the National Alliance for Autism Research and Cure Autism Now, forged research collaborations with experts through funding and developing an open-access genetic database to ramp up research.[48] According to the most recent data, 86 percent (amounting to about $64.1 million) of federal and private funding for research into autism risk and prevention is dedicated to understanding its genetic roots.[49] However, in the ambitious search for a single and common "autism gene," researchers came to recognize the complexity and challenges of phenotypical (a term that refers to observable traits) and genotypic (which refers to genetic makeup) heterogeneity.[50] In other words, the autistic population is too diverse to be accounted for by one genetic explanation. Autism genetic research then evolved into genomic research, facilitated by the incorporation of new technologies (e.g., DNA microarray), data sharing, and funding support from multiple stakeholders.[51]

The Emergence of Alternative Biomedicine

Rimland's legacy later took an interesting turn. After reorienting the dominant perspective on autism, he empowered its challengers by inspiring the alternative biomedical movement. In 1967, he founded the Autism Research Institute (ARI), which researches autism treatments. Rimland developed an interest in nutritional supplements and dietary changes, which had been investigated for the treatment of other conditions like phenyl-ketonuria, Down syndrome, and schizophrenia.[52] Applying similar principles to the case of autism, he hoped that autism could be treated with high-dose vitamin B6 and magnesium.[53] ARI launched the Defeat Autism Now! (DAN!) conference in 1995, bringing parents, researchers, and practitioners together to discuss experimental and alternative biomedical treatments for autism.[54] The DAN! conferences ended in 2011, but many of its leaders continued their work and advocacy with other organizations that supported alternative biomedicine, like Generation Rescue, TACA, Medical Academy of Pediatric Special Needs (MAPS), and AutismOne.

Rimland eventually backed away from the genetics framework he had originally proposed, reasoning that genetics could not fully account for the precipitous rise in autism cases.[55] He and other DAN! leaders, like Sidney Baker and Jon Pangborn, started to suspect the role of early childhood vaccines.[56] Toward the end of the 1990s, hypotheses about a vaccine-autism causal relationship emerged in competition with the genetics model that was establishing its dominance in autism research. Since then, numerous studies have investigated and affirmed the safety of vaccines.[57] Within science and medicine, there is no debate: vaccines do not cause autism. Yet, for a time, the vaccine-autism hypotheses were taken seriously.[58] Rimland suspected a vaccine-autism relationship and accused pharmaceutical companies of putting profits before the health and safety of children. He worried that vaccines delivered harmful toxins, like "viruses, bacteria, mercury, aluminum and formaldehyde," into children's bodies.[59] Conflating correlation with causation, he pointed to the positive relationship between the growing number of early childhood vaccines and increasing autism prevalence.[60] Even when experts disputed the vaccine-autism relationship, Rimland maintained his support.[61]

There were three vaccine-related hypotheses: about the potential role of the preservative thimerosal, the administration and timing of vaccinations, and the measles-mumps-rubella (MMR) vaccine.[62] Although no evidence connected thimerosal to autism, in 2001, the preservative was removed from vaccines administered to children under age six out of an abundance of caution. This change had no impact on the rates of diagnosis— and the prevalence of autism actually continued to rise.[63] Finally, all three hypotheses were put to rest by experts during the 2007 and 2008 Omnibus Autism Proceeding (OAP) (similar to a class action lawsuit) organized by the U.S. Court of Federal Claims. The outcomes of the OAP affirmed the legitimacy of the genetics paradigm in autism research.[64]

The popularization of the MMR-autism hypothesis is credited to Andrew Wakefield, who was a physician gastroenterologist until he lost his license to practice medicine in 2010. In 1998, Wakefield and colleagues published a research paper in *The Lancet* claiming that the twelve children in their study were all "previously normal" until they were immunized with the MMR vaccine, which led to gastrointestinal issues in all subjects and autism in nine. Wakefield proposed that vaccine-induced gastrointestinal issues[65] disrupted "normal neuroregulation and brain development," causing autistic behaviors.[66] He called this new syndrome "autism enterocolitis." Wakefield's findings were provocative and scary—and they were also false.

Almost immediately, experts found problems in Wakefield's claims.[67] The *Lancet* paper was eventually retracted in 2010 because of ethical violations, scientific misrepresentation, and fraud.[68] An investigation revealed that he had falsified and altered his findings to force the appearance of an MMR-autism relationship, a hypothesis that he had been floating long before he conducted the study.[69] Wakefield had a financial stake in the existence of autism enterocolitis and had failed to disclose major conflicts of interest. Richard Barr, a lawyer who was representing the anti-vaccination group in a suit against manufacturers of the MMR vaccine, was funding the 1998 study and had put Wakefield on his payroll. In addition, Wakefield had plans to start a company (with one of his subject's fathers) that would offer a diagnostic test for MMR-induced autism, immunotherapeutics for the treatment of autism, and a "safer" single measles shot for which he had filed a patent months before the paper was published.[70] Essentially, every aspect of his new business depended on the existence of autism enterocolitis.

It is not easy to extirpate the doubt and fear that Wakefield has sown in the minds of worried parents. Despite the paper's retraction and the research demonstrating vaccines' safety, new generations of parents still believe in a vaccine-autism relationship.[71] Public health scholars call vaccines "victims of their own success," suggesting that their efficacy has led to their underappreciation; people have either forgotten or do not fully realize the severity of vaccine-preventable diseases.[72] Autism experts have moved beyond the vaccine debate, but in a parallel world, Wakefield's and Rimland's controversial ideas about autism are kept alive within the alternative biomedical movement.

The movement's members are acutely aware that their beliefs and practices are contentious. Melissa noticed a disappointing but regular pattern in the recruitment of new members: "At our TACA meetings, you know, we'll always have a couple new faces every time we have a meeting and they're so excited and they're like this is amazing, and you'll have a few of those faces come back, but a lot of them you never see them again." She found it hard to retain new members and had a few hypotheses about why. One issue she identified was credibility, noting that some new-comers were dissuaded from joining by the medical professionals in their lives: "They're children of doctors, nurses, you know, [or] sisters, brothers of, whatever, of people in the medical field, and they listen to them, or they trust their doctor." As I will discuss in chapter 3, some level of distrust in mainstream medicine is often a precursor to entering the alternative biomedical movement. Other newcomers, Melissa said, have quickly dismissed the com-munity as an insidious project of high-profile movement lead-ers, accusing them of being "the crazy cult plan of the [Andrew] Wakefields, the [Jenny] McCarthys and the whatever."

Over the past several years, multiple doctors have gained attention for prescribing experimental and alternative treat-ments to children diagnosed with autism. For instance, in 2012, Dr. Mark Geier lost his medical license after treating autism-diagnosed children with a "Lupron protocol," a hormone inhibi-tor frequently used to delay early puberty and treat prostate cancer.[73] Later in 2014, a Chicago doctor was placed on proba-tion after being accused of endangering a child by prescribing chelation, hyperbaric oxygen therapy, and a hormone modula-tor.[74] In 2016, Dr. Bob Sears, famous for his books on modified vaccination schedules, was charged with medical negligence. The case brought forth involved one pediatric patient for whom Dr. Sears wrote an exemption from all childhood vaccines with-out adequate justification, failed to administer a neurological examination after the child was hit on the head with a hammer, and prescribed garlic for an ear infection.[75] Alternative biomedi-cal practitioners face real threats and consequences when they use treatments deemed inappropriate and dangerous.

Meanwhile, alternative biomedical parents fear accusations of medical child abuse—which can be filed when experts outside their community evaluate the medical treatment of their children as unneeded or harmful. At the time of my research, parents were anxious about their rights because of cases like that of Lou and Linda Pelletier, who lost custody of their fourteen-year-old daughter for sixteen months after being suspected of medical child abuse, and of Maryanne Godboldo, whose decision to withhold antipsychotic medication from her daughter ended in a ten-hour standoff with a SWAT team after she refused to give her daughter over to state custody.[76] These stories warned parents of the precarious position they had put themselves and their families in when they practiced alternative biomedicine. However, these parents and practitioners were not dissuaded by the real legal dangers facing their community. On the contrary, they maintained confidence in the treatments.

The Emergence of an Autistic Community

Around the same time Rimland created DAN!, laying the foundation for the alternative biomedical movement, he also played a marginal role in the early history of the autistic rights movement. In 1965, he founded the Autism Society of America (originally called the National Society for Autistic Children), which provided parents with information and support. The organization started hosting conferences in 1969. In the days before the internet, autistic people had few opportunities to meet other autistic people. Parent-centered conferences provided a workable space—not ideal, but better than nothing. During the 1991 national conference, Autism Society of America board members approached Jim Sinclair and a few other autistic people in attendance and asked if they would like to form an advisory committee. According to Sinclair, the organization wanted autistic committee members to attend board meetings, help plan the next national conference, and have space in the newsletter. Sinclair and the others enthusiastically agreed, but none of these promises came to fruition. Shortly afterward, in 1992, they formed their own organization—Autism Network International (ANI).

ANI first started as a pen pal list and newsletter that was written by autistic people for an autistic audience. In these early years, the organization prioritized community-building and cultivated the idea that there is nothing wrong with being autistic, which was—and still is—a radical perspective.[77] In 1993, Sinclair gave their famous address, "Don't Mourn for Us," at the international Autism Society of America conference in Canada (it was initially rejected at the national conference in the United States). The address drew substantial attention to the organization. In it, Sinclair challenged the notion that autism is a sickness and described it as intrinsic to the person: "Autism isn't something a person has, or a 'shell' that a person is trapped inside. There's no normal child hidden behind the autism. Autism is a way of being."[78] This idea attributed autism-related challenges to the inflexibilities of the social environment and parents' unwillingness to accept autism as a permanent, incurable reality. Sinclair asked rhetorically, "The tragedy is not that we're here, but that your world has no place for us to be. How can it be otherwise, as long as our own parents are still grieving over having brought us into the world?" While they framed parents as the problem, they also encouraged them to become part of the solution by accepting and advocating for their autistic children: "You're going to have to give up the certainty that comes of being on your own familiar territory, of knowing you're in charge, and let your child teach you a little of her language, guide you a little way into his world." The address captured the spirit of ANI and remains an important part of the autistic rights movement's history.

Decades later, parents of autistic children continue to over-power autistic people in advocacy. To autistic rights members, invisibility is perhaps worse than being outright criticized. They are often seen as nonthreatening for the very reasons that moti-vate their mobilization: autistic rights activists are too limited in power to present a real danger. Nevertheless, parent advocates see them as a potential threat to their children's resources.[79] On occasion, activists experience direct hostility from parents who see them as too "high functioning" to represent the complete spec-trum. Rick, a longtime activist, humorously recalled how one par-ent had thrown a burrito at their group during a protest against Autism Speaks. Another activist remembered the projectile as hamburgers. Neither burritos nor hamburgers are very violent, but the unusual affront was notable enough to be recounted time and time again, serving as an illustrative example of parents' hostility.

By working for the autistic rights organization ASAN, Codey wanted to empower autistic people to be better self-advocates in their own lives, but more than that, he wanted to bring about structural changes, "to make spaces more accessible and inclu-sive." He recognized that this latter goal is much more difficult, as autistic people's devaluation is maintained in the law. For instance, one major issue that activists have spoken up against is Section 14(c) of the Fair Labor Standards Act, which allows employers to pay disabled people a subminimum wage (which impacts disabled Americans in general, not just autistic indi-viduals).[80] From their perspective, the incompatibility between autistic traits and the neurotypical world engenders multiple challenges for autistic people.

Over the last two decades, the autistic rights movement has picked up more public recognition and support. In 2009, Ari Ne'eman, one of the founders of ASAN, was appointed to the National Council on Disability by President Barack Obama.

In 2021, the Interagency Autism Coordinating Committee (IACC), which coordinates efforts and provides advice to the Secretary of Health and Human Services on issues related to autism, appointed seven autistic public members (making up a third of the total) to their advisory committee. Autism Speaks has over time softened its language of undesirability and disorder.[81] Several large companies, like Ford and Microsoft, have boasted about their initiatives to hire more neurodivergent people, including autistic people.[82] Yet these gestures and invitations are small relative to what activists want to achieve ultimately: a society that is accepting and inclusive of people whose brains are "wired" differently.[83]

Autism continues to be a subject of debate and fascination. At present, the alternative biomedical and autistic rights movements are two major voices of resistance. This book examines the activities within the movements themselves, focusing on how members engage with each other, build community, and cultivate autism knowledge.

SPACES FOR REIMAGINING AUTISM

Research on public resistance to expert authority often investigates movements that seem especially antagonistic toward science and medicine, such as vaccine hesitancy, COVID-19 conspiracy theories, climate change denial, the flat earth movement, and other forms of "post-truth" politics that may negatively impact others' well-being. The two movements of this study may resist dominant actors and beliefs, but they are not completely detached from the so-called "mainstream." Autistic rights values have made some headway into popular culture, as evidenced by instances of support for neurodiversity in work and public settings.[84] *Neurodiversity* conceptualizes cognitive and neurological differences as natural variations, posing that there is not one type of "normal" brain.[85] Some alternative biomedical treatments, specifically special diets and supplements, are commonly used by parents and tolerated by doctors even though they are not evidence-based. Yet movement members actively and intentionally poise themselves as distinct from dominant experts and other authorities on autism. Setting themselves apart, members create space to radically reimagine autism.

Multiple instances of injustice have given the public good reason to be wary of experts (and their institutions) and to push back against expertise. Industry-sponsored research has misled the general public on important issues, such as the realities of global warming and the long-term health impacts of tobacco and sugar consumption.[86] Scientists and medical professionals have also leveraged their authority in ways that obfuscate—and even excuse—injustices against disenfranchised populations. Given past violations, it is understandable why the public questions the integrity of experts, especially in a time when the relationship between science, technology, and the state has become more entangled.[87] Of course, many cases of public distrust do not emerge from clear historical injustices. Today, people who are vaccine-hesitant tend to be privileged—white, middle and upper class, and educated.[88] During the ongoing COVID-19 pandemic, those who minimize its threat tend to be men, white, and Republican.[89] Yet, however these challenges arise, it is imperative to understand their cultivation and persistence. In the alternative biomedical and autistic rights movements, a sense of solidarity and the availability of an insulated, protected space are crucial to the evolution of their ideas and practices.

When it comes to autism, alternative biomedical and autistic rights members challenge the domination of medical and scientific authority, and in its place, they impose their own systems

of meaning and practices. These systems produce real consequences. Their ideas are translated into observable, experiential
realities. As scholars have documented, health social movements
can also prompt knowledge production and medical advancement through collaborations between lay activists and experts.[90]
These partnerships democratize science and empower laypeople who are impacted by research but are often left out of it.[91]
However, the movements in this study do not lend themselves to
lay-expert partnership. Alternative biomedical members distrust
mainstream medical professionals. Furthermore, their continued belief in the disproven vaccine-autism link fosters a hostile
relationship with scientists and doctors. Autistic rights activists,
for their part, are more policy-focused. They argue that autistic
people are not disordered, which means the need to collaborate
with scientists and doctors is rare, and any collaboration would
be directed at something other than understanding the biological cause of autism or developing treatment.

Even though the beliefs of alternative biomedical and autistic rights members are not completely distinct from that of the
mainstream, members purposefully emphasize differences and
conflicts. By setting themselves apart from the mainstream,
movement members generate autism knowledge within their
own spaces. Scholars have referred to such collectives as *epistemic
communities*. Burkart Holzner and John Marx described epistemic community as a "shared faith" in the scientific method.[92]
Today, however, the term is more often applied in the context of
international policy coordination.[93] In her study of how Somali
refugees approach autism, Claire Decoteau adapted the term to
characterize a group of people united around a coherent theory
of etiology, its defining features, and possible therapies.[94] Across
these iterations, in its most basic interpretation, epistemic community expresses a shared way of knowing.

Special challenges are involved in alternative biomedical and autistic rights membership. Contentious knowledge instructs its subscribers to recognize and reconcile with their marginal position. While scientific communities must work to maintain their status and legitimacy,[95] they are less burdened with these tasks compared to groups that lack authority and/or are discredited. Because contentious knowledge has limited legitimacy, movements provide a social space in which members can engage with and implement their ideas. In addition, alternative biomedical and autistic rights members depend on their respective communities for access to the resources necessary to uphold a nondominant construction of autism. For example, parents must work with specialized doctors to interpret their children's signs and symptoms through an alternative biomedical framework and access treatments, and autistic adults rely on other autistic adults to affirm the idea of neurological difference and celebrate autistic culture.

The cases of alternative biomedicine and autistic rights illustrate how science and health movements function as spaces in which their members can resist experts and cultivate competing knowledge. In this book, I show how participation within movements is essential for reimagining autism—and concomitantly, for transforming members' experiences with autism (for better and worse). In this way, the two movements behave as *free spaces*, which Sara M. Evans and Harry C. Boyte defined as "environments in which people are able to learn a new self-respect, a deeper and more assertive group identity, public skills, and values of cooperation and civic virtue. Put simply, free spaces are settings between private lives and large-scale institutions where ordinary citizens can act with dignity, independence and vision."[96] Free spaces are "free" from the surveillance of authority and protected from the ideologies imposed by dominant groups.[97] Thus, these insulated environments facilitate the cultivation of identities, counterhegemonic frames, and tactics.[98]

Free spaces take multiple physical forms—they can be churches, women's groups, schools, workplace associations, and internet groups.[99] By coming together in one place, members nurture their sense of citizenship, participate in democratic action, and forge instrumental social ties.[100] For instance, throughout Black American history, churches have been critical spaces of empowerment. Before emancipation, Black religious leaders gave voice to the congregation's oppression and communicated messages of hope and insurrection. During the civil rights movement, Black churches and colleges were instrumental in articulating political messages and training activists and political leaders.[101] While the alternative biomedical and autistic rights movements have online and offline communities, here, I explore advocacy organizations that assemble in person at meetings, conferences, retreats, and special events.

Within their respective movements, members construct microcosms of an idealized society—one where autism is a chronic illness and the other where autism is an empowered identity.[102] Such spaces do not arise out of nowhere; they exist in response to experts and the dominant autism paradigm. Within the movements, counterculture and practices reflect the evolving tensions between themselves and dominant actors.[103]

STUDYING THE ALTERNATIVE BIOMEDICAL AND AUTISTIC RIGHTS MOVEMENTS

Jim Sinclair was worried I would be another "fly-by interviewer" at Autreat, an annual retreat organized by and for autistic people.

Understandably, they and other autistic people were wary of the researchers and reporters who "showed up merely to use us for their own purposes." After giving many interviews over the years, Ari Ne'eman has learned that reporters tend to magnify small bits of his personal details and minimize the important policy issues he wants to talk about. He said, "There's an extent to which the media and society look to personalize disability in a way that can atomize our experiences and take what our systemic issues relating to policy or culture—or any number of other things that are felt at a community-wide level—and try and turn them into just personal narratives of inspiration." Sinclair wanted to ensure that anyone interested in studying their group would "have some familiarity with our community, and we with them." According to my agreement with them and the ANI planning committee, I would observe and participate in the 2013 Autreat, but I would not conduct any interviews until the following year. None of us knew at the time that there would never be another Autreat. After a dramatic incident during that 2013 retreat, Sinclair dissolved ANI and Autreat along with it. I continued my research with ASAN, ADAPT Massachusetts (MassADAPT),[104] and the Association for Autistic Community (AAC), which was founded by the former leaders of ANI (without Sinclair). These organizations are part of the autistic rights movement. They are cautious about letting neurotypical people come in, and for good reason. They have been burned by outsiders before. But once I gained entry into the organizations, the social spaces were intimate and the meetings regular, which facilitated participant observation and recruitment for interviews.

The alternative biomedical movement was also protective of its people and suspicious of outsiders—especially those they think subscribe to a more normative understanding of autism. As Mark Blaxill, coauthor of *The Age of Autism: Mercury*,

Medicine, and a Man-Made Epidemic and editor of the *Age of Autism* blog, once wrote critically about this research project: "Please understand that by putting the medicalization and neurodiversity views on an equal plane with our movement we would legitimize them. I can't support that, and understand that I would make myself a lab rat in your experiment if I did so. I can't in good conscience participate in what you label research." Alternative biomedical organizations tend to host one or two conferences a year, which are attended by hundreds of people. In this relatively large and unstructured context, it was essential to know people. At one fundraising event hosted by Generation Rescue on the last night of the 2014 Autism Education Summit, I feasted on hors d'oeuvre–sized BLTs as I wondered how I was going to maintain my access. It was my last night in Dallas, and I had failed to connect with key people. I had managed to speak one-on-one with some attendees but had few opportunities to recruit for later interviews. But then NFL running back Eric Dickerson asked what I was doing at this party, probably because everyone was in cocktail attire and I looked as though I was on my way to a business meeting. One of the executives had allowed me to attend the conference as a researcher. Dickerson had participated in the charity golf tournament earlier that day. Later that evening, he was invited to an after-party at Jenny McCarthy's suite, and he let me tag along. There I socialized with other organization leaders. No one wanted to hear about my dissertation at 2 A.M., but I told them about it anyway. Over the next two years, I observed conferences and recruited interview participants through Generation Rescue, MAPS, TACA, and the National Autism Association (NAA).

Between August 2013 and October 2016, I conducted ethnographic observations and semi-structured interviews with seventy-one participants, including autistic individuals, parents, practitioners, and allies. Here, my use of "autistic individuals" also includes people diagnosed with Asperger's syndrome, which was in the same family of pervasive developmental disorders as autistic disorder. With the publication of the *Diagnostic and Statistical Manual of Mental Disorders*, 5th ed., in 2013, it was folded into autism spectrum disorder. It is common for participants who were diagnosed with Asperger's syndrome to still use this diagnostic label. In this book, I assign pseudonyms to most participants for confidentiality. However, I use the real names of participants who are public figures and who have consented to having their identities disclosed. When discussing conference presentations, I also use the real names of presenters because these conferences were open to the public.

Observations took place in six states: California, Texas, Illinois, Florida, Pennsylvania, and Massachusetts. These observations included the sampled organizations' multiday conferences (e.g., continued medical education and retreats), regular meetings, and special events (e.g., demonstrations and social gatherings). At the end of 2015, I modified my original research design to include observations of three alternative biomedical private practices with the aim of understanding medical decision-making processes. During that time, I observed forty-nine appointments between doctors and patients' families. Most appointments included the patient, but it was not uncommon for alternative biomedical doctors to meet only with the parents and other family members.

The alternative biomedical and autistic rights movements are largely made up of organizations that are informally and formally affiliated with each other. These beliefs and practices are also observed by smaller groups and independent individuals, but I focused on the group dynamics of established, higher-profile organizations and their members. These organizations position themselves as challengers to the dominant autism framework. For this reason, they are more than self-help or support groups. With a few exceptions, most members saw themselves as participating in some kind of social movement, explicitly using the term "movement" to describe their collectivity. In one rare case, a mother who uses alternative biomedical treatments specified that she did not identify as an advocate because she only cared about helping her own child and was not very invested in advancing the organization, with which she is passively involved. The political involvement of the autistic rights participants varied, but no one denied that autistic rights is a social movement. Its history, after all, is rooted in the disability rights movement. By approaching these two groups as social movements, I explore how solidarity and identity contribute to knowledge production.

CHAPTER OVERVIEW

Chapter 2 shows how the alternative biomedical and autistic rights movements challenge experts by offering their members a competing (and more hopeful) autism framework. Members produce alternative autism knowledge to overcome the shortcomings and limits of conventional medicine that they perceive. I compare the alternative biomedical and autistic rights frameworks to illustrate how their reconstructions of autism create opportunities for action and empowerment. Hoping for the chance to recover their autistic children, alternative biomedical parents reimagine autism as a set of physiological dysfunctions triggered by harmful environmental exposures, including vaccines. However, this means accepting partial blame for compromising their children's immune systems during the critical stages between preconception and early childhood. Accordingly, parents' pursuit of treatment is also an act of repentance. In contrast, autistic rights activists resist medicalization and call for acceptance. They frame the acceptance of autism as a political, ethical, and moral issue. Rejecting individualized treatment, participants advocate for social changes that would improve autistic people's day-to-day living and increase their participation in public life. Within their respective movements, members reimagine what it means to be healthy, normal, and valuable.

In chapter 3, I trace the different paths that lead parents, practitioners, and autistic individuals into their respective movements. Parents and practitioners expressed disappointment with the limits of conventional medicine and indicated that alternative biomedical methods renewed their hope of effectively treating autistic children and patients. Comparatively, autistic adults articulated their frustration with the social consequences of having a "disorder" and joined autistic rights organizations to gain a sense of community, empower their autistic identity, and fight for social justice. The intolerability of these challenges led participants to question the authority and knowledge of experts. Participants' search for new community exposes the immediate challenges of navigating medical and support services.

Chapter 4 illustrates the process by which autistic rights activists create autistic identity and culture and learn to see autism as a natural human variation. Participation within the movement is important for accessing the social, material, and conceptual resources necessary to construct a demedicalized self and nurture an autistic culture. Activists are brought together by shared experiences of neurodivergence and marginalization. They politicize their collective identity to advance a political agenda: autism acceptance. Collective autism-as-identity is not just a political tool; it is also an objective and achievement in its own right. The autistic rights movement is a space where members construct and reinforce a shared autistic identity by comparing experiences and affirming shared knowledge. They also create temporary physical and social spaces to *enact* autistic rights. At meetings and retreats, the principles of acceptance structure the rules of interaction and the organization of the physical environment to respect autistic identity and differences.

Chapter 5 explores how the alternative biomedical framework is put into practice. In this companion to the previous chapter, participation within movement communities is important for accessing the social, material, and conceptual resources necessary to transform the hope of recovery into lived realities. Here, members learn to see autism as a physiological disorder. Members mobilize the alternative biomedical framework to create empirical and experiential knowledge about autistic bodies, inclusive of physiological dysfunctions. Through close collaboration, parents and practitioners collect and interpret laboratory tests and behavioral patterns to locate autism within—but distinct from—the child. Previously enigmatic behaviors, like self-injury and aggression, are given biological language and meaning, such as inflammation, yeast overgrowth, gluten allergy, or high levels of heavy metal concentration. This knowledge is then used to tailor and tweak alternative and experimental treatments. Most treatments are not supported by clinical research, and some are deemed potentially dangerous. Within this movement, autism becomes perceptible and measurable in a way that is not possible within mainstream medicine, a result that justifies parents' use of risky treatments on children.

In chapter 6, I compare how members of the two movements protect their unique reconstructions of autism and manage their legitimacy. I present two parallel vignettes describing significant deaths within both communities. These two vignettes illustrate how each movement understands its own vulnerability and position within the broader autism landscape. Perceived threats to their legitimacy influence the defense strategies they deploy. Autistic rights members tried to build *external* legitimacy to gain political representation and cultural recognition. Meanwhile, alternative biomedical members were concerned with maintaining *internal* legitimacy to insulate themselves from criticisms of their autism framework and treatment practices. Whether protecting their movement from quiet diminution or overt attack, discursive boundary work identifies insiders and outsiders, describes the relationship they share, and defines key characteristics that legitimize their activities. Movement participation is important to defending contentious knowledge and speaking for autism.

Lastly, in chapter 7, I revisit the participants introduced earlier in this chapter, Melissa and Codey, seven years later. Today, Melissa is bracing herself to navigate the serpentine bureaucracies of adult disability services for her son, who is about to age out of public education. Confronted with these new obstacles, her priorities have shifted closer to those of autistic rights activists (but she still supports treatment). Meanwhile, Codey is working toward his PhD in social policy and learning to manage new physical disabilities. These two participants highlight the inadequacies of autism support and services throughout the life course. Addressing the issues raised by the autistic rights and alternative biomedical movements, I propose three overlapping areas of intervention: expanding autism-specific services, developing better social safety nets, and instituting universal healthcare.

2

REIMAGINING AUTISM

As a Difference to Accept, as a Sickness to Treat

The autistic rights and alternative biomedical movements are reimagining autism: what it is, how it is experienced, and what should be done about it. Each movement offers its own framework for how to think about and do these things. The autistic rights movement reconstructs autism as an identity that should be accepted. The alternative biomedical movement reconstructs autism as a sickness that can be reversed. These frameworks shape members' worldviews, guiding their perspectives on health, risk, and self. Issues concerning the marginalization and representation of autistic people become especially important when autism is conceptualized as an identity. And treatment takes on a moral dimension when autism is conceptualized as a disorder caused by parents' choices and actions. In this chapter, I show how the beliefs held by movement members about the causes and the characteristics of autism directly influence what they insist is best for autistic people.

REIMAGINING CAUSATION
AND CHARACTERISTICS
Autism as Human Variation

Seth is a mild-mannered man who works for a global technology company. A long-time autistic rights activist, he is entrusted with a lot of responsibilities. He helps organize retreats and manages the many unpredictable issues that arise, like caring for sick attendees. He comes across as earnest, patient, and even-tempered, like the idealized fathers portrayed in family sitcoms (think Steve Keaton in *Family Ties*). I have only heard him raise his voice once; he briefly aired his aggravation—"Bullshit!"—after getting off the phone with the American Automobile Association. He received his autism diagnosis at age thirty-seven, just ten months after his son, Matty, was diagnosed.

Matty developed "atypically." Seth described Matty as having expressive speech and a "lopsided cognitive profile," so he was able to do algebra but unable to compose a paragraph. Initially, Seth's understanding of autism was bleak. Growing up in the 1960s, he associated autism with individuals who were "severely disabled" and "inscrutable"—like Noah Greenfeld, the subject of his father's (Josh Greenfeld) 1972 memoir, *A Child Called Noah*. In that era, Seth said any behavioral presentation "short of [Noah's] was not autism," meaning that the diagnostic label was reserved for people who needed the greatest support. When Matty was diagnosed, Seth feared his son would end up in an institution. However, Seth's understanding transformed after he came across two readings. First, while waiting in his therapist's office, Seth browsed an issue of *The New Yorker* and found Oliver Sacks's 1993 piece "An Anthropologist on Mars," which profiled Temple Grandin, who is now known for her autism advocacy and research on animal behavior. Shortly afterward, he read Jim Sinclair's "Don't Mourn for Us" address, published in the *Our Voice* newsletter. These two readings introduced him to a more optimistic and empowered perspective on autism.

BORN THIS WAY

After Matty was diagnosed, Seth started taking his son to autistic advocacy meetings. There, as he encountered others who shared Matty's diagnosis, he realized that autism included "people like me"—a person who has disabilities that were too mild to qualify for a diagnosis back in the 1960s (but now qualified under the new criteria). After getting diagnosed himself, Seth received professional help to understand and forgive past blunders. Reflecting on his childhood, he recalled being a "smart weird kid," a description that now carried new meaning. When Seth told his father about his new diagnosis, his father was not surprised. As a child, Seth had profoundly asymmetrical abilities—he was highly skilled in some things and seemingly incapable in others. His father revealed that he himself was hyperlexic and his grandfather had been an "arithmetic savant." Seth reasoned that neurological difference was something that ran in the family. To him, autism has a genetic component.

The causal explanation for autism, however, is not an issue of major concern in the autistic rights community. It is nearly irrelevant to members' political demands. When I asked about it, many participants expressed some degree of uncertainty about the cause of autism, leaving it up to researchers to find out. Yet they were confident that autism is something inherent to a person. They are born autistic; they are not made autistic after their birth. As one participant said, "We got to wait—wait until the science comes back. But so far, the science had made it pretty clear that you're born this way." With certainty, participants rejected claims linking autism and vaccines. "First off, I totally don't agree that autism is caused by whatchamacallit—vaccines," Trina sternly prefaced. "Autism is caused by two things mostly, probably, and some definitely—genetics and environmental factors." At the time of the interviews, the debunked vaccine-autism link and vaccine resistance were fresh in the public consciousness thanks to the Disneyland measles outbreak in December 2014 and the 2016 release of the controversial documentary *Vaxxed: From Cover-Up to Catastrophe*, which propagated the theory of a vaccine-autism causal link.

In line with the dominant perspective, many in the autistic rights movement subscribed to a genetic explanation. Seth, for instance, saw connections between himself and his son, father, and grandfather. Similarly, Bridget, a journalist and program coordinator for a disability center, referred to her family—specifically, her autistic cousins—to support a genetic explanation: "They do seem to think that some part of autism could be genetic and I could see perhaps—I have cousins that are on the autism spectrum, too. I have, probably, uncles and aunts who have autistic traits of the family. I'm not going to diagnose it for them. Even within my family, I think that my father, to me, seems like he could have gotten a diagnosis on the autism spectrum." When participants did not have autism-diagnosed family members, they sometimes referred to relatives who seemed neurologically or cognitively atypical, like older or distant relatives who lacked an official diagnosis (at least to their knowledge). They connected the spotty psychiatric histories of family members to shared neuro-histories, linking the exceptional minds of past and present generations. Paige, a spunky and fashionable young woman, was estranged from her father, but based on others' descriptions of him, she supposed he could have been autistic too. People had told her that he was intelligent and creative. They also said he had obsessive tendencies and unusual skills, like being able to memorize and recite books with great accuracy. Affectionately recalling these accounts about her father and his mannerisms, she facetiously credited him for both her autistic traits and her high cheekbones.

Autism research continues to largely focus on genetics,[1] with the hope that the findings will improve diagnoses and create opportunities for the development of biotechnologies for prevention and treatment.[2] Having observed the gay rights movement and its evolution, autistic rights activists recognize that their geneticization can be interpreted in multiple ways. Take, for instance, the search for the "gay gene." About two decades after gay rights activists successfully pressured professionals to demedicalize homosexuality and remove it from the *Diagnostic and Statistical Manual of Mental Disorders* (DSM), Dean Hamer and his colleagues published a highly publicized study associating male sexual orientation with a genetic marker on the chromosome region Xq28,[3] which sparked mixed responses among activists.[4] On the one hand, genetic findings could be interpreted as cause to remedicalize homosexuality as a disorder; on the other hand, the genetic findings could be interpreted as evidence that homosexuality is a natural variation.[5] In the case of autism, autistic rights activists were hopeful that genetic information about autism could lead to its acceptance as a category of human diversity.[6]

Participants leveraged autism genetics to justify an expansion of civil rights and inclusion—not more medicalization. Niki, an autistic rights activist and attorney, argued that a genetic explanation for autism is a reason for acceptance; it does not inherently make autism a disorder. Highlighting the social construction of disorders, participants compared brain differences to differences in eye color: "Having blue eyes is hereditary, for instance, and that's not a disorder."

Paige pondered, "But what would you do if you found the autism gene? Like, how many people who are autistic that have made wonderful things. They suspect Tesla was autistic. But diagnosing historical figures is kind of ridiculous. But Bill Gates has talked about how he has Asperger's[7] and rocks on stage when he's presenting and he's this amazing genius that stole ideas from other people." Regardless of autism's etiology, whether it is genetic or not, participants framed the acceptance of autism as an ethical and moral issue. As Lydia Brown, a disability justice activist and lawyer, expressed, "We do believe that there is nothing wrong with us, there is nothing wrong with being autistic, there is nothing wrong with accepting autism as the part of the human experience." Even if researchers were to discover pathological causes of autism, members contended that such findings do not justify efforts to eliminate autism. Bridget equated a systematic reduction of autism cases with Nazi-era eugenics:

> But even if it is caused by something like pollution. . . . Or some other thing; they were trying to say pollution causes autism. It's like; well, even if that were the case, does the cause of it mean that you have to try to eliminate it? What are you trying to go for? Are you trying to go for some sort [of] eugenic situation where everyone is perfect and therefore, what does perfect mean? And therefore, if you come up with the idea that perfect means completely neurotypical, then you claim to be, sort of Hitler. It's like, there's a lot of ethical questions around it.

There is no denying that being autistic is difficult, but as activists argued, their disabilities stem from structural exclusion. Society was designed without them in mind. Ash, a leader at the Autistic Self Advocacy Network (ASAN), stated, "I do see it as a disability, but I kind of see that as a disability within the social model of things, where society is disabling because it is not always well adapted to people who think and do things like me." Here, "What causes autism?" is not the right question to ask. The question itself implies pathology and disorder. It is a medical question that occupies experts and parents. Ash said, "I don't really think about causation as much as just the daily aspects of being autistic." The question more relevant to autistic participants is: *What causes autism to be disabling?* Buddy's circumstances illustrate the social and structural failures that make autism disabling.

BRAIN DIFFERENCE AND SOCIAL EXCLUSION

"There it is!" I gestured to a target moving across Buddy's chest. Buddy plucked the brown insect from his flannel shirt and squished it between his fingers. "The scourge of my house," he said casually, "*Cimex lectularius*, otherwise known as bed bug." The house he grew up in had fallen into dilapidation. He was living there with his brother and a guinea pig named Bernie. They could not afford a professional exterminator, so they were trying to control the infestation themselves with little success.

Buddy is living in poverty. He has a meager allowance from Social Security. After his parents died, the inheritance, which included the family house, went to his younger, non-disabled brother. He pays his brother $200 a month in rent, which is a steal compared to what he would have had to pay for subsidized housing in the city. Buddy has a college degree in electrical engineering and some work experience but perpetually struggles with securing employment. At the time of the interview, he was in his late fifties and retired. He lamented that autistic people like himself are normally relegated to work in the "food, flowers, and filth" industries—an expression that succinctly captures the limited jobs reserved for people with neurological, cognitive, and/or developmental disabilities.[8] Food refers to food service, flowers to landscaping, and filth to janitorial work.

What causes autism to be disabling? As an autistic man, Buddy's most urgent problems are unemployment, financial instability, and safe housing (of course, these things are all connected). These were the issues commonly raised by autistic rights participants. Studies have reported that between 11 and 55 percent of "higher functioning" autistic people are employed, with the majority underemployed.[9] Even those with advanced degrees are relegated to underpaid, insecure, and unskilled low-level jobs.[10] Most participants lived independently of their parents and any caregivers, requiring fewer supports than other people on the autism spectrum. Most had achieved at least a bachelor's degree (81 percent), and over a third held a postgraduate degree. Yet, despite their high levels of education, many struggled with underemployment or unemployment, and the median household income reported was $15,000–$25,000, which is above the federal poverty line but insufficient to meet basic needs (especially in a growing city).[11] Moreover, because people lose their disability benefits (like Supplemental Security Income and Medicaid) when they make more than the income limit or have counted assets above $2,000, some participants literally could not afford to take higher-paying jobs—especially if the job did not offer good health insurance.[12] In other words, it could be more costly to work than to not work. One participant, Rachel, circumvented this rule by working off the record as a nanny. While she felt safe in this arrangement, in other circumstances working under the table could expose already vulnerable populations to abuse and exploitation. Members articulated autistic problems in terms of structural, political, and cultural exclusion and devaluation—*not* individual failure. As Niki summarized the situation, "It can be hard to be autistic, mostly because we're fighting an uphill battle a lot of time, in a world that wasn't built for us, and in some cases, because things are naturally more difficult for autistic brains, but that doesn't mean that we're inherently more disordered than neurotypical people." Participants pointed to incompatibilities between their unique "brain wiring" and the social environment in which they are embedded.

Differences in "brain wiring" or "neurological expression" broadly refer to how autistic people perceive and process stimuli, which affect things like sensory processing, executive function, and social communication. These differences become barriers when autistic people navigate a neurotypical world, affecting social relationships, participation in public life, and employment.

Atypical sensory processing is prevalent among autistic individuals, manifesting differently for each person.[13] For participants, atypical sensory processing is a critical, perhaps defining, aspect of autistic embodiment. It affects experiences with auditory, visual, olfactory, tactile, and gustatory stimuli (see table 2.1). This means that certain sounds, light, smells, textures, and flavors that are unremarkable to neurotypical people can be overwhelming for autistic people.

Some participants found that the "intense world theory" accurately captures their experiences of the physical, social, and emotional world. This neurobiological theory proposes that the complete symptomology of autism is related to overly enhanced brain functioning that renders sensory experiences overwhelming.[14] Clinical studies frequently characterize autistic individuals as lacking emotional intelligence[15] and social engagement skills,[16] but intense world theory supposes that these behaviors are defensive responses to amplified stimulation—perhaps they feel *too much*. It claims that autistic individuals retreat because

TABLE 2.1 PARTICIPANTS' DESCRIPTIONS OF ATYPICAL SENSORY PROCESSING

Sensory	Illustrative example
Auditory	I have very hypersensitive hearing. . . . Well, imagine what it's like if somebody is constantly ringing loud bells; constantly, all day. Or making clapping noises or something like that. Imagine [constant] noise, but imagine it being amplified. See, that's why even quiet sounds can seem loud and disturbing. (Romy)
Visual	I get headaches from seeing—just from seeing I get headaches. It is harder to see and speak at the same time. It's hard to see and think at the same time. Certain types of things, in terms of lights and stuff, cause my brain—On that note, florescent lights are evil. (Felicity)
Olfactory	I hate perfumes, I can't wear lotions, any scented anything. (Rachel)
Tactile	I wore long sleeves and long pants all the time because I didn't want anything to touch my skin. But then I started to overheat, so the opposite was true. (Charles)
Gustatory	Really anything with flavor, I tend toward very bland stuff. Ketchup for me is extraordinarily spicy. Carrots are spicy. What other examples can I think of? I can taste the difference in brands of milk really easily and to me each brand is so distinctive. (Rachel)

the sensations of the world are too much to process. However, an intense experience of the world has its advantages, like focused attention. Vanna explained,

> I think that [autism is] a neuro-processing condition that leads to certain perceptual and processing, and sensory issues. But I also think that there are several advantages that it confers upon people. Like, I have an ability at times to hyper-focus, and that can be very useful. . . . When I'm really interested in something, I can

hyper-focus, and to like be a—not to the detriment, but to the—
and everything else just kind of falls away, and I just focus on what
I'm doing. And it definitely has its uses. . . . And a lot of autistics . . .
the special interests thing is kind of cool. And people get tired of it,
but I can spiel on and on about the things I'm interested in.

Autistic people call these intense interests "autistic passion"
and "obsessive joy,"[17] which carry a sunnier connotation than the
clinical description: "highly restricted, fixated interests that are
abnormal in intensity or focus."[18]

Despite these identified advantages, neurological and cognitive differences are often at odds with the demands of work-
places. Ash recognized that their unconventional and nonlinear
approach to completing tasks does not look like productivity
from the outside, so employers have accused them of shirking:

[My boss] would be critical, "I don't think you're being productive"
if I didn't look like I was—If I just didn't have the stereotypical
looking like I was working. When there were no calls coming in
and I was actually looking—because I was doing web design, I'm
just reading coding websites. And he would think I was not being
productive because I don't think in a very linear—I don't do things
in a very linear way. And sometimes what I'm doing is not always
intuitive. Or like a lot of times when I work, I take breaks periodically. As opposed to one long break because one of the things I do,
I don't like to change. I don't like to change things abruptly when
I'm in the middle of doing something. I like to ease in and ease
out and ease in and ease out. So instead of taking one hour long
break, a lot of the time, I'll take several five-minute breaks. Or eat
while I'm working, so I can continue doing what I'm doing and
take mini breaks. But I think a lot of bosses don't understand that.
They think that I'm slacking off while I'm working when I'm not.

During a retreat, autistic rights members exchanged ideas about how to make the office more tolerable. For those with light sensitivities, one member suggested putting a makeshift roof over the cubicle to block out the fluorescent lamps. In their experience, however, efforts to modify the workplace or acquire accommodations were rarely welcomed.

Atypical social communication is another important aspect of autistic brain wiring. Participants described difficulties with interpreting social cues and norms, keeping eye contact, and recognizing faces. These differences become problematic when engaging with neurotypical people. With so many unspoken rules of interaction, the neurotypical world is a minefield of social blunders waiting to detonate. Charles, an electrical engineer, explained, "I could do things but have no idea how they come across. Because all I can see it from is my own perspective. I don't fully take into account what the other person's experiences are or what the proper social protocol is. I used to think that if you wanted to say something, you just said it; you didn't have to code it in fancy language. But the more I live, the more I realize that's not true." Echoing the frustrations of other participants, Charles found neurotypical people to be needlessly high-maintenance: "People constantly need assurance." This requires him to actively demonstrate his affection and care: "When interacting with somebody who's not on the spectrum, I have to tell them and show them everything. If I'm invited to a party, I have to bring a gift and it has to be an appropriate gift. And I have to say the right things. And if I don't know the right things to say, I hopefully can find somebody to help me out with that."

Social communication differences can have severe, material consequences—especially when it comes to employment. "Our intelligence is irrelevant because people put so much stock in social skills," lamented Abby, who had lost her last two positions as a children's librarian after parents' complaints (discussed further in chapter 4). Russell has a master's degree in information technology but has not had the opportunity to apply his training. At the time of the interview, he was working part time, delivering auto parts. He said being autistic negatively impacted his job interviews. Moreover, he struggled with keeping organized and "reading company politics." He debated if it was worth disclosing his diagnosis at work. On one hand, he might gain accommodations from understanding employers: "I do better when tasks get written down for me than told to me verbally. Because it happens too quickly and they tell me too fast and I just can't." He had found, however, that disclosing could lead to discrimination: "I didn't really disclose really. Well, I'm open. I tell people. But I think that screws me. Because then they treat me—like, at my current job, I told them that and people treat me differently. Talk down to me."

Autistic people and the neurotypical world are discordant. Autistic rights activists argued that while autism is inextricable from the person, the social environment is malleable and adaptable. Why, then, are they solely responsible for changing to fit in? "And my point of view is that the solution is not for us to change. I mean, if we were able to change wouldn't we have changed before?" asked Ci-Ci, a diplomat. She had spent over fifty years trying to conform. Like other members, she saw only one real solution: "The solution is to get people to accept our differences. And I always refer back to LGBT because they changed in such a short period of time. It is similar, like when someone says about their gay friend that they haven't met the right girl; no, there is no right girl. And if we keep working there will be change and there will be greater acceptance." The autistic rights movement frames acceptance as the moral and practical approach to reducing disability.

Autism as Sickness

Claire is a sharp, successful executive of a restaurant group. From the very beginning, she knew there was something different about her second child, Jacob. He was so much more demanding and "fussy" than her older daughter. As a baby, he had "everything from heartburn to colic." Then, in his toddler years, he did not make eye contact or speak. The pediatrician and her family members were dismissive, explaining to Claire that boys develop social communication later than girls. Her concerns intensified, so she pushed the pediatrician for a referral. At twenty-seven months, Jacob was diagnosed with "moderate autism" by a pediatric neurologist. Claire felt both validated and devastated; she said, "you kind of grieve for knowing that you're not going to have the child you thought you were going to have. I knew at that point he wasn't going to be the President of the United States, but then there was a sense of relief because I wasn't crazy and everybody else was wrong and I was right." The diagnosis was revealing and gave her a sense of direction: "I felt like I was sword fighting with a blindfold on and it was like somebody took the blindfold off and it was like, all right, now I can see the dragon. Now, I know what I'm doing."

Claire promptly checked out two books from the library to learn about autism. One of the books was far too technical—especially for someone whose prior knowledge of autism was limited to Dustin Hoffman's Oscar-winning performance in *Rain Man*. The other book, she remembered, had larger print and was easy to read. It was written by Jenny McCarthy, whose approachable prose assured readers that their autistic children could be recovered. Claire remembered, "I was up until about three in the morning reading it. I was absolutely blown away by the chance that a child could recover, and so I went and got her other book." Although people in Claire's life called McCarthy crazy, she brushed aside their disapproval. To her, the book was inspiring. Using McCarthy's memoir as a guide, Claire reached out to the organization Talk About Curing Autism (TACA)[19] to learn more about alternative biomedical treatments. The alternative biomedical community offered parents like Claire a framework for understanding what had happened to their children and what could be done to help them. It taught her how to see and slay the dragon.

ENVIRONMENTAL EXPOSURES TRIGGERING THE FRAGILE CHILD

Alternative biomedical parents and practitioners believe that autism has genetic roots. However, they distinguish their beliefs from the way dominant experts talk about autism genetics. They argue that certain children have genetic vulnerabilities—in particular, vulnerabilities that impact their immune systems—that are acutely or cumulatively "triggered" by harmful environmental exposures. Such triggers, they claim, set off physiological dysfunctions that have biological and behavioral presentations. These behavioral presentations are the symptoms that qualify children for an autism diagnosis. In other words, they interpret autistic behaviors as signs of underlying physiological problems, like immunological, gastrointestinal, and cellular dysfunctions. They believe that common conditions that occur alongside autism,[20] like eczema, allergies, sleep difficulties, gastrointestinal problems, and dietary restrictions are not merely *co-occurring* but are "*causal* explanations for autism"[21]—they make up autism itself. Dr. Kavita Maddan, a respected doctor in the community, differentiated this interpretation of signs and symptoms from the mainstream view: "Your genetics loads the gun and the environment pulls the trigger, and then, when you get triggered or tilted, then you manifest it metabolically in different ways. And so, what you see, everybody else sees as autism. What I see is immune dysregulation, mitochondrial dysfunction, gastrointestinal inflammation, and defects in detoxification, methylation, and then probably the overlying category would be oxidative stress and inflammation."

Parents were frustrated with their former doctors' minimization of these physiological issues. To parents, autism is not a neurodevelopmental disorder but a complicated "whole-body" disorder.[22] As one mother described her shift in understanding, "I used to think autism was more of a neurological dysfunction and, and it is, it is, but that's not the root of it. Now over time, I see that the root is actually from the gut because 80 percent of the immune system is in the gut, so if the gut is not healthy . . . it causes neurological dysfunction, but it's not a neurological disease, it's more of an immune system." Conceptualizing autism as an environmentally triggered condition, participants saw it as something tragically acquired during early childhood, as opposed to something a person is born with. This framework heavily pathologizes autism. Autism, in this view, is a physical sickness in need of a cure.

Claire believes that Jacob has a "genetic predisposition." In his case, the predisposition makes it difficult for him to "detoxify" effectively, causing him to have high concentrations of metals in his blood (e.g., "arsenic, lead, mercury, nickel, aluminum, tin") and gastrointestinal issues. She said these issues manifest in atypical behaviors, like spinning, hand flapping, and lining up toys. To make sense of these genetic risks, parents searched for connections between their family's health history and children's fragile bodies. As one mother reasoned, "My grandparents all having colitis, and diabetes, and severe allergic reactions to seafood, I mean on both sides, heart disease, all those immunological, immune issues. It kind of sets the tone for it and doesn't take very much, especially with a developing baby, in the womb and outside the womb. It doesn't take very much for one thing to set a whole array of things going on, you know?" Parents and practitioners attribute vulnerabilities to different genetic mutations. Often blamed are mutations of the *MTHFR* gene (or as some parents like to playfully call it, the motherfucker gene), which makes an enzyme important to processing amino acids.[23]

While parents and practitioners traced a connection between genetics and autism, they saw environmental exposures as the primary culprit. From their perspective, a child could have genetic vulnerabilities, but autism was not inevitable. "There's no such thing as a genetic epidemic," asserted Dr. Kurt Martinek, a highly respected doctor in the alternative biomedical community, "so something's changed." His statement echoed a shared critique. Participants contended that autism research is too focused on genetic explanations and pays too little attention to environmental factors. Victoria, an organization leader at Generation Rescue, recontextualized "epidemic" to describe the pervasiveness of harmful exposures: "A child is born with their parents' genetic makeup and they have that make up, they might have some things that they inherited from their parents that can be problematic, and then, the environmental toxins pull the trigger to creating sort of what is now the autism epidemic." Members frame the autism "epidemic" as a problem unique to the modern world, which is booby-trapped with innumerable substances of unknown harms. Dr. Charlotte Langley remarked, "We've got 20,000 chemicals floating around in our body that we didn't have 200 years ago."

Explorations of environmental factors and gene-environment interaction are core areas of autism research.[24] In one of the largest twin-based studies conducted, researchers suggested that environmental factors explain 55 percent of the liability to autism.[25] Research on environmental factors have found links between autism and parental age,[26] maternal prenatal medication use,[27] maternal infections during pregnancy,[28] prenatal exposures to air pollution[29] and pesticides,[30] complications at birth,[31] and multiple births.[32] Alternative biomedical parents and practitioners, however, recognize that their understanding of environmental causality conflicts with that of dominant experts. Decoteau and Daniel found that dominant experts in the field of autism "biologize" the environment in the sense that "the environment only comes to matter in *relation to* genetics and only *during* pregnancy."[33] This construction of the environment quashes attempts to revive the discredited vaccine-autism link and any other claims that autism is caused by environmental exposures *after* birth.[34] Yet many parents believe that their children were born typical and only later became autistic.

This was a common narrative among parents who observed regression during their children's development, meaning that they observed their children losing acquired language and social skills. Regression is not uncommon—it is observed in 32.1 to 41 percent of autistic people.[35] Scholars found that parents who observed regression in their children are more likely to blame environmental causes (including vaccines) than parents who observed congenital autism (since birth or shortly after).[36] For participants, noticing a loss of developmental skills was especially devastating and tragic. This experience became a significant detail in their beliefs about causation. They interpreted loss to mean that they had a typically developing child until something external, something occurring long after their birth, took that typically developing child away. As one mother reasoned, "Kids just don't regress, you know? It's not like a phenomenon. It's something seriously going wrong." In this way, the alternative biomedical framework offered an explanation that mapped onto their experiences, making it very convincing.

Parents and practitioners believe that the time between birth and the toddler years is when children are most vulnerable to getting triggered. Dr. Maddan explained that autism risk is increased when vulnerable immune systems are "tilted" at an early age; tilting at later ages could also result in lower-impact immunological disorders. Parents identified vaccines as a key trigger. The alternative biomedical movement has since its inception maintained a belief in a vaccine-autism relationship, even though this proposed relationship has been extensively studied and debunked by experts.[37] There is substantial overlap between the beliefs of these parents and the larger population of parents who are vaccine resistant.[38] Both groups are concerned about the differential impacts of vaccines on genetically vulnerable children, the ingredients in vaccines, and the unscrupulous motives of pharmaceutical companies.[39] Despite numerous studies proving the safety of early childhood vaccines,[40] alternative biomedical parents and practitioners remain unconvinced, demanding randomized controlled trials. However, such designs are unethical because they would require child participants to "receive less than the recommended immunization schedule," which alternative biomedical parents dismiss as an unsatisfactory excuse.[41]

All the parents I interviewed insisted that vaccines had contributed to their children's autism. Some parents isolated vaccines as the main trigger, whereas others pointed to the cumulative effects of vaccines and different environmental insults. Gabriel, a former emergency room doctor, believed his son was affected by multiple environmental insults, including vaccines:

I'm pretty convinced that there was some vaccine injury. Tylenol. He spiked a couple high fevers when he was really young, and now every year we figure out more and more about the toxicities of Tylenol. Pesticides, not just on our fruits and vegetables, which we didn't have organic. And when he was super young, when he got off of formula, he loved fruit, loved grapes, strawberries, but we weren't buying organic. So just pesticide-laden, you know, Roundup. I think that's probably huge. We have dogs at home, and we had a bad tick infestation in our yard. So once a week for like three months, we were having them come spray the whole yard, so we were living in a—we weren't there when they were spraying, but we'd come home that night or whatever and we're just living in a toxic soup.

Then there were parents like Mindy, who blamed the potency of vaccines above all other exposures. She recalled that her eldest child had "severe reactions" after his vaccinations at nineteen months, including a "really high fever" and "high-pitched screams." He was later diagnosed with Asperger's syndrome. Blaming vaccines, she stopped vaccinating him and never vaccinated her two younger children. Yet Mindy's never-vaccinated daughter was diagnosed with classic autism and required even more support than her partially vaccinated son. How did Mindy make sense of that? Mindy attributed her daughter's autism to a different, unknown trigger and an underlying biological issue: "She never had the vaccines, and so, I thought 'Something else is triggering it. Something else is wrong here.' For some reason, her body created such toxic poop that she would burn her skin. Like, there's something wrong here and I thought, 'You know, there's some biological process that I haven't really uncovered yet.' I don't believe that autism is a behavioral diagnosis. I just don't buy it." Mindy supposed that if she *had* vaccinated her daughter, the outcome could have been fatal: "Thank God, I never vaccinated [my daughter], because she could have been one of those extraordinarily unfortunate ones who died, because she was already so severely affected by whatever else was going on in her body. That vaccine would probably have pushed her over the edge. So, I'm grateful that I didn't."

Offering nuance to their opposition, the parents stressed that they were not "*anti*-vaccine" but "*pro*-safe vaccines." By this, they meant they were not against immunization but were worried about the ingredients in vaccines. Some were specifically worried about the preservatives and asked their doctors for special preservative-free vaccines. In the late 1990s and early 2000s, advocacy groups voiced concern about thimerosal (a mercury-based preservative) and its possible association with autism. There was no evidence of harm, but as a precautionary measure, thimerosal was removed from most childhood vaccines in 2001.[42] Researchers have consistently found no connection between thimerosal and autism.[43] However, parents remained suspicious of preservatives and other ingredients. Jennifer, who has two autistic sons, proclaimed, "I'm a firm believer in vaccinations. I think that they are fantastic for typical kids." But her sons were not typical: "It was always a concern to me, why are my kids so wonderful and off the charts in everything, walking and talking at eight and nine months, their fine motor skills were phenomenal, and then all of a sudden, they're crashing, they get really sick and they crash. And I never in my dreams thought it was vaccines." She said that for both of her sons, vaccine ingredients—specifically egg protein—contributed to autism. She explained that her children are allergic to eggs, so to her, it made sense that they would react negatively to the vaccines that have small amounts of egg protein:[44]

So, in my mind, I don't think that vaccinations necessarily cause autism. I think it is the ingredients that are in there that our kids are allergic to and that they cannot process, so like eggs, for example. Egg is in multiple vaccines. And my—both of my boys are highly allergic to anything containing eggs. And so, when you— in my mind, when you inject a baby, who cannot process this, whose immune systems are down, whose—you know, it hasn't given them a chance to build anything up. And you inject them with something that they cannot process, in high doses, I think that that triggers the autism gene.

Vaccination was a prominent feature in parents' causation narratives, but it was seldom a "single-bullet" explanation for their children's autism. Parents and practitioners pointed to multiple environmental exposures that interacted together. While many parents blamed industries for manufacturing potentially harmful products, they were quick to take consumer responsibility. Consumer responsibilities, in this framework, were parental responsibilities.

FROM REFRIGERATOR MOTHERS TO TOXIC MOTHERS

While having lunch at a gourmet burger place with a few close friends (and me), Melissa wondered aloud what she had done to deserve so much hardship. Her son's recovery process seemed endless—for years, just as she thought she had resolved one thing, something new popped up. If God wanted to punish her, she said she would prefer that he directly harm her and spare her child. Elaine empathized with this sentiment and asked what she could have possibly done to bring all this on her own child: "I couldn't have been that bad, right?" Then she looked at me with imploring eyes: "Are you going to vaccinate your kids?" With the 1964 publication of *Infantile Autism*, Rimland had exculpated mothers, dismissing the popular belief that autism was caused by cold, uncaring "refrigerator parents." Yet the alternative biomedical community that he helped found simply shifted the reason for parental blame—from insufficient love to insufficient protection, from callousness to ignorance. And in this information age, especially when it comes to health, ignorance is regarded as an individual choice and a personal failure.[45] Alternative biomedical mothers learned to blame themselves.

What about the fathers? The fathers are encouraged but are not expected to be involved in their autistic children's recovery. Yes, this is very gendered, but then again, all parent participants were either in a heterosexual relationship or previously in a heterosexual relationship before getting divorced or separated. To my knowledge, I did not encounter any parents who were LGBTQ+. Every year at the annual Autism Education Summit, the handful of fathers in attendance are invited to stand up and receive applause from the grateful mothers who outnumber them. One year, the fathers were treated to a night out: dinner and golfing with former NFL tight end Ryan Neufeld. While the dads had a playdate with the football star, the mothers stayed back at the conference hotel to eat nachos, drink prosecco, and share treatment strategies with other mothers. This gendered division of labor is common in parenting disabled children (and really, any children)—women make deep sacrifices and perform the bulk of the care work.[46] In autism research in particular, fathers are underrepresented in the clinical and developmental literature.[47] Studies that investigate causal factors tend to focus on mothers' bodies, with fewer examining the role of the fathers' advanced age and sperm quality.[48]

Environmental dangers are problems that belong uniquely to mothers. Even beyond autism, sociologists find that public health messages often task women with the responsibility of protecting their children, their fetuses, and even "phantom fetuses" (fetuses not yet conceived) from environmental harms.[49] This framing implies that women's choices and actions—even those that seem mundane and unassuming—are deeply consequential. When autistic children are examined through an alternative biomedical lens, the failures of mothers are magnified. Claire felt that she had failed to protect her son at every stage of his existence. During her pregnancy and Jacob's early years, they lived an eighth of a mile from a coal-burning powerplant (five houses away), which she believes contributed substantially to his autism:

> I didn't know what I didn't know. So, he was conceived, in utero, and the first year of his life was in that house. It was in the air, it was in the ground, it was in everything, it was in the dust. So, I believe that was a huge contribution. The number one emission of coal is mercury. Every time I drove by that—which was every day—there was about a two-story pile of coal uncovered on the property behind the wall. So, I think that was a huge contributing factor. Now was it after he was born, in my stomach, who knows? But it was external exposure.

But it was not just the powerplant. Many other factors seemed relevant. She attributed Jacob's autism to multiple environmental exposures that she had unknowingly chosen:

> I had a housekeeper at the time, because I was working so much, that cleaned my house every ten days with the most toxic products on the planet. My house smelled like a rose garden. That's all I knew. And so, he's a baby. He's crawling around and who knows what kind of carpet cleaner and floor cleaner and he's wiping it, he's getting it on his hands and his knees and he's putting it into his mouth. I just think it was a combination of all those things. It was the food, it was all of those cleaning supplies in my house, it was the vaccines, it was the coal-burning power plant. I don't

know what his tipping point was. I don't know what was the straw that broke the camel's back, which one it was. I think it was all of those things.

It is crushing for mothers to hear that they were complicit in causing autism, that they have unwittingly betrayed their children. I was there when Crystal learned to believe it was her fault. At the time, she was in her mid-twenties and working as a housekeeper. She found it endearing that her seven-year-old autistic daughter liked to rub the tissue-thin pages of the Bible. A family member had encouraged her and her husband, Anthony, to attend the Autism Education Summit in Dallas. They were not familiar with alternative biomedicine, but they were open-minded and eager to help their only child. Crystal said the conference doubled as a little vacation. Financially strained, they rarely had the chance to take trips away from home or stay at nice hotels. Anthony even bought a new suit for $300 to attend one of the conference's special events. But the hotel room was not as nice as the ones pictured online, and the conference was far from a relaxing vacation. During a talk titled "Environmental Toxins and How We Can Manage Them Better," a doctor exposed the dangers lurking in common household and personal items. He showed an image of an extracted tooth emitting dark, smoky fumes. The fumes were purportedly the off-gassing of mercury in the dental amalgam. Crystal was startled and whispered her confession to me, "I have mercury all over my mouth. It makes me angry." She was referring to her fillings. As the doctor revealed one dangerous household item after another in rapid succession, Crystal audibly groaned and sighed—"Dammit!" She glanced over at me and gestured toward the plastic lid on my coffee, shaking her head in disapproval—that could be toxic too. A month later,

I interviewed Crystal and Anthony. Crystal said they were waiting on some laboratory test results and hoped that the tests would provide some definitive answers about how her daughter had become autistic. Crystal wondered how much of her daughter's autism was because of something she, the mother, had done: "I'm curious to see about the heavy metals and the mercury and stuff; where that is. Is it the way that they were talking about it, with all my fillings and stuff that I have. How much of that did I give to her on top of the shots and . . . stuff." Before she could see the numbers, she had already accepted the blame.

Alternative biomedical practitioners urge women to be cautious as they manage their children's environments—from womb to home. While fathers are rarely mentioned or made responsible, mothers are tasked with engineering safe environments, down to the molecules. Dr. Maddan put it bluntly: "Us moms are toxic and we're not so healthy and also our environment." This idea is not unique to this community nor is it really heterodox. Martine Lappé has argued that in the postgenomic era, shifts in autism science toward environmental and gene-environment interactions structure a medical milieu in which the womb is an environment and, as such, is a site of potential harm and autism risk.[50] Accordingly, the health of women becomes inextricably linked to the health of children. Public health promotion of preconception care has expanded the surveillance of the maternal body to the time before pregnancy, suggesting that all women of child-bearing age are individually responsible for preparing their bodies for future fetuses.[51] Such preparation requires modifications to women's lifestyles and behaviors. Even though we lack evidence of the efficacy of preconception care, alternative biomedical parents and practitioners take it very seriously. Unfortunately, it is impossible to change what was done in the past.

In search of what contributed to their children's autism, mothers reviewed their history of exposure, auditing all the lifestyle choices they made before having children—from the fingernails they painted to the polluted air they breathed. Trudy blames herself. She has two children, Cole and Alexis. Cole was born first and is autistic. Alexis "has other medical issues." Looking back on her life, Trudy enumerated all the ways her lifestyle undermined her autistic son: "I think it started with me. I mean, I never really took care of myself. I thought [I] was kind of invincible. I was working on Wall Street. I smoked, I drank, like ate whatever I could. I didn't do any kind of detoxing or cleansing before [getting pregnant]—well, we didn't really do that back then." She still feels remorseful about events that were beyond her control. During her pregnancy, she returned to work at the New York Stock Exchange six weeks after September 11, 2001, which she thinks impacted her son: "I was downtown 9/11. I think that started a load on him." She remembered, "I went back down and everything was still burning. I worked like two blocks from the site and so there was still soot. I mean there was dust everywhere and burning and the smell was really horrible." To make matters worse, Trudy believes her personal health might have benefited at the cost of her children's health. She explained that with each pregnancy, she unloaded toxic metals from her system into the fetuses: "All of the metals go into the fetus, into the baby. . . . So I was like, 'Well, Cole was first, Alexis was second, you know?' So that chelated me really well, but they had this impact and [were] genetically susceptible to it."

In most other cases in which environmental factors are blamed for sickness, advocates place the onus on industries to change their practices and the government to enforce strict regulation (e.g., Gulf War Illness, Love Canal, environmental breast cancer activism).[52] Alternative biomedical parents certainly fault industries and loose regulation, but they also take a neoliberal approach to managing their children's health, emphasizing individual choices and responsibility.[53] Most are college-educated and have the financial resources to feel that they can take control. As critical consumers, parents patrol the boundaries between their children's fragile bodies and the toxic outside world.[54] This vigilance includes a profound distrust of dominant experts, government, and corporations. Looking back on the earliest days of motherhood, Grace, who has two autistic children and works as the regional director of sales for a large corporation, blamed herself for following the mainstream without enough skepticism: "I did not make an informed choice when I vaccinated my kids. I was not informed. That was the choice of fear and following the mainstream, you know? That was not like—I had never read a vaccine insert. I had never read any of that stuff." Similarly, Claire saw her past self as ill-informed: "You do all those things thinking it's the right thing to do and then you realize it's not." She blamed herself for not being more wary: "Part of my struggle has always been the guilt involved in the fact that I did those things, you know, and [my friend] looked at me once and said, 'When you know better, you do better.'"

In general, mothers of intellectually and developmentally disabled children experience blame when their efforts to secure appropriate resources fall short; they are less often blamed for causing disabilities.[55] However, the alternative biomedical movement—including its doctors—implicitly blames parents for causing their children's autism. In return, it offers something parents desperately want but cannot find elsewhere: the hope of recovery. The hope of having a "normal" child is worth taking the blame. Accordingly, the parents in this study learned to take the blame. It is a heavy burden to bear; as Gabriel said, "I think about it every day, but I try not to obsess over it, because you could drive yourself crazy trying to figure out where you went wrong and did this to your son that you love so much." Given their beliefs about autism causation, parents framed the pursuit of treatment as a moral obligation and an act of repentance. They owed it to their children to fix what they had broken. Claire placed a lot of faith in alternative biomedical treatments, but she also saw Jacob's treatment as her path to atonement: "I said 'I got him in this mess; I have to get him out.' So, when my son is grown, he's 18, 19, 20 years old, wherever he's at, I have to be able to look him in the eyes and say, 'I did everything I could.'" But for Claire and other parents, the pursuit of recovery and redemption has no real end.

REIMAGINING SOLUTIONS

Demands for Acceptance: Autistic Rights Activism

Lorena loves her son with intense compassion and empathy. She did not scold when he shoved a friend in frustration. Instead, she softly placed her hands on his small shoulders, told him she loved him, and reminded him that he was not allowed to push people. When he marched away from her, she calmly followed him down the street and asked if he wanted to return home. He did, so they went. When he trespassed through a stranger's front gate to admire their gaudy Christmas decorations, she gently led him out and explained that they were not allowed to be there. Lorena shepherds him with ease and patience. She proudly shares pictures of the Tim Burton-esque characters he sculpts with polymer clay. She strokes his floppy brown hair and calls him "my love." At the time, her son, Luca, was eight years old. She said that some might describe him as "lowest-functioning," but she rejects the use of this sort of pathologized language to describe autistic children like Luca. She also has an adult autistic daughter whom I met only once, mainly because she is a young adult and has independence. Lorena raises her autistic children from a unique perspective, as she herself is autistic (diagnosed with Asperger's) and an autistic rights activist.

"My mother does not find me very easy to understand or interact with or deal with. And that was not lost on me," Lorena remembered. "I think the hardest thing for me being a kid, and in a lot of the autistic kids that I meet, is this idea that their parents don't like them. That their parents love them, but don't like them. That they're falling short of some perceived standard and that was an issue for me." Now, as a mother, she is especially mindful of showing her children she both likes and loves them: "[Luca would] be breaking things. And I'd really actually have to hold onto him. And I would say, 'It's all okay. It's going to be okay. I'm not going to let you hurt anybody. I'm not going to let you get hurt. I'm not going to let you break things. I'm going to keep you right here. I'm going to stay here. I love you and you're not going to be in trouble.'" Above all, she wants Luca to have "a central knowledge of being valued."

The autistic rights members want to be valued. They contend that acceptance should be the guiding principle for support-ing autistic people. Acceptance recognizes autism as a natural variation, supports inclusion, and values difference.[56] It is poised in opposition to "autism awareness," which is a campaign sup-ported by parent-led organizations (like Autism Speaks and Autism Society). The awareness campaign problematizes autism and reinforces its medicalization, suggesting that the condition is undesirable and requires treatment.[57] For instance, in a contro-versial 2009 ad, Autism Speaks anthropomorphized autism with a sinister narrator who threatened to ruin marriages, bankrupt families, and cause public embarrassment. At the end of this ad, it switched to a chorus of parents responding to these threats:

"We are coming together in all climates. We call on all faiths. We search with technology and voodoo and prayer and herbs and genetic studies and a growing awareness you never anticipated." The awareness campaign portrays autism as an entity separate from but attached to individual children. Moreover, its message about what should be done is unequivocal: autism needs to be eliminated with research, habilitative programming, and really, whatever means necessary. While the rhetoric has softened over the years, the same agenda persists.[58]

Autistic rights activists vehemently oppose programs that aim to modify their behaviors—specifically, applied behavior analysis (ABA). ABA is a popularly prescribed therapeutic program used to "influence socially significant behavior" and create behavioral change.[59] At their core, ABA programs use evidence-based behavioral practices to encourage desired behavior, extinguish undesired behavior, solicit behavioral responses to specific cues, and cultivate generalizable knowledge.[60] Autistic participants argued that ABA and programs like it merely teach children how to *appear* normal, equating them with "dog training." Granted, the basic principles behind ABA have their earliest history in animal behavior research, which were applied to human subjects starting in the late 1940s.[61] The autistic rights activists are not alone in making this critique, as educators have raised similar concerns about the method's "unnaturalness."[62]

Many autistic participants accused ABA of prioritizing the interests of parents, not the autistic person; as Charles said, "[Parents] just want their kid to act normal. That's the crux of it. If there wasn't such an emphasis on that, and if we society as a whole would accept some—not all, but some variation on what they considered normal, then there wouldn't be such a pressure to get kids to act normal while totally un-preparing them for the real world." Similarly, Lorena saw ABA as a tool to make autistic children more tolerable for their parents: "It trains the child to be able to behave in ways that will cause the parents—or usually, the mother—less distress. And young children are so dependent on their mother's regard for them and their mother's care. Do I think that they should have to be behaviorally trained [in] ways . . . that their mother will like them? No." She wished that interventions were more humanistic and less superficial: "I wish it was less about [how] to change children to fit in. And more about teaching children to express their truth in ways that people will be able [to] understand." Ari Ne'eman, the co-founder of ASAN and former chair of the National Council on Disability's Committee on Entitlements Policy, specified that members support services and programs that honor the goals of autistic people, and not those of neurotypical caregivers:

> It's important for us to understand that when we talk about fighting the "cure agenda," we're not talking about saying, "Oh, that kid who's self-injuring, let's just let him do it," or what have you. We're not talking about not providing kids with services. I've personally benefitted from services growing up. Most of ASAN's membership have had some positive, admittedly also quite a few negative, service provision experiences. But, we have to look at the goals of that service provision, and the neurodiversity movement is about having service provision that is person-centered, that is responsive to people's actual goals rather than this strange ideal of indistinguishability or normalcy, and that recognizes the purpose of support is not to teach somebody to behave neurotypical, which is something they're not, but in fact teach them to be a happy, well adjusted, successful autistic person. We're not in the business, or we shouldn't be in the business, of trying to make autistic children normal. We should be in the business of trying to help support autistic children to become happy and successful autistic adults.

Autistic rights members were tired of the expectation that they should contort themselves into the mold of neurotypicality. It is not for lack of trying that they remain atypical; Abby fumed, "Stop telling—If a kid says that they're trying, and you say, 'I don't see you trying.' That's right, you don't see them trying because you don't see what's going on in their head. . . . People have absolutely no fucking clue how hard I was trying." Because they are wired differently, there are nonnegotiable limits to their adaptation. By conceptualizing autism as inextricable from the self, the autistic rights movement focuses on changing their environment, emphasizing the need for civil rights expansion through the enactment of policies that would facilitate autistic people's participation in society. Ash pointed out that acceptance implies involved allyship and requires correcting injustices against autistic people:

> Acceptance and support, really. Not just tolerance. Not just awareness. I don't mean like, "Let's talk about autism awareness and just put a puzzle ribbon on your car." No, I mean acceptance. I mean going out there and lobbying for our rights. I mean going out there, having people do some trainings for employers. And do things like supportive employment. Like help us get jobs. Help us get good education. Help us do what we need to do in order to be successful in this world.

Autistic rights activism overlaps with and builds upon that of the disability rights movement, which has fought against social stigma and exclusion. In the wake of the civil rights and women's movements, people of diverse disabilities ("physical and mental") mobilized to achieve the shared goals of securing representation, independence, and participation.[63] The autistic rights movement makes similar demands for inclusion in all spheres of social life—especially meaningful employment. ASAN has even adopted the disability rights movement's slogan, "Nothing about us without us," and has allied itself with other disability rights organizations, such as the National Federation of the Blind. Some participants, although they are allies, argued that the disability rights movement primarily serves those with physical disabilities and lacks representation of those with cognitive and intellectual disabilities. As they carve out their own space within the broader disability rights movement, autistic rights activists are pushing for the recognition of autistic identity and authority on matters relating to autism. Their activities primarily include community building and political activism.

Their political activities cover a wide range of issues related to safety and rights, such as the regulation of legalized assisted suicide (to ensure that the decisions of disabled people are not coerced), protection of organ donation candidacy, protection of disabled parents' custody rights, police autism training, and an end to involuntary treatment. Members voice their concerns by contacting legislators and providing testimonies. At the time of this research, autistic rights members were especially upset about the use of electrical aversive conditioning devices at the Judge Rotenberg Educational Center, a residential facility in Canton, Massachusetts, for individuals with developmental and psychiatric disabilities—many of whom are poor Black and Latinx children from New York City.[64] Here, students' limbs and torsos are dotted with electrodes, which are wired to a device they carry around in backpacks. When students exhibit undesirable behaviors, electric shocks are delivered to their skin. ASAN noted that these offenses included minor things like "flapping their hands, standing up, swearing, not taking off a coat, noises or movements that they make because of their disability, screaming in pain while being shocked."[65] Some wanted to do an undercover investigation, but Anderson Cooper had already done an exposé after a video was released in 2012 (ten years after the taped events took place). The video showed a student named Andre (diagnosed with intellectual disability) strapped down and receiving multiple shocks as he screamed and pleaded for help. He was shocked thirty-one times throughout that day, as punishment for allegedly hitting a worker, for not taking off his jacket when told, and then for tensing up his body and screaming after getting shocked.[66] He was catatonic by the time his mother arrived to pick him up. In 2014, ASAN urged the Food and Drug Administration to ban the use of these devices. Yet despite the media coverage and protests from ASAN, ADAPT, and other disability groups, the devices are still used at the center.[67]

The autistic rights movement envisions a world where being autistic is not a reason for treatment or punishment.

"Recovery Is Real": Alternative Biomedical Treatments

One month after their first visit to Dr. Kurt Martinek's office, Brad and Mia returned with their autistic toddler, Benji, for a one-hour follow-up. They sat across from Dr. Martinek at his desk. Brad was visibly anxious and hurried. Mia sat quietly, letting her husband take the lead. Meanwhile, Benji occupied himself with the toy trains and tracks in the back corner of the office. Periodically, he would exclaim, "Train!"

Brad described some observed behaviors and concerns to Dr. Martinek. Brad suspected that Benji only tantrumed and self-injured around him and his wife, because no other caregiver or educator had ever reported these behaviors. He hated the contorted faces and noises Benji spontaneously made. Dr. Martinek sympathized, "Isn't that annoying?" Brad complained that his son was unable to have a conversation and said "yes" to every question asked. To prove his point, he turned around and asked Benji a series of inane questions: "Would you like to work overtime?" Benji promptly answered, "Yes." Later, when Benji softly meowed, Brad whipped around and immediately pointed it out to Dr. Martinek: "That is also annoying." Exasperated, he joked that it would be preferable if Benji could at least bark like a dog instead of meow like a cat.

"Which vaccine did this to him?" prompted Dr. Martinek. "Probably the MMR," replied Brad. Dr. Martinek said that behavioral therapies were inappropriate for Benji because his problems were fundamentally rooted in biological dysfunction and should be addressed biologically. He reviewed the laboratory test results and delivered his analysis, allowing the parents to interject with questions and provide supporting information about the child. They talked about autism almost exclusively in terms of physiological dysfunctions, as is consistent practice among alternative biomedical practitioners. Dr. Martinek identified a number of issues. He said Benji has elevated white blood cells, which meant there was probably a bacterial infection. He noted that Benji had a lot of bacteria and inflammation in the bowels. Based on the IgE levels, he called the child "Mr. Allergy." He explained that the child's eczema was caused by the allergies. While he could not determine what Benji was allergic to, he said he was worried that the allergies could be affecting the brain. The results also showed low cholesterol and low vitamin D.

Dr. Martinek described a complex treatment plan tailored to Benji's exact needs. He recommended dietary changes, an antibiotic for the child's strep, vitamin D for the deficiency, MiraLAX and fiber for regular bowel movements, and Zyrtec for the allergies. Like all alternative biomedical interventions, these treatments were designed to address the biological problems underpinning Benji's autistic behaviors. He advised that the family start the interventions one at a time, allowing two to three days before the introduction of each new one to allow time to observe the child's response. Brad inquired about the possibility of trying chelation, a more aggressive intervention (that is dangerous if used inappropriately). He was all in and even ready to escalate, but Mia was more cautious. She had been quiet for most of the consultation, but then she asked about the side effects of these prescribed treatments. Slightly annoyed with her, Dr. Martinek said that parents always belabored him with this question, doubting his methods. "Everything has side effects," he huffed sarcastically, "except for vaccines, of course."

Dr. Martinek assured Brad, "We can turn this *Titanic* around, but it's still a *Titanic*." The metaphor conveyed urgency, high stakes, and potential disaster if nothing was done. Yet it also inspired optimism because Dr. Martinek said they had not hit the iceberg yet. Brad asked whether the autism label would stick with Benji even after he was "turned around." Dr. Martinek cautioned that after Benji got better, other doctors would deny alternative biomedicine any credit and claim that he had merely been misdiagnosed all along. Before leaving, Brad told Dr. Martinek, "We want this to go away as soon as possible," implying that the condition was acute and curable. Acknowledging their shared objective and future partnership, Dr. Martinek replied sentimentally, "I want to be invited to his wedding." The idea that Benji could grow from meowing to marriage was full of hope.

WHAT DOES IT MEAN TO "RECOVER"?

Many alternative biomedical treatments lack peer-reviewed, evidence-based research. The treatments typically include dietary changes, nutritional supplements, and experimental interventions of endless types. Some of these things, like dietary changes (e.g., gluten-free, casein-free diets) and supplements (e.g., omega-3, vitamins), have been folded into the mainstream to address some autism symptoms and co-occurring issues.[68] However, the hope of "recovery" is a distinctive feature of the movement. What does it mean to "recover" a child from autism?

At a conference in 2016, Jenny McCarthy, the celebrity face of Generation Rescue, compared autism to the unfortunate circumstance of getting hit by a bus and having broken arms. She pointed out that one would not ask this victim if he had been "cured"; rather, one would ask if he had "recovered" from his injury. To recover implies having been first injured or hurt and then restored to the former state of health and functioning. Movement members believe that many autistic children were born typical and were subsequently "hit" by environmental insults, setting off a series of physiological dysfunctions. When they talk about autism recovery, they mean the process of treating the biological impacts of harmful exposures. The goal, then, is reverting the child back to their pre-"injured" self—in effect, making them as biologically and behaviorally typical as possible. To parents chasing visions of a more typical child, this goal is profoundly appealing.

Because parents and practitioners locate autism across different biological systems, many different avenues of treatment appear to be available. "And a lot of laypeople and a lot of conventionally trained medical people feel like it's an anatomical difference, it's—their brains are different, their brains are built different," said Gabriel. But even as a former doctor, he rejected the "conventional" idea that autism is neurological: "It's not that their brains are different. What you're seeing is their brain's reaction to the difference in biochemistry, in toxins that are in their body, and leaky guts and leaky blood-brain barriers and the effects that are being caused on their brain because of the disruptions in those biochemical processes." He explained that it is difficult to modify the brain, imagining it as hopelessly static and inflexible. But when autism is reconceptualized as a set of problems related to other biological systems, treatment suddenly seems possible: "There was hope, because you can fix a lot of those things and if your brain's just built different, it's hard to fix."

RECOVERY IS A MORAL OBLIGATION

Treatment in the hope of recovery is a moral obligation when parents believe that autism is caused by environmental exposures—especially problems they could have prevented. Guilt compels them to pursue recovery. "It would be so much easier if he had the other kind of autism, [if] he was just born this way," sighed Whitney, a former counselor. But she believes her son, Marcus, was not born this way. She believes he became autistic after vaccinations: "He developed normally, he had like 500 words, pretend play, he could talk on the phone . . . and then after a series of illnesses, strep, he had a febrile seizure after a number of vaccines. It was like a downward spiral. And then within a few months he no longer spoke. He didn't recognize me or anyone in the family." Because she understood the cause of autism in this way, Whitney felt that she owed it to Marcus to keep trying, no matter the emotional, social, and financial toll.

> CATHERINE: So you said if he was just born this way then you wouldn't take issue?
> WHITNEY: Probably not. Probably not. . . . Really hard. It has been hard on our family. [My husband] thinks that I am too active and it takes too much time and that it upsets me, but every parent has a different way of dealing with it. Some parents, it's just better [that] they don't get involved in anything at all and they

just focus on the child, and I do that too, but I think because my son's autism seems to me so environmentally triggered, I just . . . can't stop. And a lot of families fall apart, also because of money—costs so much money.

Furthermore, the very promise that "recovery is real" makes treatment a parental responsibility. Because they have faith in the efficacy of alternative biomedicine, parents sense a moral imperative to pursue treatments. Anything short of sincere effort would be neglectful. When Claire receives praise for her dedicated parenting, she takes offense: "Like, what was my alternative? My alternative was to watch my child fall into this black hole of autism and then burden myself and my husband—and my poor daughter when we're gone with taking care of somebody who was so low functioning—when somebody told me I could do something about it. That to me would be neglectful. That would be awful."

Alternative biomedicine consumes a tremendous number of resources and lacks a clear endpoint. When recovery is a moral obligation, parents repent with their time, effort, and money. The pursuit of treatment becomes a test of love.

LIKE EATING AT THE CHEESECAKE FACTORY

Gluten-free, casein-free, no eggs (unless from ducks or ostriches), vitamins C and D, probiotics, fish oil, turmeric, B-12 injections—the mother dreaded the prospect of having to stick a needle in her son three to four times a week, and the father said it was just too much to manage. Dr. Martinek sarcastically snapped back, "Then we are happy with autism!" But it was obvious that the parents were not happy with autism. The very suggestion seemed cruel. Dr. Martinek warned the parents that if they wanted the toddler to be ready for kindergarten, they had to follow his recommendations. Timing, he said, was critical, and waiting would mean missing the narrow window for effective treatment. As the family was getting ready to leave his office, Dr. Martinek bent down to the child's eye level and told the child that he loved him and that he wanted him to become "a real boy" one day. Today, Henry was not yet "a real boy." Real boys do not flap their hands like a bird.

For alternative biomedical parents, hope is not quite the thing with feathers, and it demands more than crumbs. "There's a string attached to that hope," said Claire. "If you do the work and you listen to your gut instincts and you read everything that's out there, you can make improvements for your kid. And some people get just a little improvement and some people get a lot of improvement and some people get total recovery. It's not always what you put into it." Hope has to be earned—and bought. It is tethered to complicated regimens and expensive protocols.

Alternative biomedical treatments are difficult to implement. When "recovery is real," unyielding effort is the only thing parents see standing between them and a recovered child. Persistence is a value that is reinforced within the movement community. Kelly, who has one teenage autistic son and is an alternative biomedical mentor in the Midwest, remembered how challenging it was to start her son's gluten-free and casein-free diet: "He didn't have the understanding that we could all eat pizza while he was eating a burger or a steak or whatever he was. It looked like punishment." In those earlier years, when her son was young, it seemed brutal to deprive him of foods her other children enjoyed, so she placed the whole family on the same diet to be fair: "We all had to stop eating the food that he was sensitive to. It was so hard. I remember telling my mom, it would be easier for me to become a Black man than it is for us to change the way that we were all eating. It was so hard."

When first starting alternative biomedicine, recovery feels like an impossible endeavor.

During her emotional keynote address, McCarthy regretfully admitted that this endeavor is indefinite, but she exhorted parents to not "give up hope" and continue experimenting. New diets, supplements, therapies, and devices are introduced at every conference, so it is impossible to exhaust the opportunities. In effort to appeal to the masses, McCarthy likened their options to the menu at The Cheesecake Factory, a restaurant chain that is famous for its tome of high-calorie American offerings: "If something doesn't work, go to the next thing, and really look at it like a menu. 'Did that, and that, and that. . . .' And this is a menu like at The Cheesecake Factory with 42 fucking pages. You sit there forever, going, 'I don't know what to pick.'" McCarthy urged parents to wend through this extensive menu of treatments until they find something that works for their child, which is either out there to be found or yet to be invented (so they must wait): "If something doesn't work in your treatment along the way, you do *not* give up hope. We could be standing in this room right now and realizing for your kid, there isn't a treatment available for another five years." Of course, eating through The Cheesecake Factory menu is an ambitious endeavor. Few families can afford to order item after item until they find something good; it is The Cheesecake Factory—they might never find anything good. But whether the search is affordable or not, movement leaders and fellow members remind each other of their moral duty to remain steadfast. For parents, alternative biomedicine, as expensive as it is, is a necessity—not a luxury.

One study estimated that, in the United States, it costs $17,000 more annually to raise a child diagnosed with autism than one without; the amount was inclusive of health care, education, autism spectrum disorder (ASD)-related therapy, family-coordinated services, and caregiver time.[69] Health insurance excludes most alternative biomedical interventions, so families typically pay out of pocket for the cost of specialized consultations, most laboratory tests, and the treatments.[70] Alternative biomedicine (maintained over the course of years) is financially draining, so it is unsurprising that the sampled participants tended to be of higher socioeconomic status. Doctors typically charge $400–$1,100 per hour, with the consultations lasting between half an hour and an hour. Many do not accept insurance. One interviewed practitioner reported that the "typical going rate is $400.00 an hour for a biomed doctor" (Dr. Charlotte Langley), and another stated that "sometimes it's $400.00 an hour, sometimes it's $1,800.00 an hour, depending on who you go to" (Dr. Martinek). Gabriel said his son's first consultation and set of baseline tests totaled $4,200 out of pocket. Parents reported paying varying amounts for treatments and consultations; one claimed to be spending between $30,000 and $60,000 a year. Claire had to sell a house and accrued $125,000 in credit card debt to finance her son's treatments.

Even among families with limited means, the high cost of treatment is not a deterrent in the search for recovery. José, Patricia, and their son Nicolas drove all the way to the Hamptons in an old, clunky minivan. A Virgin Mary statue was affixed to the dashboard. Nicholas was about five years old and did not have verbal language skills at the time. José works as a carpenter and Patricia as a waitress. This was their first consultation with Dr. Bernard Sachwell, one of the early founders of alternative biomedicine. It lasted nearly two and a half hours. During this time, Dr. Sachwell reviewed their test results, offered his expertise, discussed his personal philosophies on medicine, and recounted meandering tales about his time practicing in Chad. Like a man who has just returned home from his first mission trip, he reminisced about his time in Chad with an air of Eurocentric awe and condescension. Dr. Sachwell explained that aside from infectious diseases, Africans are very healthy and have low rates of chronic illnesses. He attributed Africans' strong immune systems to the presence of worms in their bodies, which developed from not having toilets and soap. At a snail's pace, this story led up to him prescribing therapeutic helminth worm larvae (*Hymenolepis diminuta cysticercoids* [HDCs]) (designed to treat autoimmune and inflammatory disorders), which he produced and sold. In addition, he suggested they try essential oils, which could be purchased through his secretary, a sales representative for the multilevel marketing company Young Living. At the end, when it came time to pay, Dr. Sachwell said that the consultation normally ran between $1,700 and $2,200, but for them, he would charge only $1,700. Patricia seemed very grateful to receive this discount. She handed him a credit card but then asked for it back, saying that she was not sure if there was $1,700 available. She asked if he took cash. He did, fortunately! Patricia had come prepared, and she pulled out of her purse a Bank of America envelope filled with a thick stack of hundred-dollar bills. She counted out $1,700. Dr. Sachwell passed me the stack and asked me to recount to make sure it was all there. This felt rather crass. Patricia also agreed to purchase the HDCs without asking their cost. At the time, they cost between $100 and $175 per dose (one dose every two weeks or so, with a gradual increase in the number of larvae). The family was poor but did not hesitate to pay out of pocket to help their only child.

Persistence and the desperate search for recovery have also led parents to pursue experimental interventions that fall outside the alternative biomedical rationale. Its practice often lacks an evidence-based research backing but observes its own system of reason and rationality.[71] Yet parents sometimes express a "whatever works, works" attitude that dismisses both scientific and alternative explanations. These parents are not ideologically wedded to the alternative biomedical framework—they just want their children to be healthy and to not be autistic. For example, Melissa, who blames vaccines for her son's autism, said she was willing to sacrifice anything and do whatever it took to help her son, as long as it did not cause him physical harm. Her stalwart commitment was no exaggeration. She amusingly recalled the time she took her son, Logan, to see a magic buffalo in the hope it could help him. It was rumored that a magic buffalo had once granted a nonverbal autistic girl the gift of speech. There was a well-to-do part–Native American man who owned a ranch in Calabasas—a Southern California suburb known for its celebrity denizens, like the Kardashians and Will and Jada Pinkett Smith. Some time ago, this man had saved a buffalo and brought it back to his property, where it was cared for by his live-in staff. As the story goes, one day, an autistic girl and her family came to visit the man. The girl spent some time with the buffalo and fed it whatever it is buffalos eat. When it was time to go home, her parents led her away, and for the first time in her life, she spoke: "More, more, more!" Although skeptical of the rumors, Melissa took a private plane with her son for the chance to see whether the magic buffalo was truly as magical as they claim. To her disappointment but not at all to her surprise, her son did not find his voice. At the very least, though, it was fun.

POSITION WITHIN THE FIELD

Autistic rights and alternative biomedical members resist dominant beliefs about and approaches to autism, claiming that they know what is best for autistic people. They are determined to make autistic lives happier, healthier, and easier. Despite their shared intentions, their divergent understandings of autism have led them to separate interpretations of what it means to have a good, meaningful life. For one group, a good life means having their human differences valued, being recognized as whole. For the other, a good life means recovery from injury, being made whole.

Movement members' position within the broader field of autism partly accounts for differences in their ideas about what is best. Position orients people's perspective and the knowledge they create.[72] When considering the full spectrum, autistic rights members require fewer supports. In addition, as adults, their needs are different from those of autistic children. They experience disability and embody autism in ways different from people at the other end of the spectrum—like those who do not live independently, who have limited communication skills, who struggle more with sensory processing, or who are more self-injurious. Most interviewed participants had earned at least a bachelor's degree, but many struggled with maintaining steady employment (see appendix B). While navigating the neurotypical world is unquestionably challenging and sometimes dangerous, many autistic rights members also benefit from possessing the skills that make college education possible. In these ways, autistic rights members are better positioned to recognize autism as a human difference—as opposed to a disorder in need of treatment.

During my research, I encountered only two autistic adults in the alternative biomedical movement (discussed later in chapter 4). Most movement members are neurotypical parents and practitioners. Accordingly, they make sense of autism from these positions within the broader field of autism. Parents and practitioners can only imagine what it is like to be autistic, drawing on their observations, descriptions, and some relatable experiences.[73] Their imagination surely falls short, leaving much of the autistic experience a mystery (especially if children and patients have limited communication skills). The alternative biomedical movement, however, reduces uncertainty by claiming to know autism's causation and discomforts (like gastrointestinal issues). Importantly, the movement is attractive to parents because it offers the hope of autism "recovery." Recognizing that the neurotypical world is not accepting of their children, they try to make their children more acceptable to the neurotypical world.

Positioning—as an autistic adult, as a neurotypical parent, as a neurotypical provider—may provide some insight into why people join these autism movements. However, their membership cannot be taken for granted. After all, not every parent with an autistic child joins the alternative biomedical movement and not every autistic adult joins the autistic rights movement. So, how did they enter into these two movements? What motivated their membership? In the next chapter, I explore the separate pathways into the autistic rights and alternative biomedical movements.

3

SEEKING HOPE AND SUPPORT

Pathways to Autism Movements

P eople form communities around diagnoses or health concerns to offer each other emotional support and exchange advice on navigating care. When an illness or health experience is characterized by uncertainty and contestation, such communities also serve as spaces in which to challenge experts, produce knowledge, and politicize shared experiences.[1] Autism is highly contentious.[2] This characteristic has inspired multiple cultures of advocacy, of which there are three dominant groups: (1) advocates who subscribe to the genetic and biological models of autism and are interested in increasing research on potential causes and interventions; (2) the alternative biomedical movement, which believes that autism is environmentally caused and can be reversed with alternative and experimental treatments; and (3) the autistic rights movement, which frames autism as a human difference and advocates for social and political acceptance.[3] The first group includes organizations like Autism Speaks and the Autism Society, both of which had subversive beginnings but have risen to represent a more mainstream perspective on autism.[4] The other two, the alternative biomedical and autistic rights movements, take issue with the mainstream model and resist dominant experts. This position comes with costs.

Stigma attaches to the alternative biomedical movement because of its treatment methods and controversial beliefs about vaccines. As one mother described it, "I think it's very isolating to be [an alternative] biomed parent. . . . Standing out is not—it makes you a target." Similarly, the autistic rights activists' demand for autism acceptance has attracted opposition from parent advocates who see the movement as a threat to the search for autism's cause and prevention. One member recalled the insults that have been directed at them, "We are often told very hurtful things that are—people that are like, 'you are all morons, you're idiots' which of course is also ableist." In the world of autism advocacy, the alternative biomedical and autistic rights movements are difficult paths to take. How, then, do parents, practitioners, and autistic individuals end up in these two movements? What draws them into their respective movements in the first place?

Scholars have extensively investigated the factors that influence social movement participation—demographic characteristics, social network ties, situational context, and so on[5]—but such investigations are limited when the movements concern health, illness, and disability.[6] Studies on the emergence of health social movements suggest that necessity and desperation fuel mobilization.[7] However, the reasons movements emerge and the reasons individual members join them should not be conflated. Individual pathways into health social movements represent critical moments when a person recognizes the limitations of medical knowledge, the prescribed treatments/therapies, and the available support.

The "moral career" of alternative biomedical and autistic rights members—the path along which they reconceptualize their self, identity, and purpose—is shaped by contingencies and key actors.[8] These contingencies reveal the multiple shortcomings in health care and support services that leave disabled populations and their families feeling vulnerable. Moreover, they highlight the appeal of these movements. Reflecting on what motivated their membership, alternative biomedical and autistic rights members recounted distinct narratives of discontent (see table 3.1). If alternative medicine (and the related health frameworks) had not already been normalized earlier in their lives, many participants pointed to specific moments when they felt betrayed by conventional Western medicine. Among those who felt betrayed, parents and practitioners told different narratives. For their part, most autistic individuals were introduced to autistic rights organizations after receiving their diagnosis, as they were searching for support. Through these organizations, they adopted an autism acceptance perspective and recognized the structural roots of their disabilities.

Although members joined the alternative biomedical and autistic rights movements for different reasons, their narratives similarly depicted a crisis—a crisis of caregiving, of profession,

TABLE 3.1 PARTICIPANTS' MOTIVATIONS TO JOIN AUTISM COMMUNITIES

Alternative biomedical		Autistic rights
Parents	*Practitioners*	
An affinity for alternative medicine	An affinity for alternative medicine	Desire for social support
Dissatisfaction with practitioner and/or conventional medicine	Demand from patients' parents	Desire to understand self
Dissatisfaction with prescribed therapies	Perceived need to expand medical repertoire	Social justice for autistic and disabled people

of identity, of interpersonal relationships—as a shared contingency. An autism diagnosis marked the beginning of parents' crises. Conversely, for many autistic adults, personal crises elicited an autism evaluation. Their problems did not seem to have clear or lasting solutions. The doctors, for their part, felt that they had hit the limits of their medical toolkits and needed to expand their repertoires. During these fragile moments, individuals were drawn to their respective movements, which promised to compensate for the structural and institutional shortcomings that had left people feeling desperate. For the participants in this study, movement membership transformed their worldview and reframed their past and present selves.

PATHWAYS TO ALTERNATIVE BIOMEDICINE

José was just enjoying a day at the beach with his son. A stranger was observing them from afar. Before leaving, the stranger approached José and said she had noticed that his son was on the spectrum like her daughter. She recommended that he consult with an alternative biomedical doctor in Connecticut. He and his wife had never heard of these treatment methods, and the specialized doctors were expensive, but they decided to give it a try.

Like José, many parents in this study became aware of alternative biomedicine through unremarkable circumstances. The recommendations came from any number of social connections: a relative, friend, coworker, acquaintance, or stranger. And of course, parents learned from the internet. But what inclines a parent or practitioner to adopt someone else's recommendation to alternative biomedical methods? What motivates them to consider trying something they see as "outside the box"? Why did José take health care advice from a stranger?

A few parents and practitioners traced their involvement in the alternative biomedical movement to either their upbringing or long-held beliefs about health, describing an organic and predictable trajectory. However, other parents recounted a loss of trust in their pediatrician and/or a loss of trust in conventional medicine as a whole shortly after their child was diagnosed. They pointed to instances in which pediatricians discounted their experiences or failed to present satisfactory solutions. The parents were then attracted to the alternative biomedical community because it promised what conventional medicine and popular therapies could not—the hope of radical "recovery" and new paths to neurotypicality. Similarly, several alternative biomedical practitioners recalled defining moments in which they became disenchanted with the limits of their professional toolkits. Often these moments were deeply personal. They understood alternative biomedicine as a new and potentially more effective way of helping patients.

An Affinity for the Alternative

The alternative biomedical movement is anchored by the shared goal of "recovering" autistic children, but beyond that, it promotes a particular lifestyle and worldview. Members are advised to become more conscious of their family's diet, environmental exposures, and preventative care. For a few parents and practitioners, alternative biomedicine aligned with their existing beliefs about health and their distrust of conventional Western medicine and pharmaceutical drugs. They depicted their entry into the alternative biomedical movement as a logical step that affirmed who they were and what they already believed.

Mindy holds a doctorate in education, specializing in human development, and previously worked at a small research firm. At the time of our interview, she had recently quit her job to become a full-time homemaker. She proudly appointed herself a "project manager" of the domestic sphere, coordinating the many therapists who work with her children. She had started implementing alternative biomedical treatments seven years earlier, shortly after her son was diagnosed at four and a half years old. She gravitated toward the alternative biomedical movement because she had always held "a general distrust of [the] mainstream medical community." These attitudes had also steered her research agenda during graduate school: "The reason I wanted to go to grad school was because I thought that kids were being horribly over-medicated and over-diagnosed." Mindy connected her beliefs about health and the health care system to her upbringing. Her father, who immigrated from South America, approached health in a way that was "not really very medical mainstream." She recalled that her family traditionally preferred to treat common ailments with herbs: "I guess I just grew up thinking that a more natural, sort of holistic, non-Westernized approach to life was probably—I was always a bit of a hippie, I suppose." Because she was wary of conventional medicine even before her children were diagnosed, she felt an early affinity for the alternative biomedical framework that sets her apart from most other parents.

Most parents are not like Mindy. Rather, most emphasized that alternative biomedicine was drastically different from what they were raised to believe about health and medical authority. For instance, Whitney, who has an autistic son and is a prolific blogger, said she grew up eating unhealthful foods, like "spaghetti out of a can. For dessert, we would have fruit cocktail in the can. No, I had no nutritional background at all. I didn't think it was important at all." Reflecting on their previous attitudes toward medicine, some regretted their complacency and blind trust in doctors and Western medicine. Melissa remembered that she was raised to believe that "our doctor knows everything, they're like God. You do what they say because they know." Her perspective changed after her son was diagnosed with autism and she joined the alternative biomedical movement. Most parents described their past lifestyles as uncritical and unhealthy.

Similar to Mindy, some practitioners attributed their interest in alternative medicine to family, traditions (such as Eastern medicine), and early mentors. Dr. Gwen Comte's family and professional mentors, for instance, had an enormous influence on her attitude toward health. She is a naturopathic doctor who started serving autistic patients after attending her first Defeat Autism Now! (DAN!) conference in 1999. She began her training in a traditional medical school, but the culture grated against her upbringing: "I somehow don't quite belong there and that's not quite what I want to do." When she was growing up, her mother was a professional baker. She remembered a decadent childhood in which she was constantly indulged with cakes and pies: "White flour and sugar from zero to eight [years old]." Then, one day, all the sweets and the ingredients that made them were dragged out of the house in large garbage bags. Her mother had been diagnosed with rheumatoid polyarthritis and could not effectively manage the pain with medication, so she consulted with a naturopathic doctor who prescribed a gluten-free and casein-free diet. No more flour; no more dairy. Her mother placed the whole family on this diet, which Dr. Comte said yielded extraordinary results: "A year later my mom was walking without a walking cane, she was not taking meds anymore, she was super healthy and we had been eating like this for a year." As she watched her mother improve, her perspective on health fundamentally changed: "For me, that diet—yeah, diet really could change everything. If I look for example, in my family history, I should be having asthma, I should be having arthritis, I should be having a whole bunch of problems. If we look at it just from a pragmatic point of view from my medical history, I would be prone to have all of those diseases, yet I don't have any of those." She had strong faith in the efficacy of dietary changes and wanted to work with patients as equal allies. This approach did not seem compatible with what she was learning in medical school, so she reached out to a former mentor in Mexico for guidance. He advised that she switch into naturopathic medicine but warned that it would be a "rougher road" of fewer privileges and less acceptance. She made the switch anyway. Soon afterward, the mentor introduced her to alternative biomedical treatments for autistic children. To her surprise, the methods were strikingly similar to the way her mother had treated her arthritis many years before. From there, Dr. Comte shifted her practice to focus on autism.

Unlike Dr. Comte, who pointed to early events that set her on a course toward naturopathic medicine, Dr. Charlotte Langley does not exactly remember how she became interested in naturopathy. She said, though, that this was always her calling: "I've always been very interested in what nature has to offer for our health, and what nutrition and food and lifestyle has to offer for our health, and really that's some of the biggest, most important things." She remembered when she was growing up in Alabama, her family fed her meals from Chef Boyardee, a company that produces pasta in a can. The people in her life believed that Diet Coke and fat-free cookies were "health foods." She rejected their claims with disgust: "It's not health food, that's really gross."

Her attraction to the naturopathic framework was not just a matter of intellectual compatibility; she felt a sense of belonging to its culture and a rejection from the standard medical culture: "I went through pre-med and took the MCATs and started applying to medical school and realized that the colleagues that I was in the pre-med program with were going to be my colleagues in medical school, and it wasn't my people. They weren't my people." Naturopathic medicine was not just her professional practice; it was her worldview.

The "Quickest Road to Conversion": Parents' Disenchantment with Conventional Medicine

Gabriel is from Texas, and he looks it. Embodying a stereotype, he once wore a colorful paisley shirt and snakeskin cowboy boots to a conference dinner. He is gregarious, warm, and humorous, but at the same time direct and deliberate. He and his wife have an autistic son, Peter, who was six years old when I met Gabriel in Southern California at the 2015 Medical Academy of Pediatric Special Needs (MAPS) conference, which offered continuing medical education courses on alternative biomedicine for researchers and practitioners.[9] At that time, Gabriel and his wife had been treating their son with alternative biomedicine for only six months. I ran into Gabriel a few more times at other conferences over the next year. Although the MAPS conference was not open to parents of autistic children (to the dismay and indignation of many), Gabriel gained access because he has a medical degree. In this way, he was unlike the average parent— he belonged to a professional world that he now harshly critiqued. Having trained and worked in emergency medicine, he supposed that he would have "pooh-poohed" alternative biomedicine as "quackery" had his son been typical. During our interview in 2016, he explained that alternative biomedicine was not taught when he was in medical school:

> I would've thought it was quackery and wouldn't have been as open to look at it. Conventional medicine training doesn't teach us any of this. We have to learn about chemistry and stuff, but— and, again, I graduated from medical school in '97, so we're going on how many years? Twenty years? 19 years. So, a lot of this stuff wasn't available back then, but we weren't taught any of it. So, I guess what I'm saying is, it's hard to integrate coming from a traditional medical training, something that's essentially so foreign to us, but again, to me that's my gift out of all this from God, is just that I had the foundation of having the MD and just am getting taught different ways to look at different issues and health issues and just in general.

Gabriel was now fully invested in alternative biomedicine, but just a couple of years earlier, he remembered being resistant to the very idea of getting his son diagnosed. It was his wife, a pediatric physical therapist, who first noticed developmental delays when Peter was one year old. Not wanting a diagnosis, Gabriel tried to reach a compromise with her: "Get him whatever therapy you need. I don't want a label on my son." He worried that having a label would set his son up for a life of stigma and discrimination: "It's a tough world we live in. I wanted to protect my son as much as I could and not start him off being handicapped. The world in this life does enough to handicap us." Looking back, he regretted and felt guilty about delaying the diagnostic evaluation: "I wanted to delay it as much as possible and just see if he was just a little different personality-wise and if the therapy would help enough that we could avoid a label.

Again, I mean, that's naïve. That's egotistical. That's . . . so many different things."

Swirling the ice around in his empty glass, Gabriel recalled the bleak prognosis. The pediatric neurologist had said, "You're doing everything you possibly can." This was not comforting, because Gabriel and his wife wanted to do so much more for Peter. Perhaps because the neurologist was a friend, and perhaps because Gabriel had his own critiques and discontents based on his experience as a doctor, he blamed medicine as an institution and not the individual doctor: "[The pediatric neurologist] is a good guy. I don't think he had any malice or mal-intent as most of the—we'll say, people that are in medicine that are trained in a standard fashion." Other parents were less forgiving of their children's doctors.

The diagnostic evaluation is a critical moment in parents' narratives about when they started searching for treatments outside conventional medicine and therapies. During this time of high anxiety and uncertainty, parents tend to place a great deal of importance on the way practitioners communicate with and respond to them.[10] In this study, parents pointed to poor communication during the diagnostic disclosure as a factor that eroded their trust in the doctor. Grace remembered her daughter's pediatrician's callousness when delivering the autism diagnosis: "And she said, 'Your daughter is autistic. She has classic autism.' And she said, 'And there's no cure for autism.' And, that's just basically what she said." The doctor had predicted that her daughter would never be independent, which is a devastating prognosis for anyone to hear. Not only would it be lifelong, but her daughter would "probably never be independent." Grace was shellshocked by the news, and to make matters worse, the doctor seemed insensitive and brusque: "We were overwhelmed with the reality of [the diagnosis] and the fact that it was official, but we were underwhelmed by the actual way it was delivered." She had expected the doctor to "be a lot more engaged," "to express more concern," and to "give me more resources." After that encounter, Grace never brought her child back to that doctor. On her stepsister-in-law's well-timed recommendation, she incorporated alternative biomedical treatments and stopped vaccinating her children. To alternative biomedical practitioners like Dr. Dahlia Pagani, this narrative was familiar: "Conventional medicine has to have failed [parents] in some way for them to even go searching for a better answer." Bad interactions with doctors and discouraging prognoses do not necessarily lead patients to alternative medicine, but for many parent participants, their pursuit of alternative biomedicine was contingent on negative experiences with their children's pediatrician.

Another contingency is dissatisfaction with autism services and therapies. After Peter was diagnosed, Gabriel described a profound sense of despair: "You think your whole world just came crashing down, because all these dreams that you had for your child even before they were conceived just went out the window." Not only did he struggle to accept his son's diagnosis, he was frustrated with the special therapies and programs provided at school: "You just kind of slip into that routine of going to therapy and seeing what comes of it but not really feeling that there's much more you can do for your child, and it's a hopeless, desperate place." In this place, Gabriel made a drastic decision. He quit his job as an emergency room doctor and moved his family to a different city where his son could attend a special school.

After they moved, Gabriel and his wife learned about the first annual Autism Education Summit through a network of parents at their son's new school. This was a turning point for their family. After attending this first conference, he felt uplifted

by the promises of alternative biomedicine. To him, the prospect of recovery made autism seem surmountable and palatable.
"Autism" was finally a word he could bear to utter: "Just being
there around so many people talking about autism, talking about
making their kids, family members, patients better using biomedical treatments. It just gave us so much hope. And at that
point it was so much easier to say 'autism.'" Gabriel felt empowered and in control of his son's health: "It's an ah-ha moment
because you're like, if you buckle down and just change some
things, you can have a significant impact on the future health and
recovery of your child." He returned home, made an appointment for his son with an alternative biomedical doctor, and
started the special diet immediately. He purged the kitchen of
bread, nonorganic fruits and vegetables, and dairy milk. In their
place, he stocked the kitchen with gluten-free bread, organic
fruits and vegetables, and organic almond milk. His wife even
learned to make her own gluten-free chicken nuggets.

For most parents, alternative biomedicine was the last resort
after they judged behavioral and rehabilitative therapies to be
unsuccessful or insufficiently effective. Applied behavior analysis (ABA) is one of the most commonly used therapies, as it
is proven to be effective in teaching adaptive skills and covered
by most health insurance.[11] Ole Ivar Lovaas, an ABA pioneer,
claimed that 90 percent of autistic participants demonstrated
gains and 47 percent "achieved normal intellectual and educational functioning."[12] However, parent participants did not
observe their desired progress. As Whitney put it, "I think
there is this silly idea that the research community has, 'These
people are dumb and they're taken advantage of and they don't
know what works.' Of course—we always try—I don't know
one mother who didn't try traditional ABA, speech [therapy],
and [occupational therapy] first. I can't think of one—and you

go there after it all fails. For years. You only end up there after it fails." Exemplifying this observation, Gina, who stays home full time with her young autistic son, reallocated money to support alternative biomedical treatments after trying ABA for a year (40 hours per week) without seeing any radical progress: "I said I'm not going to use up all our resources in something that's not making a lot of progress. I'm going to try a different route." She determined that it would be more sensible to spend her limited funds on a specialized doctor, laboratory testing, dietary changes, supplements, and essential oils for her son.

Gabriel is more optimistic today than he was when Peter received his diagnosis. During our interview, he visualized his son's recovery on a one-hundred-point scale, with each successful treatment incrementally moving his son toward one hundred. His son was not at one hundred yet, but it was some consolation that his kid was book smart and handsome: "Everybody's like, 'Oh, he's going to be a lady killer.' I'm like, 'Yeah, if he can just learn how to break the ice.'" By the end of my field work, Gabriel had implemented two years of alternative biomedical treatments and was receiving mentorship from respected practitioners within the community. In that short time, he had already tried a number of interventions for Peter, things he would have brushed off as "quackery" years earlier—a gluten- and casein-free diet, B-12 injections, probiotics, oral liposomal glutathione (a supplement intended to reduce inflammation), *Saccharomyces boulardii* (yeast probiotic), multivitamins (magnesium, zinc, iron, etc.), and fish oil.

Gabriel asserted that having an autistic child was the "quickest road to conversion" from conventional medicine to alternative biomedicine. Perhaps. But from parents' stories—including

Gabriel's—it seems that a quick road to conversion requires more than just an autism diagnosis. It is often contingent on parents' disenchantment with doctors and popular therapies. The parents in this study wended their way into the alternative biomedical movement along similar paths, which shows how emotional desperation and dissatisfaction can overpower confidence in medicine and dominant experts, even when the parent in question is a licensed medical doctor. Yet it remains unclear what could have been said or done by doctors and therapists to alleviate parents' disenchantment.

To enter and participate in the alternative biomedical movement, parents need more than motivation. They also need financial resources. Unlike participants in traditional health or environmental social movements,[13] they express their demands primarily through the market, rarely to regulating bodies or expert authorities.[14] Because adopting alternative biomedical treatment is expensive and time-consuming, well-resourced families are better positioned than low-resourced families to resist expertise and explore options beyond evidence-based interventions.[15] Most participants in the alternative biomedical movement are educated and middle-class, which affords them opportunities to act on their discontent and sense of medical entitlement. In addition, most interviewed participants are white[16] (and from my observations, the same is also true of conference attendees), and while they did not explicitly connect their use of alternative biomedicine to race, scholars have found that compared to parents of other races, white parents are less often scrutinized and punished by the state for their pediatric medical decisions—or for their parental decisions in general.[17] Entry into the alternative biomedical movement, then, is easiest for a privileged population.[18]

"You Broke Him, Now You Fix Him": Practitioners' Expansion of Their Medical Repertoire

Practitioners who pivoted to alternative biomedicine had trajectories similar to those of parents. At some point, they found their toolkit to be limited and believed it was necessary to expand their repertoire. Sometimes this realization was driven simply by patients' demand. For instance, one Midwestern doctor started his career in family medicine and, despite his initial skepticism, moved into functional medicine after patients started asking him to integrate different approaches. But other practitioners felt that their trusted tools had failed them during a health crisis, either their own or that of a family member. These shattering moments, which can be described as an experience of medical betrayal, pushed them to become more critical of their medical training and explore new methods.

Dr. Pagani is a naturopathic doctor who, at the time of our interview, was early in her career. She is a magnetic person— affable and sunny, but no-nonsense. As early as kindergarten, she wanted to become a pediatrician. "I was going to go and be a conventional MD [medical doctor]," she said. Then came the turning point. During her first year of college, she developed Crohn's disease, a chronic bowel disease that causes inflammation of the gastrointestinal tract. She wanted it fixed, but the doctors told her, "There's nothing you can do." Like the parents of autistic children, she refused this unsatisfactory prognosis. An overconfident and self-important nineteen-year-old student, she challenged the "five-drug regimen" that her doctor had prescribed. To her, the daily regimen did not seem sustainable, so she said to him, "Well, you're an idiot. I'm going to go find a better doctor.

You clearly don't know what you're talking about." But other doctors prescribed similar treatments: "Methotrexate, steroids, long-term antibiotic use, DMARDs [disease-modifying anti-rheumatic drugs], like other biologic agents, all this crap." Finally, she met with the head of gastroenterology, who proposed surgery as an option in the future—another intervention Dr. Pagani did not care for at all. Coming from a health-conscious family that was somewhat "alternatively minded," she wondered if dietary changes could help. She had read about diet-based interventions for Crohn's in medical journals, but the doctor was dismissive of her suggestions. She chastised him, "You are an idiot. You have no idea what you're talking about." Feeling betrayed, Dr. Pagani never saw another "conventional doctor" again. Because her confidence in Western medicine had disintegrated, she no longer wanted to be a "conventional pediatrician"—at least, not the kind who would "give antibiotics and vaccines to all of my kids." Soon afterward, she learned about naturopathic medicine from a friend's mother. Naturopathic medicine seemed more compatible with her newly honed sensibilities.

Other practitioners entered alternative biomedicine as an act of repentance and redemption. Before Dr. Kurt Martinek became a well-respected doctor in the alternative biomedical community, he was in general pediatrics. This changed when he noticed his son's developmental regression at around fifteen months: "Something got destroyed. Something got amputated." His son seemed less than whole. Dr. Martinek recalled that his wife blamed him for causing their son's autism with vaccines. He remembered her saying something to the effect of, "This really sucks. You broke him, now you fix him." This was in the late 1990s, around the time when Andrew Wakefield's controversial paper was published in *The Lancet*; the paper, which was eventually retracted, claimed a link between autism and the measles-mumps-rubella (MMR) vaccine. Dr. Martinek took his wife's accusation seriously: "Well, she knew it was after a vaccine called the MMR that we lost him. . . . Well, I don't play games. It's like, 'He's broken, I got to fix him. This is not going away.'" From there, in an effort to find treatments for his son, Dr. Martinek attended the DAN! conferences and found mentors to teach him about the "biological underpinnings" of autism and the available interventions.

Dr. Kavita Maddan told a similar story that ended in tragedy. She was in residency when she gave birth to two of her children. Both had health problems, but one child had severe allergies that could not be well managed: "I had doctors surrounding me and I could not help my kid and she actually had [an] anaphylactic reaction." Feeling that medical realities had fallen short of her expectations, she searched for doctors who were less conventional: "I had to find somebody who kind of thought outside the box, and so, I started trying to help her and find out all about food allergies and food sensitivities, and that whole thing, and asthma." Dr. Maddan had started her career in family practice but became jaded after she noticed how many pharmaceutical drugs she was prescribing. Gradually, she moved into molecular medicine and later became prominent in the alternative biomedical community. A few months before she was scheduled to give her first talk at the 2003 DAN! conference, her daughter died after going into anaphylactic shock from exposure to peanut. Neither Dr. Martinek nor Dr. Maddan began their career with the intention of entering alternative biomedicine. They recalled their entry into the field as deeply personal, motivated by love for their children and a sense of hopelessness.

Dr. Pagani, Dr. Martinek, and Dr. Maddan described experiencing a sort of awakening at the moment when they believed their trusted tools had failed them. Because of this perceived failure, they became disillusioned with conventional medicine and sought out other methods of healing. In popular media, these doctors have been collectively portrayed as quacks profiting from parents' hopes and fears. But while their work may be profitable, the practitioners in this study were not motivated merely (or at all) by money. Whether they were following the nudges of curious patients or feeling betrayed by their own expertise, the participants saw themselves as having reached the limits of their professional knowledge. Alternative biomedicine offered what seemed like a better toolkit.

PATHWAYS TO AUTISTIC RIGHTS

Luba had a lonely childhood. She felt disconnected from her peers. Social encounters with other children were confusing and inexplicably unsuccessful: "All the girls when they got to know me, they told me 'you're strange' or 'weird.' And I didn't—honestly, I didn't understand verbal cues at that time and I'm still learning. . . . When they were trying to interact with me, I guess I was making mistakes I was not supposed to make." Accordingly, she looked forward to growing up. Growing up promised a metamorphosis, a transformation into a truer self. Luba wanted to be a molecular biologist, or an assistant to someone like Dr. Gregory House from the medical drama *House*, or a lawyer like the those she saw on *Law & Order*. She dreamed of growing up to become the kind of woman who wore suits: "I wanted to do shoes that women wear in *Law & Order*, since I love those. Those dress jackets, I love these outfits. I thought I was to be 20, please. I want to be 20 so I can be—that's who I am. I like these outfits." But her early adulthood was not as glamorous as the professional lives portrayed on primetime television: "And then I turned 20 and I didn't wear [suit jackets] yet." After high school, Luba worked as a nursing aide at a hospital and briefly as a hotel housekeeper. In between, she had periods of unemployment.

A job coach encouraged her to enroll in a medical assistant training program. The admission process included a math exam, which Luba failed. This devastated her: "And I was suicidal. I admit to it. I was suicidal. I wanted to kill myself. It was the most depressing afternoon that I can remember." She had struggled with math throughout her schooling, but despite teachers' concerns, she was never formally evaluated for learning disabilities. But now, in her mid-twenties and old enough to make her own medical choices, she wanted to better understand her "math disorder." After three months of interviews with psychologists and an MRI scan, Luba was diagnosed with dyscalculia, a non-verbal learning disorder, and Asperger's syndrome. She readily accepted the first, but questioned the appropriateness of the Asperger's diagnosis. She did not know what it meant exactly, but she remembered that the character Jerry Espenson from *Boston Legal* had Asperger's. She did not think she was anything like Jerry—he was, from her perspective, "so weird." Sharing a diagnosis with Jerry seemed a bit extreme and somewhat offensive. But despite her skepticism, she tried out the recommended support groups and services.

Luba's diagnosis story is similar to that of many other participants. Not everyone who has an autism diagnosis joins the autistic rights movement, but nearly everyone in the movement is autistic with exception to the few allies.[19] All autistic participants held a formal diagnosis, which was their key into the movement. Individuals need to know—or at the least, suspect—they are autistic before they begin to search for autistic communities. As a result, acquiring a diagnosis is a critical moment along the path toward autistic rights membership. Among the study participants, a personal crisis typically preceded and motivated an autism evaluation.

Trends in movement membership evolve with the changing diagnostic criteria that determine who is autistic and who is not. Most autistic rights participants were diagnosed with either autism or Asperger's as adults (67.5 percent). Although diagnosed later in life, these participants narrated retrospective biographies that depicted a cohesive autistic self that transcended the time before diagnosis. Psychologists have referred to this group as the "lost generation" because they did not meet the *Diagnostic and Statistical Manual of Mental Disorders* (DSM) criteria for an autism diagnosis when they were children, but qualified for a diagnosis when the criteria expanded.[20] When autism first appeared as a distinct diagnosis in the DSM-III (1980), the criteria were narrow and tended to exclude more "cognitively abled" people.[21] It was not until the DSM-IV, published in 1994, that the criteria became flexible enough to include "milder" forms of the condition, like Asperger's syndrome, which was subsumed under autism spectrum disorder in the 2013 DSM-5.[22] Around the same time, public awareness of autism was growing.[23] One participant explicitly said that he "did not qualify for a DSM-III diagnosis" as a child and was diagnosed with a number of other conditions (including obsessive-compulsive disorder and depression) before receiving an Asperger's syndrome diagnosis at age eighteen. Of the autistic participants who were diagnosed as adults, over half reported either an Asperger's diagnosis or a "high-functioning" autism diagnosis.[24]

Aside from changes to the diagnostic criteria, a number of other behavioral factors contribute to the timing of diagnosis. Children tend to be diagnosed with autism later when they do not present clear signs of developmental delays, like severe language deficits, hand flapping, toe walking, sustained odd play, and hearing impairments.[25] One study suggested that referrals to clinical services are also delayed for "high-functioning" autistic adults because over the course of their lives they have developed the coping mechanisms to obscure disability.[26]

Social factors like gender, socioeconomic status, and racial inequities also influence the outcomes and timing of autism evaluation.[27] Girls are more likely to receive an early diagnosis (before 36 months), but boys are 4.3 times more likely to receive a diagnosis than girls.[28] The reasons for this gender disparity are unknown, but researchers have suggested underrecognition (particularly among higher-functioning girls/women), ascertainment bias, and problems with the diagnostic tools.[29] Higher family income is associated with an increased chance of diagnosis. In one study, children from higher-income families (income greater than $90,000) were 2.4 times more likely to receive an autism diagnosis than peers from lower-income families (income lower than $30,000).[30] Wealthier children are not inherently at higher risk, but financial resources play an important role in the likelihood that parents can advocate for their children and access diagnostic evaluations. While white and Black children share similar rates of autism prevalence, white children are more likely to receive an earlier diagnosis, which means they are likely to receive earlier access to therapy and other support services.[31] There are limited demographic data on people who were diagnosed with autism during adulthood.[32] However, one study finds that in the United States, the "most severe barrier" to an autism diagnostic evaluation in adulthood is cost.[33] This suggests that adults, like children, experience diagnostic disparities according to their socioeconomic status.[34]

Among the study participants, the circumstances that precipitated a diagnostic evaluation in adult life varied. They pointed to critical events such as academic or job-related failure (as in Luba's case), mental health crises, and suicide ideation or attempts. Participants pursued a diagnostic evaluation to either confirm a self-diagnosis or identify the root of their personal challenges. For instance, Winnie had difficulties maintaining friendships and holding down jobs. At the hospital, where she worked as a receptionist, she felt that her "confidence was going down and the stress was increasing." She consulted with a life coach who believed she met the criteria for an Asperger's syndrome diagnosis. After formal evaluations with a psychologist, Winnie was diagnosed with Asperger's syndrome in her mid-forties. She was thrilled: "I have loved having the diagnosis. It was a life-changing experience because it gave me answers then to how I've been all my life." The diagnosis offered a comprehensive explanation for why she struggled so much with social relationships.

For others, more acute circumstances prompted a diagnostic evaluation. Felix was diagnosed with Asperger's syndrome after his second suicide attempt. It happened on the heels of a traumatizing event during college when he tried to pursue a friendship with a woman but then had a harassment complaint filed against him. The complaint came as a complete shock. Despite his intentions, his actions had made someone feel unsafe. Soon afterward, he dropped out of school, and his sense of isolation deepened. It stung to have the regretted event made "permanent" in the hospital reports. Felix, a reserved and melancholy man, judged himself harshly: "Harassing is still a very bad thing. That someone else felt they had to get help to deal with me. I'm not religious but that's pretty close to evil." For most of his life, he had been diagnosed with and treated for social anxiety and depression, but he found that the drugs did not help. The Asperger's diagnosis brought relief because it finally ended the wait for antidepressants to fulfill their promise: "It was the frustration of waiting for it to end and it not ending. That led to the suicide attempts as much as anything." Felix found freedom in knowing that the drugs were never going to work for him: "Sometimes I think getting a firm no is easier than a we'll wait and see." The new diagnosis assured him that there was nothing he could do to become normal: "It wasn't the type of thing that I was going to cure. It was something that I had to adjust to. I would just have to live in a different way instead of waiting for the drugs to kick in and the therapy to reach a breakthrough."

Diagnoses are powerful classifications with medical and social consequences. They legitimize experiences of illness, prescribe action, and open access to a range of resources.[35] For those evaluated during adulthood, the diagnosis transformed their understanding of self and offered clarity. Hil, a social worker, explained this shift, "The challenges are far less than they used to be when I didn't know I was autistic. I blame[d] myself for everything, yeah. I mean I was just weird and different and broken, I felt in so many ways. . . . Now, I'm a normal autistic person. Not an abnormal neurotypical." Autistic rights participants were comforted by autism's immutability and permanence (unlike alternative biomedical parents, who invested their hopes in the reversibility of autism). Like other diagnoses, the autism label resolved major uncertainties.

For many participants, having a new autism diagnosis prompted them to search for community. Whether they had been diagnosed as children or adults, they mobilized around a shared diagnosis. They joined autistic communities (online and offline) hoping to find themselves among supportive others and to better understand their identity. At the same time, they became part of a collective voice that was challenging social and political perceptions of autistic people, promoting acceptance and inclusion, and demanding a better quality of life.

"Finally, I'm Not Alone":
Finding Self and Support

The neurologist gave Luba a list of services and organizations to help her navigate her new diagnoses. She was excited to see horse therapy on the list, but the farm was too far outside the city and catered to a much younger population. She contacted the Asperger's Association of New England (AANE),[36] hoping they could help: "I looked at their calendar, and I wasn't sure which one I should go to. So, I decided I would just try all the events that they have, just to see what I like." To her surprise and delight, she saw herself reflected in the other members: "And I just started listening to all their experience and I thought 'This is me, yes. Finally, I'm not alone.' And I just kept on going. I went to the social, pizza and game night." For the first time in her life, Luba found people with whom she could be at ease. "And I just—I got to know them and it was I could talk if I wanted to and it was so free. And I finally found my life."

Entry into autistic rights organizations depended on the participants' urge to find community after learning about their diagnosis. Regardless of when they were diagnosed, during childhood or adulthood, participants pursued organizations like AANE, Autism Network International (ANI), and the Autistic Self Advocacy Network (ASAN) because these spaces offered a community of people who had experienced similar challenges and traumas and who appreciated the uniqueness of autism. After Winnie was diagnosed with Asperger's syndrome, she was eager to locate others like herself: "I felt I just want to meet other people like me. It's like I've been an animal with spots. All my life I've been around other animals without spots and I feel I can start meeting other people like me with spots, you know?" Among fellow "spotted" people, she was not the odd one out, as she so often felt herself. Rachel, for her part, felt liberated from the pressure to conform to neurotypical expectations: "It's like I have this mask and I'm constantly, constantly having to readjust it and put it in place and I'm terrified of it slipping, and I'm terrified of people seeing who I really am. And so, what [ASAN], what the autistic community is, it's a place where you can take off the mask and you can let yourself breathe for real."

Juniper, an activist and author, explained that being around other autistic people affirms identity, "There are philosophers that say that you can't really know yourself until you see yourself reflected back at you from other people, and I think that's some of what autistic community gives autistics." When movement members entered autistic communities, they experienced *biographical illumination,* which describes a transformed conceptualization of self and identity that is facilitated by but extends beyond medical meaning and context, enriching personal biography and social relationships.[37] In other words, a diagnosis is a medical classification, but it can serve as an organizing force for the cultivation of nonmedical knowledge, identity, and culture. Autistic rights members resisted medicalization, but they recognized the importance of a diagnosis to finding others and accessing resources. As Hil put it, "Diagnosis [is] totally a medical model word. That's what we're stuck with for now. I do think that people need to be identified in order that we can meet others like us who can help us form the strategies that help us get through life." Consequently, this means that entry into the autistic rights movement is impacted by the current diagnostic criteria, screening instruments, and their accessibility. Movement members leveraged the formal diagnosis to find community, and through this community, they refined their concept of self.

Ash described this experience as a "revelation." They were diagnosed as a toddler, but for most of their life, they knew few other autistic people: "I did know one that I went to school with and went to church with but I didn't like him that much." After they quit an intolerable job at a department store, Ash's mother advised that they research autism and Asperger's to find support. They said their mother held a "medical model" perspective, implying that she approached autism as a problem to be solved. Ash did find support online, but not as their mother had intended. They encountered online forums led by autistic people and people with Asperger's. These conversations, which were vastly different from the messages they were used to hearing from family and teachers, resonated with their experience and promoted messages of acceptance. Ash remembered, "I felt like things were actually described in a way that reflected the diversity of autistic people. That reflected the different ways that we could be. That reflected all our like experiences. That didn't just look at things like a medicalized model. That didn't see us as flawed. That didn't see us all like being broken. It was kind of a revelation." Ash connected with other autistic people like themselves, but more than that, they were introduced to an empowering framework for understanding their identity and making collective demands.

Demanding Social Justice

Luba did not grow up to become a molecular biologist, nor did she become an assistant to someone like Dr. House. She did not become a lawyer like the characters on *Boston Legal.* However, she did secure a different marker of adulthood and self-actualization: she participated in disability rights activism through ASAN, which involved going to the State House with other members to voice their interests. On these important occasions, Luba would dress in a business suit, just as she had fantasized about doing when she was a misfit child: "I could wear a suit, yes. I could be who I am, yes. That was finally—[at] ASAN, Asperger Association, I was able to connect with others. I would say, 'Okay, I'm finally part of something. Finally, I'm part. I'm not weird. I am like, if I'm crazy, I'm crazy like everybody else here.' It was a beautiful experience." Luba now had meaningful friendships and a transformed sense of self. But, like many other members, she had achieved little change in her day-to-day life. At the time of our interview, Luba was working a few hours a week as a home health aide for elderly people. She wanted to get off food stamps and live alone, without a roommate, but she could not get enough hours at work. Her career and financial circumstances had not improved much over the years. She and other members knew it would take more than bootstrapping to improve their life chances. Suiting up and going to the State House was a step they could take toward lasting social and structural change.

Autistic rights participants tied their personal troubles directly to the larger issue of ableism. They were concerned about the fundamental problems that threatened the autistic community, such as discrimination, inadequate accommodations, and violence—problems that could not be solved individually. Members saw that collective action was necessary to motivate policy changes and correct cultural perceptions of autism. Ci-Ci, an activist and diplomat who was diagnosed with Asperger's in her fifties, explained that this was her reason for becoming involved in autistic rights organizations: "To me, I mean, you want to make the world a better place, and if it's an issue you care about and it is something that affects your life, there is an even stronger feeling that you want to make a difference." Similarly, Buddy said he joined ASAN not only to find other autistic people but also to advocate on the behalf of older autistic adults: "Not to be alone and also to start advocating not just for myself because there's a whole generation of us older people who have never been diagnosed or who got diagnosed late in life. Who have gone through life with it. Not just with the school issues but with the postsecondary education issues and also with employment issues."

A few members were already activists in other settings before they joined the autistic rights movement to continue their work. Long before Lydia Brown became a disability rights lawyer and well-known activist, they were a high school student who wanted to end violent encounters between the police and autistic people. While introducing a bill to require police training on how to safely engage with autistic populations in the community, Lydia encountered ASAN and joined it. Since then, they have dedicated much of their professional and personal life to disability and autistic rights activism (e.g., organizing a number of protests, lobbying on Capitol Hill, helping with community engagement and program development at ASAN). Ending violence against disabled people has been the through line of their career:

> I have a lot of different goals, I guess. Overall, my goal lifelong is to work towards a world that is less violent towards disabled people, and of course I believe violence happens in a lot of realms and not just punching and kicking. The major theme of my work for the past several years has been violence against disabled people especially multiply marginalized disabled people and so, the areas that I have tended to focus [on are] restraint, seclusion and aversive, police brutality, prosecutorial misconduct and prisoner abuse against disabled people. I have also done a lot of work in other areas too, I have done a lot of work in supportive employment, I have done work on health care access, medical abuse, inclusion in higher education so I have done work in a number of areas but I guess the general focus has been the area of violence.

Even when the social justice agenda was not the initial attraction, members eventually engaged in political activities. It would have been hard *not* to become involved in such activities. After exposure to autistic rights ideas, which reframe disability as the outcome of institutional and structural ableism—not as an individual impairment—members recognized that collective action was critical to improving their opportunities and quality of life.

WHERE INSTITUTIONS FELL SHORT

Gabriel, the doctors, and Luba found themselves in desperate places before they joined the alternative biomedical and autistic rights movements. For incoming members, these movements were immediately attractive not because of their novel ideas, but because they offered hope of the sort that was not offered by conventional doctors and other professionals. Vulnerable, they joined movements that promised different answers.

Parents like Gabriel wanted more than what doctors and therapists recommended. After receiving their children's diagnosis, in their most fragile moment, they felt abandoned by their pediatricians. Trudy, who has an autistic son and works as a consultant, remembered, "We are so traumatized. I was when I was given this diagnosis and left for dead with me and my son. It was like, 'Here, you go figure it out.'" Parents feared that an autism diagnosis would mean a bleak future for them and their children. These anxieties were not unfounded—after all, even "high-functioning" autistic individuals like Luba find it difficult to achieve stability and independence. What, then, will happen to people who need more intensive support? Just as parents felt "left for dead," the alternative biomedical movement swooped to their rescue.

Practitioners, too, some of whom were converts from conventional medicine and had undergone years of training at institutions like Yale and Boston University, found alternative biomedicine and its potential attractive. They expanded their medical repertoire after realizing the limits of their medical tool-kits. For some, this realization was coaxed by distress, like when they perceived their own health or the health of a loved one at stake. Expanding medical repertoires to include alternative and experimental treatments is objectively risky, but practitioners felt it was necessary. The alternative biomedical movement presented something they were looking for: new tools and a new intellectual community.

For autistic participants, recurring professional and interpersonal challenges precipitated a diagnostic evaluation. It was not until she was twenty-three years old that Paige pursued a diagnostic evaluation to make sense of her lifelong struggles: "I guess to understand like why I felt alienated so much growing up. And different. And why certain things made me upset that wouldn't affect the average person. . . . I guess I was just wondering why I was the way I was." Like it did for so many others, the diagnosis put a name to Paige's experiences and guided her search for support. Entering the autistic rights movement, members learned to recognize personal troubles as collective problems. Movement members were especially frustrated about the dearth of employment opportunities. Although most participants had earned at least a college degree, they could not keep a job, which directly impacted their housing, health care, and financial security. The autistic rights movement identified the root of their exclusion and disability—ableism—and directed political action.

Where institutions fell short, the autism movements promised hope and reoriented participants' understandings of self, disability, and medical authority. As I show in the next two chapters, movements provide their members the resources to transform contentious knowledge about autism into lived realities.

4

KNOWING ONE'S TRIBE

The Transformation of Autistic Rights Into Reality

When Adriana arrived at the holiday party with her mother, she waved meekly and introduced herself, "I'm the autistic one." She wore winged eyeliner, bright red lipstick, black high heels, and a knitted sweater that depicted two penguins kissing. Her mother, Ingrid, set down a small lemon tart from Trader Joe's and made a beeline for the lumpy chaise lounge in the back of the living room; she was, in that rare moment, painfully *not* autistic. Ingrid kept to herself and did not engage with the other guests, most of whom were autistic and members of the Autistic Self Advocacy Network. Like a bored mother waiting at the playground, she quietly tinkered on her phone for the full duration of the party. Adriana, however, was wide-eyed and in awe. It was apparent that she seldom socialized with other autistic people.

Adriana entered a festive scene at Ash's apartment. Some were playing a game of Apples to Apples around the coffee table, which was adorned with a bright red runner. A fat black cat lumbered around the crowded room. In the kitchen, there was an assortment of eclectic snacks, including a frozen gluten-free cheese-free cheesecake, a plastic container of thick brown purée, a pre-opened box of chocolate donut balls, a blue tin of Danish butter cookies, and cranberry Sierra Mist. In the invitation, Ash had encouraged attendees to accommodate special dietary needs—and to avoid scented products to respect others' sensitivities. Adriana hinged her arms close to her body and her limp hands rhythmically flapped as she bounced in place (this is stereotypy, "repetition, rigidity, and invariance" behaviors common among autistic people).[1] Although she had introduced herself as the "autistic one" upon her arrival, she was "astounded" that the other guests recognized her autistic traits intuitively. Perhaps she thought she was hiding it well, or perhaps she did not know how autism usually presents. She asked a guest, Rachel, how she knew. Rachel said that some autistic people have a particular way of speaking that sounds similar to a Scandinavian accent. Others identified subtle characteristics, like body language and prosopagnosia (also known as "face blindness"). These were delicate signs that they had learned to identify from being around autistic others. Adriana was giddy. She could not get enough, and she incessantly demanded further explanation from the guests—*how could they tell? How did they know?*

Rachel got annoyed with Adriana's repetitive questions and defensively snapped back: *What was wrong with appearing autistic? Was it such a bad thing?* She told Adriana that these concerns about appearing autistic stemmed from a narrow definition of normal. Agreeing with Rachel, the others assured her that it is not a bad thing to appear or to be autistic. Adriana said she had a hard time maintaining friendships and that her mother said she made people "miserable." Suddenly, all eyes turned back to Ingrid. She looked up from her paper plate of lemon tart crumbs, frozen with embarrassment. Adriana said people thought she was weird and that her family did not like her bouncing and hand flapping. Ash commiserated: their therapists used to tell them to suppress those movements and have "quiet hands." This hit a nerve. The group expressed their collective disapproval of behavioral therapy. Again, Adriana kept insisting: *How could they tell? How did they know?* Having cooled off, Rachel told her that people have a natural ability to identify others who share their "culture"—and Adriana clearly shared their culture.

This holiday party and other social spaces like it resist the medicalization of autism. Adriana arrived at the event perceiving autism as an undesirable disorder, one that isolated her and made the people in her life "miserable." Because she was a newcomer, members explicitly articulated basic ideas and norms that usually go unsaid, teaching her that autism is not an impairment and does not need fixing. The autistic rights movement, as a community, transforms autism into an empowered identity and culture through social events like this. Although the outside world is still largely designed for neurotypical citizens—those who are neurologically typical—the movement behaves as a free space set apart from the demands of dominant actors (like parents, experts, and therapists) and institutions.[2] Here, members theorize a collective autistic identity that is grounded in their embodied experiences.

In this chapter, I demonstrate that the autistic rights movement is an insulated space where members collectively *produce* and *enact* contentious knowledge. First, I describe how the coalescence of an autistic community precipitated the emergence of an autistic rights movement. Second, I show that the formation of a collective autistic identity is simultaneously the formation of contentious knowledge. Movement members generate a collective autistic identity by comparing experiences, affirming shared knowledge, and opposing medicalization. Collective autistic identity is not just a resource for mobilization; it is also an objective and achievement in its own right. Third, I demonstrate how the movement, as a socio-spatial environment, facilitates the enactment of autistic rights. In this protected space, participants incubate ideas and test strategies to improve inclusion. At meetings and retreats hosted by movement groups, the principles of acceptance structure the rules of interaction and the physical environment (e.g., accessibility, sound, lighting, scents). And finally, to highlight how movement participation empowers autistic identity, I contrast the narratives of movement members with those of two autistic individuals who pathologize autism.

BEGINNINGS

When Parents Were in Charge

Well before they could make collective demands, autistic individuals had to find each other. This was an enormous task. During the earliest days of autistic community formation, there were two main obstacles to this effort: parents' domination of autism advocacy and the limited communication technologies of the early 1990s. The priorities of parent-led advocacy were—and remain—largely oriented toward research and family support.[3] Parent conferences were not designed for autistic people, but some attended anyway because there were so few opportunities to meet autistic others.[4] Jim Sinclair, a cofounder of Autism Network International (ANI), recalled having to carve out an autistic space at parent-led conferences: "When there were autism conferences that allowed us exhibit space, we would just have an exhibit with a couple of poster boards, and they gave us one of those cool conference exhibit tables with the floor-length skirts. Autistic people would congregate there. Lots of laughter, in the middle of all the parent-oriented pity parties."

When non-autistic advocates organize events to bring autistic people together, these spaces often reflect their own presumptions and objectives. Having attended some parent-organized events, Harry, who works at an accounting firm, complained, "I don't feel they necessarily focus on the quality of the autistic individual themselves and some of the positive traits that they can bring." Although he was an adult and required little support, he found these efforts on behalf of autistic people to be infantilizing: "Even people that run groups that are supposed to be for higher-functioning people, I just feel like no matter what kind of position I am in my life I just feel like I always get treated lower than them." I observed one autism social event that was organized by a small group of young, gregarious neurotypical women who had glowing, well-hydrated skin and billowy palazzo pants. The purpose of this event was simple: light socializing and amusement. The women provided the autistic attendees—most of whom were adults—with board games, crafts, and snacks. Had I not known who the event was for, I would have guessed it was an afterschool program for young children. The attendees seemed to enjoy themselves, but this was certainly not a radical space that supported resistance and mobilization. Describing such organizations as "frenemies" (friend-enemies), Charles, an electrical engineer, explained, "They're not really providing actual help, but they're providing bits and pieces here that just get us out of our parents' basements or whatever. Like a few different activities. But that doesn't constitute community-building."

Autistic individuals recognized that they needed to create their own spaces. ANI, the first autistic self-advocacy organization, was founded in 1992. Jim Sinclair explained that the organization was formed in response to the lack of an independent autistic community.[5] In its earliest days, ANI was a pen pal list and a printed newsletter that included content written by and for autistic people. Even so, most of the initial subscribers were parents of autistic people. Rick, one of the leaders of ANI and the Association for Autistic Community, recalled that the pen pal system was limiting because letter writing is not an ideal form of communication for many autistic people. Communication and contact improved when ANI created an email listserv in 1994.

ANI: Creating an Autistic Community

The advent of the internet allowed many previously private experiences to become public.[6] In this case, online platforms fostered the coalescence of autistic and disability communities (at least among those who were literate and could access the internet),[7] which spilled over to exist offline.[8] With the formation of autistic networks, members created their own activist agenda that complemented the more established disability rights movement that arose in the 1960s. Online forums facilitated communication among autistic people, and some connected in person at parent-led conferences. In 1996, ANI hosted the first Autreat, a multiday conference intended to foster autistic community in a physical space. Unlike most other autism conferences, this one was organized by and designed for autistic people.[9] It was entirely separate from the conferences and meetings of the parent-led organizations. Autreat became an annual event, and its attendees increased from about fifty in its first year to about one hundred in its last. In 2013, ANI and Autreat ended, and in their place, the Association for Autistic Community (AAC) emerged. AAC was founded by former ANI members and hosted a similar annual conference.

In ANI's earliest years, as Sinclair noted, it aligned with the disability rights movement but lacked the organizational capacity to be politically active on its own: "We wanted to do more political advocacy, but not enough participants were into that, or had any idea how to go about it." While a social movement could not materialize overnight, the growing autistic community nurtured a collective consciousness, or a realization of shared circumstances and interests.[10] The rise of a collective consciousness gave roots to an autistic rights movement that would become larger than ANI itself. Lydia Brown, a disability justice activist and lawyer, explained, "What we know now as the autistic rights movement . . . [was] the emergence of an autistic conscience; the emergence of the ideas that would come to later be called neurodiversity really began, at least in the Western world." Sinclair also appreciated the importance of solidifying a community first: "I didn't think 'autistic' and 'community' could go together, until I realized it was already happening. In retrospect, I think that was probably a necessary precursor for organized political advocacy to be possible. There has to be a clear sense of who 'we' are and what 'we' need, before there can be a movement to get it." Having witnessed the evolution of ANI, Rick similarly recognized that the autistic community had laid the foundation for future activism: "Just getting people together. I think the fact that this has established a community. Has allowed the community to have its offshoots of advocacy."

ASAN: Entering the Political Realm and Making Demands

As the autistic community flourished and grew in numbers (both online and offline), it became apparent that political activism was necessary if equity and representation were to be achieved. It was also finally possible. Ari Ne'eman, one of the founders of the

Autistic Self Advocacy Network (ASAN), explained, "ANI and the autistic community online had done tremendously important work building cultural space for the autistic community and flushing out the ideas of neurodiversity, and now was the time to take them into the political realm." This sentiment precipitated the founding of ASAN in 2006.

At the time, Ne'eman had just graduated from high school. He was precocious. One participant remembered him from this era; Ne'eman gave her his business card at an intra-university event, which was a strange thing for a college student to do: "I remember meeting him and he gave me an ASAN card and this was before ASAN was really even a thing. And I just remember like—he was wearing a tie and I just remember being like, 'What is this?' I was like, 'Okay, thanks.' But I remember I liked him. Like he was a fun guy, but he's a very—I think he might have been born holding a briefcase." Ne'eman is academic and confident, and he speaks authoritatively. He is a large guy but carries himself in a way that makes his presence seem even bigger. He was the executive director for the first ten years of ASAN and was appointed to the National Council on Disability in 2009 by President Barack Obama.

Ne'eman recounted how, at the time when ASAN was founded, autism was gaining public visibility, but the attention and discourse excluded autistic perspectives:

In 2006, there was a rapidly growing wave of public attention surrounding autism. Autism was in the movies, on television, public service announcements, newspapers, magazines. Pretty much everywhere you went, you were going to be able to see something about autism. And yet, at the same time, there was virtually no acknowledgement of the perspectives or priorities of autistic adults ourselves. You know, we were awash in a sea of publicity that treated us as incidental to our own lives and so, there was a growing sense in the autistic adult community that something had to be done to address that. . . . We had this kind of emerging, very early autistic culture that had come about through a combination of Autreats and Jim Sinclair's efforts and this sort of growing community on the internet in various forms and list serves. And throughout that emerging autistic culture, there was a sense that we had a problem and we had to do something about it.

The autistic community and its culture evolved to include a political agenda, which aims to "advance the principles of the disability rights movement with regard to autism" through public policy, "autistic cultural activities," and leadership training.[11] Only a year after its founding, ASAN achieved its first success.

In 2007, The Child Study Center at New York University ran an advertisement campaign to raise awareness about children's mental and neurological conditions, one of which was autism.[12] The ad was stylized as a photocopied ransom note with courier typeface, threatening, "We have your son. We will make sure he will no longer be able to care for himself or interact socially as long as he lives. This is only the beginning. *[signed]* Autism." The ad campaign incited both praise and outrage. Some applauded it for raising awareness, while others decried its insensitivity. With support from other disability rights organizations, ASAN led a letter-writing protest to demand the ads' removal. ASAN criticized the ads for stigmatizing disabled people, presenting inaccurate information about autism, propagating fear, and callously suggesting "that our true selves have been 'kidnapped' by terrible 'diseases' and that we need urgent treatment to become normal again."[13] After only two weeks, the ads were pulled. The protest brought ASAN visibility and pushed the organization to publicly articulate its stance on autistic and disability rights.

The accessibility of the internet was critical to connecting autistic people, but as Ne'eman recognized, the movement depended on strong offline communities to advocate for local change:

> The role of the online; the emergence of the internet in the development of autistic culture and community cannot be overstated. But, if you're going to do work on advocacy and you're going to try and do something like convince your state legislator to expand services to cover autistic adults who don't meet the level of care requirements to qualify for most Medicaid services today, you need to be mobilizing a few dozen folks in that person's district. And if you're going to want to talk about how the library has these awful fluorescent lights and maybe we can convince them to do something about that in their upcoming renovation, you're going to be wanting to bring some folks together in your local community. So, we're making a lot of progress on that.

In-person communities, moreover, supported the development of a collective autistic identity, which is both a resource for and an achievement of mobilization.

COLLECTIVE AUTISTIC IDENTITY

Buddy remembered a difficult childhood. His home life was tumultuous, and he did not get along with the other children at school: "As a kid I was always like the walking encyclopedia, little professor.[14] Also, with the atypical with it, I was like—I could never get along with other kids, but I always was gravitated to being around adults." He attributed some of these challenges to his social communication style: "Not being able to read facial expressions or body language, you miss out on 90 percent of the time what people are saying. And I process language literally. So, if somebody says the wrong thing, in the wrong way, that other people would brush aside, let it go in one ear and out the other. I would take it mega personally. And I would have meltdowns." A week after his forty-seventh birthday, he experienced a "suicidal depressive breakdown," which prompted a psychological evaluation. His doctors diagnosed him with Asperger's syndrome. The diagnosis opened up his social world. Buddy reasoned, "There's got to be more people like me. So, I started reaching out."

Buddy became an active member of multiple autism-specific organizations. While I was doing observations, he showed up to almost every chapter meeting and special event, driving at least two hours to get into the city. He was dedicated to being fully present. When an event was held on the second floor of a building without an elevator, Buddy, who has cerebral palsy, moved his crutches and crawled up the stairs. He was impoverished and unemployed, but he was generous with the few resources he had: his time and an old but functioning car. He frequently offered to pick up others to attend various events and drop them off at home afterward without any expectation of compensation for gas. After an ASAN member lost her mother, he invited her over to celebrate the holidays with him and his brother. In these ways, Buddy was the consummate autistic rights member, committed to the cause and the community. Although his social communication differences had cut him off from his peers for most of his life, he was now a part of "an autistic subculture":

> Even though when they say autistics cannot make friends, that is
> not true. We do it in our own way. Because I have many friends,
> through my church and also through the autistic community all
> over this area. And also, the internet is a good resource to find

other people on the spectrum. Because there are many—there's probably tens if not hundreds of thousands of autistics who are online and who have formed a wider community that essentially say that there is an autistic subculture within the disability community.

Buddy had come into a *collective autistic identity*, a sense of solidarity based on shared embodied experiences (what it is like to be an autistic person) and marginalization (what it is like to be autistic in an ableist society). This identity is different from the collective *illness* identity of health social movements, which emerges from "'cognitive, moral, and emotional connection' with other illness sufferers."[15] In health social movements, activists politicize their collective illness identity to demand changes to policies, medical practice, and scientific research.[16] Autism is a medicalized condition, but because autistic rights activists do not see themselves as ill, they politicize their collective autistic identity to gain civil rights and protections (which are not limited to matters of health and health care). Their collective autistic identity involves both a sense of solidarity and a developing body of knowledge.

Comparing Notes on the Autistic Experience

One evening, after an ASAN chapter meeting adjourned, several of the members and I walked down the street to a local chain restaurant for an early dinner. This was Mara's first ASAN meeting. She had found out she was autistic just a few years earlier. Mara looked down at her berry smoothie and said that her mother lived in a semi-rural place where she grew all kinds of berries and raised chickens. Every now and then, a hawk or fox would attack the chickens. I asked where her mother lived, expecting her to say Germany because of the familiar accent. I was wrong. Her parents were originally from the northeastern United States. I admitted to her that I had thought her family was from Europe because of the way she spoke. Mara explained that when she was teaching English in Thailand, she met many English speakers from all over the world, so perhaps these linguistic exposures had modified her accent. But then Jack noted that there is such a thing as an "autistic voice" or an autistic way of speaking. Another ASAN member had described this characteristic at the holiday party a couple of months earlier. Research typically frames autistic speech and prosody as "unusual" and "abnormal," warning that these characteristics may be detrimental to social interactions.[17] Yet within the autistic rights movement, members do not treat the "autistic voice" as something that jeopardizes friendships and employment opportunities; rather, it is one of the distinctive traits that connect them to each other.[18]

Mara told us that when she was in Thailand, the locals had a harder time noticing that she was different. She supposed that they dismissed her social behaviors and mannerisms as a cultural difference, something uniquely American that did not translate well. Jack said when he went outside the country, people also attributed his idiosyncrasies to his being a foreigner. As they compared their experiences abroad, Mara and Jack agreed that autism is largely defined by cultural context and expectations. In a comparative study of how autism is constructed in three countries, Hyun Uk Kim similarly reported that the construction of autism varies by culture and argued that these findings should support an acceptance of individual differences.[19] In group settings, both formal and informal, movement members deconstruct autistic traits that are either excluded from or problematized in clinical descriptions. Together, members learn to identify fellow autistic people and to recognize their shared interests, quirks, and mannerisms.

Sinclair recounted how years earlier, before the formation of ANI, they had written to UCLA autism researchers for information about the "then-new high functioning autism." They received a packet of articles. From their perspective, these articles portrayed autism in a way that was unflattering and incongruent with how they saw themself: "The articles were all about how we lack empathy, are incapable of genuine interpersonal connections, self-centered, lacking self-awareness and insight, etc., etc., etc. Not at all the sort of person I thought I was, and definitely not the sort of people I would want to meet and associate with." After connecting with other autistic people, Sinclair found that what they learned from these new relationships contradicted the way research articles portrayed autistic people: "When I started actually reading stuff written by, and eventually corresponding directly with, autistic people, they were not at all the way those articles described us." Being among other autistic people dispelled the myths they had been told about autism and their own idiosyncrasies. Autistic people did not lack empathy and self-awareness, and they were not self-centered and incapable of interpersonal connections. Sinclair cofounded ANI partly to address "the immense chasm between our reality and the things 'everyone knew' about autism." In this way, the cultivation of a collective autistic identity is simultaneously the production of contentious knowledge. The foundation of autistic people's solidarity directly resists the way experts, parents, and therapists conceptualize autism as a disorder.

When challenging medical professionals and experts, support groups and communities provide a space to affirm health experiences.[20] Similarly, the autistic rights movement is a space where members reify autism as a human difference, rather than a disorder. Rachel remarked, "It's like a bar. It's like the equivalent of a bar where it's a lot of complaining but occasionally you get work done. And it's a very empowering thing to be around people." Participants indicated that the acquisition of an autism diagnosis served as a passport into communities of individuals to whom they could relate; as Damian remarked, "I know my tribe." For Rachel, this community lets her ease into a more "genuine" version of herself: "I'm darker and I'm snarkier in real life. . . . There's more of a sense of forgiveness in the disability community, there's more a sense of if you make a mistake, nobody's going to hate you for it. It's safer to be vulnerable." Being among similar others is a validating and authentic experience—it feels like "real life." As they participated in the movement, members realized that they were not alone in their experiences of navigating the neurotypical world. They felt not only understood but also appreciated and valued.

Of course, the movement is not free of the social divisions found in many other group settings, whether autistic or neurotypical. The movement demands acceptance, but acceptance should not be confused with an expectation of congeniality. Sinclair explained, "Autistic people, like any other group of people, are not all alike. We don't all have the same needs and desires for social interaction. Some of us don't get along with others of us. There have been misunderstandings and disagreements among us, hurt feelings, lost friendships, and worse."[21]

The movement has cliques and cattiness. Despite all his good will and dedication, Buddy was not well-liked by some of the others. He was infamous for his non sequiturs and repetitive statements. When he spoke, I would sometimes catch the others exchanging furtive glances and dismissive eyerolls across the table. Perhaps personality differences accounted for these intragroup fractures, but it was notable that Buddy's cognitive and intellectual abilities did not seem to match those of the others. He needed greater supports. During our interview, Paige expressed her disappointment with the way some members treated Buddy. She expected them to be united and was upset to find they were not:

> [Buddy's] really great, but I don't know if you noticed at that party how they were kind of making fun of him. And I don't like that at all. We're supposed to be this community where we're all ostracized and we're all sharing this similar experience. But they make fun of him so much. And he participates so much. He has the best intentions. And if he goes off topic then that's fine, whatever, he goes off topic. . . . And that's what I've noticed a lot of too is in the dialogue online and in-person, people get ignored. Outright ignored. Like, someone will say something and it won't even be acknowledged.

A collective autistic identity articulates solidarity and shared knowledge—but it does not guarantee friendship. Moreover, it reflects the shared experiences of those who participate in its construction, which means the characteristics and experiences of those who require greater support, who have limited communication, or who are intellectually disabled are either left out or underrepresented.

Constructing the Neurotypical Other

"Autistics are more likely to say what they want versus NTs [neurotypicals] [who] will leave a blank space where you have to fill it in. I'm not trying to be derogatory," said Felix. "I'm not offended," I replied. While collective autistic identity articulates who autistic people are, the construction of neurotypicals defines who they are not. Neurotypicals—or as many say, "NTs" for short—are people who are neurologically typical. Importantly, they are *not* autistic. Participants were frustrated by the experience of living in a world designed and operated by neurotypicals. In their interactions with each other, they commiserated about the neurotypicals who complicated their lives—the ones they had to work with, live with, deal with on a daily basis. I asked Vanna what she personally gained from being a part of groups like ASAN:

> VANNA: Personally? It's been kind of fun.
> CATHERINE: Kind of fun?
> VANNA: What I've personally gained? I don't know. Inner peace? No. Satisfaction? I don't know. People I can bitch to.
> CATHERINE: That's a good point.
> VANNA: It is. You can bitch about NTs. We do a lot of that actually. We do a lot of that.

The movement is also a space where members examine and analyze neurotypicals. As they contrasted neurotypicals with themselves, these conversations sharpened their collective autistic identity. Members critiqued the way parents and professionals assumed that being neurotypical was desirable, arguing that many neurotypicals are disingenuous, deceptive, impractical, overly sensitive, and socially insatiable. *What is so desirable about that?* Through their collective construction of neurotypical outsiders, they celebrated the strengths of being autistic and empowered autistic identity.

The social behaviors and norms of neurotypicals mystified Abby: "Last week I was questioning the amount of empathy I have. And I was saying, saying to my mom, 'It seems like people are constantly caring and thinking about other people and I'm not.' And she said, 'No. You just don't pretend like they do.' We got to get people to realize there is a lot of pretending going on." She argued that neurotypicals accuse autistic people of being unempathetic when perhaps neurotypicals are too insincere: "It's reciprocal altruism. Like on Facebook when somebody has a baby and they post 10,000 pictures of it and everybody says 'Oh, that baby's perfect.' And you look at it and you know it looks like Jabba the Hutt. You know half of those people have got to be lying. So, what do I do? I don't say 'Your baby is ugly.' I say, 'Congratulations. You're going to be a great mother or great father.'" Yet because autistic people live in a neurotypical world, they face real consequences when they do not follow subtle social rules. At the time of our interview, Abby had a graduate degree in library science but was working odd jobs. She had previously worked as a children's librarian, but she had been fired from her last two positions because parents complained about her personality: "They were telling my boss that their kids were afraid of me. Strangely enough the kids themselves didn't seem freaked out. I think it was more the parents." She tried to improve her interactions with parents but still lost her job: "My boss was like bitching me out about my social skills in a very patronizing way, by the way. . . . So, I put myself out there. I tried to get in the conversations with the parents. And some of the—they went pretty well, but I was like—it was very exhausting. This isn't rude. There's only so many times where I can talk about somebody's baby."

Imagining what it would be like to be neurotypical, Vanna explained, "Can be cool and it can suck, like anything else. I think that there are advantages to [being neurotypical] that need to be emphasized as much as the disadvantages. I mean, we tend to focus on the negatives of disability but disability is as normal as anything." A common argument is that being neurotypical is not objectively better than being autistic. Seth, a long-time autistic rights activist, gave the example of his niece, whom he considered to be "profoundly *non*-autistic," meaning she is highly social. He said that his neurotypical niece engaged in many risky behaviors and was susceptible to peer influence. Her social tendencies, he worried, were "beyond what is necessary to empathetically and sympathetically take people's perspective." Seth concluded that being neurotypical is not inherently a good thing and can even drive a person to make irrational choices. Part of empowering an autistic identity is whittling away at the presumption of neurotypical superiority.

As a favor, I participated in the "Ask an NT" Q&A panel at the end of two separate retreats. This panel has a theatrical and performative quality. It is a satirical critique of the way autistic people are treated as "parent resource material" at most autism conferences, where Q&As are designed to help parents understand their children's experiences and get advice.[22] "Ask an NT" borrows this Q&A format and flips the roles. Now, in an autistic-majority community, neurotypicals are the ones who are offering insights into their bewildering world. The main purpose of this event is for autistic people to poke fun at neurotypicals—and, as a lower priority, to learn about the neurotypical experience.

At one "Ask an NT," my neurotypical partner was Chad. Chad worked at the front desk of the conference site. The organizers asked him to participate at the last minute. He had a chipper demeanor and athletic build. Overall, he appeared simple and unremarkable. He was a bro. As a young, white, neurotypical, able-bodied, heterosexual man, he was perhaps the perfect representation of normativity and privilege. Sitting next to Chad, I realized that this was one of the rare times when he and I could be grouped together because of something we had in common. Together, we were strawmen in front of microphones and a charged audience.

The questions posed by the participants—replete with inside jokes—highlighted characteristics unique to their embodied experiences and characteristics of the neurotypical experience that eluded them. This was an interactive performance that defined "us" (autistics) and "them" (neurotypicals). The audience members' facetious and satirical questions referenced the stereotypes they held about neurotypicals, most of which were inspired by neurotypicals' perception of autism deficits, such as, "Do NTs get anxious when they do not get eye contact?" This question was a critique of therapists' and parents' demand for eye contact, which some participants had been subjected to when they received behavioral interventions as children. Other questions celebrated autistic strengths while mocking neurotypical weaknesses: "Is it difficult to not feel passionate for things?" This question referenced "autistic passion" and "obsessive joy," the special ability to take great pleasure in becoming wholly immersed in an interest.[23] With these questions, the autistic rights members expressed their understanding of the unique characteristics of their community. Concurrently, they expressed their discontent with the ways neurotypicals regard and mistreat autistic people.

Other questions about neurotypical experiences came from genuine curiosity, perhaps inspired by encounters that had either perplexed or annoyed the question-askers: "How come NTs are flaky in their interactions, saying one thing but meaning another?" "Do you need time away after having a lot of social interaction?" I answered that I thrive on social interaction and need it all the time, to which an attendee asked, "How can you know who you are if you're always around people?" (Ouch.) Then Chad chimed in to say he also liked being around people but sometimes hid from his wife and in-laws in the bathroom. (I felt embarrassed for both Chad and me—as neurotypicals, specifically as neurotypical heterosexuals.) Questions like these were less performative and satirical than the others. Here the neurotypical was a subject of sincere interest: "What kind of sounds bother you?" "What kind of textures do you enjoy?" Chad said he enjoyed the texture of barbells. Through the Q&A, activists reified the differences between autistic people and those who are neurotypical—delimiting who they are and who they are not.

ENACTING AUTISTIC COMMUNITIES

I drove my rental car seventy miles north from Dulles airport in Virginia, first along high-traffic city highways, then along verdant roads that were populated with small farms, quaint houses, antique shops, and conservative campaign signs. Nestled in the quiet woods of Waynesboro, Pennsylvania, I found the Jewish retreat center. The center was a few years old but still smelled of fresh construction material. Its lobby had a rustic aesthetic, decorated with a stone fireplace and deep leather sofas. On the property were a little lake and a large groundhog. Over the next five days, the center hosted the AAC conference.

Multiday conferences and regular local meetings are spaces where members of the autistic rights movement enact and apply their core principles and, at the same time, where they reinforce their collective autistic identity. These meetings are organized by and designed for autistic people, which means neurotypicals are not welcomed unless they are there as support for an autistic member.[24] Within these spaces, the attendees observe physical and social rules that aim to maximize inclusivity and the acceptance of differences. Practicing autism acceptance requires heightened mindfulness of and respect for both personal and others' needs. It is expected that attendees refrain from making assumptions about other people and provide accommodations for a variety of needs. These free spaces model the ideal society envisioned by members. Multiday conferences, even more than regular meetings, are well-equipped for such modeling because they are usually hosted in semi-remote venues that make it possible to achieve an autistic majority.

Despite special efforts to meet a range of needs, there are limits to the inclusivity at both local meetings and conferences. At the meetings and conferences I observed, the accommodations were limited by feasibility and the requirements of the members who were present. These members typically required relatively little support. Nearly everyone used verbal communication, some were employed or in school, and many lived independently (without a caregiver). Autistic people who needed greater support or who may have intellectual disabilities rarely attended. The cost of participation was also prohibitive for many, as one AAC conference attendee noticed, "So at this retreat, you will find people first off disproportionately from the region that the retreat is held in because that means less travel expenses. Secondly, you're going to meet people generally who are able to afford a retreat like this. Autreat was a bit better in that regard but not by terribly much. Frankly, this was expensive."

Governing Spaces of Inclusion and Acceptance

On the first night of the AAC conference, one of the organizers reviewed the rules at the orientation. Many of these rules encouraged collaborative accessibility, accommodating behaviors, and small personal sacrifices to maximize inclusion. Their rationale prioritized the comfort and safety of the most vulnerable and high-needs attendees above individual liberty and majority rule. Mindful of many autistic people's sensory needs, the organizers asked attendees to avoid wearing fragrances (no perfumes or scented hygiene products), using flashing lights (because of seizures), and making loud noises (like clapping). Romy, who works as a record keeper at a doors and windows company, noted that these rules and social norms are important for her participation, "I can re-charge and be in Autistic space. . . . Well, like if I have to cover my ears or go out because of loud noise, people don't question it. Or if I need to walk around people do not question why I have to do these things."

Seth said that autistic conferences like this one allow attendees the "freedom to interact socially the way that is comfortable," free of the "arbitrary expectations" found at neurotypical gatherings. Within autistic spaces, activists can freely "be autistic" among fellow autistic people. They do not have to contort themselves to appear "normal." This means that behavioral eccentricities that are usually frowned upon in the neurotypical world (like stereotypy) are accepted and anticipated. During conference presentations, attendees were free to compose themselves in the ways they found most comfortable. Attendees rocked back and forth, sat on the ground, and perused their tablets and laptops. On one occasion, a person got out of his chair and curled into the fetal position on the ground. A little girl, who was accompanied by her mother, shrieked and babbled as she pranced around the dining room.[25] No one seemed to mind or even notice. Some wore sunglasses inside when it was too bright or noise-canceling headphones when it was too loud. Among autistic people, these behaviors were unremarkable.

To create such an autistic space, the organizers established rules to manage social interactions. Attendees were asked to be mindful of others' triggers (stimuli that could provoke past traumas); this meant stopping what they were doing immediately if someone said it was a trigger. Photography was not permitted without consent because some attendees were not "out" as autistic (similar to being "out" with sexual orientation or gender identity). A communication badge system was used to clearly indicate each attendee's socializing preferences. This tool was developed by ANI for their first Autreat.[26] It consists of a rectangular badge that one pins somewhere visible, as one would a name tag. There are traditionally three colors to choose from: green, yellow, and red. During the AAC conference, the organizers debuted a fourth color, purple. Each color explicitly communicates the type of interaction the wearer is seeking (see table 4.1). If a person is flexible and invites all forms of communication, they forgo the badge.

TABLE 4.1 COMMUNICATION BADGE COLORS AND THEIR DEFINITIONS

Badge color	Definition provided by ASAN, 2016
Green	"The person is actively seeking communication; they have trouble initiating conversations, but want to be approached by people who are interested in talking."
Yellow	"The person only wants to talk to people they recognize, not by strangers or people they only know from the Internet. The badge-wearer might approach strangers to talk, and that is okay; the approached people are welcome to talk back to them in that case. But unless you have already met the person face-to-face, you should not approach them to talk."
Red	"The person probably does not want to talk to anyone, or only wants to talk to a few people. The person might approach others to talk, and that is okay; the approached people are welcome to talk back to them in that case. But unless you have been told already by the badge-wearer that you are on their 'red list,' you should not approach them to talk."
Purple (Beta)	This color means that the person is interested in interaction but not verbal interaction. This may mean that the person would rather use sign language or an assisted communication device or share an activity. (Tentative definition provided by AAC.)

Throughout the week—at both Autreat and the AAC conference—attendees regularly changed the color they displayed on their badge to reflect their current preferences. Generally, attendees were careful to respect others' badge colors. However, a few attendees pointed out that once a person had engaged with another, they sometimes forgot to check the badge colors before initiating another interaction. This was especially true when smaller groups started to form; attendees would become comfortable with one another and ignore the badge colors. While the use of badges was inconsistent, their availability was important because it normalized differences in social communication.

The physical environment was also arranged to meet the sensory needs common among autistic people. Rick replaced the fluorescent lights that many find harsh with halogen lamps propped up on ladders. During and after the presentations, instead of applauding with claps that could disturb those with auditory sensitivities, attendees wiggled their fingers in the air to express support, amusement, and approval. There were few presentations (about three per day), and they were spread out to create a relaxed experience. A separate room was designated as a "hiding cave" to provide a space for attendees to take a break and decompress.[27]

Centering Autistic Interests

At both conferences and regular local meetings, members organize activities that facilitate community building and appeal to autistic interests. Throughout the year, the local ASAN chapter hosts numerous events, such as social gatherings and demonstrations. During conferences, the presentations have included research conducted by autistic people, information about adaptive strategies, and examinations of autistic rights issues. For instance, during Autreat 2013, one autistic scholar presented her study of spatial experiences and another his study of cross-cultural attitudes toward autism. Unlike the vast majority of autism-related research, these studies were designed and conducted by autistic people.

Special social events also cater to autistic interests by leveraging sensory processing differences (like sensitivity to lights and sounds) to create an experience that is especially enjoyable to autistic individuals. At conferences, a "glow party" is traditionally held on one of the evenings. In preparation for one of these glow parties, Seth took the pooled money to buy a huge number of glow-in-the-dark sticks, bracelets, necklaces, wands, and other accessories. Attendees taped up the interior windows of a conference room to completely darken the room. The glow accessories illuminated the space with their soft fluorescent glow, creating a calm, mesmerizing ambiance. The attendees twirled, waved, and flapped the glow sticks. It was charming to see adults—many of whom are highly accomplished and professional—appreciate the playfulness of this activity. The quiet music dissolved into the background. Rick served small glasses of kosher wine, but few partook. A couple of attendees linked several of the glow sticks together with small plastic connectors, creating a long, flexible chain. They swung it like a jump rope and watched the colors sail through the air. As the rope swung around and around, Hil, a social worker and public self-advocate, whispered, "I could watch this all day." Romy got in the middle and tried to jump the glow rope, but it broke apart. Ash flapped some glow sticks that had been bent into large butterfly wings. Rick, a tall and stocky man, wrapped himself in the long glow rope and posed grandly. One attendee twisted the glow rope to form the rainbow infinity symbol that represents AAC and suggested that forming the symbol should become a tradition. I found this activity calming, but it was clear that I did not appreciate it nearly as much as the other attendees. What made the event special to the attendees was being among others who shared their intense enjoyment of this heightened sensory experience.

At the end of the conference week, the attendees gathered to give feedback on the venue, structure, and presentations. After the purple communication badge made its debut, the attendees discussed the flaws and benefits of its implementation. This also prompted a discussion of the finer rules for the use of the other communication colors. The attendees wanted to clarify the meaning of each color to reduce misinterpretations. These conversations generated ideas about how to improve the construction of autistic spaces.

A Neurotypical Reality, a Neurodiversity Dream?

Autistic spaces, however, are temporary. When members leave meetings and conferences, they are transported back to the neurotypical world, where they are made to feel alien. After an immersive week at the conference, Romy said it was difficult to leave, "Well, I really like coming to AAC conference and Autreat because I get to be in an autistic space once a year. I find it really hard to leave and go back into this world. So, when I am here it is kind of like being shielded from this crazy world."

One participant, Alfie, was especially aware of the thin, fragile boundary between autistic spaces and the neurotypical world in which they were all embedded. He saw neurodiversity as a futile, unrealistic dream. He was used to navigating worlds in which he did not fully belong. When he was in his early twenties, he came to the United States with his family as asylum seekers from the Philippines. He worked undocumented for the first seventeen years: "I didn't tell anybody I didn't have any papers or anything like that. Nobody. I didn't trust anyone except my family. I told lies for a living. I was in retail sales for seventeen years and banking and all of that." Then, in his forties, he learned about his infantile autism diagnosis, which his mother had kept secret. After hustling for most of his life, Alfie interpreted autistic empowerment in a way that emphasized individualism and self-sufficiency:

> Look at chameleons. How do you think they catch these little insects? Do you think they sit around saying "Hey, I'm a chameleon, hey come on?" Then they don't catch any insects and they die. They blend into the environment, they wait, they wait, and then *boom*. They catch the insect. It's all about the nature, duplicity, camouflage, deception. It's all part of nature. You don't have to acknowledge it. You don't have to like it. That's the way it is in the real world and it's hard for me to explain it to these guys even with my own social group.

He had little faith in the autistic rights movement or in its power to improve his quality of life:

> I think advocacy has its roles too, like ASAN for the political arena. If people want to advocate to say, "Hey we want rights for autistic people," great, wonderful. What's that got to do for me personally? Is that going to land me a job? Is that going to make me a much better person? Like I said earlier, you've got to do the homework yourself. You can get the tools. You can get help with other people. You can listen to them. You can formulate your own battle plan, but everything comes down to you. What you're going to do for yourself.

It was not the strength of the autistic rights activists that he doubted, but the willingness of policymakers: "Thing about politics, about policymakers, they're all in it for themselves I'm telling you. . . . Autistics should offer their own self-help. They should have their own organizations to provide assistance with other people in the spectrum. They don't need policymakers to do that for them. They should be able to do things themselves." Even though Alfie did not fully subscribe to the autistic rights agenda, his passive participation in the movement gave him a sense of solidarity. In these autistic spaces, he connected with "fellow travelers," he said, "I started going to these groups more often when I had the time. I did go, so I said to myself, 'You know what? I guess I belong here kind of.'" Alfie was pessimistic about social change, but within the movement, he refined his concept of self and saw opportunities for community building.

PATHOLOGIZING AUTISM: THE CASES OF WINSTON AND RITA

I have shown that participation in the autistic rights movement is important to cultivating an empowered autistic identity. Here, members access the social, material, and conceptual resources to realize a demedicalized self and nurture an autistic culture. This positive influence is brought to the foreground when members' narratives are juxtaposed with the perspectives of autistic people outside the movement. I interviewed two autistic adults—Winston and Rita—whose embodied experiences and understandings of autistic self are structured by the alternative biomedical framework. They pathologize autism and see themselves as physically sick. Their perspective is not representative of autistic people in general, or even of the autistic children of alternative biomedical parents. (There are few autistic adults who are visibly active and vocal in this community.) Their views, however, highlight the profound impact that movements can have on self-concept. In contrast to the autistic rights members, Winston and Rita present a medicalized and disempowered autistic identity.

On a warm autumn night at a kitschy resort in St. Petersburg, Florida, Winston flitted around the outdoor reception with a soprano recorder tucked under his arm. Francine, a nutritional therapist and the mother of an autistic child, found Winston inspiring and wanted to know what his parents had done right. A sociable and outspoken man in his late twenties, Winston was sort of a poster child for alternative biomedicine—and had artfully forged this reputation into a career. He was a free agent in the world of autism advocacy, traveling year-round to talk about his experiences at events and conferences like this one: "I'm a speaker and an author. . . . I am a firm believer that biomedical issues are not alongside autism, they are part of autism." At a table with parents and practitioners, Winston threw back a shot of vodka and sardonically declared that this was the only kind of shot he was willing to take. They had a good laugh. In addition to opposing vaccines, he believed he has benefited from a number of alternative biomedical treatments: a gluten-free diet, vitamin and mineral supplements, hyperbaric oxygen therapy, and specialized injections about which he was "[legally] not entitled to go into any further details." He claimed these things had helped with various medical issues he associated with autism: gastrointestinal problems, hair loss, headaches—and "invisible issues" that were not necessarily perceptible but were important to address anyway. His parents had started him on these treatments when he was a child. Winston believed that had it not been for these interventions, he could have ended up like "Jared from Subway" (who is not actually autistic and was convicted of child sex tourism and possessing child pornography) and might have been incarcerated—a grim future he was convinced he had dodged. Beyond treatments, the alternative biomedical movement had facilitated friendships with like-minded people—but few were themselves autistic. Instead, most of his friends were doctors and the mothers of autistic children. Late into the night, by the hull of a fake pirate ship, Francine danced to the Beyoncé songs that Winston played on his recorder. The sales representative for hyperbaric chambers looked on as he sipped his Cadillac margarita.

Rita was one of Winston's friends. They had met at alternative biomedical conferences. Rita dreamed of being a biathlon star, of becoming more competitive at skiing and shooting, but she felt robbed by her disability: "[Autism has] stopped me from being successful at biathlon. . . . Whenever I sit at home, I think about that all day. I can't stop thinking negatively and that's why I like work." It was unclear exactly *how* autism stunted her career in biathlon, but she saw it as the root of her troubles. At the time of our interview, she had just been laid off from Costco (a wholesale retailer known for its inexpensive rotisserie chickens and hotdogs), which had offered her some necessary distraction: "I'm actually very sad I can't go back to work anymore because when I go to work, I talk to people and I interact with customers and I think about work—rather than [about] sucking at biathlon." She also needed the job to help finance future rounds of magnetic resonance therapy (MRT), an experimental treatment for autism that uses magnetic pulses to stimulate specific areas of the brain. Recently, after she graduated high school, she and her mother drove thousands of miles to California to receive her first round of MRT—thirty minutes a day, five days a week, for four weeks. The procedure was so expensive (she estimated $10,000–$20,000) and time-consuming that they could not afford for it *not* to yield results: "I was worried that I was going to get there and it wasn't going to work. So, we paid all this money and put all this effort and time to go to California and then it's not going to work." However, Rita and her family were happy with the outcome: "Well, I could say I still have autism symptoms. Like sometimes I become a hypochondriac and I still freak out and stuff, some anxiety issues, but most of the time I don't act like I'm autistic anymore. Like I don't stim (stereotypy) or anything like that anymore. I just stopped doing that completely." Although MRT was not a cure-all, Rita noted multiple positive changes: reduced anxiety, greater adaptability, and improved comprehension (these presentations are not necessarily associated with autism). She did not instantly become a stronger biathlete, but the MRT showed promise in helping her advance. To her, all that time and money was not spent in vain.

Like autistic rights activists, Winston opposed the discrimination that autistic people experience. However, instead of advocating for social change, he and Rita emphasized the value of medical treatment. They conceptualized autism as a complex set of physiological problems, a belief that ultimately portrays autism as an individual challenge, not something institutional or structural. Accordingly, as autistic people, they saw themselves as physically sick. As Winston explained, "the *body* of a person with autism was wired differently."[28] Unlike autistic rights activists, who contend that autism is inextricable from the self, Winston and Rita separate the self and autism. Winston argued that autism, as a set of medical problems, is independent of his identity: "I believe that the individuality of people with autism should be accepted, but that medical awareness is important and that curing medical issues should not be seen, like I said before, as stifling identity, but for curing medical issues." In his defense of alternative biomedicine, he likened the treatment of autism to the treatment of chronic illnesses, like heart disease and diabetes: "I think we make a mistake when we equate a medical treatment [with] a cure that will stifle a person's identity when we do not associate treatment for heart disease stifling a person's identity. We do not associate insulin shots that type one diabetics have to have as stifling a person's identity." To Rita, autism was not who she was but an impediment to who she wanted to become: "So I can see how autism is good because you're different than everybody else, but at the same time it kind of sucks because you can't do what you want to do with life."

For autistic people, it can be demoralizing to believe that one was born non-autistic and then *made* autistic because of vaccines. This view implies brokenness, a damaged body. The self is no longer whole; parts have been stolen and spoiled. Rita blamed the MMR vaccine, "When I was born, I was born like a typical baby apparently. I was absolutely fine until I got that shot. Then I started to get worse." Comparing herself to her "normal" brother who seemed so talented—"everything he does he's so good at it"—Rita lamented the loss of her imagined potential, "I could've been a normal person. I could've been great. I wouldn't have multiple issues. I wouldn't be made fun of. I wouldn't have been struggling to make it through high school and struggling through all my life, my whole life to do what I want to be." Seen through the alternative biomedical lens, neurotypicality is the apparition of a life lost and the mirage of a life that could still be salvaged.

For some autistic people, the benefits of being a part of the autistic rights movement are not obvious or convincing. Winston and Rita traded autistic empowerment for the hope of improved physical health and a path toward neurotypicality. Winston attributed his poor physical health to autism and wanted to feel better.

Rita perceived autism as an obstacle to becoming a more competitive athlete and a more socially adjusted person. By framing autism as an individual problem, they found hope that they could do something to make themselves more acceptable to the world.

UNEVEN PARTICIPATION

The autistic rights movement is an insulated space where autistic people resist experts by reconstructing autism as human diversity and animating autistic acceptance into a lived reality. Set apart from the neurotypical world that medicalizes autism, movement members empower a collective autistic identity—a sense of solidarity and connection that they feel with each other. At the same time, this collective autistic identity is rooted in shared embodied experiences that support the belief that autism is a human difference. The autistic rights movement rejects clinical descriptions of deficit and disorder. The collective identity it has forged is both contentious knowledge and fodder for mobilization. The movement is a space where members model a society where their differences are normalized and valued. Outside of this space, autism acceptance remains an aspiration.

At the heart of their efforts is a question: What does it mean to value autistic people? Activists want equal access, rights, and opportunities, which has translated to a number of specific demands, including police training for mental health crisis response, nonpolice crisis response, banning electrical aversive conditioning devices, increasing health care access, improving access to education, reducing voting barriers, and shifting research funds toward studies that support self-determination and away from those that focus on causation and prevention. Activists also align their political agenda to support anti-racism and LGBTQ+ rights. These issues apply to autistic individuals across the spectrum with varying degrees of relevance.

But, while the movement claims to represent the interests of autistic people as a whole, active members do not reflect the complete autism spectrum. Those who participate in person tend to be autistic people with fewer support needs, and those who participate in autistic communities online have the cognitive, intellectual, and communicative skills to do so.[29] Their collective autistic identity, then, does not fully capture the embodied experiences of autistic people who have greater support needs, such as those with complex cognitive and intellectual disabilities. This is an obvious issue for a movement that aims to fully represent autistic people.

Sierra, a non-autistic disability rights activist, noticed this underrepresentation, "I think there's also a division there, where a lot of members of ASAN, both locally and nationally, are people who can communicate in words. And whether that's spoken or emailed or whatever. And who mostly don't have intellectual disabilities. Like not everyone—there are lots of people with intellectual disabilities who are involved in ASAN, but it's not the majority." In a damning observation, Codey, an autistic rights activist, said, "There's still a lot of autistic people who just viscerally hate autistic people with intellectual disabilities because they see themselves as above intellectual disability." Ash, one of the local ASAN leaders, explained that they were not trying to exclude those who have greater support needs. The problem was that it was hard to reach these populations. This means that activists can only guess what the unrepresented might want based on their own experiences. Many of the autistic rights movement's political activities try to address issues that disproportionately impact autistic people who require greater support, such as improving home- and community-based services,

opposing subminimum wages for disabled workers, and propos-
ing legislation to end organ transplant discrimination against
people with developmental and intellectual disabilities.[30] But
one can imagine that there are other needs that activists are not
privy to due to this partial representation inherent in the movement.[31] Here expanding partnerships with parents may help
reach those who are otherwise underrepresented.

Despite the uneven participation, activists assert that they
are the legitimate authorities on matters that impact the lives
of autistic people, including those who cannot voice their interests. After all, who better to represent autistic people than autistic people? Who better to speak for autistic people than autistic
people? This issue of partial representation highlights a "looping effect" in which diagnostic classification constructs a "kind of
person," and in turn, people of this "kind" interact with their classification.[32] Daniel Navon and Gil Eyal demonstrated that the
geneticization of autism expanded its diagnostic criteria, which
in turn, introduced new genetic mutations and increased genetic
heterogeneity.[33] This looping also impacted the politics of representation. The autistic rights movement could not have existed
decades earlier when the diagnostic criteria had a higher threshold and excluded those who were more "cognitively abled."[34]

Over time, diagnostic expansion stretched the autism spectrum in multiple directions and added new people. It coalesced
a heterogenous population into one "kind." As the population
changed and diversified, a portion recognized their collective
struggle. Autistic rights activists may not reflect the spectrum's
heterogeneity, but united under one diagnostic classification,
members see a cohesive population with shared experiences and
political interests. From those who require full-time support to
those who work full time, activists find solidarity in being "of a
kind," fundamentally and categorically.

5

LABORATORIES AND EXPERIMENTATION

The Tools and Strategies of "Recovery"

I met Whitney for our interview at a Starbucks near Columbus Circle. It was the middle of summer. Despite the humidity, she looked fresh and polished in her crisp white blouse and oatmeal-colored skirt. Whitney is a contributor to the *Age of Autism* blog, which is known for its vaccine skepticism.

Around the time of her son's birth, Whitney noticed that autism was gaining attention in the news. She desperately hoped her new baby would not be autistic. She recalled "not really knowing much about it and thinking, 'That's horrible. That would be awful.'" At around age two, Marcus presented some of the classic symptoms described in the *Diagnostic and Statistical Manual of Mental Disorders*, like repetitive behaviors—constantly flushing the toilets and turning the lights on and off. He also had frequent diarrhea that was "so bad it would burn a hole in his car seat."

The literature Whitney read in the beginning focused on behavioral presentations, which she felt did not answer her questions about her son's co-occurring conditions. As she expanded her search, she happened upon books that claimed a relationship between autism, vaccines, and gastrointestinal dysfunction. In these books—like David Kirby's *Evidence of*

Harm: Mercury in Vaccines and the Autism Epidemic—Whitney found descriptions of autism that explained her son's gastro-intestinal symptoms and resonated with her experiences as a mother. Whitney's self-directed research led her to an under-standing of autism that emphasized biological underpinnings. Moreover, her sources proposed a solution: if she addressed Marcus's biological issues, she could effectively treat his autis-tic behaviors.

In the waiting room of her son's speech therapist, Whitney was advised by other mothers to consult with an alternative bio-medical doctor. On one mother's recommendation, she made an appointment with Dr. Kevin Adelman, who specializes in gastrointestinal problems in autistic children. Dr. Adelman is a well-known pediatric gastroenterologist in the alternative bio-medical community. His way of practicing medicine leans on Andrew Wakefield's debunked "autistic enterocolitis" theory, which claims an association between measles-mumps-rubella (MMR) vaccination, gastrointestinal disease, and regressive autism. In addition, he was involved with the Thoughtful House Center for Children (now called The Johnson Center for Child Health and Development), a treatment and research center started by Wakefield in Texas.[1]

People in Whitney's life opposed her decision to see Dr. Adelman. Her parents, for instance, disagreed with her new-found belief that vaccines had caused her son's autism. They were suspicious of Dr. Adelman's methodology and professional affiliations; she remembered, "Everybody was saying like, 'He was a partner of Wakefield. He's a witch doctor! He's going to kill Marcus.'" Undaunted by their objections, Whitney took Marcus, then age four, to see Dr. Adelman. She was hoping he could provide new insights into her son's condition—and specif-ically its biological underpinnings. Whitney was pleased when

Dr. Adelman was willing (unlike the other specialists she had consulted) to perform an endoscopy:

> I went to hospitals and like—we went to four hospitals, like Cleveland Clinic, Boston Children's [Hospital], Cornell [Hospital]. One more useless than the next. [The doctors had] no idea what to do, trying to make it all psychosomatic. So then, I went to see Dr. Adelman in Long Island and he's like, "Let me see a stool sample. Okay this is what we're going to do, I'm going to scope him." And I was like, "Thank god! I wanted somebody to scope him."

Dr. Adelman validated her concerns. The endoscopy created a visualization. Recounting the images generated by the endoscopy, Whitney described, "Sure enough there were pictures of— it looked like Mars. [They were] angry, ulcers . . . look[ed] like mounds, and it looked horrible." The extraterrestrial landscape inside her son's body was, to Whitney, a discovery of the origins of his incomprehensible behaviors—the screaming, the head-hitting. His autistic behaviors took on shape, texture, and even an anthropomorphic temperament.

While the endoscope produced raw images, the alternative biomedical framework provided an interpretive lens to understand what she was seeing. Whitney experienced autism as a biologically observable and perceptible condition. She saw autism as something that blistered inside her child—it was not inherent to him, and it was no longer completely mysterious. When autism is constructed as a set of physical dysfunctions, parents and practitioners transform it into a condition that can be detected and monitored. Importantly, the ability to see and locate the problem suggests the potential to control it. This is the main allure of the alternative biomedical framework. When

Dr. Adelman said the Mars-like topography was inflammation, his diagnosis offered Whitney the hope that something could be done for her child.

Dr. Adelman suggested that if they treated the inflammation, they could begin to slowly treat the autism, so he prescribed anti-inflammatory drugs (Marcus was on Pentasa at the time of the interview, which is an anti-inflammatory drug prescribed to treat ulcerative colitis). Whitney noticed behavioral changes: "That really, really helped a lot and that stopped a lot of the head hitting and the screaming and it really actually led him to sleep at night for the first time in like three years. That helped a lot." Under the supervision of another alternative biomedical doctor, Marcus received intravenous immunoglobulin (IVIg, a therapy for patients with antibody deficiencies) every other week because, Whitney explained, "his T cells were like someone with late-stage AIDS." She compared the treatment to insulin for diabetic patients in its necessity. After introducing IVIg, she saw Marcus's health improve, as measured by fewer school days missed. She explained, "Before he got IVIg he was absent like 25 days and then after IVIg it was like two. And it didn't really hit me then until how much school he had been missing because he was always sick." Marcus also received glutathione treatments. Whitney said he had a glutathione deficiency and the treatments improved his mood: "He gets glutathione in that and he doesn't make enough, so it really makes him happy." These interventions are not easy because of the needles, but she was impressed by her son's cooperation, suspecting that he appreciated the benefits: "I never would have believed in a million years that I can lay him down and have an IV in him for like three hours and have him cooperate, but he does because it makes him feel better, so that was [what] we do." On top of these therapies, Marcus is also on a tailored gluten-free and potato-free diet.

At the end of our interview, Whitney showed me a picture of Marcus. He is a tall thirteen-year-old boy—tall like his father, she said. Reflecting on how she remembered him ten years ago, before they tried the alternative biomedical methods, she exhaled, "Yeah, he looks so much better." She considered the treatments a success thus far: "I think we've been successful making him healthy, healing his gut. I think if we hadn't found those things, he would be one of those kids wearing a helmet 24 hours a day and in a facility and that was always [in] the back of my head—the worst nightmare." Whitney told me Marcus had a date to the school dance later that day. She chuckled, "So funny! With his mom—how sad is that? But, you know what? That's the beauty about Marcus, he doesn't care. He doesn't care what people think about him."

Whitney's beliefs about autism and its treatment are not uncommon. The alternative biomedical movement offers parents like her the thing they desperately want for their autistic children: the hope of recovery, whatever it may mean for each family, whatever it may mean over time. Parents who participate in the movement learn how to reimagine autism as a collection of physiological dysfunctions that can be reversed with dietary changes, nutritional supplements, and experimental interventions. Ultimately, they learn to separate their children from autism itself. Alternative biomedical practices are not conventional approaches toward autism. Most of these treatments are not evidence based. What is more, medical professionals have cautioned families against interventions that are not evidence based, noting that some of these treatments are at best supplemental and at worst fatal. However, the movement is an infrastructure that animates contentious knowledge into reality. It arranges the social and material resources that members need to approach autism as a reversible disorder. In the pursuit of recovery, parents depend on the availability of specialized knowledge, tests, and treatments. Their endeavors are facilitated by a network of practitioners, functional laboratories, compound pharmacies, and a range of other businesses that partly constitute the movement itself.

The construction of physiologically dysfunctional autistic children involves two iterative processes, which I describe in this chapter. First, I show how alternative biomedical members create knowledge about the biology of individual autistic children by pairing laboratory tests and behavioral observations. Second, I show how knowledge about individual autistic children is used to inform treatment strategies and assess efficacy. Trial-and-error treatment produces nuanced new knowledge about the bodies of autistic children. By participating in the movement, parents and practitioners access the tools to measure autism, the conceptual framework to interpret the collected information, and the resources to treat autistic children.

SEEING AND MEASURING AUTISM

Alternative biomedical members transform autism into a biologically measurable and medically treatable condition. This transformation involves a number of coordinated activities: information gathering, doctor-parent collaboration, and trial-and-error experimentation. These activities are facilitated by the availability of resources organized by the movement: functional laboratories, specialized practitioners, pharmaceuticals, supplement companies, and a robust market of experimental treatments. Through the alternative biomedical framework and its practices, members make their version of autism perceptible. Accordingly, the autistic child becomes a producer of valuable information, and previously enigmatic behaviors are made intelligible.

Perceptibility suggests reality. For something to be perceptible, it must have a material existence. In Michelle Murphy's research on chemical exposure, she conceptualizes "regimes of perceptibility" as social and technical arrangements that define what can and cannot be perceived.[2] For instance, a scientific discipline defines perceptibility—and concurrently imperceptibility—by setting its criteria of detection and specifying standards of validity.[3] When investigating a phenomenon, researchers from different fields might have separate ways of conceptualizing perceptibility.[4] This means that the researchers might focus on different forms of evidence and use different tools to measure. What is perceptible and passes the threshold of being "real" in one discipline may be discounted in another discipline. Social and technical arrangements allow for certain phenomena to be seen and measured. In the context of autism science, Martine Lappé employs this framework to illustrate how shifts toward gene-environmental interaction research have directed attention toward women's bodies as sites of potential harm and risk to the fetus.[5] Here, I focus on the materialization of autism itself.

Alternative biomedicine is a regime of perceptibility. It offers ideas about which phenomena can be detected, rules about what counts as relevant information, and tools to measure things that are purportedly detectable. Alternative biomedical members believe they can detect autism's underlying biological processes, including but not limited to endocrine function, oxidative stress, methylation and transsulfuration, immune regulation, gastrointestinal function, and mitochondrial function. They do so by using functional laboratories and other screening technologies, like endoscopies to diagnose gastrointestinal health, electroencephalography (EEG) to detect seizures, and neuroimaging to examine brain functioning.

While autism has a prominent social, cultural, and clinical presence, its biological visibility is unclear. Autism research has yet to discover unambiguous and reliable biomarkers for autism. Unlike symptoms, biomarkers are measurable medical signs—"objective, quantifiable characteristics of biological processes."[6] In 2018, 44 percent of all public and private autism research funding went to projects that study the biological processes underlying autism and 19 percent went to projects that study risk factors.[7] These areas of research include investigation into genetic, molecular, and neurodevelopmental mechanisms. The hope is that discoveries will help improve diagnosis, estimate risk, define subgroups, and predict treatment response.[8] However, the search for biomarkers is a challenging endeavor because of autism's biological heterogeneity, evolving definitions, and plasticity (individuals' phenotypic manifestations can change a lot between early childhood and adulthood).[9] It is also a contentious task, as it confronts ethical questions about the subjective value of certain human traits and which should be prevented or treated.[10]

While there has been limited success in identifying autism biomarkers, the science community has demarcated where to look and where *not* to look for answers.[11] After countless studies into autism's causal explanations, its unknowns have been narrowed and are confined within the boundaries of genetic and genomic research. This circumscription forecloses certain avenues of inquiry, such as studies on postnatal environmental causes—particularly those that continue to pursue a vaccine-autism relationship.[12] Even in studies that investigate the relationship between autism and environmental factors, genetics remain important.[13] Researchers maintain the hegemony of genomic explanations by co-opting environment-centered inquiries, folding it into research on gene-environment interactions.[14] The alternative biomedical movement, however, deemphasizes the importance of genetics (see chapter 2). Its members contend that environmental triggers are the primary culprit in autism causation—and that environmental autism has biomarkers, allowing it to be seen.

The alternative biomedical framework renders autism material and perceptible in ways the dominant understanding of autism does not afford. It shows parents and practitioners where to look for meaningful signs and symptoms and how to interpret them. By conceptualizing autism in this way, parents and practitioners create opportunities to imagine the physical experiences and sensations of autistic children.[15] Imagining children's experiences, parents and practitioners create individualized knowledge about each autistic child—their problems, deficiencies, discomforts, and needs. Through this treatment process, they learn to separate autism-as-sickness from their afflicted child. Ironically, as parents become more empathetic toward their children, they also become less tolerant of autism.

Blood, Urine, and Stool

The first time I visited Dr. Kurt Martinek at his office, he pulled a patient's soiled diaper out of the garbage from behind his desk and asked, "Do want to see what it looks like?" I laughed nervously and replied, "No, thank you." The diaper was in a plastic bag, the kind markets have on a roll in the produce aisle. I did not have to hold it to know it was full and dense. It rested heavy in the bag like a grapefruit.

"Do you want to see what it looks like?" he asked again.

"I certainly do not."

"Do you want to smell what it looks like?"

"No," I replied definitively, putting the kibosh on the diaper talk.

Criticizing conventional doctors, he asked, "So, how can that be an approach, when you have foul-smelling mush coming out of a toddler, where other doctors will say, 'Well, that's toddler's diarrhea'?" He contrasted his style of practice with that of doctors who minimize the significance of autistic patients' co-occurring issues:

> I ask the parents, "Go ahead, bring that diaper into the clinician's office and open it up while you're waiting for him to come in the door." Don't tell me this is normal. So, why would you ignore that with a child, any child, whether they have autism or not? Just because they have autism doesn't mean that they're second-class citizens and don't deserve the best of medical care. So, these kids have allergies. Why wouldn't you treat allergies? These kids have food sensitivities, like celiac disease or something that's causing inflammatory bowel disease. Why wouldn't you treat that? So, people make a big deal about this being alternative medicine. No, it's pure medicine.

Although Dr. Martinek described his work as "pure medicine" and deemphasized its "alternative" nature, he adamantly believes that vaccines can cause autism (which they do not)[16] and has made a career of treating autistic patients with alternative and experimental methods (that are not evidence based). Like Whitney and Dr. Adelman, Dr. Martinek folds physiological dysfunctions into his understanding of autism. In his work, the two are inextricable. Accordingly, he sees the measurement and evaluation of biological material—like stool in a soiled diaper—as critical to the treatment process. Dr. Martinek's unorthodoxy is the thing that draws royalty, diplomats, celebrities, and everyday parents into his practice. He is well known within the alternative biomedical movement; he often gives talks at the major conferences and has coauthored a highly popular book on treatment.

While Dr. Martinek is reluctant to call his work anything other than "pure medicine" and "good medicine," Dr. Travis Drummond, who serves mainly autistic patients at his private practice in California, explicitly recognized the unorthodoxy of using laboratory testing for assessing autism. In an interview, he told me there was antagonism toward alternative biomedical practice, supposing that those outside his community might consider this way of thinking to be blasphemous. To test for indicators of immunological dysfunction, he explained, went against standard practice: "To break a religion from something considered mental health into something considered medical. We typically don't like the words 'mental health' and 'medical.' Those two words are not synonymous in the vast majority of Americans' minds or the world, because that's just not the way the culture has born itself to be."

In any clinical setting, the measurements achieved with medical technologies and procedures are important in guiding treatment. Laboratory testing and screening tools also shape patients' understandings of bodily experiences and health management strategies.[17] When experiences are difficult to access or understand—as is often the case with autistic people who have limited communication abilities—measurements can generate useful insights. In addition to tests that are typically covered by health insurance (like vitamin D, lead exposure, and cholesterol), alternative biomedical members depend on functional laboratories to perform nonstandard clinical testing to provide information about autistic children's heavy metals concentration, nutritional deficiencies, food sensitivities, and gastrointestinal health. These special tests are not usually covered by health insurance. At the time of the study, Doctor's Data, Genova, Cyrex, and Great Plains were popular laboratories within the community.

Hair, blood, urine, and stool promise to make autism perceptible. During the 2015 National Autism Conference in St. Petersburg, Florida, Dr. Dan Rossignol, president of the Medical Academy of Pediatric Special Needs (MAPS), an association of alternative biomedical practitioners, gave a presentation on the importance of laboratory testing. Dr. Rossignol has two autistic sons. He lectures in a dull and monotone narration. No matter who is in the audience, parents or peers, his presentations are dense and his slides crowded with text from his review of the literature. One mother joked that Dr. Rossignol himself might be autistic because of his mannerisms and meticulous attention to detail.

More scrupulous than his peers, Dr. Rossignol speaks like the fine print of user agreements. At the 2015 conference, he said that while there is no blood test to diagnose *autism*, there are laboratory tests to help identify the "underlying medical problems" that contribute to *autistic behaviors*. He was careful to make the distinction—the tests could not detect autism as a single entity, but they could detect the multiple problems that produced its characteristic behaviors. Dr. Rossignol explained that many metabolic abnormalities cannot be detected without a laboratory test and that autistic children are not able to effectively communicate their problems:

> Some kids will hit you or hit themselves because they are in pain and maybe they can't tell you "Hey, mommy or daddy, I am in pain" and the only way they can tell you is to hit you or hit themselves. So again, some children with autism—not all—may have self-injurious behaviors or aggressive behaviors related to gastrointestinal problems.

Parents and practitioners test for biomarkers to make visible the physiological problems that can neither be observed with the naked eye nor coherently expressed by the child. Like other laboratory tests, the quantification of autism purportedly offers "transparency and neutrality,"[18] which are incorporated into parents' and practitioners' understandings of the condition's status. Whether or not these measures are valid, alternative biomedical parents and practitioners believe they are and act on them by devising intervention plans.

Beyond laboratory testing, participants also used other clinical tools to facilitate visualization. Imaging technologies, like endoscopies and neuroimaging, provide what they believe to be a picture of autism. For instance, at the 2015 Talk About Curing Autism (TACA)[19] conference in Costa Mesa, California, Dr. Daniel Amen gave the keynote presentation on single-photon emission computed tomography (SPECT) scans. He is a spritely bald man in his sixties with a charmingly smug stage presence. He regularly peppers his talks with outrageous anecdotes and witty quips. Typically, SPECT scans are used to diagnose and track the progression of heart disease, brain disorders (e.g., Parkinson's disease, seizure disorders), and bone disorders.[20] However, in his practice, Dr. Amen extends the use of the tool to diagnose autism (among many other psychiatric conditions). He is literally a man with a vision. On his website, he advertises that SPECT scans can help identify the "underlying brain function problems associated with [autism spectrum disorder]." Furthermore, he points to tailored treatments offered by his clinic—like hyperbaric oxygen chamber therapy, neurofeedback, brain health nutrition coaching, psychotherapy, and supplement and medication management. His peers in psychiatry have accused him of fraud and quackery, calling his work the "modern equivalent of phrenology."[21]

According to Dr. Amen's explanation, the SPECT scans provide much more than a three-dimensional image—they promise solutions to a problem. He shared a story of one pediatric patient, a nine-year-old named Aaron. Aaron was not autistic, but he exhibited behavioral issues. He drew violent pictures of people getting shot and of himself hanging in a noose. Right on cue, the audience gasped. They were horrified by the illustrations projected on the screen. Dr. Amen surmised that Aaron was a school shooter "waiting to happen." Aaron's SPECT scan revealed a large cyst on his left temporal lobe. Dr. Amen recalled how three separate neurologists refused to operate until "real symptoms" emerged. However, he was eventually able to find a neurosurgeon to remove the large cyst, potentially saving the boy's life. He said that after the cyst was removed, the boy finally smiled for the first time in a year and his behaviors returned to "normal." The audience erupted in applause.

Dr. Amen explicitly pointed out that the SPECT scans, aside from offering the hope of treatment, help reduce stigma because they show that the problem is *medical* and not *moral*, that there is nothing inherently wrong with the children or their character. The same may be true of all the clinical tests alternative biomedical members use to identify the underlying causes of autistic behaviors. When parents and practitioners formulate autism as measurable and visual, they differentiate autism from the child. This suggests the idea of autistic duality—that there is autism and the "true" child, a sick and a well child, an abnormal and an aspirational child. In Dr. Amen's story, Aaron was not inherently violent; rather, it was the cyst that caused him to have violent thoughts. Reconstructed as a "medical" problem, autism's undesirable traits are separated out, leaving the child unstained.

Through the alternative biomedical framework, the autistic child becomes a goldmine of biological indicators. These tests, however, are not especially useful on their own because they lack context and meaning. Believing that every autistic child is medically unique, practitioners cannot easily compare a patient's test results to those of other children or even other autistic children. They recalibrate their understanding of healthy and unhealthy for every patient. For instance, when Dr. Kavita Maddan tested the blood lead level of an autistic patient, his result was 1 μg/dL, which is below the Environmental Protection Agency's (EPA) level of concern for children (5 μg/dL).[22] Even though the patient's blood lead level was low, Dr. Maddan said that it was enough to pose serious harm for *this* specific child. Patients' test results, in isolation, are not especially meaningful because practitioners do not compare patients' scores against standard reference ranges. Instead, practitioners consider changes in patients' test results over time and interpret results in light of behavioral observations, which are provided by parents. Behavioral observations are just as important as test results. The construction of the autistic child arranges parents and practitioners into close partnership.

Making Sense of Autistic Behavior

While educating an audience of parents, a practitioner said that children with parasites may exhibit unusual behaviors when there is a new or full moon. During the same conference, another practitioner associated erratic behaviors, anal itching, poor sleep, and increased appetite with the colonization of undesirable parasites. For these patients, he suggested using probiotics, herbs, and pharmaceutical drugs. Dr. Maddan explained that during a full moon, intestinal parasites come out to lay eggs, which can affect children with weak immune systems. She considered chlorine dioxide (widely used as a bleach) the best treatment protocol but warned her patients' parents of its controversial status and apprised them of the rumors about child protective services pursuing those who dared to disclose their practices online. The U.S. Food and Drug Administration (FDA) warns that taking chlorine dioxide can cause "severe vomiting, severe diarrhea, life-threatening low blood pressure caused by dehydration, and acute liver failure."[23]

On one observed occasion, a mother and father arrived at Dr. Maddan's office with two autistic teenage sons who had limited communication skills and needed full-time supervision. The younger son arrived at the appointment wearing a harness that his parents used to keep him from wandering away. His mother described him as technologically savvy; he had attempted to buy real estate and listed his neighbors' houses for sale online. The mother suspected that he had parasites and asked if they could test fecal and blood samples. Dr. Maddan asked whether his symptoms worsened around the full moon. His mother confirmed that she did in fact observe correlations between the phase of the moon and his behavioral changes—the boy would obsessively try to get on the computer. Dr. Maddan explained that a full moon can disrupt sleep because the parasites are out reproducing. The boy's mother found it impressive that there could be a "scientific" reason for her son's symptoms. To treat the boy, Dr. Maddan suggested that on nights with a full moon, at 2:00 A.M., the parents try giving him one tablespoon of castor oil and one tablespoon of brandy (this is not evidence based). This should help clean out his system, she said. The treatment was expected to yield a clear response. The mother took the suggestion seriously as the father laughed. He found the idea of prescribing brandy to a teen comically unusual.

Parents like the mother in this narrative want to know why their children behave the way they do, why they behave atypically. In this case, "bad parasites" was a satisfying explanation because it offered the mother a reason for her son's obsession (it was not *him*; it was the parasites) and, more importantly, it suggested a treatment protocol. Physiological insights explicated his behaviors, and the behaviors implied a physiological dysfunction. Knowledge about individual autistic children is produced through an iterative process of collecting and interpreting information. Taken altogether, these interpretations facilitate parents' imagination of how their children experience autism physically, which then informs their medical decision-making and gives them a sense of control.

Furthermore, when parents conceptualize autism as physical sickness, behaviors that were indecipherable start to become more relatable. For example, participants likened the effects of certain foods to recreational drug use and addiction. Gabriel, a former emergency room doctor and father to a young autistic boy, said his child did not "act neurotypical" because he was "stoned" off gluten and casein. Alternative biomedical doctors taught him that gluten can behave like an opioid for some children and produce similar effects. Parents may or may not have personal experiences with recreational drug use, but perhaps addiction and withdrawal resonate because of their cultural visibility. Seeing autism as a physical sickness, Gina empathized with her son by drawing connections between the physical discomforts she has experienced and what she imagines her son to experience: "If I have a yeast infection, how uncomfortable is that, right? And that's just one, that's just one thing. And a child at four or five having yeast overgrowth, bacterial dysfunction in the gut, leaky gut, food sensitivities, I mean, the list goes on. . . . You can only imagine how that can affect the brain, right? I mean, me, alone, if I don't have breakfast, I can't concentrate." Through an alternative biomedical lens, parents rationalized their children's seemingly abnormal behaviors and found answers in uncertain circumstances.

Parents and professionals keep track of behavioral patterns in other therapeutic settings for autistic children as well. For instance, in applied behavior analysis (ABA), the most widely recommended autism intervention method, therapists collect behavioral observations to track learning progress and steer programming. However, within the alternative biomedical movement, members use information gathered about the child's behaviors to identify physiological dysfunctions. By now, Mindy knows when her son has had too much gluten: "He'll come up to me and he'll say, 'I need a hug.' And sometimes he needs it emotionally, but sometimes he doesn't. Sometimes he's completely emotionally fine, but he needs a squeeze, he needs physical compression. And I can tell if he requires more of those hugs when he's been having more gluten." Similarly, Melissa said she could tell when her son, Logan, was having intestinal problems based on changes in his behaviors. She recalled conventional doctors dismissing the severity of her son's digestive issues and supposed that they thought "the mental health is causing the [gastrointestinal] problems." In other words, Melissa believed that her son's medical issues were often minimized or neglected by doctors because they interpreted these challenges as resulting from intellectual and cognitive disability—for instance, if the child is a picky eater, the doctors could attribute digestive or nutritional problems to pickiness. After consulting with a chiropractor and multiple alternative biomedical doctors, Melissa said they targeted "[*Clostridium difficile*], *Clostridium*, yeast" infections as a few of Logan's underlying medical issues.

Over the years, Melissa has honed her interpretative skills. Although she feels confident in her ability to diagnose her son based on behavior, she uses stool tests for confirmation: "We would then do a CDSA [comprehensive digestive stool analysis], so another stool test and we would confirm with the stool test results. But it got to the point where we knew by behavior what was going on and so—well, we always confirm everything with the test." For Melissa, Logan's observable behaviors are indicative of harder-to-see physiological problems—irregular events inside his body. As he grew older, the behaviors associated with gastrointestinal health changed. The relationship between behavior and physiological dysfunction is ever-evolving and dynamic, which requires parents to be adaptive in their meaning-making processes.

The alternative biomedical framework differentiates autism from the child, but the distinction is not always clear, which muddles the significance of observations. It is hard for parents to see the child within when they have been trained to render autism hypervisible by pathologizing bad behaviors. Mindy, who has two autistic children and one non-autistic child, sometimes struggles to separate atypical behaviors that may be biologically meaningful from undesirable behaviors that are developmentally typical. Thinking of her daughter, Jewel, she pondered, "Is she just being an obnoxious little six-year-old or is she being somebody who can't regulate herself?" Sometimes Jewel exhibited "sneaky misbehaviors," as when she climbed furniture to steal chips from a high cupboard. Mindy said she had to remind herself to not conflate all undesirable behaviors with autism: "That's Normal Kid, but it's easy to kind of forget that some of that stuff is just that, and it's not necessarily like 'Oh, no, it's a regression, she's not listening to me.'" Mindy noticed that other parents in the movement seem to also experience similar difficulty in interpreting undesirable behaviors:

> Sometimes a cigar is just a cigar. Sometimes a kid is just a kid and it's not always autism. I see that on the Facebook groups, too, a lot of the times. [Parents] are like "Oh no, my daughter was really defiant with me, she refused to go to bed at 9:00 P.M. when I told her to." And a lot of parents chime in and they're like "Oh, melatonin, maybe you need to increase her Vitamin D, maybe because of da-da." I sometimes am the one who's just like, "Look, she's like seven, right? She doesn't want to go to bed. It doesn't mean that she's like deficient in some—you know, she needs more iron or zinc or selenium. Like, sometimes she just doesn't want to go."

The alternative biomedical lens does not offer perfect vision even on its own terms. While the framework resolves general uncertainties about autism as a condition, uncertainties about individual autistic children remain. As Mindy pointed out, it is not always clear which behaviors are acceptably problematic and which are unacceptably pathological.

PARENT AND PRACTITIONER COLLABORATION

Knowledge about individual autistic children is produced through an iterative process of collecting and interpreting information. This process is a collaborative effort between practitioners and parents—autistic children rarely give their input. This arrangement is not unique to alternative biomedical practice; in pediatric medical encounters, children are often assigned limited and passive roles in their own consultations and medical decision-making processes (though there is growing effort to support pediatric decision-making).[24] When advocating on their children's behalf, parents assume dynamic and influential roles in medical encounters—and in health care more broadly.[25] In cases of autism in which the child has limited verbal speech, parents are tasked with mitigating communication barriers between their child and others.[26] Even when autistic patients have verbal communication skills, their experiences may be discredited or deemed unreliable.[27] However, in alternative biomedical practice, the notable exclusion of autistic patients during consultations emphasizes practitioners' and parents' active roles in the construction of physiologically dysfunctional children.

Parents and practitioners dovetail their specialized knowledges to assemble a cohesive autism profile.[28] Parents possess information about observed behavioral patterns and certain accessible physiological findings (things one can see by simply looking, like eczema and stool characteristics). Meanwhile, practitioners interpret parents' observations and test results together. As Dr. Martinek explained, "When I get labs, it just tells me what area of the pond to go fishing, where I'm more likely to catch something. But it's not enough treating a piece of paper. Ultimately, I'm treating a child." Yet, based on my observations at three alternative biomedical practices, treating the child involves the child only minimally. Typically, the patient accompanies the parent(s) and other caregivers, but it is not uncommon for the parents to arrive without their child or to conference call the doctors from home. Even when the patient is there, they rarely have much of a voice in the proceedings (they play in the office or wait outside). For instance, when a verbal teen boy and his mother arrived at Dr. Maddan's office for a consultation, the boy briefly protested his gluten-free and casein-free diet. He wanted more options, desiring Mexican food. Dr. Maddan did not think he was ready to have gluten and dairy reintroduced. (Mexican cuisine has a lot of gluten-free and casein-free options, so I am not sure why he was not allowed.) Disappointed, he stepped out so his mother and the doctor could discuss his case. Alone with Dr. Maddan, the mother talked about her son's average grades, his lack of motivation, how he snuck into the kitchen and ate two entire boxes of gluten-free cookies, how he damaged a wall at home, his paleness, the large bags under his eyes. Parents serve as their children's representatives and proxies—even when they are physically present, communicative, capable, and nearing adulthood.

On one occasion, a mother and father arrived at Dr. Martinek's office without the patient. In the child's place was not just "a piece of paper" but a thick, well-organized binder. From the binder, the mother showed Dr. Martinek a calendar that had been carefully color-coded with behavior notes for each day. Yellow and orange markings indicated days with no self-injury and no aggression. In addition to looking over the parents' records, Dr. Martinek reviewed the recent stool culture results from a functional laboratory. The mother reported that her autistic son was responding well to the IVIg treatments over the last six months, so she wanted to continue for another six months. Dr. Martinek admitted that no one knows why IVIg shows positive results, but observationally, it does seem to help patients. The mother noticed that her son had recently developed irrational fears—of raccoons coming into the house, of bees, and of eating so much food that his body would explode. She suspected that these fears were caused by pediatric autoimmune neuropsychiatric disorders associated with streptococcal infections (PANDAS), which is characterized by a sudden onset of obsessive-compulsive disorder following a strep infection. In addition, she said the child flexed his fingers in a strange way.

Dr. Martinek said the child's immune system was abnormal and advised that they try *Hymenolepis diminuta cysticercoids*

(HDCs), or helminth worm therapy, which is designed to treat autoimmune and inflammatory disorders (though there is limited research on HDCs' efficacy as a therapeutic). He was growing the helminths in beetles. The beetles fed on organic oats from Whole Foods, a detail that he facetiously added. Aware that an outsider might be startled by the idea of worm therapy, the mother turned around in her chair to face me and commented that I had probably not expected to hear about these things. Dr. Martinek and the parents reviewed the child's behaviors and laboratory test results to modify the treatments. Before the parents left his office, Dr. Martinek compiled a list of different interventions they could try.

Between consultations, I asked Dr. Martinek about his process for evaluating patients. He said that parent reports are critical to interpreting the lab results. When he works with a child, he simply asks parents whether they perceive a behavior to be "normal or abnormal." For Dr. Martinek, questions of normal and abnormal are fundamentally biological questions. For instance, when a mother asked Dr. Martinek about her autistic son's violent obsession with his daycare provider (he bit and kicked her), wondering if he thought the child was merely infatuated with the woman, he immediately stopped her to ask, "You can't go there and wonder 'Why?' Is it normal or abnormal?" He dissuaded her from rationalizing her son's behaviors. Concurrently, he dissuaded her from attributing the bad behaviors to the child's character; the problem was the autism, not the boy. Reframing the problem, Dr. Martinek told the mother that she could not train behaviors out of the boy as if he were a dog. Instead, he redirected the conversation to focus on the child's bacteria problems and supplements. Like many of his colleagues, he works with the parents to identify physiological and behavioral problems and to bring them into relationship. In effect, the parents play a large role in defining atypicality and abnormality, which is subjective.

I wondered whether the practitioners had concerns about the reliability of parents' reports; after all, they carry enormous weight since the laboratory results are not supposed to make sense on their own. Practitioners interpret laboratory results together with parents' observations. Dr. Drummond explained, "Ultimately if a parent tells me 'My child's getting better,' unless they're going to pay me to lie to me . . . I mean, if they're going to do that, [then] they have an even bigger problem than autism, you know. So, I tend to believe my moms and dads, because they're coming to me. They're paying their time." He trusts parents' integrity because, from his perspective, they have no reason to lie.

PURSUING TYPICALITY

The alternative biomedical market is vast and ever-evolving, as new supplements, devices, and procedures are introduced continually. Parents and practitioners accept that the effects of these treatments are not predictable, so they have to carefully tailor regimens to each individual child. Accordingly, the treatment process relies on the perceptibility of autism to gauge progress. Parents and practitioners collaboratively monitor autistic bodies with laboratory tests and autistic behaviors with observation. They imbue patterns and changes with significance, interpreting these signs as cues about how to proceed. Their evaluations of the treatments' efficacy are iterative processes of knowledge production.

In December 2015, Dr. Bernard Sachwell and his wife invited me to their home and offices in the quiet, charming village of Sag Harbor, located in East Hampton, New York. Dr. Sachwell, who is nearing retirement, sees far fewer patients these days than he used to. He does, however, run a small laboratory on the first floor of the guest apartment. The laboratory smelled of new paint. It was sparsely furnished with a long workbench and two microscopes. In a corner was a metal shelving unit. Each shelf held three or four shallow containers with mesh screen lids; they looked like frozen food trays. But instead of a dry disk of Salisbury steak, inside were grain beetles at various stages of development. They were arranged from mealy worms on the bottom shelf to fully developed beetles on the top shelf. Dr. Sachwell opened a container to show me the beetles. They were lean and moved fast. He had supplied them with carrots and a damp paper towel. The accommodations seemed thoughtful, almost loving.

Dr. Sachwell said he had a "Costa Rican assistant" who comes during the week to dissect the beetles and harvest the helminth worm larvae, called HDCs. She was not professionally trained to work with any sort of specimen, but Dr. Sachwell had recognized her dexterity and tasked her with this project. To collect the HDCs, the assistant he hired first breaks off the beetle's head and then cuts into the abdomen. The HDCs are stored in clear plastic vials with saline. I held one under a lamp. They were tiny, teardrop-shaped flecks. In one magnified photo of an HDC, it looked like a pirouetting figure with a soft face. After harvest and preparation, the HDCs are shipped out to patients on Tuesdays via FedEx. At the time of my visit, he had between twenty and thirty customers. He was charging $100 for 1–10 HDCs, $125 for 11–20, $150 for 21–30, and $175 for 31–60. He affectionately refers to the HDCs as "little dudes," but a patient thought the term was too cute to market as a serious health product, so he renamed them "primobiotics" and had it trademarked.

Like Dr. Sachwell, other practitioners sell treatments directly to patients. This is made possible in several ways: selling supplements on site, formulating their own supplements (which are not subject to FDA approval), holding a nonpharmacy dispensing permit,[29] and establishing a compound pharmacy.[30] For instance, Dr. Maddan has her own compound pharmacy. Dr. Martinek has a personal laboratory where he makes leuprolide injections and grows HDCs. Dr. Theoharis Theoharides, a researcher at Tufts University School of Medicine and an active member of the alternative biomedical community, sells his own trademarked supplement, NeuroProtek, which is a combination of flavonoids that are meant to reduce oxidative stress and inflammation. Because the alternative biomedical framework locates autism across various physiological systems beyond the brain, multiple avenues of treatment seem to be available—along with multiple entrepreneurial opportunities for practitioners and purveyors.

Researchers have not identified a medical treatment or cure for the core symptoms of autism,[31] but the alternative biomedical movement offers a market for autism treatment that seems inexhaustible: hyperbaric chamber therapy, LED light therapy, craniosacral therapy, camel's milk, homeopathy, stem cell therapy, essential oils. These are all unproven interventions. These recovery efforts largely exclude psychiatric drugs.[32] However, parents do not reject pharmaceutical drugs altogether. Like other groups of vaccine-hesitant parents, they strategize about which pharmaceutical drugs their children need.[33] The parents I interviewed were not opposed to the use of off-label pharmaceutical drugs when they fit with the logic of alternative biomedicine. For instance, Namenda, which is usually prescribed for dementia, was popular at the time.

At the most basic level, the alternative biomedical approach includes dietary changes and nutritional supplements, but many parents and practitioners also integrate other experimental interventions. Most alternative biomedical treatments have not gone through systematic clinical research. Instead, practitioners translate research from different biological science disciplines into experimental treatments for patients. Unlike evidence-based medicine, this process pushes treatments straight from the bench to bedside, skipping many of the regulatory practices that normally happen in the middle. This is not to say that the treatments do not appear to "work," as participants have reported success. Moreover, despite a lack of scientific support, many families outside the movement have implemented specialized diets, such as gluten-free and casein-free diets, to help their autistic children.[34]

Sponsors and vendors at conferences introduce new interventions and tools that they claim can help with autistic children's underlying issues. In 2015, alternative biomedical conferences buzzed with excitement about helminth worm larvae and GcMAF (Gc protein–derived macrophage-activating factor), a protein extracted from human blood.[35] In 2016, experimental stem cell therapy captured attendees' attention. Like the helminths and GcMAF, this is not approved by the FDA. The majority of stem cell therapy clinics are outside of the United States in low- and middle-income countries, like India, Panama, and Mexico.[36] At conferences, this sort of medical tourism was sometimes packaged as a luxury vacation. For around $17,000, the World Stem Cells Clinic, located in Cancún, Mexico, bundled the multiday procedure with flights and hotel stay.[37] The clinic's website promised "fun for the whole family," mixing autism treatment with pleasure: "Although the main reason for the trip is to make the most out of [stem cell therapy] for your child, visiting Cancún can also be a great way to get away from routine and make memories with your family."[38] In other words, come for the stem cell therapy, stay for the cochinita pibil! At two observed conferences, representatives from the World Stem Cells Clinic presented their services to an audience of parents. Medical experts, however, warn against the risks of receiving unproven and unregulated stem cell treatments, which could result in infection, rejection, tumorigenesis, and even death.[39]

Treatment fads come and go (which perhaps speaks to their inefficacy). As Dr. Maddan recalled, when she first entered alternative biomedical practice, secretin (a hormone normally used in diagnostic procedures) was in high demand as a therapy because a popular news program had reported that an autistic boy had recovered after receiving secretin during an endoscopy. But its popularity waned. Dr. Maddan told me, "Secretin was one of those things that there's different protocols and ideas that have just kind of come and gone that haven't really stuck, and that's been one of them that hasn't really stuck. I use homeopathic secretin now." The ever-evolving and expanding market of alternative biomedical intervention offers new opportunities for recovery, but simultaneously, it deepens parents' journey into the abyss of treatments.

Outside the movement, autistic children typically receive educational and behavioral interventions, such as ABA.[40] Alternative biomedical parents also use educational and behavioral programs, but these tools are seen as auxiliary treatment plans. For instance, after her son was diagnosed, Gina placed him in an ABA program for a year (forty hours a week), but she did not think he was making enough progress. After learning about alternative biomedicine from the internet, she reduced his ABA services and invested her limited funds in getting her son "tested and treated." Gina, who has unfulfilled dreams of becoming a nurse, believed that addressing her son's physiological issues would optimize the therapeutic benefits of ABA: "My theory is that the body needs to be healthy first, before it can learn the [ABA] therapies, so I think the reason why my son wasn't progressing like he should have was because he had all of these issues going on internally and, that needed to get worked out and resolved first."

Trial and Error

Parents and practitioners described the pursuit of recovery as interminable and immensely complicated. A common saying within the broader autism community goes: "If you've seen one child with autism, you've seen one child with autism"—that is, presentations of autism vary from child to child. In line with this view, movement members contend that because each autistic child is unique, the efficacy of interventions varies. Accordingly, parents anticipate a tedious process of fine-tuning the treatment through trial and error. The same can be said about the design of special educational and behavioral programs, which are also tailored to the child.[41] One difference is that navigating alternative biomedical interventions is perhaps even more unwieldy and confusing. Given the unpredictability of the responses and the seemingly limitless intervention options, the treatment process may seem dauntingly enigmatic and byzantine.

Practitioners follow a general theory of how certain treatment methods *should* work, but they do not expect patients to reliably respond in the same way. For instance, Dr. Darren Jesson explained that he cannot predict with certainty how a patient might respond to an intervention: "We have them trial and error, go off and think, like, gluten and casein, because we see a lot of kids have problems with breaking down gluten and casein, and so that's again a sort of a shotgun approach. There's not really a good test yet that tells you 100 percent who's going to do better on that, but it's fairly simple to tell them for a few weeks to remove those foods and see how they do."

Because the treatment process is so unpredictable and individually tailored, members rely on the perceptibility of autism to evaluate efficacy and guide next steps. When Lucille and her autistic ten-year-old daughter, Allie, came in for a consultation, Dr. Martinek prescribed various treatments and discussed the significance of the anticipated responses. Allie is a thin, small-framed girl. During the visit, as her mother and the doctor reviewed their intervention strategies, she sat quietly on the sofa and looked out the window. Occasionally she climbed into her mother's lap and stayed for a few moments. Lucille reported that Allie was hyperactive, had limited verbal language, self-injured, and made grunting noises. Dr. Martinek agreed with Lucille that the most urgent issue at hand was getting Allie to calm down, as the problem was weighing heavily on the family. Dr. Martinek asked whether Allie was still "bossy" and "controlling." Lucille noted that all her daughters were bossy and controlling. She wondered if this could be a personality trait and not autism; if it was, she did not want to take her daughter's personality away. When autism is separated from the child and undesirable traits are problematized, the child becomes harder to see.

Pointing to the placid girl, Lucille said, "Don't be tricked. This is not her." She said that Allie was being good because she knew she was in the doctor's office. Lucille, a fashionable and polished woman, looked over at me. She hesitated and then shared that her daughter laughed even after getting spanked. She told Dr. Martinek that she had found a reasonably clean and suitable marijuana dispensary in Beverly Hills, but the marijuana had helped only with her daughter's appetite and not with behavior. THC wound her up even more. However, Lucille observed that the hyperbaric chamber therapy had helped curb Allie's penchant for destruction; at least she was no longer hurting the family's cat. Dr. Martinek claimed that the person who invented the hyperbaric chambers had worked with Mother Teresa. Disappointed, Lucille said, "I was expecting a miracle—because some kids had a miracle when they were there." She lamented to Dr. Martinek that her husband had expended all his patience and that Allie's hyperactivity was no longer sustainable.

Dr. Martinek outlined a multistep treatment plan, reiterating that the goal was to get her to sit still on the couch long enough to read a book. He advised Lucille to continue with the Prozac (a selective serotonin reuptake inhibitor usually prescribed for depression, panic disorders, and obsessive-compulsive disorder) and add Motrin (ibuprofen). He said if the Motrin worked to calm Allie down, then the underlying issue could be inflammation. If inflammation was the issue, he advised they next try administering HDCs (helminth worm therapy). Lucille said she would like to try the HDCs and explained that they had previously delayed their introduction because Allie had seizures. He said that if the issue was hormonal, they could try "shutting down" her hormones and delaying puberty, which would cost $750 per month for the inhibitor. He semi-jokingly noted that "9 out of 12 fathers" supported this intervention method.

Lucille gently resisted the idea, saying that she did not want to prevent her daughter from going through puberty. Dr. Martinek sternly contradicted her, "You do." He rhetorically asked if she could imagine what Allie would be like a week before her period, alluding to premenstrual syndrome. Seemingly distraught by this thought, Lucille said that she did not want to. He cautioned her that Allie would continue to be hyperactive into puberty. Figuratively speaking, he warned, "She will kill you. She has already killed dad." He assured her that the drug, leuprolide, had been tested for over thirty years and did not cause cancer. Furthermore, he said they could stop the medication at any time, so the risks seemed minimal.

The plan was set—first, they would try Motrin, and if that worked, they would try the HDCs; if neither worked, they would delay puberty with leuprolide injections. Conveniently, Dr. Martinek produced both HDCs and leuprolide in his private laboratory and sold them directly to patients. He explained to Lucille that the leuprolide would tell her daughter's body to not produce the hormones, which would mean no breasts, no body hair, no odor, and importantly, no hyperactivity. During my observations, I encountered a few other patients on the drug. Dr. Martinek explained that he prescribes leuprolide when autistic children exhibit aggression and/or start masturbating, which he said really "disrupts the family." For one patient, leuprolide disrupted his growth, so he needed a separate growth hormone injection. This experimental treatment has been condemned by leading autism researchers, such as Simon Baron-Cohen, because it interferes with normal development and risks the health of children's hearts and bones. Baron-Cohen told the *Chicago Tribune* in a 2009 interview, "The idea of using it with vulnerable children with autism, who do not have a life-threatening disease and pose no danger to anyone, without a careful trial to determine the unwanted side effects or indeed any benefits, fills me with horror."[42]

In this community, the very tools that are used to treat also serve to illuminate the dysfunctions of autistic bodies, like the Motrin that Dr. Martinek uses to diagnose inflammation. The process of treating autistic children's physiological and behavioral issues demands nuanced and specified knowledge about each individual patient, which is developed over time through the careful monitoring and interpretation of responses. The way a child responds to treatment gives new insight into deficits and dysfunctions.

Searching for Signs of Success

Practitioners and parents note that the meaning of behavioral responses to treatment is not always intuitive. Positive behavioral reactions are obviously desirable. However, negative (or undesirable) behavioral responses can paradoxically be a sign of treatment efficacy. Melissa explained that waiting to see improvement can be extremely difficult: "Sometimes you start a treatment and you literally go to hell. It's like worse than you can even imagine. I thought my child was very difficult to deal with. I put him on this medicine, this supplement or whatever and it is a thousand times worse." One father, Gabriel, said that his son's practitioner calls these reactions "positive negatives." He said one positive negative is "hyperactivity, those are positive things, the kid's actually coming alive again." Parents explained that "regression," the deterioration of skills or worsening of behavior, can sometimes be a temporary sign of a physiological issue that has been accurately pinpointed and provoked.

When asked how he knows a treatment was successful, Dr. Jesson said matter-of-factly, "Well, the parents will tell you that." Practitioners defer to parents when assessing efficacy. Dr. Jesson's successes are measured in what he terms "tingle moments" and "high-five moments." These are moments when parents tell him things like: "'My kid said his first word and he's starting to look us in the eye, and communication's improving. His behavior's improving. His sleep is improving,' or 'He has a

bowel movement three times a day and it's been a normal one.'"
Dr. Maddan is less trusting of her patients' parents. She said
that some parents overreport success, whereas others underre-
port success. She acknowledged that there might be a "placebo
effect," by which she meant the effect on parents: the parents
might perceive their children to be doing better than they actually are. Yet, despite possible inaccuracies, she believes that the
overreporting of success is good because it generates a certain
"energy" that comes from love, which can have its own healthful effects. She suggested that part of treatment is treating the
family's relationship to the autistic child. Whether or not a given
child actually responds well to treatment, both Dr. Jesson and
Dr. Maddan recognize the importance of the parents' perception.

Parents ultimately determine the success of treatments, but
making such a determination is not easy. Aware that their own
deep desire for improvement could bias their perception, parents search for ways to objectively measure treatment efficacy
at home. The alternative biomedical movement provides an
observational tool: the Autism Treatment Evaluation Checklist
(ATEC), which was developed by Bernard Rimland (a founder
of the movement) and Stephen M. Edelson.[43] This questionnaire
contains seventy-seven items organized into four categories:
speech and language communication, sociability, sensory and
cognitive awareness, and health and physical behavior. It includes
descriptive items, such as "speech tends to be meaningful/
relevant," "disagreeable/not compliant," "constipation," and "often
agitated"; for each one, parents indicate the applicability on
three- and four-point Likert scales. The final scores are between
0 and 180, with 0 representing no autism and 180 severe autism.
Many parents complete the ATEC before and after the start of
a new treatment to calculate change. Because it relies on parents'
judgment, the tool is highly subjective by design.

Jennifer uses the ATEC to measure the progress of her two autistic sons, Leon and Landon. She is a state-level beauty queen who has perfectly coiffed blonde hair and bright white teeth. She often attends alternative biomedical conferences both as a sponsor and as a parent. In the exhibit hall, she prepares water basins for ionic footbath demonstrations and extols the device's detoxification capabilities (though there is no evidence that these footbaths work).[44] The footbaths are not just for her sons; she uses the basin too. She said ionic footbaths keep her skin glowing and her bowel movements regular. While joking with a dowdy mother, Jennifer said the footbath had transformed her so that she looked like Heidi Klum. This device was no ordinary treatment, she explained—it was a lifestyle change and an investment. Jennifer said she had been skeptical of the ionic footbath at first. Her husband's friend, Nathan, was selling the device, and as a favor, she agreed to enroll her two autistic sons in his study to assess its efficacy. Nathan asked her to complete the ATEC before and after a one-month trial period. In that time, she noticed improvements in her sons' behaviors and was excited to see their progress reflected in the dropped scores:

> So, when we started Leon, Leon's ATEC was at—I have it written down right here. Oh, gosh, I believe it was a 66, and today he's at a 12. And anything below a 10 is considered recovery. And then, Landon was at an 88, and he's down to a 66. So, we were required to measure our gains by the ATEC, so everyone could see progress being made, and within the first month, both boys' ATEC scores dropped a lot of points.

Some parents questioned the ATEC's accuracy. Sitting at lunch, Claire and another mother discussed the ATEC's problem of parental bias. Claire said that while *she* was able to maintain objectivity, other mothers had a hard time accurately evaluating their children. Claire criticized companies that conduct studies with the ATEC (like the study Jennifer had been involved in), reasoning that these results were not reliable because they were based solely on parent reports. Sharing a personal experience with the ATEC, Claire recalled completing the questionnaire with a friend whose child was observably more "severe" than her own son. While her son received a score of 88, her friend's child received only a score of 55. Claire determined that her friend did not fill it out critically because the score should have been higher. Despite its inaccuracies, Claire said parents were left with no other assessment tools to use at home.

To control for placebo effect by proxy, a phenomenon in which others perceive a patient's treatment to work without evidence or indication of efficacy, some parents deliberately withhold information about treatment changes to gain unsolicited feedback from family members, friends, therapists, and educators.[45] After starting an intervention, parents like Claire wait for people from their social network to volunteer their observations. Distrusting their own ability to be objective, parents value these observations to gauge the effects of a treatment. Claire explained, "I would look for a therapist or teacher to say, 'Hey, he's having a really good week,' you know? I'll never, ever tell them if I'll change anything because I want them to tell me unsolicited. I don't want them to be looking for it, so I'll never tell them." This strategy is also recommended by practitioners. Dr. Gwen Comte, for example, said that these outside observations are "very precious" because they are not "tainted" by parents' biases, or a placebo effect by proxy. She advises the parents of her patients not to disclose intervention changes to family members and to allow them to volunteer their "pure comments" when a change is truly notable.

Trust the Method

When physiological events cannot be easily detected by parents' or others' observations, the alternative biomedical framework provides members with a theoretical structure for understanding their children's health and progress. During a MAPS conference, as we toured the sponsor exhibits, Gabriel pointed out the compound pharmacy where he buys his son's vitamin B-12 shots. Recently, with guidance from a respected alternative biomedical doctor, he increased his son's dosage from three times a week to daily. I asked him about its efficacy. Gabriel provided an analogy. You can grow an oak tree and a tomato plant at the same time, he said, and initially, they will both poke up from the ground at the same rate of growth. While the tomato plant will continue to grow quickly, the oak tree's growth becomes gradual and steady. But with patience, over time, the oak tree will grow to be taller and mightier than the tomato plant. He compared the effects of the B-12 shots to the oak tree: he found the initial improvement to be drastic and exciting, but then progress plateaued. Despite the slowing improvement, Gabriel remained committed to the B-12 shots.

At times, however, change is imperceptible and trust in the framework proves insufficient. When an intervention elicits a behavioral reaction—either positive or negative—parents perceive it to hold promise. Yet often in the treatment process, the indicators of efficacy are frustratingly ambiguous. Parents find that the worst type of sign is no sign at all—no skill advancement or "positive negative" reaction. The costs of alternative biomedical treatments are high, so when a method is difficult to evaluate, parents must decide whether it is worth the financial investment. Melissa described the challenge of isolating the ineffective interventions from the effective ones for elimination:

"There are [a] number of things that we would do and he wouldn't react one way or the other, and those are the most frustrating ones, 'Eh, I don't really see anything.'" At least with "bad" reactions, she could see an "obvious" sign that something was happening and make a judgment. When there is ambiguity, parents are unable to construct new knowledge about autism or its treatment trajectory.

Failure is not without value. Laurel, who has two autistic sons, explained that many of the treatments she had tried over the last sixteen years did not seem to deliver "earth-shattering" progress, but she wanted to continue because stopping would mean quitting: "With a lot of the therapies I've tried with my kids, they are just nonresponders you know for a lot of this stuff so. . . . But it doesn't . . . dissuade me from trying because I always want them to have a better quality of life so . . . I'm never going to give up on them, and just say that I'm going to accept the autism." Despite the lack of noticeable success, the promise of recovery remained tantalizing, and for some parents like Laurel, the promise alone bound them to treatment as a moral obligation.

TOO BIG TO FAIL

The alternative biomedical movement transforms autism into a collection of physiological dysfunctions, transforming the autistic child into a sick child. An entire world emerges on this premise and, within it, new technologies, strategies, opportunities, and relationships. Enacting contentious knowledge about autism, members collectively turn unproven and disproven methods into a lived reality. Despite objections and ambivalence from researchers and medical professionals, members see "autism recovery" dangling within reach.

The movement is an arrangement of relationships, ideas, and tools that reimagine autism as a perceptible and treatable condition. In this movement, parents learn to see autism as a sickness that is separate from their child. As parents pathologize and surveil undesirable behaviors, autistic experiences seem more relatable while the purported child "within" becomes harder to see. The child that parents hope to recover becomes lost in their medical translation. In the pursuit of recovery, parents and practitioners depend on each other to produce individualized knowledge about autistic children. Parents gather observations and identify behaviors in need of intervention. Practitioners interpret laboratory test results and parent reports. Together, they rely on and sustain a market of specialized testing, diagnostic procedures, and an inexhaustible menu of experimental treatments. The alternative biomedical framework nurtures a powerful sense of control. Members believe they know what autism *is* and what can be *done* about it. Differentiating their methods from those of the mainstream, the movement's members embrace an experimental spirit.

Of course, there are limitations to the hope that the movement offers. Rejecting the "mainstream" framework and accepting the alternative biomedical framework means trading a set of seemingly bleak unknowns for a set of promising unknowns. While community members derive order and explanation from this framework, they also encounter a unique brand of chaos. Their individualized approach to understanding and taming autistic bodies creates a situation where treatment is a circuitous and indefinite journey. The interpretation of signs and symptoms could mean one thing or its opposite. A negative reaction after treatment could be bad . . . or it could be good! It all depends on the individual autistic child! Treatment is approached as an iterative process of trial and error, which demands patience and the willingness to regularly fail.

Yet those who maintain their participation tolerated these challenges with the trust that both successes and failures are intrinsic to the process and that uncertainties are accounted for by a system of reason. Members also trust in their wealth of choices. When parents are willing to explore options outside of evidence-based medicine, the market opens up wide. If a treatment disappoints them, there is something new to try and future innovations to look forward to. Even if an intervention proves unsuccessful, the consolation is that something new has been learned about that autistic child, which might suggest a different and more effective strategy. In its sophisticated design, the alternative biomedical movement anticipates and normalizes uncertainty, which obfuscates failure and nourishes hope.

The movement makes it hard to lose hope. After investing so much time, effort, and money, the pursuit of autism recovery grows into a project that is too big and too complicated to fail. Movement members and leaders exhort parents to stay the course despite difficulty and unpredictable outcomes. Families reorganize their lifestyle, priorities, and finances around the elusive promises of recovery. For instance, Mindy said her family revolves around her autistic daughter: "Our lives are so focused on her and her recovery, her healing, her progression." Recognizing the strain, she spun her family's situation as a positive, character-building experience for her two other children: "I think [the other children are] benefiting a lot from being that way, from our family being that way. I think it outweighs the negative aspects of it, which, I mean, there are plenty of those. We can't really do grand family vacations." As it is for so many other members of the alternative biomedical movement, recovery becomes a central force.

Disability has enormous social and material impacts on families; this is not unique to those with autistic children or those who use alternative biomedical treatments.[46] However, the alternative biomedical movement makes grand promises and asks its members to make grander sacrifices. Recall Claire (chapter 2), who sold her house and accrued $125,000 in credit card debt, or José and Patricia (chapter 2), who desperately wanted to help their son but did not have the credit line to cover his consultation and treatments. Importantly, consider the experiences of autistic children and patients, the recipients of treatment, who are acted upon and are often excluded from their own medical decision-making.[47] Within the movement, parents learn to frame their persistence as a moral obligation and treatment as a test of love. Given everything they have invested into autism recovery and the disruption these decisions have had on their families, ultimate failure is unacceptable.

6

THE OUTSIDERS

Resisting Criticism and Claiming Legitimacy

P arents and practitioners of the alternative biomedical movement see themselves in a precarious place. Over the past several years, a few of their prominent doctors have gained public attention—of the bad sort. One lost his medical license for treating autistic children with a hormone inhibitor that is typically used to treat prostate cancer, endometriosis, and early puberty.[1] Another was placed on probation after being accused of endangering a child by prescribing chelation, hyperbaric chamber therapy, and a hormone modulator.[2] And toward the end of my field work, a well-known pediatrician was charged with medical negligence and writing vaccine exemptions without an adequate record of medical reasons for school-aged patients.[3] Meanwhile, parents feared that they would be accused of medical child abuse, so much so that a lawyer was invited to give a keynote address on parents' medical rights at an annual conference. This lawyer gave advice to parents about how to prepare for legal battles and respond to Child Protective Services should they show up at the door without warning. When experimenting with treatments on disabled children, parents and practitioners have to resign themselves to the omnipresent risk of severe legal consequences.

While the alternative biomedical movement is on the public radar, the autistic rights movement often goes undetected. Their demands for acceptance are not fervently attacked by other advocates outside their community (i.e., parents, educators, therapists). In their efforts to become widely recognized as the ultimate authorities on autism, they face a different threat: invisibility. The autistic rights movement does not have nearly as much political and financial power as parent-led organizations, like Autism Speaks, which is the largest autism advocacy organization in the United States. The parents of autistic children dominate autism advocacy and have fought to represent the interests of autistic people. Parental expertise eclipses the experiential knowledge of autistic individuals. Autistic rights members understand that they do not yet have a secure place in the network of expertise forged by parents, therapists, educators, researchers, and medical professionals.[4] When asked why they protest Autism Speaks, Lydia Brown, a disability rights activist and lawyer, said, "Most people aren't aware that there is controversy. It again goes back to the lack of disability representation and to the pathology paradigm that treats disability as people's individual private health problems that they need to fix. So, people don't know that there are problems with Autism Speaks. Let alone, with autistic people, of all people, are ones objecting most loudly to them."

Both alternative biomedical and autistic rights members see themselves as contentious and vulnerable. This chapter illustrates how they protect their ideas about autism and advance their respective agendas. Movement members perform discursive *boundary work* to claim legitimacy, resist outside criticism, and represent the interests of autistic people. Boundary work is the process of attributing qualities to insiders and outsiders, which creates distinction between groups and articulates a group's collective identity.[5] When boundaries are porous or murky, the strategy is used to argue that one group is more authoritative and legitimate than a competing group. In the context of knowledge and expertise, demarcating boundaries is instrumental to securing resources, power, and control.[6]

Research on boundary work tends to focus on dominant ways of knowing (or how certain epistemologies come to dominate) and the creation of outsiders. Much less attention is paid to the ways marginal actors use these same strategies to protect contentious knowledge. In the world of autism, boundary work is performed by self-proclaimed outsiders to sustain ideas that challenge medical providers, researchers, therapists, and parent advocates. As a discursive strategy, boundary work does not necessarily reflect reality. Instead, it reflects the way participants perceive the world. Autistic rights members differentiate their knowledge from that of parent advocates, positioning themselves as the true representatives on issues concerning autistic people. They direct their strategies *outward* to convince outsiders to recognize their authority. Meanwhile, alternative biomedical members differentiate themselves from conventional practitioners and other parents of autistic children, portraying themselves as more innovative, intelligent, and dedicated. They direct their boundary-work strategies *inward* to guard their practices against outside interference. An analysis of these boundary-work activities reveals how members perceive their relationships to other actors and how they respond to these tensions.[7]

THE DAY OF MOURNING: THE AUTISTIC RIGHTS MOVEMENT'S BOUNDARY WORK

In early spring of 2016, on a Sunday afternoon, autistic rights members and allies held signs written in bright, colorful script:

Disabled lives matter!
Disability rights are human rights!
Remember the dead and fight like hell for the living!
In the past 10 years 300 disabled people have been murdered by their
caregivers. Today we are mourning them.

The Boston Day of Mourning was an understated demonstration hosted by the local chapter of the Autistic Self Advocacy Network (ASAN). Sixteen autistic and disabled adults stood quietly, displaying their signs. A few distributed informational flyers to passersby.

The weather was chilly, but the sun was out, and it seemed that winter was finally coming to an end. The area around Harvard was buzzing. Nearby, families and students continuously flowed in and out of Crema Café, leaving with coffee and small paper bags of baked goods and sandwiches. As they passed the concrete center platform of Brattle Square, some continued on and others glanced quickly over at the signs out of curiosity. The square is a popular public space for demonstrations and community events, so this display was nothing out of the ordinary. It blended right into the neighborhood's bustling life.

Rachel, who is often grumpy and sardonic, exclaimed with agitation, "This happens every year!" She was upset about the way the demonstrators were arranging themselves, which she judged to be ineffective for engaging with the public. Some held their posters inward, away from the foot traffic. Some talked only to other demonstrators. She said that autistic quirks can be self-defeating in situations that require social savviness. After Rachel's admonishment, the group gradually reorganized themselves into a line.

The Day of Mourning is an ASAN national event that is organized in multiple cities by local chapters and coordinators.

It was started by Zoe Gross, an ASAN member, in response to the death of George Hodgins. George was an autistic man who was killed in a murder-suicide by his mother, Elizabeth Hodgins, in 2012. Gross found that journalists and readers frequently sympathize with parents who murder their autistic children.[8] She argued that the framing of these stories propagates the idea that the autistic victims are partly to blame because they are difficult to live with and implies that parents' violence is understandable. Gross indicated that in the news coverage of George's murder, he was described as "low functioning and high maintenance,"[9] while his mother was "devoted and loving."[10] Many autistic rights activists wondered: *How could a "devoted and loving" woman kill her son?* Paige, an ASAN member, accused parent-led advocacy organizations such as Autism Speaks of being complicit in perpetuating narratives that portray parents as the true victims and normalize their filicidal impulses:

> That's what you see, the horror stories. And Autism Speaks, one of their documentaries has this woman who has her autistic daughter in the background and is trying to give her a hug, and the mom keeps pushing her off. And she's like, "Sometimes I think about strapping us into the car with my regular daughter and driving off a bridge." Which is so bad because the amount of caregivers who kill their children in the past year is so sky high. And then, you get like the apologists, "Oh, it must be so hard to take care of someone with a disability." And it's almost like, "Well, you take that chance when you have a child. That they may have a disability. And if they don't have one they may develop it later on in life."

Autistic and disability rights activists worry that such biased framing has the power to justify violence against disabled people and send the message to parents and caregivers that they would receive sympathy if they committed these crimes. Moreover, these messages affirm the perception that children with disabilities are undesirable.

ASAN estimates that between 2016 and 2021, over 700 disabled people were killed by parents, relatives, and other caregivers—people who were entrusted with their safety and well-being.[11] Although there is insufficient research on violence against disabled populations,[12] a systemic review finds that globally, disabled adults are 1.5 times more likely than non-disabled adults to experience the risk of physical and sexual violence; among those with intellectual disabilities, it is 1.6 times.[13] In the United States, disabled adults are almost four times more likely than non-disabled adults to experience violent victimization (including aggravated assault, rape/sexual assault, and robbery).[14] Of this group, disabled adults with cognitive disabilities experience the highest rate of victimization. Relatives (including parents, children, and other relationships) account for 14 percent of the violence perpetrated against disabled people (compared to 7 percent among non-disabled victims). These crimes are less likely to be reported to the police (38 percent) compared to crimes committed against non-disabled people (45 percent). Another study finds that disabled children are 3.68 times more likely to experience physical and sexual violence than their non-disabled counterparts.[15]

The Day of Mourning remembers these lost community members. It also directs public attention to the cruel injustices that result from the devaluation of disabled lives. The tone is urgent. The issue is a matter of literal life or death. As per tradition, the demonstrators took turns reading an abbreviated list of names of disabled people who were killed by their caregivers, dating back to the 1980s. In the middle of this reading, a man walked by, and in response to one of the attendee's "disabled lives matter" sign, he taunted, "*All* disabled lives matter!" It seemed that he had intended to say, "All lives matter," which is the counter-slogan used to oppose the Black Lives Matter movement. Despite his failure to effectively insult, his antagonism was unambiguous. Lydia Brown yelled back, "I will have to politely ask you to FUCK OFF!" The man turned around to shout a retort and continued on his way. Brown appeared shaken and wandered away for several minutes, returning later with a lox bagel.

To close the demonstration, Brown forcefully recited a poem they had written about ableism and the callous treatment of autistic life, focusing on George's death. Brown is an incredibly commanding speaker and has a way of making abstract ideas accessible without sacrificing profundity. Even in conversations about the most trivial things, like their love for Ethiopian cuisine (to which they have dedicated an entire blog), Brown's words are deliberate and precise. Brown read their poem thunderously: "He was part of our world, with colors and tastes and sounds and smells, saw beauty, suffered pain, longed for love—but they don't want you to imagine him seeing his mom with a gun to his head and wonder how he must have felt." Two women with a stroller stopped to listen. This was perhaps the longest anyone paid attention to the demonstration all morning. One of the women picked up a flyer that had blown to the ground.

Autistic rights members perceive social and cultural devaluation as the fundamental threat to their community. They assert that this devaluation underlies all of the other challenges they face as autistic people. Accordingly, they aim to change social attitudes and policies. Their demands for autistic acceptance and inclusion follow a path previously forged by early disability rights and identity-based movements (i.e., the gay rights movements).[16] The autistic rights movement demands an expansion of civil rights protections that would increase employment opportunities, safe housing, health care access, and participation in public life.

At first glance, autistic rights members' demands are hard to refuse: they want their human differences to be accepted and valued. These demands, on the surface, do not seem controversial. However, the goal of autism acceptance would require a radical shift in cultural values, social norms, and disability rights laws. The autistic rights agenda is also controversial because activists are not only challenging the medicalization of autism but also making claims about which stakeholders get to represent the interests of autistic people and which do *not*. Movement members contend that autistic people are the rightful authorities on all issues concerning autism. *Who knows more about the autistic experience and autistic needs than autistic people? Who better to represent the interests of autistic people than autistic people?* This stance means that the fight for autistic rights is waged against the incumbent authorities on autism. Although autistic rights members blame many stakeholders for pushing an autism-as-disorder discourse (including medical professionals, therapists, and educators), they target parents of autistic children as the most prominent threat. However, this is not specific to autism; tensions between parents' designs and activists' embodied experiences exist throughout disability advocacy and pediatric gender-affirming medical care.[17]

Why target parents? First, parents are the ones who are directly responsible for the care of autistic children; autistic children's immediate welfare is in their hands. Second, autistic rights members recognize that parents have played an enormous role in steering the field of autism research, education, and health care.[18] In this medical and historical context, parents too have challenged experts. They have fought tirelessly to be seen as experts on their own children—and not as the cause of their children's condition.[19] For autistic people who have limited communication skills, parental expertise is critical to their translation and participation.[20] Parents serve as their autistic children's ambassadors, representing their interests in the neurotypical world.[21] Autistic rights activists, however, accuse parents' representation of being biased in favor of their own interests as caregivers.

Autistic rights members recognize parents' substantial influence in caregiving and advocacy. They perceive most parents—including their own—as supporting the treatment of autism and autistic behaviors, which goes against their messages of acceptance. Movement members rarely discuss the challenges that parents experience in providing care for autistic people, and they seldom mention that these issues may stem from the same structural problems that create barriers in their own lives. Arguing that they know what autistic people need, they focus on becoming the definitive authorities on autism. They direct their boundary work strategies outward, toward other autism stakeholders and the general public. To increase their legitimacy and authority in the eyes of this audience, autistic rights members perform boundary work that differentiates the depth of their experiential knowledge from the partial representation of parental expertise.

Personal Parental Problems

"I grew up in a family where they couldn't appreciate my differences. They wanted me to be as normal as possible because the stress of dealing with someone with different interests and different talents that they couldn't appreciate was too much for my parents," said Harry. He was not officially diagnosed until he was in his mid-twenties, but throughout his life, he remembered his mother being intolerant of his developmental delays and idiosyncrasies: "My mom was bothered by the fact that I was so different from other people. She couldn't stand that I wasn't normal. Not liking sports, the way I grew up not being able to speak until I was five. Having a hard time with eye contact, and not being able to socialize with people very well." His atypicality clashed with his parents' desire for a "normal" child.

Autistic rights members were once autistic children. Whether they had been diagnosed early or later in life, most described unhappy childhoods and strained relationships with their parents. They attributed this tension to their parents' difficulty with accepting their autistic behaviors. These fraught parent-child relationships shape the autistic experience that they politicize as activists.

When I met with Vanna, she was living on disability benefits and spent her time working on fiber art (like weaving and rug hooking) at a day shelter. Her older brother was diagnosed with "classic autism" in the early 1970s when he was about six years old. He needed a lot of support. More than three decades later, Vanna herself was diagnosed with "high-functioning autism." Reflecting on their shared childhood, she said, "I don't think my parents knew what was best for my brother." She disagreed with her parents' decision to place her brother in behavioral therapy, saying it was "kind of abusive." She found it demeaning that the programs had him working for "little treats" (food and sweets). To make matters worse, he had to tote his treats around school in a small cooler until he could earn them. She remembered, "Little tiny autistic kids carrying around their own coolers of treats. Very sad." Vanna also hated that her parents underestimated his ability to comprehend and would openly discuss the dreadfulness of his existence:

> My mom used to think that about my brother, and, having a horrible—"Oh my god, his life must be so awful." I don't know if his life was that awful really. She doesn't know either, but she said that in front of him so many times. And then people start thinking, "Oh, my life is awful and horrible," because people . . . everyone says so. And that's not fair to do to someone. My mom said she thought about killing herself and my brother, and like she said that kind of stuff in front of him. And it's like, "Why would you do that?"

Unlike her parents, Vanna said she accepted her brother just as he was: "I never thought autism was terrible because I never pitied my brother. No, I always thought he was fine the way he was. He was my brother. You know, I always just accepted him. Yeah, he was an asshole at times, but, you know, everyone is." She joined the autistic rights movement to represent the interests of fellow autistic people. As noted earlier in this book, parental expertise often serves as a proxy for autistic experience, especially when there are barriers to communication.[22] From Vanna's perspective, however, parents have their own agendas and cannot truly understand the desires of autistic people. As an autistic person herself and as someone whose brother had greater support needs, she believed she had a strong understanding of what autistic people required:

> When we speak, when someone like me who's able to speak and walk around and advocate for myself, I'm not just advocating for myself and for people that look and sound like me. By advocating for myself, I'm also advocating I always think for all autistics,

whether they can talk or not, or whether they can . . . whether they're able to talk or not. . . . In some ways I got into this for my brother as much as myself.

Ash shared Vanna's activist agenda. However, Ash's rejection of parental expertise stemmed from growing up with the diagnosis: "I'm just kind of tired of people assuming all autism parents are like wonderful and self-sacrificing and helpful. Mine were emotionally abusive." Ash disagreed with the interventions implemented by their parents and educators. In particular, they remembered how much they hated behavioral therapy, which included training on how to increase eye contact and reduce hand flapping. Before they learned about neurodiversity and the autistic rights movement, Ash felt stigmatized:

Well, I thought of [autism] as like a bad thing. I thought it was bad thing that was shameful to talk about. I thought it was a bad thing and it was shameful to talk about and something I was supposed to fight off. Like I was supposed to fight off the symptoms and something you didn't talk about. Something you didn't really do anything about. Something that was shameful. Something that made you less than other people. Something that made you worse.

At the time of our interview, Ash had been estranged from their parents for a number of years.

Parents are entrusted with the sacred responsibility of protecting and advocating on behalf of their children.[23] The participants in this study perceived their parents as having abdicated this responsibility. They described their parents as people who failed to appreciate their differences and adequately support their needs. With disappointment, they said their parents subscribed to a medical model of autism that pathologized and problematized autistic behaviors. Participants dismissed their parents' attempts to help as misguided and, at times, cruel. Inspired by these struggles with their parents, many movement members challenge the authority of parental expertise, arguing that their embodied knowledge confers a more legitimate authority.

"Not Like My Kid": Embodied Knowledge Versus Parental Expertise

Ash believes that fundamentally, both parents and autistic rights activists want "a good quality of life" for autistic people. However, they have different interpretations of what "a good quality of life" entails and how it can be achieved: "[Parents are] more focused on cures and early intervention and ABA, applied behavioral analysis. That's what they're focused on whereas we're focused on acceptance. We're focused on treatment that works with us as autistic people as opposed to trying to make fake neurotypicals out of us. I think we're more focused on like the practical issues." Autistic rights activists argue that parents do not know what autistic people truly want because they are not autistic themselves. Yet parents serve as proxies for their autistic children, determining how to meet children's immediate and long-term needs. Parents whose children require greater support continue to make decisions on their behalf long into adulthood. Vanna worried that neurotypical parents were not qualified to make these important decisions: "Parents come at things with their own bias because they're separate beings."

Autistic rights activists contend that their embodied knowledge qualifies them to represent the interests of autistic people. Even as the diagnostic category evolves, expanding to include more people and contracting to trim outliers,[24] activists imagine that autistic people across the spectrum share biological citizenship—that they are biologically and genetically linked.[25] Autism is heterogenous, but movement members perceive a unified autistic identity and a shared political agenda. Furthermore, they assert that their embodied knowledge provides relevant insights into the lived experiences of other autistic people, even those who seem very different from them.

Autistic rights activists see a cohesive autistic population, one that cuts across the full spectrum. Parent advocates do not. This difference is a crucial point of contention. Both groups see the other as guilty of partial representation.[26] When demanding acceptance, activists experience invalidation from parent advocates. Parents dismiss activists' credibility, arguing that autistic rights activists do not share the same characteristics as their autistic children and thus should not speak on their behalf. Charles, an electrical engineer, said that parents have accused him and other members of being "not like my child":

CHARLES: It can get depressing when the parents shout us down.
CATHERINE: Does that happen?
CHARLES: Oh yeah. All the time. Because they're saying, "You're not enough like my kid." And we use the acronym NLMC, because it happens so much. So, all we need to say is "NLMC" and everybody in the advocacy community knows exactly what that means. "Not like my child." So, that's because they're only seeing us now, as adults. If they saw us as children, then they'd think differently. But they aren't.

How are autistic rights activists different from the autistic children of parent advocates? Participants said that parents tend to highlight two key differences: age and required supports. Autistic rights members who attend in-person events are typically adults and require relatively few supports. Hil, a social worker, did not find the age difference between members and parents' children particularly meaningful. As they explained, "Number one, your child is 10 years old. I'm 56. You don't know what I was like at 10 years old. You don't know what your child will be like at 56. You don't know that we're not the same." Movement members note that autistic people change over time, so parents should not assume that their children are so different from activists or that activists cannot remember what it was like to be an autistic child.

Most participants live independently, and nearly everyone I observed or interviewed has verbal language. As one participant noticed, "A lot of [parents] don't really seem to care what you have to say if they perceive you as being less affected by autism than their child, so that's a bit tough." When parents categorize them as "less affected" and "high functioning," the terms suggest that their demands are of lower priority and their needs are less urgent than those of young and "low-functioning" autistics. Hil explained that such differentiation reinforces parental expertise while diminishing the value of their embodied knowledge: "See, these divisions and functioning labels are never used to help us. They are always used against us. Either you're too low functioning to participate in your own advocacy. Or you're too high functioning to count. So, who does that leave? Non-autistic people to make the decisions about our lives. That's not acceptable."

In a landscape where services are insufficiently funded and access to them is unequal,[27] what is at stake is the privilege of representing autistic people and steering the allocation of these limited resources.[28] Charles supposed that parent advocates see them as competitors: "I think the concern, assuming this is a general concern, is that everybody's competing for resources, and things that will help adult quote-unquote 'high functioning autistics' would take resources away from children." Participants were frustrated with parents' failure to recognize the full scope of their advocacy. Vanna insisted, "We care about the autistics who can't speak for themselves, right, that we do care about them, and we do care about our siblings who can't speak for themselves." She reasoned that parents of "classically autistic children" do not believe the autistic rights movement is "interested in their children" because, reciprocally, "[parents] are not interested in us." Like many other members, Vanna joined the movement to represent the full autism spectrum—not just people who have problems similar to her own:

> And we are interested in their kids because we have solidarity with our own. So . . . and we are thinking about their kids, because we consider them a part of our own group. So, of course, we're interested in them. Just because [parents are] not interested in us does not mean that we're not interested in their kids, so it's a whole bizarre thing, and there's kind of . . . I think kind of a war on about who is going to speak for autistics.

Because they occupy this liminal position—in the view of outsiders, they are simultaneously too autistic to speak for themselves and yet not autistic enough to speak for the broader autism community—activists fear they will be erased from autism advocacy. Ash said,

> Well, organizations like Autism Speaks, people who spread the idea that autism is a horrible disease that needs to be cured and that we can't advocate for ourselves. And parents and other—parents and professionals who think we can't speak for ourselves and keep speaking for us. And trying to determine what we need

and like basically acting as though autism self—like autistic self-advocates' words are not important. I mean I see a lot of organizations out there with no autistic self-advocates involved at all. It's just parents, just professionals, nobody on the spectrum. I see like legislation and all kinds of things where nearly everybody doing recommendations for autism is not on the spectrum.

Participants were infuriated that parent advocates do not fully understand the autistic experience, yet they seem to enjoy more authority and voice than autistic people.

Individual parents, however, are not their biggest enemy. The autistic rights movement positions itself against the behemoth organization Autism Speaks, which caters to parents. When asked why Autism Speaks is the primary organization they challenge, Lydia Brown offered a direct and clear explanation: power. They explained,

> Because they have a lot of political power, they have a lot of clout in the public sphere, the National Autism Association is little known.[29] They don't have much influence; most people don't know who they are. So, while we think that [the National Autism Association is] ridiculous, there is not any need to go out picketing against them because they don't have influence. Autism Speaks has politicians that work with them, they have gone internationally, they work with heads of states internationally, they work with pioneers in scientific research, they work with a lot of celebrities. They were founded by Bob and Suzanne Wright. Bob is a former chairman of NBC Universal and then he became the chairman of General Electric, they are very wealthy people with a lot of connections politically and socially. And so, it's imperative that we fight against them because of the amount of influence that they have.

Autistic rights activists protest the way Autism Speaks wields its influence. Rachel depicted the organization as an oppressive force: "Autism Speaks and that type of organization don't see themselves in a position of power but they are and they refuse to acknowledge that they are complicit in the oppression of others." By oppression, she and other members were referring to the way Autism Speaks promotes an autism-as-disorder model. At the time of this research, Autism Speaks framed itself as an organization that provides information and resources to families, supports autism awareness, and funds research on "causes, prevention, treatments and a cure for autism."[30] Today, the organization has incorporated the language of "acceptance" and the "aesthetics of neurodiversity," but autistic rights activists contend that the organization has not changed in any meaningful way.[31] Cynthia, a writer and artist, was one of many autistic rights members who disagreed with Autism Speaks' priorities: "It seems that [Autism Speaks] send[s] a lot of money to research and trying to find a cure for autism, but autism's not a disease." Bridget, a journalist, argued that because these priorities are envisioned by non-autistic people, they serve the desires of non-autistic people. Moreover, what makes the lives of parents and caregivers easier is not necessarily beneficial to autistic people:

"Autism Speaks. It's time to listen."[32] But the people they want you to listen to are not people on the autism spectrum, but they want you to listen to their opinions about, like how their lives are very hard because they have someone in it with autism or something. It's like, well, what about how it's hard for people who have autism? And maybe you're making it harder by trying to say that their identity is something that should be cured.

Autistic rights members perceive a struggle between themselves and parent advocacy organizations, between the hope of acceptance and the dominance of medicalization. Responding to these tensions, their boundary work strategies depict the shortcomings of parental expertise and the legitimacy of their embodied knowledge. Because their goal is to effect change in policy and social attitudes, they articulate these ideas in public forums: demonstrations, protests, community events, and legislative hearings.

Who Is Being Represented and By Whom?

To enact autistic rights principles outside the movement, members need to collaborate with people outside their community, including their own detractors. Autism acceptance is a call for radical social change. Accordingly, they direct their strategies outward.

Along a wide suburban street lined with foliage and manicured lawns, six autistic rights demonstrators from ASAN stood quietly with white posters that read: "Autism Speaks Does Not Speak for Me!," "Civil Rights Not a Cure!," "People Not Puzzles," "Nothing About Us Without Us," and "Acceptance." Ash had designed the posters with Sharpie markers. They had a creative flair and playful penmanship. Across the street was a modest entrance to the open-air amphitheater where the Autism Speaks Walk, a fundraising event, was taking place. The ASAN members wanted to gain the attention of people turning their cars into the amphitheater, but they had been assigned a space where it was difficult to garner attention, and the text on the posters was too small to be seen from so far away.

At the ASAN meeting the day before, Paige had asked if they should anticipate any violence or harassment while protesting the Autism Speaks Walk. Rachel said she should expect to hear parents saying their children were "not like you." She said parents would point to their children's aggressive behaviors to illustrate how different they were from the autistic rights activists at the protest. But on the day of the protest, there was no one to argue, no one to confront. When they first arrived at the amphitheater, Ash approached two Autism Speaks staff members and asked where they should set up their protest. Ash specified that they wanted to be visible. The staff cheerfully invited the group to set up across the street from the parking lot. The parking lot stretched half a mile from the event space. Ash accepted the suggestion without much negotiation. They held up their signs as they walked out of the center to make the most of their brief visibility.

As demonstrated by this protest and its rather anticlimactic outcome, autistic rights activists are competing against far larger and more powerful stakeholders. Gaining representation would mean becoming the definitive authorities on autism and influencing decisions that impact autistic people. Vanna summarized,

One of the things we're pushing for, and I'm trying to push for wherever I can, is if decisions are going to be made about us at the table, there needs to be a super majority of us autistics at the table helping to decide things and what policy is and stuff, and there's been a lot of resistance to that, a lot of things about parents and professionals need to be making these decisions, but they're not autistics, right? So, for all that they can speculate and for all that they know their child maybe or maybe not, they don't know autism. There's only one way to know what autism is, and that's to have it.

At this moment, in the broad field of autism advocacy, limited space is reserved for autistic activists. Inequalities within the autistic rights movement make it even more complicated to negotiate who gets to occupy these rare spaces. From Vanna's perspective, those who are privileged do not really understand the average autistic experience, yet they are often called to serve as token representatives. She complained that the tokens tend to be "super-autistic," meaning they are articulate, poised, and successful. They are the kind of people who make autism palatable to neurotypical stakeholders such as parents and lawmakers. Thinking about one specific person, Vanna said, "He's like a really wealthy autistic whose family is politically involved, I think, so the president—not the president, the last governor, appointed him [to the state autism committee] because he knew him." She argued that his wealth and social connections made him an outlier: "It's like, these aren't representative of the average autistic person's life. He has a horse . . . he has a horse." I asked her what that means. She said, "I think your average autistic person doesn't have a job, may be on disability. . . . Is on disability or [Supplemental Security Income], they haven't worked, and might live with a parent or might live on their own, and is probably on [Medicaid], and tries to figure out what to do with their day so that they're not in front of the TV all day or on the computer all day." For now, autism rights activists perceive parent advocates to be some of their greatest opponents in the struggle for authority and representation. But as Vanna suggested, even when activists are given opportunities to speak for autism, representing the full spectrum is a difficult thing to do.

THE DEATH OF DR. BRADSTREET: THE ALTERNATIVE BIOMEDICAL MOVEMENT'S BOUNDARY WORK

The ice sculpture stood like a magnificent trophy, towering about five feet tall. The middle ice block read, "God Bless, Dr. James Jeffrey Bradstreet." At the base was the logo of OxyHealth, a hyperbaric chamber company and one of the major sponsors of this continuing medical education conference. Multicolored disco lights illuminated the glassy sculpture. It was outlandish, commanding, and a little ostentatious. At the center of attention during cocktail hour, it set a mood that was both austere and uncomfortably humorous. Drinks in hand, a few guests—medical professionals and sponsors—posed with it for pictures. Others cautiously reached out to glide their fingers along the slick sides of the ice.

Later that evening, during dinner, the waiters circulated in the hotel ballroom, distributing plastic shot cups filled with Dr. Bradstreet's favorite cocktail. Guests approached the memorial ice sculpture and poured their shots into the drilled-in tunnel. The luge chilled the liquid as it slid through the tunnel and dripped into a plastic cup at the other end. Some people looked around incredulously and chuckled at the sculpture's novelty. A few guests at my dinner table appeared uneasy, perhaps discomfited by the asymmetry between the dignity of the gesture and the garishness of the ice luge. Dr. Bradstreet's close colleagues and friends came up to share one last drink with him before closing the evening at the fold-out blackjack, roulette, and poker tables.

The man being commemorated, Jeff Bradstreet, had died in Chimney Rock, North Carolina, on June 19, 2015, just three months prior. He was found in a river with a bullet in his chest. In the days before his death, Dr. Bradstreet's office had been raided by the federal Food and Drug Administration (FDA) and the Georgia Drugs and Narcotics Agency. They were investigating his prescription of globulin component macrophage-activating factor (GcMAF) injections to autistic patients. While the efficacy of GcMAF as a treatment is unsupported by research, some believe it has curative effects for a number of conditions, from autism to cancer to AIDS. Drugs that are unproven and unapproved, like GcMAF, can pose serious health risks because they have not been formally reviewed for quality, safety, and efficacy. The successes of GcMAF were anecdotal, and its failures had counted in the deaths of at least five people.[33] The FDA raid was precipitated by Dr. Bradstreet's connections to First Immune, the company through which he acquired GcMAF injections for patients. Four months earlier, in February 2015, the British laboratory producing First Immune GcMAF had been raided by the United Kingdom's Medicine and Healthcare Products Regulatory Agency (a regulating body similar to U.S. FDA). It was then discovered that the blood plasma used to produce First Immune's GcMAF was deemed unsuitable for humans or drug production.[34] If convicted of violating interstate commerce statutes, Dr. Bradstreet could have faced up to twenty years in prison.[35]

In the news, he was portrayed as a dangerous quack. But that night, his colleagues and supporters tearfully remembered him as a dedicated and gracious doctor. They praised him for answering patients' calls after business hours and for occasionally offering resources to patients without charge. At the same time, the eulogies painted him as an impulsive man who was quick to promote new intervention methods. One colleague humorously recounted that whenever he saw Dr. Bradstreet getting excited about a new intervention, he would mark his calendar and wait a year to see if the excitement was sustained before taking the recommendation seriously. While other medical professionals might have interpreted Dr. Bradstreet's practices as pseudoscientific and dangerous, here, among his close colleagues, his experimental spirit and inventiveness were regarded as celebrated quirks that had made him a good doctor.

The reported cause of death was suicide, but some of his supporters suggested it was murder. Gema, a highly involved parent in the alternative biomedical community, dispelled the rumors. She personally knew his family and had heard that before his death, he had left a folder on the kitchen table filled with information and documents his wife would need, such as the will. These seemed to be clear signs that his suicide was carefully planned. She explained that he was a generous and kind man but arrogant. Dakota, who worked for a supplement company that sponsors many alternative biomedical conferences, expressed similar sentiments. During our conversation, an old episode of *Full House* played in the background of the hotel room. She had no doubt that it was suicide but was confused about why a former pastor like Dr. Bradstreet would commit such a sin. Furthermore, she questioned his technique, noting that shooting oneself in the chest leaves too much room for error and is not the surest way to die. The laugh track playing on the television disruptively chimed in and out. Dakota brushed aside her questions, but for others in the community, they were the breadcrumbs that led toward the theory of homicide.

Rumors connected his death to the recent deaths of other alternative practitioners, telling a conspiratorial story of related mobster-esque killings motivated by intense objections to their unconventional practices and research. Parents and practitioners tended to distance themselves from these stories, dismissing them as mere conspiracy, too gauche for serious discussion. Dr. Dahlia Pagani was familiar with the rumors but skeptical of their veracity: "Right after Dr. Bradstreet died there was a whole thing of like—there have been four MDs in the last three months who are doing alternative therapies who are dead all under like suspicious terms—you can't believe anything that you read ever, research paper, internet, whatever." Yet the murder mystery was so sensational that many had to mention it, even if only to dismiss it.

Some members of the community found these stories plausible. Christine, a mother of a teenage autistic son who resides in a small Nebraskan town, admitted to me, "I can subscribe to the theory that they were targeted and killed." I first met Christine in Dallas at an alternative biomedical conference that catered to parents of autistic children. We had been seated side-by-side with our feet soaking in white plastic basins filled with water that had browned and grown opaque with the toxins purportedly excreting from our bodies. Christine had done her investigation online, reading what others had theorized about Dr. Bradstreet on various internet forums. He was one of the doctors she had considered consulting to treat her son. When I spoke with her shortly after the conference, she informed me that there was a "whole movement of people" who believed his death was due to something more sinister than suicide: "It's like a huge conspiracy theory." In her portrayal, he was an intellectual renegade who had encroached upon forbidden knowledge—a cure for autism—and now burned at the stake.

Christine sensed tension and wariness among alternative biomedical practitioners at the parent conference. This perception was not unfounded. A few months earlier, the 2015 Medical Academy of Pediatric Special Needs (MAPS) conference for alternative biomedical practitioners was underattended because a number of attendees had pulled out at the last minute. Dakota, whose work in health supplements had brought her close to the alternative biomedical community, surmised that this hesitance was attributable to the FDA raid that preceded Dr. Bradstreet's death. She supposed that many practitioners had decided not to attend at the last minute, fearing that an association with MAPS might attract a similar investigation of their practices.

Dr. Ravi Zahin, one of Dr. Bradstreet's colleagues and collaborators, described the situation with hushed delicacy. His usual spritely demeanor was clouded over. We would all die one day, he said, and so we should not be afraid to do the work we need to do while living. Whether or not individuals chose to believe the rumors, these widely circulated narratives conveyed the community's perception of its outsider status, its vulnerability, and its potential endangerment. Dr. Kavita Maddan, a well-known alternative biomedical practitioner and a close friend of Dr. Bradstreet, explained that these were the risks of being unconventional: "It just hits too close to home that our—what we do is not looked upon well by whatever agencies and, so, none of us want that. So, regardless of whether he was shot or shot himself, whatever happened with the FBI and FDA, that pushed him to that point, it's our world."

Dr. Bradstreet and his like-minded colleagues provide parents something they desperately want: the precious hope of recovery, the chance of neurotypicality. Their methods, however, have attracted harsh criticism from medical professionals who accuse them of malpractice, child abuse, and bad science. Because of these longstanding tensions, Dr. Bradstreet's death reinforced and magnified the friction between the alternative biomedical community and their detractors. Alternative biomedical members portrayed him as a martyr, embodying the community's fundamental values, its purpose, and most of all, the realization of its deepest fear—that one day, government authorities could intervene and cut off access to what they believe are effective treatments for autism. Practitioners and parents wanted to be left alone. Most were not actively trying to change the minds of experts or the public. Their objectives were focused on individual treatment. As Christine said, "I'm just sitting here in my house in the Midwest, in Nebraska, mostly trying to figure out how to help my son. But also, being aware of the bigger picture. This type of treatment is definitely controversial."

The alternative biomedical members in this study tried to protect their beliefs and practices from outsiders. This protective behavior was necessary to preserve their hope of recovering autistic children. Perceiving themselves to be under siege, they directed their strategies inward with an emphasis on managing stigma and affirming their own legitimacy.[36] Practitioners, defending their professional qualification to treat autistic children, carefully aligned their education and credentials with those of conventional doctors. They pointed to their medical training and use of peer-reviewed research in the design of experimental treatments. To justify their methods, parents and practitioners differentiated themselves from experts and other parents by boasting their intellectual and moral superiority. The practitioners emphasized their inventiveness and the parents their unwavering dedication. For all of the participants, these two strategies—professional alignment and expulsion boundary work—reinforced their sense of collective identity and solidified their position in the larger field of autism. Within the movement, these processes helped members neutralize criticism.

Good Medicine: Aligning with Mainstream Medicine

A mother came into Dr. Kurt Martinek's office to ask for a vaccine exemption letter and discuss her autistic daughter's co-occurring condition, which she thought was causing sensitivity to sound and certain fabrics. The mother said she had tried "modern medicine" (perhaps to mean Western or allopathic medicine), but it did not work. Dr. Martinek quickly snapped back to correct her: he too practiced modern medicine. Relaxing into a joke, he asked whether he was too old to be modern.

The mother corrected herself, "natural medicine." Dr. Martinek is one of the best-known doctors in the alternative biomedical community and has coauthored a popular book on specialized treatments. He grows therapeutic helminth worm larvae in his lab. He discourages vaccination. He once told a patient's family that driving a Chevy Bolt could cause "cancer of private parts." Yet he was reluctant to label the type of medicine he practices as anything other than regular medicine. "There's nothing unique about the biomedical approach," he claimed. "It's just medicine." He distinguished his type of practice as "good medicine," defining "good" as spending more time with each patient, which he can afford because he and many of his peers do not accept health insurance. Describing his practice as "modern," "nothing unique," and "good," he implied that his peers are comparable to but better than conventional doctors.

Although some of their treatments are too experimental to be accepted by medical experts, alternative biomedical practitioners and parents position their methodologies within the "reason and rationality" of biomedicine.[37] Recall that the movement was facilitated by Bernard Rimland, who earned wide respect for shifting the autism paradigm from psychogenic to biological, but later lost credibility for supporting a vaccine-autism link and promoting unorthodox treatments.[38] The alternative biomedical movement, then, has historical roots in the medical mainstream. In the pursuit of autism treatment, parents and practitioners described a divergence, rather than a complete break, from dominant experts and professionals. Pointing to institutional markers such as credentials, education, and peer-reviewed publications, they delicately positioned their practice as simultaneously distinct from and an extension of conventional medicine. Through discursive alignment strategies, members actively invoked professional similarities to highlight alternative biomedical practitioners' qualifications to treat and the legitimacy of their practices. Practitioners strategically blurred the professional boundaries between the alternative and conventional, seeking refuge within the very system they challenged.

Because they challenge experts and because their practices are not evidence based (and sometimes dismissed as outright dangerous), alternative biomedical members cannot expand the boundaries of their community into the domain of conventional medicine (and they cannot force conventional medicine to accept them).[39] However, through alignment, they claim conventional forms of institutionalized cultural capital and authority.[40] Members see their practitioners as concurrently competing within the broader boundaries of medicine and outside its conventions. Participants noted that their specialized practitioners have credentials (e.g., doctor of medicine, doctor of osteopathic medicine, doctor of naturopathic medicine) and the same basic medical education as conventional counterparts, plus additional training to set them apart. The alternative biomedical movement may be critical of medical orthodoxy, but its members leverage the authority conferred by medical education and credentials.

Parents, for their part, trust practitioners because of their formal training. During an interview, Trudy, the mother of an autistic son, contrasted the credentials of her child's alternative biomedical practitioners with images of sinister witches: "[T]his is done by MDs and DOs and doctorates. They're not like some crazy person back stirring a big caldron of like bubbling stuff to give to our kids or some quack doctor website, you know?" She argued that the interventions, although they may appear unconventional, are prescribed by medical authorities, rather than by someone unqualified and dangerous. Her child's practitioners did not toil over caldrons; they used laboratory tests and prescribed drugs.

Practitioners argued that they were more educated, and thus better educated, than conventional doctors. On top of their formal medical training, they had to learn additional sciences, like osteopathy and naturopathy, to understand patients' physiological dysfunctions and intervention needs. For instance, Dr. Zahin sees himself as having extra education. He is a naturopathic doctor who owns a couple of wellness spas. He works with a general population, which includes autistic children and other pediatric patients with neurodevelopmental conditions. He said he originally planned to apply for "regular medical school," but after attending an informational lecture about a program in which "you could learn conventional medicine plus this other thing called 'herbs,'" he interviewed and gained admission into a naturopathic medicine program. Dr. Zahin said he received the same education as other doctors and more, which he framed as a positive attribute:

> [In] comparison to a medical school in Harvard and all these other [institutions]—it's probably still on their website—but and you see how many class hours you get in pathology, oncology, neurology, and so it was, it was cool to me that I get all of that, plus I get like stuff that I didn't know, so I just thought it was more education.

Unlike Dr. Zahin, Dr. Darren Jesson started in family practice, but he too had to learn more to expand his repertoire into alternative biomedical practice. He was skeptical when his patients first asked about alternative treatments, but then he attended conferences to explore these methods: "The more I learned, the more I became a believer in it." He said the new content reminded him of the "pure sciences" he was taught in the first couple years of medical school (like microbiology, neuroscience, pathology). By incorporating these new methods, he could indulge his curiosity and feel like a "scientist":

> I think just in the first few years of medical school, they're pure sciences. So, you're really learning biochemical pathways. You're learning anatomy as well as pathology, and you're really, taking a pure science approach to problems. . . . And so really, I would say the integrated and functional training I received in the first few classes I went to [at conferences], they started throwing up slides that were from the basic sciences from my first few years at medical school, and it was actually back to the basics. And really, think through these problems from a scientific standpoint, and look at pathways, and figure out what things were breaking down. So, for me, it really felt like a refreshing return to my roots of being a scientist again.

Dr. Jesson was never a scientist; rather, he perhaps meant to say that learning about alternative biomedical treatments and how they work in theory felt exciting and creative. Like him, the other practitioners prided themselves on being "scientific." They pointed to their use of published research in medical decision-making, claiming the legitimacy associated with peer-reviewed studies. Dr. Travis Drummond, who works mostly with autistic patients in California, emphasized that his experimental methods are informed by research conducted at high-prestige universities and hospitals:

> [W]hat makes this my approach or the approach I try to employ—I don't know if it's unique, but perhaps, discriminates it from the standard professional. . . . Again, I'm really looking at the research that has been done on these children. . . . Let me give you an example. UC Davis, UC San Francisco, Mount Sinai, Einstein

have all done work with something called intranasal oxytocin. And I use intranasal oxytocin in my practice as a trial. Is that biomedical? I don't know. They certainly would not want to say that [*laughing*], because biomedical is to hold a stigma that it's some sort of voodoo kind of, it's kind of out there. And most of these centers are very, very kosher biologically based research facilities.

Here, Dr. Drummond separated himself from both "the standard professional" and the bad reputation of "voodoo," while loosely associating himself with top scientists and claiming that his methods drew from knowledge generated at trusted institutions. While researchers working on intranasal oxytocin at universities find mixed results and call for more studies on its benefits for autistic people,[41] Dr. Drummond takes it directly from the bench to patients' bedside. He presented his experimental practice as unorthodox but not witchcraft; rather, it was unorthodox and cutting edge.

Of course, it is important to emphasize that Dr. Jesson, Dr. Drummond, and their alternative biomedical colleagues are not scientists and the experimental treatments that they implement do not follow the rigorous procedures required in clinical trials. When participants made claims about "doing science" or "doing research," they meant to say that their treatments were partly inspired by published research—often, early findings that only suggest certain interventions should be studied further. Practitioners followed their own sense of logic, but methodologically, their experimentation was unstructured and rather haphazard.

Because many of their treatments are experimental, practitioners were eager to point to research papers that appear to validate their methods. Dr. Charlotte Langley understood that good research is critical to the acceptance of alternative biomedical treatments; she lamented, "[Oxytocin therapy for kids with autism] is a therapy that I use all the time and yeah, it's not evidence-based. There's not enough evidence on it. There's some, but there's not as much evidence as there would need to be to make it a 'conventional' or a widely accepted treatment. It's still pretty fringe." Insufficient evidence was the problem for many of the treatments she and her colleagues prescribed, including specialized diets and supplements. So, when a prominent pediatrics journal published a review paper on gastrointestinal complaints among autistic children, Dr. Langley interpreted it as a small victory: "I think that it's kind of coming around and the science is actually backing up some of the biomed therapies that we've been doing for years, which is awesome. That's great news." Even when published studies do not fully validate their work, practitioners still find that these tenuous links reduce stigma and legitimize their methodologies.

These discursive strategies work within the alternative biomedical community to legitimize unconventional practices. They suggest that members respect conventional forms of medical and scientific authority and understand themselves as entitled to the same privileges as those who avail themselves of conventional medicine. Furthermore, professional alignment sends a powerful message to parents, especially when their practitioner is educated in both allopathic and alternative medicine but has made a career in the latter. First, it implies that after surveying the medical landscape, the practitioner has rationally selected what they believe to be the better way to treat patients. Second, it suggests that the practitioner continues to be dually informed by both paradigms in their treatment decision-making. The alignment with the medical mainstream communicates that alternative biomedical practice is well informed and engages with an orthodox paradigm, as opposed to being insular and dogmatic.

Practitioners' alignment strategies express a complex relationship with conventional medicine and its experts. They perceive themselves as better educated and more knowledgeable than mainstream medical professionals. Yet, by identifying their resemblances to conventional counterparts, these practitioners demarcate their medical jurisdiction and defend their right to treat autistic children. However, as I illustrate in the next section, to empower their unorthodoxy and neutralize the attacks against them, both practitioners and parents point to intellectual and moral strengths that distinguish them from other actors in the field of autism.

Out of the Box: Diverging from Mainstream Medicine

On the last day of a 2014 conference in Dallas, Texas, attendees gathered to see the special guest—the man whose work had significantly influenced their knowledge about autism and its causation and whose biography was an allegory of their collective struggle. Mark Blaxill, a vocal vaccine skeptic and writer, presented the 2014 Galileo Award for someone who embodies a heretical and innovative spirit to Andrew Wakefield, a British physician gastroenterologist, who, in 1998, had published a paper that controversially suggested a relationship between autism and the MMR (measles-mumps-rubella) vaccine. This publication was retracted from *The Lancet* in 2010 because investigations found ethical violations and fraud. This led the United Kingdom's General Medical Council to strip Wakefield of his medical license.[42] At what would seem to have been the nadir of his career, Wakefield began to enjoy a life of celebrated infamy within the alternative biomedical community.

In his speech, Blaxill drew parallels between the brave but tortured lives of Galileo and Wakefield. Galileo was to heliocentrism as Wakefield was to autistic enterocolitis, a condition that describes gastrointestinal disease associated with autism and has been discredited by the medical community. He compared Galileo's experience of being condemned and placed under house arrest until his death to Wakefield's loss of his medical license. However, Blaxill asserted that whereas Galileo had "chickened out" and retracted his theory under coercion, Wakefield had not succumbed, which made him more morally resolute and admirable than his illustrious forebear. The theatre of the Galileo Award ceremony captured the community's conscious and proud divergence from the mainstream medical and scientific communities, which have rejected Wakefield's work.

The practitioners and parents in this study admired unorthodoxy. Because alternative biomedicine is experimental by design, unorthodoxy is embraced as an inherent characteristic. As Dr. Langley explained, outsiders may criticize their lack of evidence, but she and her colleagues believe they are on the cusp of something worthwhile: "The main criticism I get is that the treatments that I'm recommending are not evidence-based and I can't disagree. There's some evidence to support. Some of it is presumptive, some of it is [that] I'm really having to translate the research to support our clinical application even though the clinical trials haven't been done on outcomes. So, I get it. That's true. However, that's how a lot of good medicine starts, right?" To her, worthwhile medicine comes from tinkering and translating early research findings into experimental treatments for patients.

Describing his peers in MAPS, a professional association for alternative biomedical practitioners, Dr. Martinek said, "If they're involved with MAPS, they're interested in thinking outside the box." In my interview with Dr. Dahlia Pagani, a naturopathic doctor, she expressed the same sentiment nearly verbatim: "I don't consider any of these MAPS doctors conventional MDs. They are MDs who are . . . thinking outside the box." When comparing their training to that of their "mainstream" and "conventional" counterparts, practitioners criticized their peers for undereducation, rote learning, and inflexibility. Practitioners hold degrees in a range of disciplines, such as medicine, osteopathic medicine, naturopathic medicine, chiropractic medicine, and nursing. However, they recognized a paradigmatic difference between themselves, as a collective, and their mainstream counterparts.

Participants portrayed conventional doctors as complacent pawns of a flawed medical system. They argued that traditional medical education and training are designed to produce staunchly compliant and unimaginative doctors. For instance, Claire, the mother of an autistic boy, criticized her son's former pediatric neurologist for being unthinkingly stubborn in her commitment to traditional practice. Claire recalled that the doctor had noticed her child's improvement but attributed all the progress to behavioral therapy, denying any credit to alternative biomedicine:

> And so, I told [the pediatric neurologist] about all the traditional therapies he was getting, which he was, and I told her about the biomedical interventions that we had done, and she shook her head "no" and she said, "I hate to see you waste your money like that." And I said to her, "You honestly think that a little bit of ABA [applied behavior analysis] therapy at my house has made the impact that you're seeing right now?" and she said, "Yep. It's the only thing I know that works." And I said, "Well then, I'm done here." . . . I think because of her medical training she just simply can't imagine it to be true, and I think that she is also probably not, has not seen a lot of parents at that point.

Claire interpreted this exchange as an indication that the doctor's training had prevented her from even "imagining" the potential of unorthodox interventions. Subsequently, Claire continued to use alternative biomedical practice and stopped seeing this pediatric neurologist: "And we never went back again and I never paid for that appointment either." Robyn, a nurse practitioner by training, similarly observed that conventionally trained doctors were less willing to diverge from their training. She characterized them as less effective and slower to adopt new methods because, for one, they chose to passively wait for scientific evidence: "They've done what they know, or if research isn't out about it, they won't teach it and so they're waiting for that research instead of being proactive and saying, 'Well, here's what we see,' or you know, 'What's been tried and what works.'" Robyn suggested that, by comparison, alternative biomedical practitioners were admirably innovative and experimental.

During her interview, Dr. Maddan differentiated the world in which she received her medical training from the world in which she currently practices. She indicated that the conventional standard for "good" doctoring is the ability to memorize information and thus that conventional doctors are "not good at thinking outside or freely," which she equated with "brainwashing." Pointing to a similar sort of rote medical practice in his interview, Dr. Jesson described his medical school clinical training as primarily drug dispensation: "It sort of feels like a lot of the basic science is thrown out the window, and it felt like we were just matching a pill to a problem." Where they perceived their medical education to fall short, alternative biomedicine expanded their repertoire (see chapter 3).

In contrast to the flaws and rigidity of traditionally trained medical professionals, participants portrayed specialized practitioners as dynamic, innovative pioneers. Fiona, a professional

234 • THE OUTSIDERS

disability advocate, has an adult son who was diagnosed with Asperger's syndrome at age five. She described alternative bio-medical practitioners as being more sophisticated and knowl-edgeable than their conventional counterparts: "Mainstream basically does not—my experience has been that they really don't understand a lot of the complicated health issues that go with autism. And the biomed practitioners clearly have pro-tocols and have an understanding of these complex medical challenges that traditional medical practitioners are just in the dark about."

Dr. Maddan contrasted her peers' search for the root of a con-dition with the shallow assessment done by their conventional counterparts: "Our thinking process is different. We look at the body and we try to figure out where the symptoms are coming from. Whereas, when I was trained from a regular perspective, you look at the symptoms and you make a diagnosis based on the symptoms and some lab testing." While she and her alterna-tive biomedical colleagues also look at symptoms and lab tests, she suggested that their interpretations go deeper. Furthermore, Dr. Maddan argued that conventional doctors lack the induc-tive reasoning to experimentally translate research from mul-tiple biological science disciplines into treatment. She used the example of joint pain: a "regular doctor" would prescribe anti-inflammatories to treat the symptom, while an alternative bio-medical doctor would design a treatment protocol informed by research on possible underlying issues, such as fat absorption, Lyme disease, chronic gut infection, and omega-3 deficiencies: "And there's no double blind and placebo control studies to prove that what you do is going to help the patient, but there are studies to say that if you have omega-3 issues, then you could have joint problems. But [regular doctors] can't make that leap." Dr. Drummond similarly differentiated his work from that of "the average doctor," drawing attention to his application of early research findings. To justify and legitimize his methods to patients' parents, he would show them the publications that inspired his treatment plans: "So I have to be able to [show] research and evidence behind my decisions. That's part of what I do, and the other part of it is what makes it different is that I really arduously—to the point of, maybe, the point of overkill—put research on the table in front of my parents [for] everything that I do. The average doctor does not do that, as you already could guess." Parents, however, are perhaps even less prepared to make sense of these studies than their practitioners. Early research may recommend further studies to better understand an intervention, but they do not advise application. Yet practitioners proudly boasted about snuggling the lab bench right up to the patient's bed.

As they criticize mainstream medicine, members share a sense of pride in being different and nonconforming, often wearing their heresy as a badge of honor. During a 2015 parent-oriented conference in Costa Mesa, California, one doctor proudly admitted that he had been called a "charlatan" and "snake oil salesman," but he had a retort for all those criticisms: "Don't you know? Snake oil has omega-3 fatty acids." The audience roared with laughter. A snake oil salesman, in this cheeky reappropriation, possessed inventive cleverness and was underestimated by others. While there is insufficient scientific evidence to support the efficacy of omega-3 fatty acids for improving autistic behaviors, within the movement community, they are commonly prescribed to address issues from hyperactivity to seizures.[43] As illustrated here, the movement's members use boundary-work strategies not only to differentiate alternative biomedical practitioners from their conventional counterparts but also to elevate them above other doctors.

Unlike the "Meek" and "Lazy" Parents

Like the practitioners, parents prided themselves on "thinking outside the box," but they also emphasized that the alternative biomedical framework requires them to be proactive and make sacrifices. Parents support alternative and experimental treatment not only because they hope their children will recover but also because they believe their dedication is necessary for good parenting, a message that is reinforced within the community. Yet, outside the movement, they experienced stigma and criticism.

Parent participants understood that their friends, family, and doctors questioned their medical choices. Grace, a mother of two autistic children, reflected, "Probably a lot of them think we're really crazy, because a lot of people think biomed people are crazy. I think some of them get it." In response to critiques, parents like Grace performed discursive boundary work to set themselves apart from parents who relied on conventional models to understand and treat their autistic children. Her peers in the community, she noticed, "judge other parents harshly who don't want to do biomed." Contrasting themselves with parents outside their community, participants constructed a collective identity marked by empowerment, savviness, and tenacity.

Participants took pride in their community and in what membership signified. By reconstructing autism as a recoverable condition, the alternative biomedical framework demands parents' perseverance and tests their character. During her interview, Claire emphasized members' shared priorities and extreme sacrifice: "Having a network of people who do not give up on their children, who are willing to put a second mortgage on their house, and not have a social life, and lose family and friends for their child's health, those are the people I want to know. Those are the people I want to be friends with." Certainly, not all parents can be so devoted, as treatments are time-consuming and costly. But although parents' investments in the pursuit of treatment varied, participants consistently perceived themselves as more dedicated than other parents of autistic children. Alternative biomedical practice was integral to their parent identity.

At the end of a conference day, I attended an informal dinner with several of the organization leaders and members, all of whom are mothers of autistic children. The women reflected on the siblings' panel hosted earlier that afternoon, during which the neurologically typical children of the alternative biomedical movement shared their experiences of growing up with an autistic sibling. The women at dinner praised the children's eloquence and maturity. One mother, Paula, remarked that alternative biomedical parents simply raise better children than do parents outside their community. Another mother interjected to say that they should not be so dismissive of other families, to which Paula clarified that the children of "passionate" parents—like themselves—are particularly special. This inspired a frank conversation comparing their community members to parents of autistic children outside the movement. Paula said she knew of families who instrumentally sought out an autism diagnosis to take advantage of the free respite care services. Another asserted that some parents she knew even took pleasure in complaining about their autistic children for attention. In this conversation and many other interactions during conference weekends, parents depicted themselves as generally superior to parents outside their community in their devotion and resourcefulness.

From working with many different families as a disability advocate, Fiona noticed that her fellow alternative biomedical parents—particularly mothers—were highly knowledgeable, networked, and capable of providing treatment for their children, even when it came to something as challenging as injections (the most common being B-12 vitamin injections):

> [T]he moms who pursue biomed have really done their research and done their homework, and they understand—they really understand what's going on medically for their kids. And, they're strong networking with other moms. . . . I think they're some of the brightest moms I've ever met, because they've educated themselves to understand what's going on with their kids and how to intervene and how to deliver, you know, whatever kind of supplements, including injections.

Aside from just being well-read, parent participants said that they had to be assertive when challenging mainstream medicine. Implementing unorthodox treatments requires steadfast confidence. For instance, one interviewed mother, Melissa, judged herself as more tenacious than other parents of autistic children. Recounting her interactions with her son's pediatrician, she portrayed herself as an uncompromising force, unintimidated by the authority of conventional doctors:

> [M]any of those women hadn't done all of the reading, so they weren't as knowledgeable, and I feel like their personality was a little bit more subdued and kind of meek and mild about it. Because they were just overwhelmed themselves and I think they go in there and say, "Uh, wondering about that diet. . . ." Whereas I am like, "We are doing this diet, and this is what I need. Don't question me."

Similarly, Whitney, who has an autistic son, said that fighting against mainstream medical professionals required self-education and conviction. In addition, she noted that some characteristics, such as libertarian attitudes, are cultivated when parents take treatment into their own hands and resist interference from medical and government authorities. Whitney's insights into parental resistance are reminiscent of Jennifer Reich's work on neoliberal mothering and vaccine hesitancy; mothers perceive themselves as the true experts on their children's health and exercise their privilege to decide what is best for their individual children, even if it is contrary to expert advice.[44] For cases in which children responded to traditional interventions (like behavioral therapy), Whitney imagined that those parents, in their fortunate circumstance, had never been forced to develop these respected traits:

> I think biomedical parents have to just read a lot more, go to lectures, talk with other parents. . . . They are telling me to give [my son] [an antipsychotic medication] and that will solve his [gastrointestinal] problems, and I'm like, "To me that sounds stupid and I'm not going to do that." Biomedical parents, I think, have more self-confidence in dealing with the medical community. Because it hasn't worked for us, versus with more traditional autism it mostly works for them, so. . . . Also, you become much more of a libertarian. Like, with the medical marijuana, "Get out of my life!"

Some participants accused other parents of autistic children of being lazy and unwilling to inconvenience themselves for the sake of their child's recovery. For example, Kelly, the mother of an autistic boy, opined, "I really think they're lazy. I think that it's a cop-out, that doing the diet is hard. It's easier to drive through the McDonald's driveway and feed your kids crap all the time; it is." In this damning portrayal, those who do not take advantage of these intervention methods are bad and selfish parents—especially those who are aware of but choose to forego these treatment options.

The alternative biomedical way of treating autistic children involves vigilant policing of the child's physiological environment. It is a meticulous and laborious process of removing toxins, allergens, "bad" bacteria, and "bad" parasites, and introducing healthful foods and supplements, "good" bacteria, and "good" parasites. Intervention efforts also address the fortification of internal boundaries, such as tightening intestinal villi junctions to prevent "leaky gut"[45] (which is Andrew Wakefield's idea about autistic enterocolitis) and "leaky brain."[46] Just as they patrol the boundaries of children's bodies, practitioners and parents perform discursive boundary work to protect their beliefs and practices from becoming compromised or weakened by outside criticism. They align themselves with conventional medicine to reinforce their qualifications, but they also distinguish themselves from their detractors.

To validate their continuing efforts to recover their children, parents pointed to the key characteristics and values that connect them to fellow insiders and separate them from outsiders. Parent participants see their treatment strategies as the best form of care for autistic children, but as they find, these strategies require intense effort that test their dedication and, implicitly, their love for their children. Their struggles to provide treatment presented opportunities to demonstrate parental commitment and concurrently distinguish alternative biomedical parents from other parents of autistic children.

Several months after the MAPS conference, another alternative biomedical organization hosted a conference that catered to parents. There, the hyperbaric chamber company supplied yet another ice sculpture and luge to honor the memory of Dr. Bradstreet. Before plunging their skewered fruit into the chocolate fountain, parents, practitioners, and vendors took each other's hands, forming a large circle, and collectively sang the Bill Withers song "Lean on Me." They swayed and hugged, sharing a poignant moment. The song is not about mourning or remembrance. Rather, it is a song about how friends strengthen each other to weather adversity. While Dr. Bradstreet's death signified the threats facing the community, the shared suffering generated a renewed sense of solidarity and hopefulness. Despite everything that seemed to be against them, the community members could validate each other's beliefs and practices and together make sense of the risks of being controversial.

SELF-PROCLAIMED OUTSIDERS

Boundary-work strategies do not reveal objective truths. Rather, they reflect how science and health movement members locate themselves and conceptualize their relationships to others, whether opponents or allies. These perceived relationships highlight the ways members understand their group identity. Their condemnation of other stakeholders captures the qualities and beliefs that they value; if others are bad, then they are good. Moreover, how they position themselves in relation to other actors helps explain their rationale and actions. Their understanding of threat, whether it is real or not, shapes their defense strategies.

Both the alternative biomedical and autistic rights movements challenge the dominant autism framework, but in different ways. They manage separate forms of vulnerability and identify different opponents. Because the autistic rights activists want representation rights, they compete against others who try to speak for autistic people—namely, parents and the parent-led organization Autism Speaks. Meanwhile, the alternative biomedical movement is heavily defined by its experimental treatment practices, so its members position themselves in opposition to mainstream medical professionals, researchers, and parents of autistic children outside their community. Autistic rights members turn outward to claim authority and convince others to respect their embodied knowledge. In contrast, alternative biomedical members turn inward to legitimize their practice, discredit critiques, and portray dominant actors as intellectually and morally inferior. As movement members situate their place within the broader field of struggle, they identify rivals and discursive strategies for protecting their beliefs.

In reality, the boundaries separating conventional from unconventional, orthodoxy from unorthodoxy, authority from subordinate are blurry and flexible. The Interagency Autism Coordinating Committee, a federal advisory committee that coordinates federal efforts and provides advice on issues related to autism, brings together a diversity of stakeholders, including people from the alternative biomedical and autistic rights movements. Within the alternative biomedical movement, there are medical doctors and researchers appointed at reputable universities, so they are not entirely separate from the experts and institutions that they challenge. Many families who do not subscribe to the alternative biomedical framework also use specialized diets to help their autistic children. Similarly, parent-led organizations, like Autism Speaks and Autism Society, have also incorporated the language of autism acceptance into their advocacy work (although their agenda has remained more or less the same).[47]

Although there is some overlap with the mainstream, autistic rights and alternative biomedical movements use discursive boundary work to construct themselves as outsiders. Regardless of how others may perceive them, they are outsiders because they say so. There is an advantage to taking this position. By setting themselves apart from other groups and actors, movement members sharpen their collective identity and make space to reimagine autism.

7

MAKING SPACE FOR
THE SPECTRUM

About seven years after our last interview, I revisited Melissa and Codey. When I first introduced the two of them in chapter 1, they were in the thick of it. Melissa was fully invested in her autistic son Logan's recovery, regularly attending conferences and experimenting with a number of alternative biomedical treatments. Desperate to help her son, she even took him to see a magic buffalo, but the buffalo did not live up to its incredible rumors. Codey, at the time, was fresh out of college. Like Melissa's son, he was given alternative biomedical treatments as a child, but he had taken himself off and become active in the autistic rights movement during college. Where are they now?

"Life is still about poop. Will always be about poop," said Melissa. Logan was now seventeen years old and a junior in high school. In some ways, not much had changed. Melissa's life was "still about poop" in the sense that she was still managing Logan's physiological dysfunctions, like gastrointestinal and immunological issues. She continued to tweak and adjust his treatments, including vitamin C, magnesium, mitochondrial support supplements, sublingual immunotherapy, oxytocin, Namenda,[1] and naltrexone.[2] She was still fighting with her son's health insurance to get his medication reimbursed. In fact, she had recently taken a week off from work at the functional medicine clinic to tackle this very task. Stacks of medical papers were piled on her desk. Logan "still has his moments where he loses his cool," but he was not nearly as aggressive as he once was. The "Tasmanian devil" days were behind them. Yet in other ways, caring for Logan had changed significantly. The last time I saw Melissa, she was focused on treating the health issues that she associated with autism, but now, she said, "the biggest thing is transition and a career."

Logan was growing up. He wanted to go to college and become a video game content creator. "Even though we were in the hurricane of health stuff back in the day, I always knew this was coming. It was too far out, not necessarily enough to think about it," said Melissa. She had spent more than a decade channeling all her resources into his recovery, but she felt unprepared for this next stage: "We help him with so much and he's not at the point where he can do any of these things really independently. How do you figure out what they want to do, and then do a resume, find a job, do interviews? College? What does that look like when you need support? How is that even going to happen?" Melissa knew how to deal with Logan's physiological dysfunctions at the molecular level, but the things he needed to be an independent and fulfilled adult did not come in a pill or a cleanse.

When Logan ventures into the world, many things will be beyond Melissa's control and foresight. She and her husband have started planning safety nets should Logan fail to launch: "For Logan, somehow, I'll have to figure out how he makes whatever that leap is. But yet have a great big net to catch him if he falls underneath." Recently, they purchased a new home on a large property where they could build a smaller house for

Logan. This plan, however, did not bring them much peace of mind. Melissa sighed, "It's just a lot of the unknowns, really. I don't think we'll know for a few years until we get there and have to figure it out. And then, who knows? Maybe it's another five years of working and continuing to find new programs to help him grow and mature. I don't know. That keeps me up at night, is the unknown of his future." The strategies she had expertly honed to tame the uncertainties of his recovery were no longer applicable.

There was a time when Melissa and her husband had an agreement—if oxygen masks were to drop down during their flight, they would ignore the safety instructions and place the mask on Logan before putting on their own masks. She eventually recognized that if she were to delay her own masking, she might fall unconscious and leave Logan without help. This was a bad idea. Later, Melissa applied these flight safety principles to everyday parenting. She reminded herself and other mothers that caring for their own health was critical to caring for their children—their lives were linked. Alternative biomedical parents expressed fears about their eventual death because they did not know what would happen to their autistic children after they were gone. Parents like Melissa care for their autistic children with a meticulousness that comes from love (and guilt). Who can be trusted—who would be willing—to take over these responsibilities? These concerns are not unique to parents of the alternative biomedical movement or to parents of autistic children; they are shared by parents of disabled children in general. In a system without guaranteed safety nets, parents feel the high-stakes pressure of raising children who will become independent, productive members of society.[3] The stakes are high because failure to become self-reliant means poverty and increased risk of victimization.

Melissa could not trust Logan to live independently—at least not yet. She described him as "super high functioning"; he can communicate verbally and is mainstreamed in school. Even so, access to disability services will be critical as he ages out of high school and into adulthood.[4] Years ago, she attended a twelve-week course called "Partners in Policy Making," where she was warned about the bureaucratic traps that keep disabled adults in poverty. In particular, she remembered listening to autistic self-advocates describing their struggles with the asset limits of benefits programs (e.g., Medicaid, Supplemental Security Income): "There's the challenge too that if you are super high functioning—wonderful, hopefully, you get a job—but then, there's also the point of a lot of the individuals, even if they have a degree or get [a] part-time job, you can only make so much money and then you lose your services." She recalled their grievances: "I remember the self-advocates were like, 'What am I supposed to do with my time? I can only have $2,000 in my account and I can only work this many hours or lose my benefits. If I lose my benefits, I don't have a place to live. Now, instead, I'm at home losing my mind because there's nothing to do and I want to contribute to society, but I can't.'" At that time, her son was only three years old, but now their frustrations were becoming her frustrations.

As an autistic rights activist, Codey has dedicated much of his time and early career to addressing related policy failures. The last time we spoke, he had just graduated from college and had taken a program coordinator job with the Autistic Self Advocacy Network (ASAN). Now, seven years later, he is in a PhD program for social policy and is working as a consultant to translate policy jargon into plain language. Communication access is something he cares about tremendously. In the academic setting, he sees it as a way to increase opportunities for research engagement "to both make the research they're publishing more accessible to people, and also make it so people with disabilities ourselves are more centered in the research, both in the planning and the process of doing the research." One of his ongoing projects is creating an accessible research and ethics certification program, which he hopes will one day be an accepted alternative to the training programs[5] required by institutional review boards and encourage more research headed by neurodivergent people.

While his professional life is picking up, Codey has been set back by emerging health issues. Doctors suspect he has Ehlers-Danlos syndrome, which is a set of hereditary disorders that affect connective tissues. He has noticed that other autistic people experience similar health problems and thinks there might be a connection: "It probably has to do with whatever genetic component of autism exists. But I'm not a geneticist. . . . I think it's now people are just starting to look more into autism and physical health and those relations." I asked if he is worried that such findings might further pathologize autism. Commenting on the arbitrariness of the ways genetic differences are problematized, Codey replied, "People with red hair are more likely to get sunburn, but that doesn't mean we tell people with red hair to stop having red hair or that they should somehow dye their hair, otherwise change the color. So, imagine having red hair is being autistic and then the sunburn is the physical disabilities that are associated with that." Even if autism is associated with health risks, he argued, autism itself is not an inherent disorder in need of a cure.

Codey's objections to treatment are also deeply personal. He wondered if there is a relationship between his current physical disabilities and the experimental treatments he received during childhood: "Recently I've been thinking, I don't know how the treatments that I had affected my body and if any of the health problems I have now were at all related to or exacerbated by the things that happened when I was a kid." He had undergone many alternative and experimental treatments designed for autism recovery—antibiotic for strep throat, antidepressants, blood pressure medication, vitamin supplements, iron supplement, acidophilus, and herpes medication. With so little research on their long-term effects, he could only guess at their cascading impacts on his quality of life and finances: "I can't really know for sure what causes what, but let's say some of the treatments I had as a kid did contribute to my health issues, that's now money that I am losing from not being able to work, money that I am paying for treatments for things that I'm struggling with." He differentiated treatments that aim to make autistic people appear more neurotypical from the health care that autistic people want—like disability and mental health support.

Melissa and Codey have maintained their separate understandings of autism. Yet, over the years, their concerns have come to overlap a little. Melissa was always aware of the social and institutional obstacles that exclude autistic people from public life and limit their independence. But now, as she is preparing her autistic teen for adulthood, these problems have become personal and urgent. These obstacles have pressed her to devise a financial strategy to keep her son well-resourced but technically under the asset limit for disability benefits. Few other autistic and disabled people can rely on a safety net woven by family wealth. Codey certainly could not expect his parents to set up a trust. From his experience, navigating services through the state departments is a circuitous process:

> The first time I tried to get services from [the state Department of Mental Health], I was denied because they said you're autistic you should be getting services from the Department of

Developmental Disability. And I said, "But my main issue I'm having right now is more to do with my mental health than my autism. So, I don't understand." . . . When I went to the Developmental Disability Services, they said that they would probably deny me and tell me to go back to the mental health people.

The siloing of services is a challenge faced by many other disabled people and their families. It is difficult to receive services when a person's diagnoses do not neatly fall under the purview of a specific agency.[6] The person may end up being passed along from agency to agency without receiving much help in the end. Codey sees health care access as an issue of social justice and civil rights, emphasizing the complexity of the care that disabled people require:

> When we talk about justice and civil rights and talk about how the way that different issues affect people's lives, it's never just one way. It's always thinking about intersectionality. And that's how I feel about when we talk about disability as this is the one disability that someone has. Because that's very often not true. Almost everyone that has some kind of neurodivergence also is autistic or ADHD, almost always has some kind of trauma or some kind of mental health disability, and usually some kind of physical disability.

The evolution of their struggles illustrates the weak and inadequate system of autism support and services. Melissa and Codey joined their respective social movements to manage these gaps and, ultimately, to speak for an autistic population that they believe is underrepresented and misrepresented. As I conclude this book, I want to highlight the infrastructures that allow Melissa, Codey, and their fellow members to create and sustain contentious knowledge—knowledge that aims to challenge expert authority and orthodoxy. In addition, addressing some of the underlying concerns of my participants, I recommend three general changes to policies and programming, including the diversification of support for autistic people, improved social safety nets, and the adoption of universal health care.

SPACES FOR CREATING KNOWLEDGE

Health and science movements animate contentious knowledge into lived realities. Members of the alternative biomedical and autistic rights movements position themselves in opposition to the mainstream, organizing themselves around a shared sense of marginalization. They see themselves as the underdogs, sharpening the boundaries between their community and others. There is an advantage to being an underdog (whether or not this is truly the reality of their position within the field of autism). As alternative biomedical users or autistic rights activists, they incorporate this underdog status into their understanding of themselves: they are formidable mothers, innovative doctors, or complete and empowered persons. In this way, members of these movements are not just reimagining autism but also reimagining their own identities.

Within their respective social movements, among like-minded people and insulated from the intrusion of outsiders, members find the freedom to cultivate and enact their ideas. Alternative biomedical parents and practitioners agree that autism falls under the jurisdiction of medical experts, but they take autism beyond disability to pathologize it as a sickness. They reconstruct autism as a set of physiological dysfunctions that has materiality, allowing them to measure, interpret, and treat the purported problems. Recognizing the controversial nature of their beliefs and practices, members establish internal legitimacy by admonishing mainstream doctors and parent advocates. Autistic rights activists, however, conceptualize autism as a human difference and identity that should be accepted, not treated or cured. Together, they have developed an autistic culture and a body of nonmedical knowledge about autism, identifying shared characteristics (like behaviors, tendencies, and aversions). The movement provides a space for activists to model autism acceptance, as they hope to see it widely adopted one day. Wrestling with parent advocates, they contend that autistic people are the best and most appropriate representatives for fellow autistic people. Social movements, as socio-spatial environments, nurture the production of contentious knowledge. In these spaces, members access the social and material resources necessary to legitimize their ideas and turn them into action. Autism is transformed into sickness or into human difference.

Social movements that concern health, medicine, and science have real consequences. They are empowering spaces where people find the freedom to incubate and deploy ideas that may lack external legitimacy or may be stigmatized. Even when beliefs are questioned or disputed by experts, movement members transform contentious ideas into shared realities. And in some cases, as illustrated by the alternative biomedical movement, interacting with these beliefs can have substantive impacts on people's lives. Some of the more experimental treatments, like chelation and unregulated stem cell therapy, have the potential to seriously endanger children.[7] It is important to examine how movement members produce knowledge and perceive their relationship to other stakeholders, as these processes can help identify the needs and concerns of underrepresented groups. A similar lens can also be applied to other science and health movements, such as those centered on contested illnesses, vaccine hesitancy, and climate change denial, to explore why and how people challenge experts. Such orientation points to what members gain from movement participation and, relatedly, what experts and institutions might be failing to provide.

A focus on social movements also reveals why it is not easy to disabuse individuals of ideas that challenge those of expert authority. It is not easy to simply educate people on the safety of vaccines, on the seriousness of climate change, or on the spherical shape of the Earth. From nuanced contradictions to "fake news" to conspiracy theories, these beliefs are difficult to correct individually. This is because contentious knowledge is not isolated or created in a vacuum; rather, it is entrenched in a complex system of beliefs and becomes part of people's realities—people can see it, act on it, and exchange it. Ideas that may seem irrational or ignorant are made to make sense within a system of belief. Furthermore, a sense of solidarity unites challengers against their identified opponents (like experts, the government, or the mainstream public), validating their experiences and toughening them against outside persuasion. When encountering resistance against expert authority, understanding challengers' social infrastructure helps to reveal the features that sustain belief.

MAKING SPACE FOR THE SPECTRUM

During my last interaction with Dr. Martinek, he did not detail promising treatments; rather, he was dreaming of a resort in St. Croix. His autistic son was on the cusp of adulthood without a clear future, so Dr. Martinek started researching places to build a large residence for autistic adults like his son. This imagined resort-like residence would not be like any institution of the dark past, but a happy place where each person could decorate their own bedrooms, socialize with others, pursue their interests, and go on trips to Disney World. They would receive the best care and live happily ever after. Even Dr. Martinek, the greatest proponent of alternative biomedicine, was well aware that, at some point, the realities of disability would outpace the hope of recovery. Yet his solution accepted society for what it is: a place his child did not belong. Somehow it seemed easier to build a new world for his son than to fix the one he was already living in. Autistic rights activists, of course, are acutely aware that they do not belong here. Juniper, an autistic rights activist and author, once hoped for a spaceship to take them back to their planet: "I remember as a child laying in bed, waiting for sleep to come and wondering where I was actually from because it seemed impossible that I could actually be a human and the child of my parents. And so, sometimes I would think I must be from another planet and maybe my people would come back and get me and take me home." Juniper could not remember if they sincerely believed this or if it was just a way to make sense of how they felt. Activists recognize the incongruence between autistic people and the neurotypical world, but they have nowhere else to go. Then what should be done for people like Codey and Juniper or like the children of Melissa and Dr. Martinek? There is no separate planet to deport autistic people to and no island resort to hide them away. We have to make space for autism here and now.

Autism services and support demand greater investment, but researchers continue to gaze at the mirage of autism's causes and prevention. After decades of research and millions of dollars dedicated to identifying a clear set of "autism genes," autism has proven itself to be incredibly elusive and difficult to pin down.[8]

In 2018, similar to previous years, about 63 percent of autism research funding was dedicated to understanding its biology and risks (primarily genetic relationships), compared to a measly 6 percent for services and supports and even less, 3 percent, for autistic adulthood.[9]

Perhaps it is time to shift our priorities. What we need is more funding to understand and meet the diverse needs of autistic people and their families. More broadly, helping autistic people and their families requires better social safety nets, which would have universal benefit. Such measures are in everyone's interest because most people will experience some form of disability in their lifetimes, either personally or as caregivers.[10] With these issues in mind, I propose three overlapping areas of intervention: expanding autism-specific services, developing better social safety nets, and instituting universal health care.

First, to address autism's heterogeneity, we need to expand autism-specific medical, educational, and social services across the life course, from point of diagnosis into adulthood. For instance, as parent participants in this study revealed, doctors need to be more sensitive when presenting an autism diagnosis. During this delicate time, doctors would benefit from demonstrating greater compassion to maintain families' trust and inspire hopefulness. This way, even if families explore alternative and experimental treatments, doctors have a better chance of staying involved to help guide decision-making and advise against riskier interventions.

Improvements to autism education and therapy should incorporate the perspectives of autistic people. After diagnosis, a commonly prescribed therapy for autistic children is applied behavior analysis (ABA). While experts find that ABA helps autistic children improve their intellectual abilities, communication, adaptive behavior, and socialization,[11] recent studies draw attention to the trauma experienced by adults who received ABA as children and are criticizing the method for being unethical.[12] This is alarming because ABA is popular; in addition, because it is often covered by health insurance, it is one of the more accessible interventions for families. Although autistic rights activists oppose ABA, they support many other interventions that "help autistic people get what we want and need, not what other people think we need"; helpful therapies include physical therapy, speech therapy, occupational therapy, and augmentative and alternative communication.[13] Their insights are valuable and necessary to improving autism education.

Beyond childhood interventions, more funding is needed to support autistic people throughout adulthood. Compared to the general population, autistic adults experience higher rates of unemployment and underemployment (which impacts all other forms of material security),[14] chronic illness,[15] suicidal ideation,[16] and interpersonal violence.[17] Addressing these issues is critical. Importantly, researchers and policymakers will have to be cognizant of how these issues manifest across the spectrum—from those with the greatest support needs to those who live and work independently.

Second, federal and state governments need to build real social safety nets, like guaranteed housing, universal basic income, and quality home and community-based services. Up until the age of twenty-one, autistic people are entitled to free appropriate public education (FAPE) (outlined in the Individuals with Disabilities Education Act), which provides specialized education and services. However, on their twenty-second birthday, all these entitlements disappear.[18] Parents call this dreaded milestone "the cliff." However, autism and disability do not end when a person turns twenty-two. Disabled people and their families must then navigate a byzantine and meager network of adult services.[19] As it goes for anything else, money is protective. A popular advice is to set up a trust, but most people cannot fall back on personal wealth.[20]

Current residential, employment, and socialization services for autistic adults fall short.[21] Instead of optimizing the lives of disabled adults, existing programs minimally maintain them. For instance, an increasing number of autistic adults rely on Supplemental Security Income (SSI),[22] which is hardly enough to cover basic necessities (in 2023, the federal amount is $914 per month, plus state-administered supplement)[23] and keeps people in poverty (because of the resource cap that limits how much a person can save). A meaningful life is more than mere survival.

Although I have focused on autism, expanding social safety nets is in the best interest of most Americans. One in four American adults experience disability (of hearing, vision, cognition, mobility, self-care, or independent living).[24] These recommendations would help to protect people should disability severely impact their material resources. On this issue, Irving Zola wrote: "Only when we acknowledge the near universality of disability and that all its dimensions (including the biomedical) are part of the social process by which the meanings of disability are negotiated will it be possible fully to appreciate how general public policy can affect this issue."[25] The challenges of disability are largely tied to poor social policies. Arguing for a universal policy toward disability, Zola imagined one that is "not based on breaking the rules of order for the few but on designing a flexible world for the many."[26] We should demand a society where being disabled and caring for disabled people are not devastating circumstances. Disability is mostly frightening because we allow it to be.

Third, I want to draw attention to one specific social safety net: universal health coverage. The United States needs universal health coverage in which everyone is guaranteed access to health care. Recall Rachel, an autistic participant who could not afford to lose Medicaid so she took a nannying job that paid under the table. This allowed her to create some financial security and keep her public health coverage. Luckily, she felt that her work environment was safe, but one can easily see how in other circumstances, working under the table could expose an already vulnerable population to abuse and exploitation. If health care access was guaranteed, Rachel would have been able to take a formal job without having to worry about the heavy cost and coverage of private insurance. Autistic people have more health care needs than non-disabled counterparts.[27] Families of autistic children who are privately insured are five times more likely to spend out of pocket than those who receive Medicaid, illustrating the inadequacy of private insurance coverage and its financial burdens on families.[28] Similarly, disabled adults under sixty-five years old (who do not qualify for Medicare) experience higher rates of unmet health care needs because of costs—31.4 percent among those between ages 18 and 44 and 25.9 percent among those between ages 45 and 64.[29] Expanding public health coverage is important to lifting access barriers. The added post-insurance costs of health care are a burden to the very people who can least afford it.

Of course, inadequate coverage is not unique to autistic and disabled people. In 2022, 8 percent of Americans were uninsured[30] and 43 percent were underinsured, meaning their coverage does not enable affordable access to health care.[31] Because of health care's high costs, 38 percent of Americans delayed medical treatment in 2022, and 27 percent delayed medical treatment for "very/somewhat serious" conditions.[32] Not having universal health care impacts more than an individual's health. More than half of Americans have gone into debt because of medical and/ or dental bills, which undermines their opportunities to achieve financial security, such as preparing for emergencies, buying a home, paying for their children's education, and saving for retirement.[33] Public health experts, medical professionals, and most Americans recognize the necessity of health care for all.[34] During the COVID-19 pandemic, researchers estimated that universal health care could have saved 212,000 lives in 2020 alone and over 338,000 lives between the start of the pandemic and March 2022.[35] Health care has to be a right and not a commodity.

Despite the differences in their worldview, the autistic rights and alternative biomedical movements express shared concerns: insufficient support for a heterogeneous autistic population and the absence of adequate safety nets. Issues related to social safety nets, however, are not exclusive to autistic or presently disabled people. In an economically developed country like the United States, it is inexcusable to leave health and disability up to neoliberal forces. We are all insecure when the shortcomings of social policy devalue and punish human diversity. As a society, we should strive toward a kind of anti-ableism that rejects the idea that there is an ideal body and an ideal mind. Anti-ableism is not only a matter of social justice, but promises to enhance our society by pulling in a diversity of skills and talents from the margins. When we make space for the spectrum, everyone has something to gain.

APPENDIX A

INTERVIEW PROTOCOLS

INTERVIEW PROTOCOL: PARENT/CAREGIVER

Introduction

1. Tell me a little bit about yourself. (*Or, lead off with things you already know about participant.*)

   Probe: Are you employed? *If so*, tell me about your job.

2. Tell me about your family.

   Probe: Who in your family is autistic?

3. Tell me about [*CHILD(REN) DIAGNOSED WITH AUTISM*].

   Probe: Autism spectrum disorder (ASD) presentation.

Caring for autistic child(ren)

4. Tell me about how you learned that [*CHILD*] is autistic.

   Probe: Early signs/concerns; diagnosis.

   Probe: How did getting a diagnosis change the way you think about [*CHILD*]'s needs/challenges?

5. What is it like to be [*CHILD*]'s mom/dad?

   Probe: What would a typical day look like? Tell me about what your role and responsibilities are in caring for [*CHILD*]. What is it like to be a caregiver for your child?

(*continued*)

Probe: What have been some challenges/rewards in caring for [*CHILD*]?

Probe: What would you want other people in your life to know or understand about the experience of caring for an autistic child?

6. Who else has an important role in caring for [*CHILD*]? What are their responsibilities?

7. What do you think [*CHILD*] needs most from the care they receive?

8. How do you think parenting an autistic child is similar or different to parenting a child without autism?

    Probe: If they have neurotypical children, then ask for concrete examples.

9. Do you think parenting an autistic child has changed you as an individual? How so?

Perspectives on autism

10. Before [*CHILD*] was diagnosed, were you familiar with autism? What did you think about it?

11. How would you define autism?

    Probe: How do you think the other people in your life think about autism?

12. Do you think autism has a cause? *If so*, how would you explain the cause of autism?

    Have you always believed this? *If not*, how have your ideas about the cause of autism changed?

    Probe: How did you come to know this?

13. For you, what does it mean to be autistic or to have autism?

    Probe: How do you think this experience compares to not being autistic?

Autism and alternative biomedical practice

14. Tell me a little bit [*more*] about [*CHILD*]. What do you see as some of your child's skills and challenges?

15. What do you identify as some of [*CHILD*]'s needs?

16. [*If applicable*] I met you at/ through [*point of contact*], tell me about why you decided to attend and what you hoped to get from [*point of contact*].

This question will vary. In most cases, I refer to a conference. Link to first point of contact.

17. Tell me about some of the interventions or treatments that [*CHILD*] is currently receiving.

Use parent's language of "intervention" or "treatment" or "therapy" or whatever else.

How did you discover or learn about these interventions/ treatments?

Probe: What attracted you to these intervention methods? What makes it the appropriate option for your child?

Before adopting [alternative] biomedical interventions for [*CHILD*], did you (or someone in your family) have prior interests that inclined you to seek [alternative] biomedical interventions?

Probe: What interventions/ treatments were tried before?

18. What kind of resources do you turn to for guidance?

Do you have someone who helps you with intervention/ treatment decision-making? If so, who? How does this person help you?

19. When using these interventions, describe how you know if a particular intervention is working for your child.

Probe: Examples of intervention results.

What kinds of signs, evidence, or patterns indicate success?

(*continued*)

What have been some of the
successes you experienced
in providing intervention/
treatment?

20. Describe how you know if a
    particular intervention is *not*
    working for your child.

    Probe: Examples of intervention
    results.

    What have been some of the
    frustrations you experienced
    in providing intervention/
    treatment?

21. How has having [*CHILD*]
    on [alternative] biomedical
    interventions affected the way
    you think about your own health
    and/or the rest of your family's
    health?

    What do other people around
    you think about your use
    of [alternative] biomedical
    interventions for [*CHILD*]?

22. What do you hope to achieve
    with these treatments and
    interventions?

    What would successful
    treatment/intervention
    ultimately look like?

Autism advocacy and outreach

23. Could you tell me about your
    involvement with [*organization,
    point of contact*]? How did you
    decide to join this organization?

    Probe: What attracted you to this
    organization?

    Could you tell me a bit about
    your roles and participation in
    [*organization*]?

24. In addition to [*organization, point of contact*], are you actively involved with any other organizations related to autism, [*area of expertise*], or otherwise?

If applicable, could you tell me a little bit about your involvement in this/these other organization(s)?

Note: If participant is involved in many organizations, ask about which organization they are most involved with. With which do they have a lot of responsibilities? Focus on that organization for subsequent questions.

25. Why did you decide to become active in this/these organization(s)?

Probe: What do you hope to achieve in your work with this/these organization(s)?

Probe: What have you personally gained from working with this/these organization(s)?

Probe: What have been some of the challenges you have faced as [*title*] affiliated with [*organization*]? How have you responded to these challenges?

Probe: Tell me about some of your successes in working with [*organization*].

26. How are these organizations similar to or different from other autism advocacy groups?

27. Are there other ways you participate in advocacy? If so, could you please describe these ways?

28. What would you consider to be some of the threats to [alternative] biomedical interventions for autism?

(*continued*)

29. What do you think is important to the growth and expansion of [alternative] biomedical interventions for autism?

    Probe: How do you envision the future of [alternative] biomedical interventions/treatments and autism?

Conclusion

30. Is there anything else that I did not ask but you think is important for me to know or understand?

31. If I have follow-up questions, would it be okay if I get back in touch with you?

INTERVIEW PROTOCOL: PRACTITIONERS

Introduction

1. What is your job title?

2. How long have you been [*occupation/title*]? How long have you been with [*name of organization/company/practice/institute*]?

3. Tell me about your work and what you do.

4. What populations do you serve? What kind of care do you provide?

    Of your patients, could you estimate what percentage are autistic patients? Or how many autistic patients do you typically serve each year?

Alternative biomedical practice

5. Tell me about how you decided to enter into [*area of expertise*].

    Probe: Motivation, previous interests, decision-making process.

6. Could you describe your training process before entering into [*area of expertise*]—either formal or informal?

    Probe: Critical points of decision-making.

7. Tell me about [*area of expertise*]. What is unique about [*area of expertise*]?

Perspectives on autism

8. How would you define autism?

   How does this definition compare to that of other health care professionals?

9. Do you think autism has a cause? *If so*, how would you explain the cause of autism?

   Have you always believed this? *If not*, how have your ideas about the cause of autism changed?

   Probe: How did you come to know this?

10. For you, what does it mean to be autistic or to have autism?

    Probe: How do you think this experience compares to not being autistic?

Autism and alternative biomedical practice

11. Tell me about how you started working with autistic patients.

    Probes:

    If also PARENT/CAREGIVER for someone with autism/special needs: How has being a parent/caregiver to an autistic child influenced the direction of your career?

    If PARENT/CAREGIVER for someone with autism/special needs: Could you tell me about your child?

    Tell me about how you learned that [*CHILD*] has autism.

    What did you do after you learned that [*CHILD*] has autism?

12. Tell me about how you approach a patient with autism.

    Probe: How might your approach be similar to or different from the way other practitioners might approach a patient with autism?

    Probe: What kind of resources do you refer to for guidance in your practice? How are these resources helpful?

    (continued)

13. Describe how you know if a particular intervention is effective for a patient.

    What kinds of signs, evidence, or patterns indicate success?

    Probe: Case example.

14. Describe how you know if a particular intervention is *not* working for a patient.

    What kinds of signs, evidence, or patterns indicate that an approach is not a good fit?

    When an intervention is judged to be ineffective, what do you do next?

    Probe: Case example.

15. What have been some personal challenges or frustrations you have experienced working with autistic patients? How do you address these challenges?

    When working with a patient, what do you hope to achieve? What does a successful case look like?

    Examples: What have been some personal successes working with autistic patients?

    Probe: Case example.

Autism advocacy and outreach

16. Could you tell me about your involvement with [*organization, point of contact*]? Why did you decide to join this organization?

    Could you tell me a bit about your roles and responsibilities in [*organization*]?

    Probe: What attracted you to this organization?

17. In addition to [*organization, point of contact*], are you actively involved with any other organizations related to autism, [*area of expertise*], or otherwise?

    If applicable, could you tell me a little bit about your involvement in this/these other organization(s)?

Note: If participant is involved in many organizations, ask which organization they are most involved with. With which do they have a lot of responsibilities? Focus on that organization for subsequent questions.

18. How did you decide to become active in this/these organization(s)?

Probe: What do you hope to achieve in your work with this/these organization(s)?

Probe: What have you personally gained from working with this/these organization(s)?

Probe: What have been some of the challenges you have faced as [*title*] affiliated with [*organization*]? How have you responded to these challenges?

Probe: Tell me about some of your successes in working with [*organization*].

19. How are these organizations similar to or different from other autism advocacy groups?

20. Are there other ways you participate in advocacy? If so, could you please describe these ways?

21. What would you consider to be some of the threats to [alternative] biomedical interventions for autism?

22. What do you think is important to the growth and expansion of [alternative] biomedical interventions for autism?

Probe: How do you envision the future of [alternative] biomedical interventions/treatments and autism?

(*continued*)

Conclusion

23. Is there anything else that I did not ask but you think is important for me to know or understand?

24. If I have follow-up questions, would it be okay if I get back in touch with you?

INTERVIEW PROTOCOL: AUTISTIC ADULTS

Introduction

1. Tell me about yourself; for example, what are some of your interests? Are you employed? If so, what is your job?

Autism diagnosis and early experiences

2. Do you identify yourself as an autistic person? *If not*, how do you identify?

   Probe: When did you start to identify as [*autistic or participant's language*]? How did this come about?

3. Do you have an official diagnosis? *If so*, describe how you obtained the diagnosis. *If not*, describe how you came to identify as autistic.

   Probe: Did the diagnosis tell you anything new about yourself? If so, what?

   Probe: When were you diagnosed? What initiated the pursuit of a diagnosis?

4. Describe/tell me about your earliest memory of hearing the term *autism* or *autistic*.

Perspectives on autism

5. How would you define autism?

   Probe: How does your definition of autism compare to the definition held by other people in your life?

6. How do the other people in your life think about autism? How do they think about you being autistic?

7. Do you think autism has a cause? *If so,* how would you explain the cause of autism?

   Have you always believed this? *If not,* how have your ideas about the cause of autism changed?

   Probe: How did you come to know this?

8. For you, what does it mean to be autistic?

   Probe: How do you think this experience compares to not being autistic?

Autistic needs

9. Do you think you have specific needs or challenges associated with autism? *If so,* could you describe some of these needs/challenges?

10. Do you have specific needs or challenges that you think are not associated with autism? Explain. *If so,* how do you know which needs/challenges are related to autism and which ones are not related to autism?

    Probe: Could you describe some of the strategies or interventions you use to manage these challenges?

11. Could you describe some of the strategies or interventions you use to manage these challenges?

    How do [*specified strategies/interventions*] help you? How do you know if an intervention is effective/ineffective?

    How did you discover or learn about these strategies/interventions?

    Probe: What kind of resources do you turn to for guidance?

(*continued*)

12. Do you think you have special strengths or advantages associated with autism? *If so,* could you describe some of these strengths/advantages?

    How have you been able to use these strengths/advantages?

13. What do you think you need for general well-being?

    Probe: Of these, which have you achieved? Please describe.

    Probe: Which have been challenging to achieve? Why?

    Probe: How do the other people in your life think about general well-being for autistic individuals?

Autism advocacy and outreach

14. I contacted you because you identified yourself as an "autistic self-advocate/activist." How do you participate as an autistic self-advocate/activist?

    Probe: Members/membership.

    Probe: Could you describe your objectives as an autistic self-advocate?

    Probe: How do the people in your life think about your involvement with autism self-advocacy?

15. Tell me about how you started your involvement or interest in autism self-advocacy.

    Probe: What have been some of the challenges you have faced as a self-advocate?

    Probe: How have you responded to these challenges?

    Probe: Tell me about some of your successes as a self-advocate.

16. Could you tell me about your involvement with [*organization, point of contact*]? Why did you decide to join this organization?

    Probe: What attracted you to this organization?

Could you tell me a bit about your roles and participation in [*organization*]?

Probe: What do you hope to achieve in your work with this/these organization(s)?

Probe: What have you personally gained from working with this/these organization(s)?

17. In addition to [*organization, point of contact*], are you actively involved with any other organizations related to autism, neurodiversity, or otherwise?

Note: If participant is involved in many organizations, ask which organization they are most involved with. With which do they have a lot of responsibilities? Focus on that organization for subsequent questions.

If applicable, could you tell me a little bit about your involvement in this/these other organization(s)?

18. How are these organizations similar to or different from other autism advocacy groups?

19. What would you consider to be some of the threats to autistic self-advocacy?

20. What do you think is important to the growth and expansion of autistic self-advocacy?

21. How do you envision the future of autistic self-advocacy and autism?

Conclusion

22. Is there anything else that I did not ask but you think is important for me to know or understand?

23. If I have follow-up questions, would it be okay if I get back in touch with you?

APPENDIX B
PARTICIPANTS

TABLE B.1 INTERVIEWEE DEMOGRAPHICS*

	Alternative biomedical family % (n = 18)	Alternative biomedical providers % (n = 10)	Autistic rights members % (n = 37)
Age of official autism diagnosis			
0–5 years of age	94.1 (16)		10.8 (4)
6–10 years of age			
11–17 years of age			5.4 (2)
18+ years of age	5.9 (1)		67.5 (25)
Childhood (age uncertain)			16.2 (6)
Gender			
Woman	88.9 (16)	50.0 (5)	43.2 (16)
Man	11.1 (2)	50.0 (5)	37.8 (14)
Nonbinary			18.9 (7)
Race			
Black			10.8 (4)
Asian		20.0 (2)	8.1 (3)
Latinx and/or Hispanic	11.1 (2)		
White	88.8 (16)	70.0 (7)	81.0 (30)
Other		10.0 (1)	

(*continued*)

	Alternative biomedical family % (n = 18)	Alternative biomedical providers % (n = 10)	Autistic rights members % (n = 37)
Highest level of education			
High school			5.4 (2)
Some college/associate	27.8 (5)		13.5 (5)
Bachelor's degree	22.2 (4)		43.2 (16)
Master's degree	22.2 (4)		27.0 (10)
Doctorate/professional	11.1 (2)	100.0 (10)	10.8 (4)
Not applicable (N/A)	16.7 (3)		
Employment status			
Employed	55.6 (10)	100.0 (10)	64.8 (24)
Student			8.1 (3)
Unemployed	44.4 (8)		27.0 (10)
Household income			
Median	$125,000+	$125,000+	$15,000–25,000

*Table B.1 does not include three autistic rights participants who are not autistic, two alternative biomedical participants who are autistic, and one academic researcher.

TABLE B.2 INTERVIEWED PARTICIPANTS—AUTISTIC RIGHTS MOVEMENT

Name	Pronoun	Race/ethnicity	Age in 2016	Age of autism spectrum disorder (ASD) diagnosis	Highest level of education completed	Occupation
Trina	She/her	White	34	Late 20s	High school	Unemployed
Rick	He/him	White	65	50	Postgraduate	Lawyer
Alfie	He/him	Asian	51	Childhood	Postgraduate	IT support
Ci-Ci	She/her	Black	58	54	Postgraduate	Diplomat, foreign service officer
Stephen Shore	He/him	White	54	Childhood	Postgraduate	Professor
Filene	She/her	White	—	31	College	Operatic singer
Bridget	She/her	White	27	23	College	Journalist
Temple Grandin	She/her	White	69	Childhood	Postgraduate	Professor
Lydia Brown	They/them	Asian	22	Childhood	College	Student and advocate
Mike	He/him	White	32	Not autistic	—	Student
Jim Sinclair	They/them	White	55	Childhood	College	Unemployed
Willow	She/her	White	51	Not autistic	Some college	Unemployed
Ash	They/them	Black	30	3	College	Professional advocate
Abby	She/her	White	36	36	Postgraduate	Unemployed
Vanna	She/her	White	48	39	College	Unemployed
Felicity	She/her	White	27	22	College	Math tutor
Niki	They/them	White	29	22	Postgraduate	Lawyer
Seth	He/him	White	—	37	College	Tech
Luba	She/her	White	35	28	—	Home health aid

(continued)

TABLE B.2 (CONTINUED)

Name	Pronoun	Race/ethnicity	Age in 2016	Age of autism spectrum disorder (ASD) diagnosis	Highest level of education completed	Occupation
Sierra	She/her	White	27	Not autistic	College	Community organizer
Paige	She/her	White	26	23	Some college	Administrative assistant
Buddy	He/him	White	58	47	College	Unemployed/retired
Cynthia	She/her	Black	—	Adulthood	College	Writer and artist
Russel	He/him	White	43	Adult	Postgraduate	Executive director of nonprofit
Lorena	She/her	White	41	28	College	Student and social work intern
Molly	She/her	Black	40	Childhood	High school	Freelance musician
Charles	He/him	White	34	3	Postgraduate	Electrical engineer
Rachel	She/her	White	32	28	Postgraduate	Nanny
Ronald	He/him	White	51	42	Some college	Unemployed
Hil	They/them	White	56	46	College	Social worker
Winnie	She/her	White	48	45	Some college	Unemployed
Harry	He/him	Asian	37	26	Postgraduate	Financial associate
Connor	He/him	White	34	18	Postgraduate	Unemployed
Romy	She/her	White	30	5	Some college	Records specialist
Ari Ne'eman	He/him	White	29	Childhood	College	Nonprofit activist
Felix	He/him	White	34	Adulthood	College	Unemployed
Juniper	They/them	White	49	Adulthood	College	Unemployed
Codey	He/him	White	24	2	College	Leadership programs coordinator
Tobias	He/him	White	28	12	College	PhD student
Lea	They/them	White	—	23	Postgraduate	Nonprofit program assistant

TABLE B.3 INTERVIEWED PARTICIPANTS—ALTERNATIVE BIOMEDICAL MOVEMENT

Name	Pronoun	Race/ethnicity	Age in 2016	Age of ASD child(ren) at interview	Highest level of education completed	Occupation
Riley	She/her	White	44	~10	—	Program coordinator
Crystal	She/her	White	—	7	—	Housekeeper
Anthony	He/him	White	—	7	—	Construction
Gina	She/her	White	35	5	College	Unemployed
Victoria	She/her	White	38	N/A	College	Executive director
Robyn	She/her	White	34	N/A	Postgraduate	Nurse practitioner
Whitney	She/her	White	48	13	Postgraduate	Unemployed
Fiona	She/her	White	54	23	Postgraduate	Professional disability advocate
Melissa	She/her	White	45	10	Some college	Unemployed
Christine	She/her	White	—	18	College	Unemployed
Mindy	She/her	White	41	12 and 6	Postgraduate	Unemployed
Laurel	She/her	White	52	22 and 23	Postgraduate	Engineer
Jennifer	She/her	White	29	4.5 and 3	Some college	Unemployed
Sandra	She/her	White	42	15	College	Director of visitor services
Kelly	She/her	White	—	15	Some college	Unemployed
Trudy	She/her	White	47	14	Postgraduate	Consultant
Claire	She/her	White	44	9	Some college	Restaurant executive

(continued)

TABLE B.3 (*CONTINUED*)

Name	Pronoun	Race/ethnicity	Age in 2016	Age of ASD child(ren) at interview	Highest level of education completed	Occupation
Gabriel	He/him	White/Hispanic	45	6	Postgraduate	Former doctor
Grace	She/her	White	33	6 and 4	Some college	Regional director of sales
Robyn	She/her	White	34	N/A	Postgraduate	Nurse practitioner
Gwen Comte	She/her	White	—	N/A	Postgraduate	Naturopathic doctor
Ravi Zahin	He/him	Asian	45	N/A	Postgraduate	Naturopathic doctor
Darren Jesson	He/him	White	42	N/A	Postgraduate	Integrative/functional medicine
Travis Drummond	He/him	—	57	N/A	Postgraduate	Medical doctor
Kurt Martinek	He/him	White	—	19	Postgraduate	Medical doctor
Bernard Sachwell	He/him	White	—	N/A	Postgraduate	Medical doctor
Kavita Maddan	She/her	Asian	—	N/A	Postgraduate	Medical doctor
Dahlia Pagani	She/her	White	33	N/A	Postgraduate	Naturopathic doctor
Charlotte Langley	She/her	White	41	N/A	Postgraduate	Naturopathic doctor
Patrick	He/him	White	—	N/A	Postgraduate	Researcher
Winston	He/him	White	28	N/A	Some college	Author and speaker
Rita	She/her	White	20	N/A	High school	Unemployed

NOTES

1. WARRIORS AND ALIENS

1. Institute of Medicine, *Immunization Safety Review: Vaccines and Autism* (Washington, DC: National Academies Press, 2004).
2. World Health Organization, "Ten Threats to Global Health in 2019," https://www.who.int/news-room/spotlight/ten-threats-to-global-health -in-2019.
3. Gil Eyal, Brendan Hart, Emine Onculer, Neta Oren, and Natasha Rossi, *The Autism Matrix* (Cambridge, UK: Polity, 2010).
4. Hyperbaric oxygen therapy is most commonly prescribed to treat carbon monoxide poisoning and decompression sickness (particularly among scuba divers).
5. Chelation is a treatment to remove heavy metals and minerals from the body. When improperly used, it can cause hypocalcemia, renal impairment, and death. Stephen James, Shawn W. Stevenson, Natalie Silove, and Katrina Williams, "Chelation for Autism Spectrum Disorder (ASD)," *Cochrane Database Systematic Reviews* 5, no. 5 (May 2015), https://doi.org/10.1002/14651858.CD010766.pub2.
6. Oliver Sacks, "An Anthropologist on Mars," *New Yorker*, December 27, 1993.
7. Sacks, "An Anthropologist on Mars"; Jim Sinclair, "Don't Mourn for Us," *Our Voice* 1, no. 3 (1993).
8. Mylène Legault, Jean-Nicolas Bourdon, and Pierre Poirier, "From Neurodiversity to Neurodivergence: The Role of Epistemic and Cognitive

Marginalization," *Synthese* 199, no. 5 (2021): 12843–68, https://doi.org/10.1007/s11229-021-03356-5.

9. Leo Kanner, "Autistic Disturbances of Affective Contact," *Nervous Child* 2 (1943): 242. Emphasis in original.

10. American Psychiatric Association, *Diagnostic and Statistical Manual of Mental Disorders*, 5th ed. (Washington, DC: American Psychiatric Publishing, 2013).

11. Matthew J. Maenner et al., "Prevalence and Characteristics of Autism Spectrum Disorder Among Children Aged 8 Years—Autism and Developmental Disabilities Monitoring Network, 11 Sites, United States, 2020," *MMWR Surveillance Summaries* 72, no. 2 (March 2023): 1–14, https://doi.org/10.15585/mmwr.ss7011a1.

12. Edward R. Ritvo et al., "The UCLA-University of Utah Epidemiological Survey of Autism: Prevalence," *American Journal of Psychiatry* 146, no. 2 (February 1989): 194–99, https://doi.org/10.1176/ajp.146.2.194.

13. Eyal et al., *The Autism Matrix*.

14. "Mental retardation" was once a clinical and legal term. In 2010, President Barack Obama signed a law to replace the term "mental retardation" with "intellectual disability" in all federal health, education, and labor statutes. The *Diagnostic and Statistical Manual of Mental Disorders*, 5th ed., published in 2013, also revised "mental retardation" to "intellectual disability."

15. Ka-Yuet Liu, Marissa King, and Peter Bearman, "Social Influence and the Autism Epidemic," *American Journal of Sociology* 115, no. 5 (March 2010): 1387–434, https://doi.org/10.1086/651448.

16. Daniel Navon and Gil Eyal, "Looping Genomes: Diagnostic Change and the Genetic Makeup of the Autism Population," *American Journal of Sociology* 121, no. 5 (March 2016): 1416–71, https://doi.org/10.1086/684201.

17. Ian Hacking, *The Social Construction of What?* (Cambridge, MA: Harvard University Press, 1999).

18. Meng-Chuan Lai et al., "Prevalence of Co-occurring Mental Health Diagnoses in the Autism Population: A Systematic Review and Meta-Analysis," *Lancet Psychiatry* 6, no. 10 (October 2019): 819–29, https://doi.org/10.1016/s2215-0366(19)30289-5; Arlene Mannion and Geraldine Leader, "Comorbidity in Autism Spectrum Disorder: A Literature

Review," *Research in Autism Spectrum Disorders* 7, no. 12 (December 2013): 1595–616, https://doi.org/10.1016/j.rasd.2013.09.006.

19. Allison C. Carey, Pamela Block, and Richard Scotch, *Allies and Obstacles: Disability Activism and Parents of Children with Disabilities* (Philadelphia: Temple University Press, 2020); Matthew S. McCoy et al., "Ethical Advocacy Across the Autism Spectrum: Beyond Partial Representation," *American Journal of Bioethics* 20, no. 4 (May 2020): 13–24, https://doi.org/10.1080/15265161.2020.1730482.

20. Carey, Block, and Scotch, *Allies and Obstacles*, 180.

21. Linda Blum, *Raising Generation Rx: Mothering Kids with Invisible Disabilities in an Age of Inequality* (New York: New York University Press, 2015); Carey, Block, and Scotch, *Allies and Obstacles*.

22. Carey, Block, and Scotch, *Allies and Obstacles*; McCoy et al., "Ethical Advocacy."

23. Looking at pro-breastfeeding and anti-circumcision movements, Harmony Newman and Laura Carpenter introduced the concept of "embodiment by proxy," which refers to the way "activists draw on physical sensations that they imagine for other people's bodies, rather than on those they experience themselves." Harmony D. Newman and Laura M. Carpenter, "Embodiment Without Bodies? Analysis of Embodiment in US-Based Pro-Breastfeeding and Anti-Male Circumcision Movements," *Sociology of Health and Illness* 36, no. 5 (June 2014): 640, https://doi.org/10.1111/1467-9566.12095.

24. Carey, Block, and Scotch, *Allies and Obstacles*.

25. Mary Langan, "Parental Voices and Controversies in Autism," *Disability & Society* 26, no. 2 (February 2011): 193–205, https://doi.org/10.1080/0968 7599.2011.544059; Claire Laurier Decoteau and Meghan Daniel, "Scientific Hegemony and the Field of Autism," *American Sociological Review* 85, no. 3 (May 2020): 451–76, https://doi.org/10.1177/000312242092253; Jennifer S. Singh, *Multiple Autisms: Spectrums of Advocacy and Genomic Science* (Minneapolis: University of Minnesota Press, 2016).

26. McCoy et al., "Ethical Advocacy."

27. McCoy et al., "Ethical Advocacy."

28. Phil Brown, *Toxic Exposures: Contested Illnesses and the Environmental Health Movement* (New York: Columbia University Press, 2007), 18.

29. Chloe Silverman, *Understanding Autism: Parents, Doctors, and the History of a Disorder* (Princeton, NJ: Princeton University Press, 2011).

30. Pier Jaarsma and Stellan Welin, "Autism as a Natural Human Variation: Reflections on the Claims of the Neurodiversity Movement," *Health Care Analysis* 20, no. 1 (March 2012): 20–30, https://doi.org/10.1007/s10728-011-0169-9.

31. Phil Brown et al., "The Health Politics of Asthma: Environmental Justice and Collective Illness Experience in the United States," in *The Sociology of Health and Illness: Critical Perspectives*, 9th ed., ed. Peter Conrad and Valerie Leiter (New York: Worth, 2012); Phil Brown et al., "Policy Issues in Environmental Health Disputes," *Annals of the American Academy of Political and Social Science* 584, no. 1 (November 2002): 175–202, https://doi.org/10.1177/000271620258400113; Scott Frickel et al., "Undone Science: Charting Social Movement and Civil Society Challenges to Research Agenda Setting," *Science, Technology, & Human Values* 35, no. 4 (2010): 444–73, https://doi.org/10.1177/0162243909345836; Maren Klawiter, *The Biopolitics of Breast Cancer: Changing Cultures of Disease and Activism* (Minneapolis: University of Minnesota Press, 2008).

32. In 2019, the organization renamed itself The Autism Community in Action (TACA).

33. Jonann Brady and Stephanie Dahle, "Celeb Couple to Lead 'Green Vaccine' Rally," *ABC News*, last modified October 9, 2009, https://abcnews.go.com/GMA/OnCall/story?id=4987758.

34. Jennifer A. Reich, "Neoliberal Mothering and Vaccine Refusal: Imagined Gated Communities and the Privilege of Choice," *Gender & Society* 28, no. 5 (October 2014): 679–704, https://doi.org/10.1177/0891243214532711; Norah MacKendrick and Kate Cairns, "The Polluted Child and Maternal Responsibility in the US Environmental Health Movement," *Signs* 44, no. 2 (Winter 2019): 307–32, https://doi.org/10.1086/699340.

35. Verta Taylor, "Gender and Social Movements: Gender Processes in Women's Self-Help Movements," *Gender & Society* 13, no. 1 (February 1999): 8–33, https://doi.org/10.1177/089124399013001002; Stephen M. Haas et al., "Communicating Thin: A Grounded Model of Online Negative Enabling Support Groups in the Pro-Anorexia Movement," *New Media & Society* 13, no. 1 (2011): 40–57, https://doi.org/10.1177/1461444810363910.

36. Phil Brown et al., "Embodied Health Movements: New Approaches to Social Movements in Health," *Sociology of Health & Illness* 26, no. 1 (January 2004): 50–80, https://doi.org/10.1111/j.1467-9566.2004.00378.x.

37. Lydia X. Z. Brown, "Ableism/Language," Autistic Hoya, last modified September 14, 2022, https://www.autistichoya.com/p/ableist-words-and -terms-to-avoid.html; Fiona Kumari Campbell, *Contours of Ableism: The Production of Disability and Abledness* (London: Palgrave Macmillan, 2009).

38. Catherine Lord, Cory Shulman, and Pamela DiLavore, "Regression and Word Loss in Autistic Spectrum Disorders," *Journal of Child Psychology and Psychiatry* 45, no. 5 (July 2004): 936–55, https://doi.org /10.1111/j.1469-7610.2004.t01-1-00287.x; Fritjof Norrelgen et al., "Children with Autism Spectrum Disorders Who Do Not Develop Phrase Speech in the Preschool Years," *Autism* 19, no. 8 (November 2015): 934–43, https://doi.org/10.1177/1362361314556782; John Baio et al., "Prevalence of Autism Spectrum Disorder Among Children Aged 8 Years—Autism and Developmental Disabilities Monitoring Network, 11 Sites, United States, 2014," *MMWR Surveillance Summaries* 67, no. 6 (2018): 1–23, https://doi.org/10.15585/mmwr.ss6706a1.

39. Kanner, "Autistic Disturbances of Affective Contact," 248.

40. National Center For Education Statistics, *120 Years of American Education: A Statistical Portrait* (Washington, DC: U.S. Department of Education, 1993), https://nces.ed.gov/pubs93/93442.pdf.

41. Kanner, "Autistic Disturbances of Affective Contact," 250.

42. Kanner, "Autistic Disturbances of Affective Contact," 250.

43. Kanner, "Autistic Disturbances of Affective Contact," 250.

44. James Harris and Joseph Piven, "Correcting the Record: Leo Kanner and the Broad Autism Phenotype," SpectrumNews.org, April 26, 2016, https:// www.spectrumnews.org/opinion/viewpoint/correcting-the-record-leo -kanner-and-the-broad-autism-phenotype/; Silverman, *Understanding Autism*; Theodore Shapiro, "Autism and the Psychoanalyst," *Psychoanalytic Inquiry* 20, no. 5 (2000): 648–59, https://doi.org/10.1080/07351692009348914; Jeffrey P. Baker, "Autism in 1959: Joey the Mechanical Boy," *Pediatrics* 125, no. 6 (2010): 1101–1103, https://doi.org/10.1542/peds.2010-0846; Majia Holmer Nadesan, *Constructing Autism: Unravelling the 'Truth' and Understanding the Social* (London: Routledge, 2005).

45. Bruno Bettelheim, *The Empty Fortress: Infantile Autism and the Birth of the Self* (New York: Free Press, 1967), 125.

46. Bettelheim, *The Empty Fortress*, 127.

47. Singh, *Multiple Autisms*; John Donvan and Caren Zucker, *In a Different Key: The Story of Autism* (New York: Crown, 2016); Eyal et al., *Autism Matrix*; Chloe Silverman and Jeffrey P. Brosco, "Understanding Autism: Parents and Pediatricians in Historical Perspective," *Archives of Pediatrics & Adolescent Medicine* 161, no. 4 (April 2007): 392–98, https://doi.org/10.1001/archpedi.161.4.392.

48. Singh, *Multiple Autisms*.

49. Including genetic risk factors, gene-environment interactions, and epigenetics. Interagency Autism Coordinating Committee, "Autism Research Database," U.S. Department of Health and Human Services, https://iacc.hhs.gov/funding/data/.

50. Singh, *Multiple Autisms*; Francesca Happé, Angelica Ronald, and Robert Plomin, "Time to Give Up on a Single Explanation for Autism," *Nature Neuroscience* 9 (2006): 1218–20, https://doi.org/10.1038/nn1770.

51. Singh, *Multiple Autisms*.

52. Silverman, *Understanding Autism*.

53. Bernard Rimland, "Controversies in the Treatment of Autistic Children: Vitamin and Drug Therapy," *Journal of Child Neurology* 3, no. 1_suppl (1988): S68–72, https://doi.org/10.1177/0883073888003001S13.

54. Silverman, *Understanding Autism*; Jon Pangborn and Sidney MacDonald Baker, *Autism: Effective Biomedical Treatments* (San Diego, CA: Autism Research Institute, 2005).

55. Bernard Rimland, "The Autism Epidemic, Vaccinations, and Mercury," *Journal of Nutritional & Environmental Medicine* 10, no. 4 (2000): 261–66, https://doi.org/10.1080/13590840020013248.

56. Silverman, *Understanding Autism*.

57. Matthew Z. Dudley et al., "The State of Vaccine Safety Science: Systematic Reviews of the Evidence," *Lancet Infectious Diseases* 20, no. 5 (May 2020): E80–89, https://doi.org/10.1016/S1473-3099(20)30130-4.

58. Anna Kirkland, "The Legitimacy of Vaccine Critics: What Is Left After the Autism Hypothesis?," *Journal of Health Politics, Policy and Law* 37, no. 1 (February 2012): 69–97, https://doi.org/10.1215/03616878-1496020.

59. Bernard Rimland, "Do Children's Shots Invite Autism?," *Los Angeles Times*, April 26, 2000, A13, https://www.latimes.com/archives/la-xpm-2000-apr-26-me-23718-story.html.

60. Rimland, "Do Children's Shots Invite Autism?"

61. Rimland, "Autism Epidemic."

62. Stanley Plotkin, Jeffrey S. Gerber, and Paul A. Offit, "Vaccines and Autism: A Tale of Shifting Hypotheses," *Clinical Infectious Diseases* 48, no. 4 (February 2009): 456–61, https://doi.org/10.1086/596476.

63. Centers for Disease Control and Prevention, "Timeline: Thimerosal in Vaccines (1999–2010)," last modified August 19, 2020, https://www.cdc.gov/vaccinesafety/concerns/thimerosal/timeline.html.

64. Claire Laurier Decoteau and Kelly Underman, "Adjudicating Non-Knowledge in the Omnibus Autism Proceedings," *Social Studies of Science* 45, no. 4 (2015): 471–500, https://doi.org/10.1177/0306312715600278.

65. The gastrointestinal issues included "the incomplete breakdown and excessive absorption of gut-derived peptides from foods, including barley, rye, oats, and casein from milk and dairy produce." A. J. Wakefield et al., "Retracted: Ileal-Lymphoid-Nodular Hyperplasia, Non-Specific Colitis, and Pervasive Developmental Disorder in Children," *Lancet* 351, no. 9103 (February 1998): 640, https://doi.org/10.1016/S0140-6736(97)11096-0.

66. Wakefield et al., "Retracted: Ileal-Lymphoid-Nodular Hyperplasia," 640.

67. Brent Taylor et al., "Autism and Measles, Mumps, and Rubella Vaccine: No Epidemiological Evidence for a Causal Association," *Lancet* 353, no. 9169 (June 1999): 2026–29, https://doi.org/10.1016/S0140-6736(99)01239-8; Frank DeStefano and Robert T. Chen, "Negative Association Between MMR and Autism," *Lancet* 353, no. 9169 (June 1999): 1987–88, https://doi.org/10.1016/S0140-6736(99)00160-9.

68. Fiona Godlee, Jane Smith, and Harvey Marcovitch, "Wakefield's Article Linking MMR Vaccine and Autism Was Fraudulent," *BMJ* 342, no. 7788 (January 2011): 64–66, https://doi.org/10.1136/bmj.d1678.

69. Brian Deer, "How the Case Against the MMR Vaccine Was Fixed," *BMJ* 342 (January 2011): 77–82, https://doi.org/10.1136/bmj.c5347.

70. In his patent application for a new measles vaccine, Wakefield claimed that the current MMR vaccine caused inflammatory bowel disease (IBD) in some patients but that his vaccine would protect against measles and treat IBD. By protecting against IBD, he said the vaccine

would prevent IBD-induced regressive autism. Brian Deer, "How the Vaccine Crisis Was Meant to Make Money," *BMJ* 342 (January 2011): 136–42, https://doi.org/10.1136/bmj.c5258; Owen Dyer, "Andrew Wakefield Is Accused of Paying Children for Blood Samples," *BMJ* 335, no. 7611 (July 2007): 118–19, https://doi.org/10.1136/bmj.39280.513310.4E.

71. Jennifer A. Reich, *Calling the Shots: Why Parents Reject Vaccines* (New York: New York University Press, 2016).

72. Tara C. Smith, "Vaccine Rejection and Hesitancy: A Review and Call to Action," *Open Forum Infectious Diseases* 4, no. 3 (Summer 2017), https://doi.org/10.1093/ofid/ofx146; Jason L. Schwartz and Arthur L. Caplan, "Vaccination Refusal: Ethics, Individual Rights, and the Common Good," *Primary Care: Clinics in Office Practice* 38, no. 4 (December 2011): 717–28, https://doi.org/10.1016/j.pop.2011.07.009v; Heidi J. Larson et al., "Addressing the Vaccine Confidence Gap," *Lancet* 378, no. 9790 (August 2011): 526–35, https://doi.org/10.1016/s0140-6736(11)60678-8.

73. Deborah L. Shelton, "Autism Doctor Loses License in Illinois, Missouri," *Chicago Tribune*, November 5, 2012, https://www.chicagotribune.com/news/ct-xpm-2012-11-05-ct-met-autism-doctor-20121106-story.html; Trine Tsouderos, "'Miracle Drug' Called Junk Science," *Chicago Tribune*, May 21, 2009, https://www.chicagotribune.com/lifestyles/health/chi-autism-lupron-may21-story.html.

74. Patricia Callahan, "Naperville Doctor Disciplined in Controversial Autism Case," *Chicago Tribune*, December 30, 2014, https://www.chicagotribune.com/lifestyles/health/ct-autism-anjum-usman-discipline-met-20141229-story.html.

75. Tara Haelle, "Dr. Bob Sears Could Lose License for Medical Negligence—Not Vaccine Choice," *Forbes*, last updated September 11, 2016, https://www.forbes.com/sites/tarahaelle/2016/09/11/dr-bob-sears-could-lose-license-for-medical-negligence-not-vaccine-choice/#74962e4625f6; Elissa Strauss, "Leading Vaccination Skeptic Dr. Bob Sears Is at Risk of Losing His Medical License," *Slate*, September 15, 2016, http://www.slate.com/blogs/xx_factor/2016/09/15/leading_vaccination_skeptic_dr_bob_sears_is_at_risk_of_losing_his_medical.html.

76. Neil Swidey and Patricia Wen, "A Medical Collision with a Child in the Middle," *Boston Globe*, December 15, 2013, https://www.bostonglobe.com/metro/2013/12/15/justina/vnwzbbNdiodSD7WDTh6xZI/story

.html; Zachary T. Sampson, "After 16-Month Battle, Justina Pelletier Returns Home," *Boston Globe*, June 19, 2014, https://www.bostonglobe.com /metro/2014/06/18/justina-pelletier-returns-her-family-home-connecticut -ending-medical-and-legal-odyssey/ON7QhGURgprYZoVS7uuxeL /story.html; "Ten Hour Siege, a SWAT Team . . . and a TANK: How Police Dealt with Mother Who Refused to Give Her Child Medication," *DailyMail.com*, last modified April 15, 2011, http://www.dailymail.co.uk /news/article-1377178/SWAT-teams-10-hour-siege-mother-Maryanne -Godboldo-Detroit.html.

77. Jim Sinclair, "History of ANI," Autism Network International, January 2005, http://www.autreat.com/History_of_ANI.html.

78. Sinclair, "Don't Mourn for Us."

79. Carey, Block, and Scotch, *Allies and Obstacles*.

80. U.S. Department of Labor, "Subminimum Wage," https://www.dol.gov /general/topic/wages/subminimumwage.

81. Autism Speaks' 2013 mission statement depicted autism as undesirable and burdensome by phrasing one goal as bringing "hope to all who deal with the hardships of this disorder," but by 2018, the organization had minimized its tone of despair and—clearly inspired by autistic rights rhetoric—had included "increasing understanding and acceptance of people with autism spectrum disorder." Autism Speaks, "Mission," http://www.autismspeaks.org/about-us/mission.

82. Robert D. Austin and Gary P. Pisano, "Neurodiversity as a Competitive Advantage," *Harvard Business Review* 95, no. 3 (May–June 2017): 96–103, https://hbr.org/2017/05/neurodiversity-as-a-competitive-advantage.

83. Francisco Ortega, "The Cerebral Subject and the Challenge of Neurodiversity," *BioSocieties* 4, no. 4 (December 2009): 425–45, http://dx.doi.org /10.1017/S1745855209990287.

84. Joanne Cleaver, "Combating Sensory Overload: How Zoos and Museums Are Redefining Inclusion," *New York Times*, April 22, 2022, https:// www.nytimes.com/2022/04/22/travel/sensory-disabilities-travel.html; Erin Blakemore, "Celebrating Media-Makers on the Autism Spectrum," *Washington Post*, April 23, 2022, https://www.washingtonpost.com/health /2022/04/23/autism-creativity/.

85. Robert Chapman, "Defining Neurodiversity for Research and Practice," in *Neurodiversity Studies: A New Critical Paradigm*, ed. Hanna Rosqvist,

Nick Chown, and Anna Stenning (London: Routledge, 2020), 218–20; Ortega, "Cerebral Subject."

86. Naomi Oreskes and Erik Conway, *Merchants of Doubt: How a Handful of Scientists Obscured the Truth on Issues from Tobacco Smoke to Global Warming* (London: Bloomsbury Press, 2010); Cristin E. Kearns, Laura A. Schmidt, and Stanton A. Glantz, "Sugar Industry and Coronary Heart Disease Research: A Historical Analysis of Internal Industry Documents," *JAMA Internal Medicine* 176, no. 11 (November 2016): 1680–85, https://doi.org/10.1001/jamainternmed.2016.5394.

87. Gil Eyal, *The Crisis of Expertise* (Hoboken, NJ: Wiley, 2019); Sheila Jasanoff, *The Fifth Branch: Science Advisers as Policymakers* (Cambridge, MA: Harvard University Press, 2009).

88. Reich, *Calling the Shots*; Mariam Siddiqui, Daniel A. Salmon, and Saad B. Omer, "Epidemiology of Vaccine Hesitancy in the United States," *Human Vaccines & Immunotherapeutics* 9, no. 12 (December 2013): 2643–48, https://doi.org/10.4161/hv.27243.

89. Wändi Bruine de Bruin, Htay-Wah Saw, and Dana P. Goldman, "Political Polarization in US Residents' COVID-19 Risk Perceptions, Policy Preferences, and Protective Behaviors," *Journal of Risk and Uncertainty* 61, no. 2 (2020): 177–94, https://doi.org/10.1007/s11166-020-09336-3; Alec Tyson, "Republicans Remain Far Less Likely than Democrats to View COVID-19 as a Major Threat to Public Health," Pew Research Center, July 22, 2020, https://www.pewresearch.org/fact-tank/2020/07/22/republicans -remain-far-less-likely-than-democrats-to-view-covid-19-as-a-major -threat-to-public-health/; Michael Niño et al., "Race and Ethnicity, Gender, and Age on Perceived Threats and Fear of COVID-19: Evidence from Two National Data Sources," *SSM-Population Health* 13 (March 2021): 100717, https://doi.org/10.1016/j.ssmph.2020.100717; John H. Evans and Eszter Hargittai, "Who Doesn't Trust Fauci? The Public's Belief in the Expertise and Shared Values of Scientists in the COVID-19 Pandemic," *Socius* 6 (2020): 2378023120947337, https://doi.org/10.1177 /2378023120947337.

90. Frickel et al., "Undone Science"; Brown et al., "Embodied Health Movements."

91. Sabrina McCormick, "From 'Politico-Scientists' to Democratizing Science Movements: The Changing Climate of Citizens and Science,"

Organization & Environment 22, no. 1 (April 2009): 34–51, https://doi.org /10.1177/1086026609333419.

92. Burkart Holzner and John Marx, *Knowledge Affiliation: The Knowledge System in Society* (Boston: Allyn and Bacon, 1979).

93. Peter M. Haas, "Introduction: Epistemic Communities and International Policy Coordination," *International Organization* 46, no. 1 (Winter 1992): 3, https://doi.org/10.1017/S0020818300001442.

94. Claire Laurier Decoteau, "The 'Western Disease': Autism and Somali Parents' Embodied Health Movements," *Social Science & Medicine* 177 (March 2017): 169–76, https://doi.org/10.1016/j.socscimed.2017.01.064; Claire Laurier Decoteau, *The Western Disease: Contesting Autism in the Somali Diaspora* (Chicago: University of Chicago Press, 2021).

95. Thomas F. Gieryn, *Cultural Boundaries of Science: Credibility on the Line* (Chicago: University of Chicago Press, 1999); Sheila Jasanoff, "Contested Boundaries in Policy-Relevant Science," *Social Studies of Science* 17, no. 2 (May 1987): 195–230, https://doi.org/10.1177/030631287017002001.

96. Sara M. Evans and Harry C. Boyte, *Free Spaces: The Sources of Democratic Change in America* (Chicago: University of Chicago Press, 1986), 7.

97. Evans and Boyte, *Free Spaces*; Eric L. Hirsch, *Urban Revolt: Ethnic Politics in the Nineteenth-Century Chicago Labor Movement* (Oakland: University of California Press, 1990); Rick Fantasia and Eric L. Hirsch, "Culture in Rebellion: The Appropriation and Transformation of the Veil in the Algerian Revolution," in *Social Movements and Culture*, ed. Hank Johnston and Bert Klandermann (London: Routledge, 1995), 144–60.

98. Francesca Polletta, "'Free Spaces' in Collective Action," *Theory and Society* 28, no. 1 (February 1999): 1–38, https://www.jstor.org/stable/3108504.

99. Evans and Boyte, *Free Spaces*; Pete Simi and Robert Futrell, "Cyberculture and the Endurance of White Power Activism," *Journal of Political and Military Sociology* 34, no. 1 (Summer 2006): 115–42, https://www.jstor.org /stable/45294188.

100. Maria Lowe, "'Sowing the Seeds of Discontent': Tougaloo College's Social Science Forums as a Prefigurative Movement Free Space, 1952–1964," *Journal of Black Studies* 39, no. 6 (July 2009): 865–87, https://doi.org/10 .1177/0021934707305401; Evans and Boyte, *Free Spaces*.

101. Lowe, "'Sowing the Seeds of Discontent'"; Evans and Boyte, *Free Spaces*.

102. Polletta, "'Free Spaces' in Collective Action."

103. Fantasia and Hirsch, "Culture in Rebellion."
104. MassADAPT is a disability rights organization that includes many autistic rights activists.

2. REIMAGINING AUTISM

1. One of the earliest studies examining autism genetics was published in 1977; it compared twenty-one pairs of same-sex twins, concluding that autism is possibly a combination of genetic predisposition (influencing the cognitive development involving language) and organic brain damage. See Susan Folstein and Michael Rutter, "Infantile Autism: A Genetic Study of 21 Twin Pairs," *Journal of Child Psychology and Psychiatry* 18, no. 4 (September 1977): 297–321, https://doi.org/10.1111/j.1469-7610.1977.tb00443.x.

2. Kristin Bumiller, "The Geneticization of Autism: From New Reproductive Technologies to the Conception of Genetic Normalcy," *Signs* 34, no. 4 (Summer 2009): 875–99, https://doi.org/10.1086/597130; Jennifer S. Singh, *Multiple Autisms: Spectrums of Advocacy and Genomic Science* (Minneapolis: University of Minnesota Press, 2016).

3. The study was not replicated. Dean Hamer, Stella Hu, Victoria L. Magnuson, Nan Hu, and Angela M. L. Pattatucci, "A Linkage Between DNA Markers on the X Chromosome and Male Sexual Orientation," *Science* 261, no. 5119 (1993): 321–27, https://doi.org/10.1126/science.8332896.

4. Peter Conrad and Alison Angell, "Homosexuality and Remedicalization," *Society* 41, no. 5 (July 2004): 32–39, https://doi.org/10.1007/BF02688215; Peter Conrad and Susan Markens, "Constructing the 'Gay Gene' in the News: Optimism and Skepticism in the US and British Press," *Health* 5, no. 3 (July 2001): 373–400, https://doi.org/10.1177/136345930100500306.

5. Conrad and Angell, "Homosexuality and Remedicalization."

6. Scholars contended that genetic information gathers meaning from its social and temporal context and indicate that if medicalization preceded genetic research, then subsequent genetic information reinforces medicalization. The "geneticization of autism" emerges from a history of medicalization, suggesting the challenge of achieving a paradigmatic shift. For autism, it is unlikely that geneticization will reduce medicalization. See Sara Shostak, Peter Conrad, and Allan V. Horwitz,

"Sequencing and Its Consequences: Path Dependence and the Relationships Between Genetics and Medicalization," *American Journal of Sociology* 114, no. S1 (2008): S287–316, https://doi.org/10.1086/595570.

7. Before it was subsumed under autism spectrum disorder in the *Diagnostic and Statistical Manual of Mental Disorders*, 5th ed. (DSM-5), Asperger's syndrome was in the same family of pervasive developmental disorders as autistic disorder.

8. Gregory G. Garske and Jay R. Stewart, "Stigmatic and Mythical Thinking: Barriers to Vocational Rehabilitation Services for Persons with Severe Mental Illness," *Journal of Rehabilitation* 65, no. 4 (October–December 1999): 4–8.

9. June L. Chen et al., "Trends in Employment for Individuals with Autism Spectrum Disorder: A Review of the Research Literature," *Review Journal of Autism and Developmental Disorders* 2, no. 2 (2015): 115–27, https://doi.org/10.1007/s40489-014-0041-6.

10. Chen et al., "Trends in Employment."

11. A few of the autistic rights participants who did not disclose their income either lived with parents and/or were unsure.

12. Medicaid provides health coverage to children, pregnant women, parents, seniors, and individuals with disabilities who are considered low income. Coverage varies from state to state. In states that adopted the Affordable Care Act's (ACA) Medicaid expansion, eligible adults cannot make more than 138 percent above the federal poverty level, which is $20,120 per year for 2023.

13. Scott D. Tomchek and Winnie Dunn, "Sensory Processing in Children with and Without Autism: A Comparative Study Using the Short Sensory Profile," *American Journal of Occupational Therapy* 61, no. 2 (March–April 2007): 190–200, https://doi.org/10.5014/ajot.61.2.190; Janet K. Kern et al., "The Pattern of Sensory Processing Abnormalities in Autism," *Autism* 10, no. 5 (September 2006): 480–94, https://doi.org/10.1177/1362361306066564.

14. Kamila Markram and Henry Markram, "The Intense World Theory—A Unifying Theory of the Neurobiology of Autism," *Frontiers in Human Neuroscience* 4 (2010): 224, https://doi.org/10.3389/fnhum.2010.00224.

15. Danielle I. Brady et al., "Cognitive and Emotional Intelligence in Young Adults with Autism Spectrum Disorder Without an Accompanying Intellectual or Language Disorder," *Research in Autism Spectrum*

Disorders 8, no. 9 (September 2014): 1016–23, https://doi.org/10.1016/j.rasd .2014.05.009.

16. Jill Locke et al., "A Tangled Web: The Challenges of Implementing an Evidence-Based Social Engagement Intervention for Children with Autism in Urban Public School Settings," *Behavior Therapy* 46, no. 1 (2015): 54–67, https://doi.org/10.1016/j.beth.2014.05.001.

17. Julia Bascom, *The Obsessive Joy of Autism* (London: Jessica Kingsley, 2015).

18. American Psychiatric Association, *Diagnostic and Statistical Manual of Mental Disorders*, 5th ed. (Washington, DC: American Psychiatric Publishing, 2013).

19. Now called "The Autism Community in Action."

20. Arlene Mannion and Geraldine Leader, "Comorbidity in Autism Spectrum Disorder: A Literature Review," *Research in Autism Spectrum Disorders* 7, no. 12 (December 2013): 1595–616, https://doi.org/10.1016/j.rasd.2013.09.006.

21. Claire Laurier Decoteau, "The 'Western Disease': Autism and Somali Parents' Embodied Health Movements," *Social Science & Medicine* 177 (March 2017): 171–72, https://doi.org/10.1016/j.socscimed.2017.01.064.

22. Chloe Silverman, *Understanding Autism: Parents, Doctors, and the History of a Disorder* (Princeton, NJ: Princeton University Press, 2011); Claire Laurier Decoteau and Meghan Daniel, "Scientific Hegemony and the Field of Autism," *American Sociological Review* 85, no. 3 (May 2020): 451–76, https://doi.org/10.1177/000312242092253.

23. National Library of Medicine, "MTHFR Gene," MedLine Plus, last modified October 1, 2019, https://ghr.nlm.nih.gov/gene/MTHFR.

24. Singh, *Multiple Autisms*; Amirhossein Modabbernia, Eva Velthorst, and Abraham Reichenberg, "Environmental Risk Factors for Autism: An Evidence-Based Review of Systematic Reviews and Meta-Analyses," *Molecular Autism* 8 (March 2017): 13, https://doi.org/10.1186/s13229-017 -0121-4; Martine D. Lappé, "The Maternal Body as Environment in Autism Science," *Social Studies of Science* 6, no. 4 (October 2016): 675–700, https://doi.org/10.1177/0306312716659372; Decoteau and Daniel, "Scientific Hegemony."

25. Joachim Hallmayer et al., "Genetic Heritability and Shared Environmental Factors Among Twin Pairs with Autism," *Archives of General Psychiatry* 68, no. 11 (November 2011): 1095–102, https://doi.org/10.1001 /archgenpsychiatry.2011.76.

26. Maureen S. Durkin et al., "Advanced Parental Age and the Risk of Autism Spectrum Disorder," *American Journal of Epidemiology* 168, no. 11 (December 2008): 1268–76, https://doi.org/10.1093/aje/kwn250; Modabbernia, Velthorst, and Reichenberg, "Environmental Risk Factors."

27. Hannah Gardener, Donna Spiegelman, and Stephen L. Buka, "Prenatal Risk Factors for Autism: Comprehensive Meta-Analysis," *British Journal of Psychiatry* 195, no. 1 (July 2009): 7–14, https://doi.org/10.1192/bjp.bp.108.051672.

28. Hjördis O. Atladóttir et al., "Maternal Infection Requiring Hospitalization During Pregnancy and Autism Spectrum Disorders," *Journal of Autism and Developmental Disorders* 40, no. 12 (December 2010): 1423–30, https://doi.org/10.1007/s10803-010-1006-y.

29. Heather E. Volk et al., "Autism Spectrum Disorder: Interaction of Air Pollution with the MET Receptor Tyrosine Kinase Gene," *Epidemiology* 25, no. 1 (January 2014): 44–47, https://doi.org/10.1097/ede.0000000000000030.

30. Janie F. Shelton et al., "Neurodevelopmental Disorders and Prenatal Residential Proximity to Agricultural Pesticides: The CHARGE Study," *Environmental Health Perspectives* 122, no. 10 (October 2014): 1103–9, https://doi.org/10.1289/ehp.1307044.

31. Hannah Gardener, Donna Spiegelman, and Stephen L. Buka, "Perinatal and Neonatal Risk Factors for Autism: A Comprehensive Meta-Analysis," *Pediatrics* 128, no. 2 (August 2011): 344–55, https://doi.org/10.1542/peds.2010-1036.

32. Lisa A. Croen, Judith K. Grether, and Steve Selvin, "Descriptive Epidemiology of Autism in a California Population: Who Is at Risk?," *Journal of Autism and Developmental Disorders* 32, no. 3 (June 2002): 217–24, https://doi.org/10.1023/a:1015405914950.

33. Emphasis in original. See Decoteau and Daniel, "Scientific Hegemony," 454.

34. Decoteau and Daniel, "Scientific Hegemony."

35. Robin L. Hansen et al., "Regression in Autism: Prevalence and Associated Factors in the CHARGE Study," *Ambulatory Pediatrics* 8, no. 1 (January–February 2008): 25–31, https://doi.org/10.1016/j.ambp.2007.08.006; Brian D. Barger, Jonathan M. Campbell, and Jaimi D. McDonough, "Prevalence and Onset of Regression Within Autism Spectrum Disorders:

A Meta-Analytic Review," *Journal of Autism and Developmental Disorders* 43, no. 4 (April 2013): 817–28, https://doi.org/10.1007/s10803-012 -1621-x.

36. Robin P. Goin-Kochel and Barbara J. Myers, "Congenital Versus Regressive Onset of Autism Spectrum Disorders: Parents' Beliefs About Causes," *Focus on Autism and Other Developmental Disabilities* 20, no. 3 (Fall 2005): 169–79, https://doi.org/10.1177/10883576050200030501; Eric Fombonne et al., "Beliefs in Vaccine as Causes of Autism Among SPARK Cohort Caregivers," *Vaccine* 38, no. 7 (February 2020): 1794–803, https://doi.org /10.1016/j.vaccine.2019.12.026.

37. Silverman, *Understanding Autism*.

38. Jennifer A. Reich, *Calling the Shots: Why Parents Reject Vaccines* (New York: New York University Press, 2016).

39. Reich, *Calling the Shots*.

40. Matthew Z. Dudley et al., "The State of Vaccine Safety Science: Systematic Reviews of the Evidence," *Lancet Infectious Diseases* 20, no. 5 (May 2020): E80–89, https://doi.org/10.1016/S1473-3099(20)30130-4.

41. Institute of Medicine, "Methodological Approaches to Studying Health Outcomes Associated with the Current Immunization Schedule: Options, Feasibility, Ethical Issues, and Priorities," in *The Childhood Immunization Schedule and Safety: Stakeholder Concerns, Scientific Evidence, and Future Studies*, ed. Institute of Medicine (Washington, DC: National Academies Press, 2013), 106–7.

42. Centers for Disease Control and Prevention, "Timeline: Thimerosal in Vaccines (1999–2010)," last modified August 19, 2020, https://www.cdc .gov/vaccinesafety/concerns/thimerosal/timeline.html; C. J. Clements et al., "Thiomersal in Vaccines: Is Removal Warranted?," *Drug Safety* 24, no. 8 (2001): 567–74, https://doi.org/10.2165/00002018-200124080 -00001.

43. Institute of Medicine, *Immunization Safety Review: Vaccines and Autism* (Washington, DC: National Academies Press, 2004).

44. Vaccines that include traces of egg protein include yellow fever, influenza, measles/mumps/rubella, and some rabies vaccines. Allergic reactions are rare. See Robert A. Wood, "Allergic Reactions to Vaccines," *Pediatric Allergy and Immunology* 24, no. 6 (September 2013): 521–26, https://doi.org/10.1111/pai.12102.

45. Victoria Pitts, "Illness and Internet Empowerment: Writing and Reading Breast Cancer in Cyberspace," *Health (London)* 8, no. 1 (January 2004): 33–59, https://doi.org/10.1177/1363459304038794.

46. Linda Blum, *Raising Generation Rx: Mothering Kids with Invisible Disabilities in an Age of Inequality* (New York: New York University Press, 2015); Ellen K. Scott, "'I Feel as if I Am the One Who Is Disabled': The Emotional Impact of Changed Employment Trajectories of Mothers Caring for Children with Disabilities," *Gender & Society* 24, no. 5 (September 2010): 672–96, https://doi.org/10.1177/0891243210382531.

47. Valerie L. Braunstein et al., "The Inclusion of Fathers in Investigations of Autistic Spectrum Disorders," *Research in Autism Spectrum Disorders* 7, no. 7 (July 2013): 858–65, https://doi.org/10.1016/j.rasd.2013.03.005.

48. Stefanie Atsem et al., "Paternal Age Effects on Sperm FOXK1 and KCNA7 Methylation and Transmission into the Next Generation," *Human Molecular Genetics* 25, no. 22 (November 2016): 4996–5005, https://doi.org/10.1093/hmg/ddw328; Christina M. Hultman et al., "Advancing Paternal Age and Risk of Autism: New Evidence from a Population-Based Study and a Meta-Analysis of Epidemiological Studies," *Molecular Psychiatry* 16, no. 12 (December 2011): 1203–12, https://doi.org/10.1038/mp.2010.121.

49. Norah MacKendrick and Kate Cairns, "The Polluted Child and Maternal Responsibility in the US Environmental Health Movement," *Signs* 44, no. 2 (Winter 2019): 307–32, https://doi.org/10.1086/699340; Miranda R. Waggoner, *The Zero Trimester: Pre-Pregnancy Care and the Politics of Reproductive Risk* (Oakland: University of California Press, 2017); Lappé, "The Maternal Body."

50. Lappé, "The Maternal Body."

51. Miranda R. Waggoner, "Motherhood Preconceived: The Emergence of the Preconception Health and Health Care Initiative," *Journal of Health Politics, Policy and Law* 38, no. 2 (2013): 345–71, https://doi.org/10.1215/03616878-1966333.

52. Sabrina McCormick, "From 'Politico-Scientists' to Democratizing Science Movements: The Changing Climate of Citizens and Science," *Organization & Environment* 22, no. 1 (April 2009): 34–51, https://doi.org/10.1177/1086026609333419; Maren Klawiter, "Breast Cancer in Two Regimes: The Impact of Social Movements on Illness Experience,"

Sociology of Health & Illness 26, no. 6 (2004): 845–74, https://doi.org
/10.1111/j.1467-9566.2004.421_1.x; Phil Brown et al., "The Health Politics of Asthma: Environmental Justice and Collective Illness Experience in the United States," in *The Sociology of Health and Illness: Critical
Perspectives*, 9th ed., ed. Peter Conrad and Valerie Leiter (New York:
Worth, 2012).

53. Jennifer A. Reich, "Neoliberal Mothering and Vaccine Refusal: Imagined
    Gated Communities and the Privilege of Choice," *Gender & Society* 28,
    no. 5 (October 2014): 679–704, https://doi.org/10.1177/0891243214532711.

54. Andrew Szasz, *Shopping Our Way to Safety: How We Change from Pro-
    tecting the Environment to Protecting Ourselves* (Minneapolis: University
    of Minnesota Press, 2007); Norah MacKendrick and Lindsay M. Ste-
    vens, "'Taking Back a Little Bit of Control': Managing the Contami-
    nated Body through Consumption," *Sociological Forum* 31, no. 2 (June
    2016): 310–29, https://doi.org/10.1111/socf.12245.

55. Blum, *Raising Generation Rx*; Amy C. Sousa, "From Refrigerator
    Mothers to Warrior-Heroes: The Cultural Identity Transformation
    of Mothers Raising Children with Intellectual Disabilities," *Symbolic
    Interaction* 34, no. 2 (Spring 2011): 220–43, https://doi.org/10.1525/si.2011
    .34.2.220.

56. Autistic Self Advocacy Network, "About," Autism Acceptance Month:
    Acceptance is an Action, http://www.autismacceptancemonth.com/about/.

57. Mitzi Waltz, "Images and Narratives of Autism within Charity Dis-
    courses," *Disability & Society* 27, no. 2 (2012): 219–33, https://doi.org/10.1080
    /09687599.2012.631796.

58. Sara Luterman, "The Biggest Autism Advocacy Group Is Still Failing Too
    Many Autistic People," *Washington Post*, February 14, 2020, https://www
    .washingtonpost.com/outlook/2020/02/14/biggest-autism-advocacy
    -group-is-still-failing-too-many-autistic-people/.

59. John O. Cooper, Timothy E. Heron, and William L. Heward, *Applied
    Behavior Analysis*, 2nd ed. (Columbus, OH: Merrill Prentice Hall,
    2007), 2.

60. Doreen Granpeesheh, Jonathan Tarbox, and Dennis R. Dixon, "Applied
    Behavior Analytic Interventions for Children with Autism: A Descrip-
    tion and Review of Treatment Research," *Annals of Clinical Psychiatry*
    21, no. 3 (July–September 2009): 162–73, https://pubmed.ncbi.nlm.nih

.gov/19758537/; Richard M. Foxx, "Applied Behavior Analysis Treatment of Autism: The State of the Art," *Child and Adolescent Psychiatric Clinics* 17, no. 4 (October 2008): 821–34, https://doi.org/10.1016/j.chc.2008.06.007.

61. Dennis R. Dixon, Talya Vogel, and Jonathan Tarbox, "A Brief History of Functional Analysis and Applied Behavior Analysis," in *Functional Assessment for Challenging Behaviors and Mental Health Disorders*, ed. Johnny L. Matson (Cham, Switzerland: Springer, 2012), 3–24, https://doi.org/10.1007/978-1-4614-3037-7_2; Cooper, Heron, and Heward, *Applied Behavior Analysis*; Paul R. Fuller, "Operant Conditioning of a Vegetative Human Organism," *American Journal of Psychology* 62, no. 4 (1949): 587–90, https://doi.org/10.2307/1418565.

62. Catherine D. Tan and Gil Eyal, "'Two Opposite Ends of the World': The Management of Uncertainty in an Autism-Only School," *Journal of Contemporary Ethnography* 44, no. 1 (2015): 34–62, https://doi.org/10.1177/0891241613515000.

63. Richard K. Scotch, "Politics and Policy in the History of the Disability Rights Movement," *Milbank Quarterly* 67, suppl 2 (1989): 380–400, https://doi.org/10.2307/3350150; Doris Zames Fleischer and Frieda Zames, *The Disability Rights Movement: From Charity to Confrontation* (Philadelphia: Temple University Press, 2001).

64. Chistina Bosch, "Time to End Public Funding of Judge Rotenberg Center," *Commonwealth Magazine*, April 20, 2021, https://commonwealth magazine.org/education/time-to-end-public-funding-of-judge-roten berg-center/; Jennifer Gonnerman, "31 Shocks Later," *New York Magazine*, August 31, 2012, https://nymag.com/news/features/andre-mccollins -rotenberg-center-2012-9/.

65. Autistic Self Advocacy Network, "#StopTheShock: The Judge Rotenberg Center, Torture, and How We Can Stop It," https://autisticadvocacy .org/actioncenter/issues/school/climate/jrc/.

66. Gonnerman, "31 Shocks Later."

67. The FDA banned the electric shock devices in 2020, but the federal appeals court in Washington, DC, overturned the ban in 2021. Brendan Pierson, "D.C. Circuit Overturns FDA Ban on Shock Device for Disabled Students," Reuters, July 7, 2021, https://www.reuters.com/legal /litigation/dc-circuit-overturns-fda-ban-on-shock-device-disabled-students -2021-07-06/.

68. Nila Sathe et al., "Nutritional and Dietary Interventions for Autism Spectrum Disorder: A Systematic Review," *Pediatrics* 139, no. 6 (June 2017): e20170346, https://doi.org/10.1542/peds.2017-0346; David Fraguas et al., "Dietary Interventions for Autism Spectrum Disorder: A Meta-Analysis," *Pediatrics* 144, no. 5 (November 2019): e20183218, https://doi.org/10.1542/peds.2018-3218.

69. Tara A. Lavelle et al., "Economic Burden of Childhood Autism Spectrum Disorders," *Pediatrics* 133, no. 3 (March 2014): e520–529, https://doi.org/10.1542/peds.2013-0763.

70. Health insurance coverage for autism-related care varies by state. Most will cover screening, diagnosis, and treatment. Treatment can include behavioral health treatment (e.g., applied behavior analysis and early intervention), pharmacy care, psychiatric care, psychological care, and therapeutic care (e.g., speech and language therapy, occupational therapy). See National Conference of State Legislatures, "Autism and Insurance Coverage State Laws," last modified August 24, 2021, https://www.ncsl.org/research/health/autism-and-insurance-coverage-state-laws.aspx.

71. Silverman, *Understanding Autism*.

72. Donna Haraway, "Situated Knowledges: The Science Question in Feminism and the Privilege of Partial Perspective," *Feminist Studies* 14, no. 3 (Autumn 1988): 575–99, https://doi.org/10.2307/3178066.

73. Harmony D. Newman and Laura M. Carpenter, "Embodiment Without Bodies? Analysis of Embodiment in US-Based Pro-Breastfeeding and Anti-Male Circumcision Movements," *Sociology of Health and Illness* 36, no. 5 (June 2014): 639–54, https://doi.org/10.1111/1467-9566.12095.

3. SEEKING HOPE AND SUPPORT

1. Kristin K. Barker, "Electronic Support Groups, Patient-Consumers, and Medicalization: The Case of Contested Illness," *Journal of Health and Social Behavior* 49, no. 1 (March 2008): 20–36, https://doi.org/10.1177/002214650804900103; Jennifer A. Reich, "'We Are Fierce, Independent Thinkers and Intelligent': Social Capital and Stigma Management Among Mothers Who Refuse Vaccines," *Social Science & Medicine* 257 (July 2020): 112015, https://doi.org/10.1016/j.socscimed.2018.10.027; Steven Epstein, *Impure Science: AIDS, Activism, and the Politics of Knowledge*

(Oakland: University of California Press, 1996); Maren Klawiter, *The Biopolitics of Breast Cancer: Changing Cultures of Disease and Activism* (Minneapolis: University of Minnesota Press, 2008).

2. Claire Laurier Decoteau and Meghan Daniel, "Scientific Hegemony and the Field of Autism," *American Sociological Review* 85, no. 3 (May 2020): 451–76, https://doi.org/10.1177/000312242092253; Jennifer S. Singh, *Multiple Autisms: Spectrums of Advocacy and Genomic Science* (Minneapolis: University of Minnesota Press, 2016).

3. Mary Langan, "Parental Voices and Controversies in Autism," *Disability & Society* 26, no. 2 (February 2011): 193–205, https://doi.org/10.1080/09687599.2011.544059; Ginny Russell and Susan Kelly, "Looking Beyond Risk: A Study of Lay Epidemiology of Childhood Disorders," *Health, Risk & Society* 13, no. 2 (2011): 129–45, https://doi.org/10.1080/13698575.2010.515738.

4. Singh, *Multiple Autisms*; John Donvan and Caren Zucker, *In a Different Key: The Story of Autism* (New York: Crown, 2016).

5. Jocelyn S. Viterna, "Pulled, Pushed, and Persuaded: Explaining Women's Mobilization Into the Salvadoran Guerrilla Army," *American Journal of Sociology* 112, no. 1 (July 2006): 1–45, https://doi.org/10.1086/502690; Doug McAdam, "Recruitment to High-Risk Activism: The Case of Freedom Summer," *American Journal of Sociology* 92, no. 1 (July 1986): 64–90, http://www.jstor.org/stable/2779717; Bert Klandermans, "Mobilization and Participation: Social-Psychological Expansions of Resource Mobilization Theory," *American Sociological Review* 59, no. 5 (1984): 583–600, https://doi.org/10.2307/2095417.

6. Santosh Vijaykumar, Ricardo J. Wray, Trent Buskirk, Himakshi Piplani, Joya Banerjee, Michael Furdyk, and Reshma Pattni, "Youth, New Media, and HIV/AIDS: Determinants of Participation in an Online Health Social Movement," *Cyberpsychology, Behavior, and Social Networking* 17, no. 7 (July 2014): 488–95, https://doi.org/10.1089/cyber.2013.0124.

7. Joseph Dumit, "Illnesses You Have to Fight to Get: Facts as Forces in Uncertain, Emergent Illnesses," *Social Science & Medicine* 62, no. 3 (February 2006): 577–90, https://doi.org/10.1016/j.socscimed.2005.06.018; Klawiter, *Biopolitics of Breast Cancer*; Phil Brown, *Toxic Exposures: Contested Illnesses and the Environmental Health Movement* (New York: Columbia University Press, 2007); Epstein, *Impure Science*.

8. Erving Goffman, "The Moral Career of the Mental Patient," *Psychiatry* 22, no. 2 (1959): 123–42; Erving Goffman, *Asylums: Essays on the Social Situation of Mental Patients and Other Inmates* (Piscataway, NJ: Aldine Transaction, 1961).

9. Described on the MAPS website, the organization hosts "CME [continuing medical education] conferences to help medical professionals understand, explore, and share the underlying concepts and findings associated with integrative pediatrics and care of those that have outgrown the pediatric label," https://www.medmaps.org/.

10. Mandy Abbott, Paul Bernard, and Jenny Forge, "Communicating a Diagnosis of Autism Spectrum Disorder—A Qualitative Study of Parents' Experiences," *Clinical Child Psychology and Psychiatry* 18, no. 3 (July 2013): 370–82, https://doi.org/10.1177/1359104512455813; Aspasia Stacey Rabba, Cheryl Dissanayake, and Josephine Barbaro, "Parents' Experiences of an Early Autism Diagnosis: Insights Into Their Needs," *Research in Autism Spectrum Disorders* 66 (October 2019): 101415, https://doi.org/10.1016/j.rasd.2019.101415.

11. Richard M. Foxx, "Applied Behavior Analysis Treatment of Autism: The State of the Art," *Child and Adolescent Psychiatric Clinics* 17, no. 4 (October 2008): 821–34, https://doi.org/10.1016/j.chc.2008.06.007; Johnny L. Matson et al., "Applied Behavior Analysis in Autism Spectrum Disorders: Recent Developments, Strengths, and Pitfalls," *Research in Autism Spectrum Disorders* 6, no. 1 (January–March 2012): 144–50, https://doi.org/10.1016/j.rasd.2011.03.014; Nienke Peters-Scheffer, Robert Didden, Hubert Korzilius, and Peter Sturmey, "A Meta-Analytic Study on the Effectiveness of Comprehensive ABA-Based Early Intervention Programs for Children with Autism Spectrum Disorders," *Research in Autism Spectrum Disorders* 5, no. 1 (January–March 2011): 60–69, https://doi.org/10.1016/j.rasd.2010.03.011.

12. Ole Ivar Lovaas, "Behavioral Treatment and Normal Education and Intellectual Functioning in Young Autistic Children," *Journal of Consulting and Clinical Psychology* 55 (February 1987): 7, https://doi.org/10.1037//0022-006x.55.1.3.

13. Phil Brown et al., "Embodied Health Movements: New Approaches to Social Movements in Health," *Sociology of Health & Illness* 26, no. 1 (January 2004): 50–80, https://doi.org/10.1111/j.1467-9566.2004.00378.x.

14. Andrew Szasz, *Shopping Our Way to Safety: How We Change from Protecting the Environment to Protecting Ourselves* (Minneapolis: University of Minnesota Press, 2007).

15. Sally J. Rogers and Laurie A. Vismara, "Evidence-Based Comprehensive Treatments for Early Autism," *Journal of Clinical Child & Adolescent Psychology* 37, no. 1 (January 2008): 8–38, https://doi.org/10.1080/15374410701817808; Jessica R. Steinbrenner et al., *Evidence-Based Practices for Children, Youth, and Young Adults with Autism* (Chapel Hill, NC: Frank Porter Graham Child Development Institute, 2020); Jennifer A. Reich, *Calling the Shots: Why Parents Reject Vaccines* (New York: New York University Press, 2016).

16. Although there is limited demographic data on families who actively participate in the alternative biomedical movement, other studies find that complementary and alternative medicine use for the treatment of autism is more common among non-Hispanic white families. See Kathleen Pillsbury Hopf, Eric Madren, and Kirsten A. Santianni, "Use and Perceived Effectiveness of Complementary and Alternative Medicine to Treat and Manage the Symptoms of Autism in Children: A Survey of Parents in a Community Population," *Journal of Alternative and Complementary Medicine* 22, no. 2 (2015): 25–32, https://doi.org/10.1089/acm.2015.0163; Ashli A. Owen-Smith et al., "Prevalence and Predictors of Complementary and Alternative Medicine Use in a Large Insured Sample of Children with Autism Spectrum Disorders," *Research in Autism Spectrum Disorders* 17 (September 2015): 40–51, https://doi.org/10.1016/j.rasd.2015.05.002; James M. Perrin et al., "Complementary and Alternative Medicine Use in a Large Pediatric Autism Sample," *Pediatrics* 130, suppl 2 (November 2012): S77–82, https://doi.org/10.1542/peds.2012-0900E.

17. Jennifer Randles, "'Willing to Do Anything for My Kids': Inventive Mothering, Diapers, and the Inequalities of Carework," *American Sociological Review* 86, no. 1 (2021): 35–59, https://doi.org/10.1177/0003122420977480; Dorothy Roberts, *Shattered Bonds: The Color of Child Welfare* (New York: Civitas, 2009).

18. Of course, there are underresourced families who use alternative biomedicine. In her book *The Western Disease: Contesting Autism in the Somali Diaspora*, Claire Decoteau examines Somali refugees in Toronto and Minneapolis who use alternative biomedical treatment. Their knowledge

about and approaches to autism were shaped by experiences with forced migration, discrimination, and the Western lifestyle. See Claire Laurier Decoteau, *The Western Disease: Contesting Autism in the Somali Diaspora* (Chicago: University of Chicago Press, 2021).

19. Access to autistic communities can be prohibited by disability (i.e., not having the appropriate support to navigate the internet) and social and material resources (i.e., not having transportation to participate in person).

20. Meng-Chuan Lai and Simon Baron-Cohen, "Identifying the Lost Generation of Adults with Autism Spectrum Conditions," *Lancet Psychiatry* 2, no. 11 (November 2015): 1013–27, https://doi.org/10.1016/s2215 -0366(15)00277-1.

21. Fred R. Volkmar, Brian Reichow, and James McPartland, "Classification of Autism and Related Conditions: Progress, Challenges, and Opportunities," *Dialogues in Clinical Neuroscience* 14, no. 3 (2012): 229–37, https://doi.org/10.31887/DCNS.2012.14.3/fvolkmar.

22. Volkmar, Reichow, and McPartland, "Classification of Autism."

23. Yunhe Huang et al., "Diagnosis of Autism in Adulthood: A Scoping Review," *Autism* 24, no. 6 (August 2020): 1311–27, https://doi.org/10.1177 /1362361320903128.

24. A 2021 study estimates that almost half (42.8 percent) of autistic people have average or high IQ. See Maja Z. Katusic et al., "IQ in Autism Spectrum Disorder: A Population-Based Birth Cohort Study," *Pediatrics* 148, no. 6 (2021): e2020049899, https://doi.org/10.1542/peds.2020-049899.

25. David S. Mandell, Maytali M. Novak, and Cynthia D. Zubritsky, "Factors Associated with Age of Diagnosis Among Children with Autism Spectrum Disorders," *Pediatrics* 116, no. 6 (December 2005): 1480–86, https://doi.org/10.1542/peds.2005-0185.

26. Francesca G. Happé et al., "Demographic and Cognitive Profile of Individuals Seeking a Diagnosis of Autism Spectrum Disorder in Adulthood," *Journal of Autism and Developmental Disorders* 46, no. 11 (November 2016): 3469–80, https://doi.org/10.1007/s10803-016-2886-2.

27. Matthew J. Maenner et al., "Prevalence of Autism Spectrum Disorder Among Children Aged 8 Years—Autism and Developmental Disabilities Monitoring Network, 11 Sites, United States, 2016," *MMWR Surveillance Summaries* 69, no. 4 (March 2020): 1–12, https://doi.org/10.15585/mmwr .ss6904a1; Kathryn A. Smith et al., "Disparities in Service Use Among

Children with Autism: A Systematic Review," *Pediatrics* 145, suppl 1 (April 2020): S35–46, https://doi.org/10.1542/peds.2019-1895g.

28. Maenner et al., "Prevalence of Autism Spectrum Disorder."

29. Meng-Chuan Lai et al., "Sex/Gender Differences and Autism: Setting the Scene for Future Research," *Journal of the American Academy of Child & Adolescent Psychiatry* 54, no. 1 (January 2015): 11–24, https://doi.org/10.1016/j.jaac.2014.10.003.

30. Pauline Thomas et al., "The Association of Autism Diagnosis with Socioeconomic Status," *Autism* 16, no. 2 (March 2012): 1–13, https://doi.org/10.1177/1362361311413397v.

31. Maenner et al., "Prevalence of Autism Spectrum Disorder."

32. Happé et al., "Demographic and Cognitive Profile"; Huang et al., "Diagnosis of Autism in Adulthood."

33. Comparatively, in the United Kingdom, respondents named cost as the least severe barrier to accessing an autism diagnostic evaluation in adulthood. See Laura Foran Lewis, "A Mixed Methods Study of Barriers to Formal Diagnosis of Autism Spectrum Disorder in Adults," *Journal of Autism and Developmental Disorders* 47, no. 8 (August 2017): 2410–24, https://doi.org/10.1007/s10803-017-3168-3.

34. As might be imagined, there are greater socioeconomic disparities among adult than pediatric populations because private insurances tend to stop covering autism-related services after age 21, which means adults seeking diagnosis are more often in the position of paying out of pocket. See National Conference of State Legislatures, "Autism and Insurance Coverage State Laws," last modified August 24, 2021, https://www.ncsl.org/research/health/autism-and-insurance-coverage-state-laws.aspx.

35. Annemarie Jutel, *Putting a Name to It: Diagnosis in Contemporary Society* (Baltimore, MD: Johns Hopkins University Press, 2011); Phil Brown, "Naming and Framing: The Social Construction of Diagnosis and Illness," *Journal of Health and Social Behavior* 35, extra issue (1995): 34–52, https://doi.org/10.2307/2626956.

36. Now renamed the Asperger/Autism Network.

37. Catherine D. Tan, "'I'm a Normal Autistic Person, Not an Abnormal Neurotypical': Autism Spectrum Disorder Diagnosis as Biographical Illumination," *Social Science & Medicine* 197 (January 2018): 161–67, https://doi.org/10.1016/j.socscimed.2017.12.008.

4. KNOWING ONE'S TRIBE

1. Allison B. Cunningham and Laura Schreibman, "Stereotypy in Autism: The Importance of Function," *Research in Autism Spectrum Disorders* 2, no. 3 (July–September 2008): 469–79, https://doi.org/10.1016/j.rasd.2007.09.006.

2. Francesca Polletta, "'Free Spaces' in Collective Action," *Theory and Society* 28, no. 1 (February 1999): 1–38, https://www.jstor.org/stable/3108504; Verta Taylor and Nancy E. Whittier, "Collective Identity in Social Movement Communities: Lesbian Feminist Mobilization," in *Frontiers in Social Movements Theory*, ed. Aldon D. Morris and Carol McClurg Mueller (New Haven, CT: Yale University Press, 1992), 104–29; Robert Futrell and Pete Simi, "Free Spaces, Collective Identity, and the Persistence of US White Power Activism," *Social Problems* 51, no. 1 (February 2004): 16–42, https://doi.org/10.1525/sp.2004.51.1.16; Sara M. Evans and Harry C. Boyte, *Free Spaces: The Sources of Democratic Change in America* (Chicago: University of Chicago Press, 1986).

3. John Donvan and Caren Zucker, *In a Different Key: The Story of Autism* (New York: Crown, 2016); Chloe Silverman, *Understanding Autism: Parents, Doctors, and the History of a Disorder* (Princeton, NJ: Princeton University Press, 2011); Jennifer S. Singh, *Multiple Autisms: Spectrums of Advocacy and Genomic Science* (Minneapolis: University of Minnesota Press, 2016).

4. Jim Sinclair, "History of ANI," Autism Network International, January 2005, http://www.autreat.com/History_of_ANI.html.

5. Sinclair, "History of ANI."

6. Peter Conrad, Julia Bandini, and Alexandra Vasquez, "Illness and the Internet: From Private to Public Experience," *Health* 20, no. 1 (2016): 22–32, https://doi.org/10.1177/1363459315611941.

7. Chloe J. Jordan, "Evolution of Autism Support and Understanding via the World Wide Web," *Intellectual and Developmental Disabilities* 48, no. 3 (June 2010): 220–27, https://doi.org/10.1352/1934-9556-48.3.220.

8. Joyce Davidson, "Autistic Culture Online: Virtual Communication and Cultural Expression on the Spectrum," *Social & Cultural Geography* 9, no. 7 (2008): 791–806, https://doi.org/10.1080/14649360802382586.

9. Sinclair, "History of ANI."

10. Taylor and Whittier, "Collective Identity"; Bernd Simon and Bert Klandermans, "Politicized Collective Identity: A Social Psychological Analysis," *American Psychologist* 56, no. 4 (April 2001): 319–31, https://doi.org/10.1037/0003-066X.56.4.319.

11. Autistic Self Advocacy Network, "About," Autism Acceptance Month: Acceptance Is an Action, http://www.autismacceptancemonth.com /about/.

12. Joanne Kaufman, "Ransom-Note Ads About Children's Health Are Canceled," *New York Times*, December 20, 2007, https://www.nytimes.com /2007/12/20/business/media/20child.html.

13. Ari Ne'eman, "An Urgent Call to Action: Tell NYU Child Study Center to Abandon Stereotypes Against People with Disabilities," Autistic Self Advocacy Network, December 8, 2007, http://autisticadvocacy .org/2007/12/tell-nyu-child-study-center-to-abandon-stereotypes/.

14. Hans Asperger called the patients from his 1944 study "little professor" because of their deep knowledge on specific topics of interest.

15. Phil Brown et al., "Embodied Health Movements: New Approaches to Social Movements in Health," *Sociology of Health & Illness* 26, no. 1 (January 2004): 60, https://doi.org/10.1111/j.1467-9566.2004.00378.x.

16. Phil Brown et al., "The Health Politics of Asthma: Environmental Justice and Collective Illness Experience in the United States," in *The Sociology of Health and Illness: Critical Perspectives*, 9th ed., ed. Peter Conrad and Valerie Leiter (New York: Worth, 2012); Steven Epstein, *Impure Science: AIDS, Activism, and the Politics of Knowledge* (Oakland: University of California Press, 1996); Maren Klawiter, *The Biopolitics of Breast Cancer: Changing Cultures of Disease and Activism* (Minneapolis: University of Minnesota Press, 2008).

17. Joanne McCann and Sue Peppé, "Prosody in Autism Spectrum Disorders: A Critical Review," *International Journal of Language & Communication Disorders* 38, no. 4 (October–December 2003): 325–50, https://doi.org/10 .1080/1368282031000154204; Sarai Holbrook and Megan Israelsen, "Speech Prosody Interventions for Persons with Autism Spectrum Disorders: A Systematic Review," *American Journal of Speech-Language Pathology* 29, no. 4 (November 2020): 2189–2205, https://doi.org/10.1044/2020_ajslp-19-00127.

18. Anne-Marie R. Depape et al., "Use of Prosody and Information Structure in High Functioning Adults with Autism in Relation to

Language Ability," *Frontiers in Psychology* 3 (March 2012): 72, https://doi.org/10.3389/fpsyg.2012.00072.

19. Hyun Uk Kim, "Autism Across Cultures: Rethinking Autism," *Disability & Society* 27, no. 4 (2012): 535–45, https://doi.org/10.1080/09687599.2012.659463.

20. Kristin K. Barker, "Electronic Support Groups, Patient-Consumers, and Medicalization: The Case of Contested Illness," *Journal of Health and Social Behavior* 49, no. 1 (March 2008): 20–36, https://doi.org/10.1177/002214650804900103; Jennifer A. Reich, "'We Are Fierce, Independent Thinkers and Intelligent': Social Capital and Stigma Management Among Mothers Who Refuse Vaccines," *Social Science & Medicine* 257 (July 2020): 112015, https://doi.org/10.1016/j.socscimed.2018.10.027; Joseph Dumit, "Illnesses You Have to Fight to Get: Facts as Forces in Uncertain, Emergent Illnesses," *Social Science & Medicine* 62, no. 3 (February 2006): 577–90, https://doi.org/10.1016/j.socscimed.2005.06.018.

21. Sinclair, "History of ANI."

22. Sinclair, "History of ANI."

23. Julia Bascom, *The Obsessive Joy of Autism* (London: Jessica Kingsley, 2015).

24. After respecting their boundaries and proving that I was not a "fly-by interviewer," an exception was made for me. See chapter 1 for the discussion on field access.

25. To increase inclusion, autistic attendees were allowed to bring caregivers and support aids.

26. Sinclair, "History of ANI."

27. "Hiding cave" was used instead of "quiet room," which evokes negative associations with behavioral therapy.

28. Emphasis added.

29. There is limited research on the internet use of certain autistic subpopulations, including autistic women, transgendered autistic people, nonwhite autistic people, low-income autistic people, and minimally speaking and/or autistic adults with co-occurring intellectual disability. See Elizabeth McGhee Hassrick et al., "Benefits and Risks: A Systematic Review of Information and Communication Technology Use by Autistic People," *Autism in Adulthood* 3, no. 1 (March 2021): 72–84, https://doi.org/10.1089/aut.2020.0048.

30. Autistic Self Advocacy Network, "All Aboard! ASAN 2021 Annual Report," https://autisticadvocacy.org/wp-content/uploads/2021/11/All-Aboard -ASAN-Annual-Report-2021.pdf.

31. Matthew S. McCoy et al., "Ethical Advocacy Across the Autism Spectrum: Beyond Partial Representation," *American Journal of Bioethics* 20, no. 4 (May 2020): 13–24, https://doi.org/10.1080/15265161.2020.173 0482; Allison C. Carey, Pamela Block, and Richard Scotch, *Allies and Obstacles: Disability Activism and Parents of Children with Disabilities* (Philadelphia: Temple University Press, 2020).

32. Ian Hacking, *The Social Construction of What?* (Cambridge, MA: Harvard University Press, 1999); Majia Holmer Nadesan, *Constructing Autism: Unravelling the 'Truth' and Understanding the Social* (London: Routledge, 2005).

33. Daniel Navon and Gil Eyal, "Looping Genomes: Diagnostic Change and the Genetic Makeup of the Autism Population," *American Journal of Sociology* 121, no. 5 (March 2016): 1416–71, https://doi.org/10.1086/684201.

34. Fred R. Volkmar, Brian Reichow, and James McPartland, "Classification of Autism and Related Conditions: Progress, Challenges, and Opportunities," *Dialogues in Clinical Neuroscience* 14, no. 3 (2012): 229–37, https://doi.org/10.31887/DCNS.2012.14.3/fvolkmar.

5. LABORATORIES AND EXPERIMENTATION

1. Alex Hannaford, "Andrew Wakefield: Autism Inc.," *Guardian*, April 6, 2013, https://www.theguardian.com/society/2013/apr/06/what-happened -man-mmr-panic.

2. Michelle Murphy, *Sick Building Syndrome and the Problem of Uncertainty: Environmental Politics, Technoscience, and Women Workers* (Durham, NC: Duke University Press, 2006).

3. Murphy, *Sick Building Syndrome*.

4. In the case of sick building syndrome, Murphy illustrates how toxicology and popular epidemiology, two conflicting regimes of perceptibility, have different ways of assessing toxic exposure.

5. Martine D. Lappé, "The Maternal Body as Environment in Autism Science," *Social Studies of Science* 6, no. 4 (October 2016): 675–700, https:// doi.org/10.1177/0306312716659372.

6. Kyle Strimbu and Jorge A. Tavel, "What Are Biomarkers?," *Current Opinion in HIV and AIDS* 5, no. 6 (November 2010): 464, https://doi.org/10.1097/COH.ob013e32833ed177.

7. Interagency Autism Coordinating Committee, "Autism Research Database," U.S. Department of Health and Human Services, https://iacc.hhs.gov/funding/data/.

8. George M. Anderson, "Autism Biomarkers: Challenges, Pitfalls and Possibilities," *Journal of Autism and Developmental Disorders* 45, no. 4 (2015): 1103–13, https://doi.org/10.1007/s10803-014-2225-4; Pat Walsh et al., "In Search of Biomarkers for Autism: Scientific, Social and Ethical Challenges," *Nature Reviews Neuroscience* 12, no. 10 (2011): 603–12, https://doi.org/10.1038/nrn3113.

9. Walsh et al., "In Search of Biomarkers."

10. Walsh et al., "In Search of Biomarkers."

11. Claire Laurier Decoteau and Kelly Underman, "Adjudicating Non-Knowledge in the Omnibus Autism Proceedings," *Social Studies of Science* 45, no. 4 (2015): 471–500, https://doi.org/10.1177/0306312715600278.

12. Decoteau and Underman, "Adjudicating Non-Knowledge"; Claire Laurier Decoteau and Meghan Daniel, "Scientific Hegemony and the Field of Autism," *American Sociological Review* 85, no. 3 (May 2020): 451–76, https://doi.org/10.1177/000312242092253.

13. Chloe Silverman, *Understanding Autism: Parents, Doctors, and the History of a Disorder* (Princeton, NJ: Princeton University Press, 2011); Jennifer S. Singh, *Multiple Autisms: Spectrums of Advocacy and Genomic Science* (Minneapolis: University of Minnesota Press, 2016).

14. Decoteau and Daniel, "Scientific Hegemony."

15. Harmony D. Newman and Laura M. Carpenter, "Embodiment Without Bodies? Analysis of Embodiment in US-Based Pro-Breastfeeding and Anti-Male Circumcision Movements," *Sociology of Health and Illness* 36, no. 5 (June 2014): 639–54, https://doi.org/10.1111/1467-9566.12095.

16. Institute of Medicine, *Immunization Safety Review: Vaccines and Autism* (Washington, DC: National Academies Press, 2004), https://www.nap.edu/catalog/10997/immunization-safety-review-vaccines-and-autism.

17. Susanne Dalsgaard Reventlow, Lotte Hvas, and Kirsti Malterud, "Making the Invisible Body Visible: Bone Scans, Osteoporosis and Women's

Bodily Experiences," *Social Science & Medicine* 62, no. 11 (June 2006): 2720–31, https://doi.org/10.1016/j.socscimed.2005.11.009.

18. Kirsten Bell, "Biomarkers, the Molecular Gaze and the Transformation of Cancer Survivorship," *BioSocieties* 8, no. 2 (2013): 124–43, http://dx .doi.org/10.1057/biosoc.2013.6.

19. In 2019, the organization renamed itself The Autism Community in Action (TACA).

20. National Institute of Biomedical Imaging and Bioengineering, "Nuclear Medicine," U.S. Department of Health and Human Services, last modified July 2016, https://www.nibib.nih.gov/science-education /science-topics/nuclear-medicine#1006.

21. Neely Tucker, "Daniel Amen Is the Most Popular Psychiatrist in America. To Most Researchers and Scientists, That's a Very Bad Thing," *Washington Post*, August 9, 2012, https://www.washingtonpost.com/lifestyle /magazine/daniel-amen-is-the-most-popular-psychiatrist-in-america -to-most-researchers-and-scientists-thats-a-very-bad-thing/2012/08/07 /467ed52c-c540-11e1-8c16-5080b717c13e_story.html; Robert Burton, "Brain Scam," *Salon*, May 12, 2008, http://www.salon.com/2008/05/12/daniel _amen/.

22. U.S. Environmental Protection Agency, "America's Children and the Environment (ACE): Biomonitoring—Lead," last modified June 29, 2022, https://www.epa.gov/americaschildrenenvironment/biomonitoring-lead.

23. U.S. Food and Drug Administration, "Danger: Don't Drink Miracle Mineral Solution or Similar Products," Consumer Updates, last modified August 12, 2019, accessed June 12, 2023, https://www.fda.gov/consumers /consumer-updates/danger-dont-drink-miracle-mineral-solution-or -similar-products.

24. Jonathan Gabe, Gillian Olumide, and Michael Bury, "'It Takes Three to Tango': A Framework for Understanding Patient Partnership in Paediatric Clinics," *Social Science & Medicine* 59, no. 5 (September 2004): 1071–79, https://doi.org/10.1016/j.socscimed.2003.09.035.

25. Michelle O'Reilly et al., "Parents' Constructions of Normality and Pathology in Child Mental Health Assessments," *Sociology of Health & Illness* 42, no. 3 (March 2020): 544–64, https://doi.org/10.1111/1467 -9566.13030; Tanya Stivers, "Participating in Decisions About Treatment: Overt Parent Pressure for Antibiotic Medication in Pediatric

Encounters," *Social Science & Medicine* 54, no. 7 (April 2002): 1111–30, https://doi.org/10.1016/S0277-9536(01)00085-5; Anny T. Fenton, "Abandoning Medical Authority: When Medical Professionals Confront Stigmatized Adolescent Sex and the Human Papillomavirus (HPV) Vaccine," *Journal of Health and Social Behavior* 60, no. 2 (2019): 240–56, https://doi.org/10.1177/0022146519849895; Amanda M. Gengler, "'I Want You to Save My Kid!': Illness Management Strategies, Access, and Inequality at an Elite University Research Hospital," *Journal of Health and Social Behavior* 55, no. 3 (2014): 342–59, https://doi.org/10.1177/0022146514544172.

26. Brendan Hart, "Autism Parents & Neurodiversity: Radical Translation, Joint Embodiment and the Prosthetic Environment," *BioSocieties* 9, no. 3 (September 2014): 284–303, https://doi.org/10.1057/biosoc.2014.20; Nevena Dimitrova, Şeyda Özçalışkan, and Lauren B. Adamson, "Parents' Translations of Child Gesture Facilitate Word Learning in Children with Autism, Down Syndrome and Typical Development," *Journal of Autism and Developmental Disorders* 46, no. 1 (January 2016): 221–31, https://doi.org/10.1007/s10803-015-2566-7.

27. Melanie Yergeau, "Clinically Significant Disturbance: On Theorists Who Theorize Theory of Mind," *Disability Studies Quarterly* 33, no. 4 (2013), https://doi.org/10.18061/dsq.v33i4.3876.

28. Silverman, *Understanding Autism.*

29. A nonpharmacy dispensing site (taxonomy code #332900000X) is, by definition, "a site other than a pharmacy that dispenses medicinal preparations under the supervision of a physician to patients for self-administration (e.g., physician offices, ER, Urgent Care Centers, Rural Health Facilities, etc.)," https://npidb.org/taxonomy/332900000X/.

30. Compound pharmacies customize medication for individual patients who cannot take an FDA-approved drug. There are many reasons why some patients require a compounded drug, like allergy to an ingredient in the FDA-approved drug. Compounded drugs are not FDA approved. Physicians who compound drugs are exempt from Current Good Manufacturing Practice requirements, which means their drugs are not subjected to the high quality and safety standards of drugs produced on a large scale.

31. Centers for Disease Control and Prevention, "Facts About ASD," last modified December 9, 2022, http://www.cdc.gov/ncbddd/autism/facts.html.

32. In conventional practice, it is not uncommon for doctors to prescribe drugs like antidepressants, stimulants, tranquilizers/antipsychotics, anticonvulsants, hypotensive agents, anxiolytic/sedative/hypnotics, and benzodiazepines to manage comorbid conditions for autistic patients. See Donald P. Oswald and Neil A. Sonenklar, "Medication Use Among Children with Autism Spectrum Disorders," *Journal of Child and Adolescent Psychopharmacology* 17, no. 3 (June 2007): 348–55, https://doi.org/10.1089/cap .2006.17303. See also Jon Pangborn and Sidney MacDonald Baker, *Autism: Effective Biomedical Treatments* (San Diego, CA: Autism Research Institute, 2005).

33. Jennifer A. Reich, "Vaccine Refusal and Pharmaceutical Acquiescence: Parental Control and Ambivalence in Managing Children's Health," *American Sociological Review* 85, no. 1 (2020): 106–27, https://doi.org /10.1177/0003122419899604.

34. Nila Sathe et al., "Nutritional and Dietary Interventions for Autism Spectrum Disorder: A Systematic Review," *Pediatrics* 139, no. 6 (June 2017): e20170346, https://doi.org/10.1542/peds.2017-0346.

35. Marco Ruggiero, Heinz Reinwald, and Stefania Pacini, "Is Chondroitin Sulfate Responsible for the Biological Effects Attributed to the GC Protein-Derived Macrophage Activating Factor (GcMAF)?," *Medical Hypotheses* 94 (September 2016): 126–31, https://doi.org/10.1016/j.mehy .2016.07.012.

36. Edna F. Einsiedel and Hannah Adamson, "Stem Cell Tourism and Future Stem Cell Tourists: Policy and Ethical Implications," *Developing World Bioethics* 12, no. 1 (April 2012): 35–44, https://doi.org/10.1111/j.1471 -8847.2012.00319.x; Samantha Lyons, Shival Salgaonkar, and Gerard T. Flaherty, "International Stem Cell Tourism: A Critical Literature Review and Evidence-Based Recommendations," *International Health* 14, no. 2 (March 2022): 132–41, https://doi.org/10.1093/inthealth/ihab050.

37. Honor Whiteman, "Stem Cell Therapy: Is the US Missing a Trick?," *Medical News Today*, last modified February 25, 2016, https://www.medical newstoday.com/articles/306974.

38. Michelle Ibarra, "Why Should You Travel to Cancun for SCT?," World Stem Cells Clinic, July 21, 2019, https://worldstemcellsclinic.com/blog /why-should-you-travel-to-cancun-for-sct.

39. Lyons, Salgaonkar, and Flaherty, "International Stem Cell Tourism."

40. ABA operates on the principles of reinforcing desired behaviors and extinguishing undesirable behaviors. See Doreen Granpeesheh, Jonathan Tarbox, and Dennis R. Dixon, "Applied Behavior Analytic Interventions for Children with Autism: A Description and Review of Treatment Research," *Annals of Clinical Psychiatry* 21, no. 3 (July–September 2009): 162–73, https://pubmed.ncbi.nlm.nih.gov/19758537/; Richard M. Foxx, "Applied Behavior Analysis Treatment of Autism: The State of the Art," *Child and Adolescent Psychiatric Clinics* 17, no. 4 (October 2008): 821–34, https://doi.org/10.1016/j.chc.2008.06.007.

41. Stanley I. Greenspan and Serena Wieder, *Engaging Autism: Using the Floortime Approach to Help Children Relate, Communicate, and Think* (Boston: Da Capo Lifelong Books, 2006); O. Ivar Lovaas and Tristram Smith, "Early and Intensive Behavioral Intervention in Autism," in *Evidence-Based Psychotherapies for Children and Adolescents*, ed. John R. Weisz and Alan E. Kazdin (New York: Guilford, 2003), 325–40; John O. Cooper, Timothy E. Heron, and William L. Heward, *Applied Behavior Analysis*, 2nd ed. (Columbus, OH: Merrill Prentice Hall, 2007).

42. Trine Tsouderos, " 'Miracle Drug' Called Junk Science," *Chicago Tribune*, May 21, 2009, https://www.chicagotribune.com/lifestyles/health/chi-autism-lupron-may21-story.html.

43. Bernard Rimland and Stephen M. Edelson, "Autism Treatment Evaluation Checklist," Autism Research Institute, https://autism.org/autism-treatment-evaluation-checklist/.

44. Deborah A. Kennedy, Kieran Cooley, Thomas R. Einarson, and Dugald Seely, "Objective Assessment of an Ionic Footbath (IonCleanse): Testing Its Ability to Remove Potentially Toxic Elements from the Body," *Journal of Environmental and Public Health* 2012 (2012): 258968, https://doi.org/10.1155/2012/258968.

45. Ben Whalley and Michael E. Hyland, "Placebo by Proxy: The Effect of Parents' Beliefs on Therapy for Children's Temper Tantrums," *Journal of Behavioral Medicine* 36, no. 4 (2013): 341–46, https://doi.org/10.1007/s10865-012-9429-x.

46. Linda Blum, *Raising Generation Rx: Mothering Kids with Invisible Disabilities in an Age of Inequality* (New York: New York University Press, 2015); Susan L. Parish et al., "Material Hardship in US Families Raising Children with Disabilities," *Exceptional Children* 75, no. 1 (2008): 71–92,

https://doi.org/10.1177/00144029080750104;SusanL.Parishetal.,"Economic Implications of Caregiving at Midlife: Comparing Parents with and Without Children Who Have Developmental Disabilities," *Mental Retardation* 42, no. 6 (December 2004): 413–26, https://pubmed.ncbi .nlm.nih.gov/15516174/.

47. Petronella Grootens-Wiegers et al., "Medical Decision-Making in Children and Adolescents: Developmental and Neuroscientific Aspects," *BMC Pediatrics* 17, no. 1 (2017): 1–10, https://doi.org/10.1186/s12887 -017-0869-x; Vida Jeremic et al., "Participation of Children in Medical Decision-Making: Challenges and Potential Solutions," *Journal of Bioethical Inquiry* 13, no. 4 (December 2016): 525–34, https://doi.org/10 .1007/s11673-016-9747-8.

6. THE OUTSIDERS

1. Deborah L. Shelton, "Autism Doctor Loses License in Illinois, Missouri," *Chicago Tribune*, November 5, 2012, https://www.chicagotribune.com /news/ct-xpm-2012-11-05-ct-met-autism-doctor-20121106-story.html; Trine Tsouderos, "'Miracle Drug' Called Junk Science," *Chicago Tribune*, May 21, 2009, https://www.chicagotribune.com/lifestyles/health/chi -autism-lupron-may21-story.html.

2. Patricia Callahan, "Naperville Doctor Disciplined in Controversial Autism Case," *Chicago Tribune*, December 30, 2014, https://www.chicago tribune.com/lifestyles/health/ct-autism-anjum-usman-discipline-met -20141229-story.html.

3. Tara Haelle, "Dr. Bob Sears Could Lose License for Medical Negligence—Not Vaccine Choice," *Forbes*, last modified September 11, 2016, https://www.forbes.com/sites/tarahaelle/2016/09/11/dr-bob-sears -could-lose-license-for-medical-negligence-not-vaccine-choice /#74962e4625f6; Elissa Strauss, "Leading Vaccination Skeptic Dr. Bob Sears Is at Risk of Losing His Medical License," *Slate*, September 15, 2016, http://www.slate.com/blogs/xx_factor/2016/09/15/leading_vaccination _skeptic_dr_bob_sears_is_at_risk_of_losing_his_medical.html.

4. Gil Eyal, "For a Sociology of Expertise: The Social Origins of the Autism Epidemic," *American Journal of Sociology* 118, no. 4 (January 2013): 863–907, https://doi.org/10.1086/668448.

5. Thomas F. Gieryn, *Cultural Boundaries of Science: Credibility on the Line* (Chicago: University of Chicago Press, 1999); Verta Taylor and Nancy E. Whittier, "Collective Identity in Social Movement Communities: Lesbian Feminist Mobilization," in *Frontiers in Social Movements Theory*, ed. Aldon D. Morris and Carol McClurg Mueller (New Haven, CT: Yale University Press, 1992), 104–29; Paige L. Sweet and Danielle Giffort, "The Bad Expert," *Social Studies of Science* 51, no. 3 (2021): 313–38, https://doi.org/10.1177/0306312720970282.

6. Gieryn, *Cultural Boundaries*; Sheila Jasanoff, "Contested Boundaries in Policy-Relevant Science," *Social Studies of Science* 17, no. 2 (May 1987): 195–230, https://doi.org/10.1177/030631287017002001; Andrew Abbott, *The System of Professions: An Essay on the Division of Expert Labor* (Chicago: University of Chicago Press, 1988).

7. Pierre Bourdieu, *Science of Science and Reflexivity* (Chicago: University of Chicago Press, 2004); Pierre Bourdieu and Loïc J. D. Wacquant, "The Logic of Fields," in *An Invitation to Reflexive Sociology*, ed. Pierre Bourdieu and Loïc J. D. Wacquant (Chicago: University of Chicago Press, 1992), 94–114; Alberto Melucci, "The Process of Collective Identity," in *Social Movements and Culture*, ed. Hank Johnston and Bert Klandermans (Minneapolis: University of Minnesota Press, 1995), 41–63.

8. Zoe Gross, "Foreword: Killing Words," in "Anti-Filicide Toolkit," Autistic Self Advocacy Network, 3–4, last modified January 2022, http://autistic advocacy.org/wp-content/uploads/2015/01/ASAN-Anti-Filicide-Toolkit -Complete.pdf.

9. Joe Rodriguez and Lisa Fernandez, "Parents of Autistic Children Speak Out on Sunnyvale Murder-Suicide," *Mercury News*, March 8, 2012, last modified August 13, 2016, https://www.mercurynews.com/2012/03/08 /parents-of-autistic-children-speak-out-on-sunnyvale-murder-suicide/.

10. Nicki Pecchenino, "Guest Opinion: Death by Legislature," *Santa Cruz Sentinel News*, March 9, 2012, http://www.santacruzsentinel.com/general -news/20120309/guest-opinion-death-by-legislature.

11. Autistic Self Advocacy Network, "Disability Day of Mourning 2021," March 26, 2021, https://autisticadvocacy.org/2021/03/disability-day-of -mourning-2021.

12. Carolyn O. Mueller, Anjali J. Forber-Pratt, and Julie Sriken, "Disability: Missing from the Conversation of Violence," *Journal of Social Issues* 75,

no. 3 (September 2019): 707–25, https://doi.org/10.1111/josi.12339; Karen Hughes et al., "Prevalence and Risk of Violence Against Adults with Disabilities: A Systematic Review and Meta-Analysis of Observational Studies," *Lancet* 379, no. 9826 (April 2012): 1621–29, https://doi.org/10.1016/s0140-6736(11)61851-5.

13. Hughes et al., "Prevalence and Risk of Violence Against Adults with Disabilities."

14. Erika Harrell, "Crime Against Persons with Disabilities, 2009–2019—Statistical Tables," Bureau of Justice Statistics, U.S. Department of Justice, November 2021, https://bjs.ojp.gov/library/publications/crime-against-persons-disabilities-2009-2019-statistical-tables.

15. Lisa Jones et al., "Prevalence and Risk of Violence Against Children with Disabilities: A Systematic Review and Meta-Analysis of Observational Studies," *Lancet* 380, no. 9845 (September 2012): 899–907, https://doi.org/10.1016/s0140-6736(12)60692-8.

16. Jerry Alan Winter, "The Development of the Disability Rights Movement as a Social Problem Solver," *Disability Studies Quarterly* 23, no. 1 (Winter 2003): 33–61, https://doi.org/10.18061/dsq.v23i1.399; Allison C. Carey, Pamela Block, and Richard Scotch, *Allies and Obstacles: Disability Activism and Parents of Children with Disabilities* (Philadelphia: Temple University Press, 2020).

17. Carey, Block, and Scotch, *Allies and Obstacles*; Samuel Dubin et al., "Medically Assisted Gender Affirmation: When Children and Parents Disagree," *Journal of Medical Ethics* 46, no. 5 (May 2020): 295–99, https://doi.org/10.1136/medethics-2019-105567.

18. Jennifer S. Singh, *Multiple Autisms: Spectrums of Advocacy and Genomic Science* (Minneapolis: University of Minnesota Press, 2016); Gil Eyal et al., *The Autism Matrix* (Cambridge: Polity, 2010); Martine D. Lappé, "Taking Care: Anticipation, Extraction and the Politics of Temporality in Autism Science," *BioSocieties* 9, no. 3 (September 2014): 304–28, https://doi.org/10.1057/biosoc.2014.14; Chloe Silverman, *Understanding Autism: Parents, Doctors, and the History of a Disorder* (Princeton, NJ: Princeton University Press, 2011).

19. Linda Blum, *Raising Generation Rx: Mothering Kids with Invisible Disabilities in an Age of Inequality* (New York: New York University Press, 2015); Eyal et al., *Autism Matrix*; Singh, *Multiple Autisms*.

20. Brendan Hart, "Autism Parents and Neurodiversity: Radical Translation, Joint Embodiment and the Prosthetic Environment," *BioSocieties* 9, no. 3 (September 2014): 284–303, https://doi.org/10.1057/biosoc.2014.20.

21. Kelly Underman, Paige L. Sweet, and Claire Laurier Decoteau, "Custodial Citizenship in the Omnibus Autism Proceeding," *Sociological Forum* 32, no. 3 (September 2017): 544–65, https://doi.org/10.1111/socf.12348.

22. Underman, Sweet, and Decoteau, "Custodial Citizenship"; Kobie Boshoff et al., "Parents' Voices: 'Why and How We Advocate': A Meta-Synthesis of Parents' Experiences of Advocating for Their Child with Autism Spectrum Disorder," *Child: Care, Health and Development* 42, no. 6 (November 2016): 784–97, https://doi.org/10.1111/cch.12383; Brendan Hart, "Autism Parents & Neurodiversity: Radical Translation, Joint Embodiment and the Prosthetic Environment," *BioSocieties* 9, no. 3 (September 2014): 284–303, http://dx.doi.org/10.1057/biosoc.2014.20.

23. Boshoff et al., "Parents' Voices"; Blum, *Raising Generation Rx*.

24. Isaac C. Smith, Brian Reichow, and Fred R. Volkmar, "The Effects of DSM-5 Criteria on Number of Individuals Diagnosed with Autism Spectrum Disorder: A Systematic Review," *Journal of Autism and Developmental Disorders* 45, no. 8 (2015): 2541–52, https://doi.org/10.1007/s10803-015-2423-8; Marissa King and Peter Bearman, "Diagnostic Change and the Increased Prevalence of Autism," *International Journal of Epidemiology* 38, no. 5 (October 2009): 1224–34, https://doi.org/10.1093/ije/dyp261.

25. Nikolas Rose and Carlos Novas, "Biological Citizenship," in *Global Assemblages: Technology, Politics, and Ethics as Anthropological Problems*, ed. Aihwa Ong and Stephen J. Collier (Hoboken, NJ: Blackwell, 2005), 439–63, https://doi.org/10.1002/9780470696569.ch23; Adriana Petryna, "Biological Citizenship: The Science and Politics of Chernobyl-Exposed Populations," *Osiris* 19 (2004): 250–65, https://www.jstor.org/stable/3655243.

26. Matthew S. McCoy et al., "Ethical Advocacy Across the Autism Spectrum: Beyond Partial Representation," *American Journal of Bioethics* 20, no. 4 (May 2020): 13–24, https://doi.org/10.1080/15265161.2020.1730482.

27. Natasha Malik-Soni et al., "Tackling Healthcare Access Barriers for Individuals with Autism from Diagnosis to Adulthood," *Pediatric Research* 91, no. 5 (April 2022): 1028–35, https://doi.org/10.1038/s41390-021-01465-y; Rebecca Elias and Susan W. White, "Autism Goes to College:

Understanding the Needs of a Student Population on the Rise," *Journal of Autism and Developmental Disorders* 48, no. 3 (2018): 732–46, https://doi .org/10.1007/s10803-017-3075-7; Jennifer S. Singh and Garrett Bunyak, "Autism Disparities: A Systematic Review and Meta-Ethnography of Qualitative Research," *Qualitative Health Research* 29, no. 6 (May 2019): 796–808, https://doi.org/10.1177/1049732318808245; Sandra Hodgetts, Lonnie Zwaigenbaum, and David Nicholas, "Profile and Predictors of Service Needs for Families of Children with Autism Spectrum Disorders," *Autism* 19, no. 6 (August 2015): 673–83, https://doi.org/10.1177/1362361314543531.

28. Carey, Block, and Scotch, *Allies and Obstacles*.

29. An organization that supports alternative biomedicine.

30. Autism Speaks, "2015 Annual Report," https://www.autismspeaks.org /sites/default/files/2018-08/2015-annual-report.pdf.

31. Sara Luterman, "The Biggest Autism Advocacy Group Is Still Failing Too Many Autistic People," *Washington Post*, February 14, 2020, https://www .washingtonpost.com/outlook/2020/02/14/biggest-autism-advocacy -group-is-still-failing-too-many-autistic-people/.

32. Autism Speaks had a campaign that stated, "Autism Speaks. It's time to listen."

33. Emily Willingham, "Conspiracy Fears Dominate Life and Death of Autism Doctor Bradstreet," *Forbes*, July 20, 2015, https://www.forbes.com /sites/emilywillingham/2015/07/20/conspiracy-fears-dominate-life-and -death-of-autism-doctor-bradstreet/#31af721e7f6f.

34. Michael E. Miller, "The Mysterious Death of a Doctor Who Peddled Autism 'Cures' to Thousands," *Washington Post*, July 16, 2015, https://www .washingtonpost.com/news/morning-mix/wp/2015/07/16/the-mysterious -death-of-a-doctor-who-peddled-autism-cures-to-thousands/.

35. Emily Willingham, "Here's Why Authorities Searched the Offices of Controversial Autism Doctor Bradstreet," *Forbes*, July 9, 2015, https:// www.forbes.com/sites/emilywillingham/2015/07/09/government -search-of-autism-doctor-bradstreets-office-related-to-experimental -autism-treatment/?sh=65002b52b07e/.

36. Catherine D. Tan, "Defending 'Snake Oil': The Preservation of Contentious Knowledge and Practices," *Social Studies of Science* 51, no. 4 (August 2021): 538–63, https://doi.org/10.1177/0306312721992543.

37. Silverman, *Understanding Autism*.

38. Steve Silberman, *NeuroTribes: The Legacy of Autism and the Future of Neurodiversity* (New York: Avery, 2015).

39. Paul Offit, *Autism's False Prophets: Bad Science, Risky Medicine, and the Search for a Cure* (New York: Columbia University Press, 2010).

40. Pierre Bourdieu, "The Forms of Capital," in *Handbook of Theory and Research for the Sociology of Education*, ed. J. Richardson (Westport, CT: Greenwood, 1986), 241–58.

41. Evdokia Anagnostou et al., "Intranasal Oxytocin Versus Placebo in the Treatment of Adults with Autism Spectrum Disorders: A Randomized Controlled Trial," *Molecular Autism* 3, no. 1 (2012): 16, https://doi.org/10.1186/2040-2392-3-16; Karen L. Bales et al., "Chronic Intranasal Oxytocin Causes Long-Term Impairments in Partner Preference Formation in Male Prairie Voles," *Biological Psychiatry* 74, no. 3 (August 2013): 180–88, https://doi.org/10.1016/j.biopsych.2012.08.025; Linmarie Sikich et al., "Intranasal Oxytocin in Children and Adolescents with Autism Spectrum Disorder," *New England Journal of Medicine* 385, no. 16 (2021): 1462–73, https://doi.org/10.1056/NEJMoa2103583.

42. John F. Burns, "British Medical Council Bars Doctor Who Linked Vaccine with Autism," *New York Times*, May 24, 2010, https://www.nytimes.com/2010/05/25/health/policy/25autism.html; Madison Park, "Medical Journal Retracts Study Linking Autism to Vaccine," CNN, last modified February 2, 2010, http://www.cnn.com/2010/HEALTH/02/02/lancet.retraction.autism/index.html.

43. Stephen James, Paul Montgomery, and Katrina Williams, "Omega-3 Fatty Acids Supplementation for Autism Spectrum Disorders (ASD)," *Cochrane Database of Systematic Reviews* 11 (November 2011), https://doi.org/10.1002/14651858.cd007992.pub2.

44. Jennifer A. Reich, "Neoliberal Mothering and Vaccine Refusal: Imagined Gated Communities and the Privilege of Choice," *Gender & Society* 28, no. 5 (October 2014): 679–704, https://doi.org/10.1177/0891243214532711.

45. The term refers to the problem of permeable intestines, which allow food to "leak" into the bloodstream, causing inflammation and affecting brain functioning. Medical studies report no significant relationship between gastrointestinal disorders and autism. See Rafail I. Kushak et al., "Evaluation of Intestinal Function in Children with Autism and Gastrointestinal Symptoms," *Journal of Pediatric Gastroenterology and Nutrition* 62, no. 5 (2016): 687–91, https://doi.org/10.1097/mpg.0000000000001174.

46. The term is used to describe a compromised blood-brain barrier.
47. Luterman, "Biggest Autism Advocacy Group."

7. MAKING SPACE FOR THE SPECTRUM

1. Namenda is typically prescribed to help with dementia.
2. Naltrexone is typically prescribed to help with alcohol and opioid addiction.
3. Jennifer A. Reich, *Calling the Shots: Why Parents Reject Vaccines* (New York: New York University Press, 2016); Linda Blum, *Raising Generation Rx: Mothering Kids with Invisible Disabilities in an Age of Inequality* (New York: New York University Press, 2015).
4. Valerie Leiter, *Their Time Has Come: Youth with Disabilities on the Cusp of Adulthood* (New Brunswick, NJ: Rutgers University Press, 2012).
5. Like the Collaborative Institutional Training Initiative (CITI) program.
6. Leiter, *Their Time Has Come.*
7. Tonya N. Davis et al., "Chelation Treatment for Autism Spectrum Disorders: A Systematic Review," *Research in Autism Spectrum Disorders* 7, no. 1 (January 2013): 49–55, https://doi.org/10.1016/j.rasd.2012.06.005; Samantha Lyons, Shival Salgaonkar, and Gerard T. Flaherty, "International Stem Cell Tourism: A Critical Literature Review and Evidence-Based Recommendations," *International Health* 14, no. 2 (March 2022): 132–41, https://doi.org/10.1093/inthealth/ihab050.
8. Jennifer S. Singh, *Multiple Autisms: Spectrums of Advocacy and Genomic Science* (Minneapolis: University of Minnesota Press, 2016); Claire Laurier Decoteau and Meghan Daniel, "Scientific Hegemony and the Field of Autism," *American Sociological Review* 85, no. 3 (May 2020): 451–76, https://doi.org/10.1177/0003122420922253; Daniel Navon and Gil Eyal, "Looping Genomes: Diagnostic Change and the Genetic Makeup of the Autism Population," *American Journal of Sociology* 121, no. 5 (March 2016): 1416–71, https://doi.org/10.1086/684201.
9. Interagency Autism Coordinating Committee, "Autism Research Database," U.S. Department of Health and Human Services, https://iacc.hhs.gov/funding/data/.
10. Catherine A. Okoro et al., "Prevalence of Disabilities and Health Care Access by Disability Status and Type Among Adults—United States, 2016," *Morbidity and Mortality Weekly Report* 67, no. 32 (August 2018): 882–87, https://doi.org/10.15585/mmwr.mm6732a3.

11. Maria K. Makrygianni et al., "The Effectiveness of Applied Behavior Analytic Interventions for Children with Autism Spectrum Disorder: A Meta-Analytic Study," *Research in Autism Spectrum Disorders* 51 (July 2018): 18–31, https://doi.org/10.1016/j.rasd.2018.03.006.

12. Laura K. Anderson, "Autistic Experiences of Applied Behavior Analysis," *Autism* 27, no. 3 (April 2023): 737–50, https://doi.org/10.1177/13623613221118216; Henny Kupferstein, "Evidence of Increased PTSD Symptoms in Autistics Exposed to Applied Behavior Analysis," *Advances in Autism* 4, no. 1 (2018): 19–29, https://doi.org/10.1108/AIA-08-2017-0016; Daniel A. Wilkenfeld and Allison M. McCarthy, "Ethical Concerns with Applied Behavior Analysis for Autism Spectrum Disorder," *Kennedy Institute of Ethics Journal* 30, no. 1 (2020): 31–69, https://doi.org/10.1353/ken.2020.0000.

13. Autistic Self Advocacy Network, "What We Believe: Autism Research and Therapies," https://autisticadvocacy.org/about-asan/what-we-believe/.

14. June L. Chen et al., "Trends in Employment for Individuals with Autism Spectrum Disorder: A Review of the Research Literature," *Review Journal of Autism and Developmental Disorders* 2, no. 2 (2015): 115–27, https://doi.org/10.1007/s40489-014-0041-6; Derek K. Nord et al., "Employment in the Community for People with and Without Autism: A Comparative Analysis," *Research in Autism Spectrum Disorders* 24 (April 2016): 11–16, https://doi.org/10.1016/j.rasd.2015.12.013.

15. Elizabeth Weir, Carrie Allison, and Simon Baron-Cohen, "Autistic Adults Have Poorer Quality Healthcare and Worse Health Based on Self-Report Data," *Molecular Autism* 13, no. 1 (2022): 23, https://doi.org/10.1186/s13229-022-00501-w.

16. Sarah Cassidy et al., "Suicidal Ideation and Suicide Plans or Attempts in Adults with Asperger's Syndrome Attending a Specialist Diagnostic Clinic: A Clinical Cohort Study," *Lancet Psychiatry* 1, no. 2 (July 2014): 142–47, https://doi.org/10.1016/s2215-0366(14)70248-2.

17. Vicki Gibbs and Elizabeth Pellicano, "'Maybe We Just Seem Like Easy Targets': A Qualitative Analysis of Autistic Adults' Experiences of Interpersonal Violence," *Autism* (January 2023): 13623613221150375, https://doi.org/10.1177/13623613221150375; Michelle A. Fardella et al., "A Qualitative Investigation of Risk and Protective Factors for Interpersonal Violence in Adults on the Autism Spectrum," *Disability & Society*

33, no. 9 (October 2018): 1460–81, https://doi.org/10.1080/09687599.201
8.1498320.

18. Leiter, *Their Time Has Come*; Daniel J. Laxman et al., "Loss in Services
Precedes High School Exit for Teens with Autism Spectrum Disorder:
A Longitudinal Study," *Autism Research* 12, no. 6 (June 2019): 911–21,
https://doi.org/10.1002/aur.2113.

19. Leiter, *Their Time Has Come*.

20. Martha C. White, "Planning for Your Retirement, and for a Child's
Special Needs, All at Once," *New York Times*, August 27, 2022, https://
www.nytimes.com/2022/08/27/business/retirement-special-needs.html.

21. Janet E. Graetz, "Autism Grows Up: Opportunities for Adults with
Autism," *Disability & Society* 25, no. 1 (2010): 33–47, https://doi.org/10
.1080/09687590903363324; Paul T. Shattuck et al., "Services for Adults
with an Autism Spectrum Disorder," *Canadian Journal of Psychiatry* 57,
no. 5 (2012): 284–91, https://doi.org/10.1177/070674371205700503.

22. Kristy A. Anderson et al., "National and State Trends in Autistic
Adult Supplemental Security Income Awardees: 2005–2019," *Journal of
Autism and Developmental Disorders* 52, no. 8 (August 2022): 3547–59,
https://doi.org/10.1007/s10803-021-05215-1.

23. Social Security Administration, "Understanding Supplemental Security
Income SSI Benefits—2023 Edition," accessed March 27, 2023, https://
www.ssa.gov/ssi/text-benefits-ussi.htm.

24. Okoro et al., "Prevalence of Disabilities and Health Care Access."

25. Irving Kenneth Zola, "Toward the Necessary Universalizing of a Disability Policy," *Milbank Quarterly* 67, suppl 2 pt 2 (1989): 401–28, https://doi
.org/10.1111/j.1468-0009.2005.00436.x, 20.

26. Zola, "Toward the Necessary Universalizing," 21.

27. Behzad Karami Matin et al., "Contributing Factors to Healthcare Costs
in Individuals with Autism Spectrum Disorder: A Systematic Review,"
BMC Health Services Research 22, no. 1 (May 2022): 1–20, https://doi.org
/10.1186/s12913-022-07932-4.

28. Susan L. Parish et al., "Autism and Families' Financial Burden: The
Association with Health Insurance Coverage," *American Journal on
Intellectual and Developmental Disabilities* 120, no. 2 (2015): 166–75,
https://doi.org/10.1352/1944-7558-120.2.166.

29. Okoro et al., "Prevalence of Disabilities and Health Care Access."

30. Aiden Lee et al., "National Uninsured Rate Reaches All-Time Low in Early 2022," Office of the Assistant Secretary for Planning and Evaluation, U.S. Department of Health and Human Services, August 2, 2022, https://aspe.hhs.gov/reports/2022-uninsurance-at-all-time-low.

31. Sara R. Collins, Lauren A. Haynes, and Relebohile Masitha, "The State of US Health Insurance in 2022: Findings from the Commonwealth Fund Biennial Health Insurance Survey," Commonwealth Fund, September 2022, https://www.commonwealthfund.org/sites/default/files/2022-09/Collins_state_of_coverage_biennial_survey_2022_db.pdf.

32. Megan Brenan, "Record High in US Put Off Medical Care Due to Cost in 2022," Gallup, January 17, 2023, https://news.gallup.com/poll/468053/record-high-put-off-medical-care-due-cost-2022.aspx.

33. Noam Levey, "Sick and Struggling to Pay, 100 Million People in the US Live with Medical Debt," National Public Radio, June 16, 2022, https://www.npr.org/sections/health-shots/2022/06/16/1104679219/medical-bills-debt-investigation.

34. Bradley Jones, "Increasing Share of Americans Favor a Single Government Program to Provide Health Care Coverage," Pew Research Center, September 29, 2020, https://www.pewresearch.org/fact-tank/2020/09/29/increasing-share-of-americans-favor-a-single-government-program-to-provide-health-care-coverage; Janice Hopkins Tanne, "US Needs Universal Access to Health Care, American College of Physicians Says," *BMJ* 335, no. 7632 (2007): 1228, https://doi.org/10.1136/bmj.39423.499560.DB.

35. Alison P. Galvani et al., "Universal Healthcare as Pandemic Preparedness: The Lives and Costs That Could Have Been Saved During the COVID-19 Pandemic," *Proceedings of the National Academy of Sciences* 119, no. 25 (June 2022): e2200536119, https://doi.org/10.1073/pnas.2200536119.

BIBLIOGRAPHY

Abbott, Andrew. *The System of Professions: An Essay on the Division of Expert Labor*. Chicago: University of Chicago Press, 1988.

Abbott, Mandy, Paul Bernard, and Jenny Forge. "Communicating a Diagnosis of Autism Spectrum Disorder—A Qualitative Study of Parents' Experiences." *Clinical Child Psychology and Psychiatry* 18, no. 3 (July 2013): 370–82. https://doi.org/10.1177/1359104512455813.

American Psychiatric Association. *Diagnostic and Statistical Manual of Mental Disorders*. 5th ed. Washington, DC: American Psychiatric Publishing, 2013.

Anagnostou, Evdokia, Latha Soorya, William Chaplin, Jennifer Bartz, Danielle Halpern, Stacey Wasserman, A. Ting Wang, Lauren Pepa, Nadia Tanel, Azadeh Kushki, and Eric Hollander. "Intranasal Oxytocin Versus Placebo in the Treatment of Adults with Autism Spectrum Disorders: A Randomized Controlled Trial." *Molecular Autism* 3, no. 1 (2012): 16. https://doi.org/10.1186/2040-2392-3-16.

Anderson, George M. "Autism Biomarkers: Challenges, Pitfalls and Possibilities." *Journal of Autism and Developmental Disorders* 45, no. 4 (2015): 1103–13. https://doi.org/10.1007/s10803-014-2225-4.

Anderson, Kristy A., Jeffrey Hemmeter, David Wittenburg, Julia Baller, Anne M. Roux, Jessica E. Rast, and Paul T. Shattuck. "National and State Trends in Autistic Adult Supplemental Security Income Awardees: 2005–2019." *Journal of Autism and Developmental Disorders* 52, no. 8 (August 2022): 3547–59. https://doi.org/10.1007/s10803-021-05215-1.

Anderson, Laura K. "Autistic Experiences of Applied Behavior Analysis." *Autism* 27, no 3 (April 2023): 737–50. https://doi.org/10.1177/13623613221118216.

Atladóttir, Hjördis O., Poul Thorsen, Lars Østergaard, Diana E. Schendel, Sanna Lemcke, Morsi Abdallah, and Erik T. Parner. "Maternal Infection Requiring Hospitalization during Pregnancy and Autism Spectrum Disorders." *Journal of Autism and Developmental Disorders* 40, no. 12 (December 2010): 1423–30. https://doi.org/10.1007/s10803-010-1006-y.

Atsem, Stefanie, Juliane Reichenbach, Ramya Potabattula, Marcus Dittrich, Caroline Nava, Christel Depienne, Lena Böhm, Simone Rost, Thomas Hahn, and Martin Schorsch. "Paternal Age Effects on Sperm FOXK1 and KCNA7 Methylation and Transmission into the Next Generation." *Human Molecular Genetics* 25, no. 22 (November 2016): 4996–5005. https://doi.org/10.1093/hmg/ddw328.

Austin, Robert D., and Gary P. Pisano. "Neurodiversity as a Competitive Advantage." *Harvard Business Review* 95, no. 3 (May–June 2017): 96–103. https://hbr.org/2017/05/neurodiversity-as-a-competitive-advantage.

Autism Speaks. "2015 Annual Report." https://www.autismspeaks.org/sites /default/files/2018-08/2015-annual-report.pdf.

Autism Speaks. "Mission." http://www.autismspeaks.org/about-us/mission.

Autistic Self Advocacy Network. "About." Autism Acceptance Month: Acceptance Is an Action. http://www.autismacceptancemonth.com/about/.

Autistic Self Advocacy Network. "All Aboard! ASAN 2021 Annual Report." https://autisticadvocacy.org/wp-content/uploads/2021/11/All-Aboard -ASAN-Annual-Report-2021.pdf.

Autistic Self Advocacy Network. "Disability Day of Mourning 2021." March 26, 2021. https://autisticadvocacy.org/2021/03/disability-day-of-mourning-2021/.

Autistic Self Advocacy Network. "#StopTheShock: The Judge Rotenberg Center, Torture, and How We Can Stop It." https://autisticadvocacy.org /actioncenter/issues/school/climate/jrc/.

Autistic Self Advocacy Network. "What We Believe: Autism Research and Therapies." https://autisticadvocacy.org/about-asan/what-we-believe/.

Baio, John, Lisa Wiggins, Deborah L. Christensen, Matthew J. Maenner, Julie Daniels, Zachary Warren, Margaret Kurzius-Spencer, Walter Zahorodny, Cordelia Robinson Rosenberg, Tiffany White, Maureen S. Durkin, Pamela Imm, Loizos Nikolaou, Marshalyn Yeargin-Allsopp, Li-Ching Lee, Rebecca Harrington, Maya Lopez, Robert T. Fitzgerald, Amy Hewitt, Sydney Pettygrove, John N. Constantino, Alison Vehorn, Josephine Shenouda, Jennifer Hall-Lande, Kim Van Naarden Braun, and Nicole F. Dowling.

"Prevalence of Autism Spectrum Disorder Among Children Aged 8 Years—Autism and Developmental Disabilities Monitoring Network, 11 Sites, United States, 2014." *MMWR Surveillance Summaries* 67, no. 6 (2018): 1–23. https://doi.org/10.15585/mmwr.ss6706a1.

Baker, Jeffrey P. "Autism in 1959: Joey the Mechanical Boy." *Pediatrics* 125, no. 6 (2010): 1101–3. https://doi.org/10.1542/peds.2010-0846.

Bales, Karen L., Allison M. Perkeybile, Olivia G. Conley, Meredith H. Lee, Caleigh D. Guoynes, Griffin M. Downing, Catherine R. Yun, Marjorie Solomon, Suma Jacob, and Sally P. Mendoza. "Chronic Intranasal Oxytocin Causes Long-Term Impairments in Partner Preference Formation in Male Prairie Voles." *Biological Psychiatry* 74, no. 3 (August 2013): 180–88. https://doi.org/10.1016/j.biopsych.2012.08.025.

Barger, Brian D., Jonathan M. Campbell, and Jaimi D. McDonough. "Prevalence and Onset of Regression within Autism Spectrum Disorders: A Meta-Analytic Review." *Journal of Autism and Developmental Disorders* 43, no. 4 (April 2013): 817–28. https://doi.org/10.1007/s10803-012-1621-x.

Barker, Kristin K. "Electronic Support Groups, Patient-Consumers, and Medicalization: The Case of Contested Illness." *Journal of Health and Social Behavior* 49, no. 1 (March 2008): 20–36. https://doi.org/10.1177/002214650804900103.

Bascom, Julia. *The Obsessive Joy of Autism*. London: Jessica Kingsley, 2015.

Bell, Kirsten. "Biomarkers, the Molecular Gaze and the Transformation of Cancer Survivorship." *BioSocieties* 8, no. 2 (June 2013): 124–43. https://doi.org/10.1057/biosoc.2013.6.

Bettelheim, Bruno. *The Empty Fortress: Infantile Autism and the Birth of the Self*. New York: Free Press, 1967.

Blakemore, Erin. "Celebrating Media-Makers on the Autism Spectrum." *Washington Post*, April 23, 2022. https://www.washingtonpost.com/health/2022/04/23/autism-creativity/.

Blum, Linda. *Raising Generation Rx: Mothering Kids with Invisible Disabilities in an Age of Inequality*. New York: New York University Press, 2015.

Bosch, Christina. "Time to End Public Funding of Judge Rotenberg Center." *Commonwealth Magazine*, April 20, 2021. https://commonwealthmagazine.org/education/time-to-end-public-funding-of-judge-rotenberg-center/.

Boshoff, Kobie, Deanna Gibbs, Rebecca L. Phillips, Lousie Wiles, and Logan Porter. "Parents' Voices: 'Why and How We Advocate': A Meta-Synthesis of Parents' Experiences of Advocating for Their Child with

Autism Spectrum Disorder." *Child: Care, Health and Development* 42, no. 6 (November 2016): 784–97. https://doi.org/10.1111/cch.12383.

Bourdieu, Pierre. *Science of Science and Reflexivity*. Chicago: University of Chicago Press, 2004.

Bourdieu, Pierre, and Loïc J. D. Wacquant. "The Logic of Fields." In *An Invitation to Reflexive Sociology*, edited by Pierre Bourdieu and Loïc J. D. Wacquant, 94–114. Chicago: University of Chicago Press, 1992.

Brady, Danielle I., Donald H. Saklofske, Vicki L. Schwean, Janine M. Montgomery, Adam W. McCrimmon, and Keoma J. Thorne. "Cognitive and Emotional Intelligence in Young Adults with Autism Spectrum Disorder Without an Accompanying Intellectual or Language Disorder." *Research in Autism Spectrum Disorders* 8, no. 9 (September 2014): 1016–23. https://doi.org/10.1016/j.rasd.2014.05.009.

Brady, Jonann, and Stephanie Dahle. "Celeb Couple to Lead 'Green Vaccine' Rally." ABC News. Last modified October 9, 2009. https://abcnews.go.com/GMA/OnCall/story?id=4987758.

Braunstein, Valerie L., Nicole Peniston, Andrea Perelman, and Michael C. Cassano. "The Inclusion of Fathers in Investigations of Autistic Spectrum Disorders." *Research in Autism Spectrum Disorders* 7, no. 7 (July 2013): 858–65. https://doi.org/10.1016/j.rasd.2013.03.005.

Brenan, Megan. "Record High in US Put Off Medical Care Due to Cost in 2022." Gallup, January 17, 2023. https://news.gallup.com/poll/468053/record-high-put-off-medical-care-due-cost-2022.aspx.

Brown, Lydia X. Z. "Ableism/Language." Autistic Hoya. Last modified September 14, 2022. https://www.autistichoya.com/p/ableist-words-and-terms-to-avoid.html.

Brown, Phil. "Naming and Framing: The Social Construction of Diagnosis and Illness." *Journal of Health and Social Behavior* 35, extra issue (1995): 34–52. https://doi.org/10.2307/2626956.

Brown, Phil. *Toxic Exposures: Contested Illnesses and the Environmental Health Movement*. New York: Columbia University Press, 2007.

Brown, Phil, Brian Mayer, Stephen Zavestoski, Theo Luebke, Joshua Mandelbaum, and Sabrina McCormick. "The Health Politics of Asthma: Environmental Justice and Collective Illness Experience in the United States." In *The Sociology of Health and Illness: Critical Perspectives*, 9th ed., edited by Peter Conrad and Valerie Leiter, 81–92. New York: Worth, 2012.

Brown, Phil, Stephen Zavestoski, Brian Mayer, Sabrina McCormick, and Pamela S. Webster. "Policy Issues in Environmental Health Disputes." *Annals of the American Academy of Political and Social Science* 584, no. 1 (November 2002): 175–202. https://doi.org/10.1177/000271620258400113.

Brown, Phil, Stephen Zavestoski, Sabrina McCormick, Brian Mayer, Rachel Morello-Frosh, and Rebecca Gaisor Altman. "Embodied Health Movements: New Approaches to Social Movements in Health." *Sociology of Health & Illness* 26, no. 1 (January 2004): 50–80. https://doi.org/10.1111/j.1467-9566.2004.00378.x.

Bumiller, Kristin. "The Geneticization of Autism: From New Reproductive Technologies to the Conception of Genetic Normalcy." *Signs* 34, no. 4 (Summer 2009): 875–99. https://doi.org/10.1086/597130.

Burns, John F. "British Medical Council Bars Doctor Who Linked Vaccine with Autism." *New York Times*, May 24, 2010. https://www.nytimes.com/2010/05/25/health/policy/25autism.html.

Burton, Robert. "Brain Scam." Salon, May 12, 2008. http://www.salon.com/2008/05/12/daniel_amen/.

Callahan, Patricia. "Naperville Doctor Disciplined in Controversial Autism Case." *Chicago Tribune*, December 30, 2014. https://www.chicagotribune.com/lifestyles/health/ct-autism-anjum-usman-discipline-met-20141229-story.html.

Campbell, Fiona Kumari. *Contours of Ableism: The Production of Disability and Abledness*. London: Palgrave Macmillan, 2009.

Carey, Allison C., Pamela Block, and Richard Scotch. *Allies and Obstacles: Disability Activism and Parents of Children with Disabilities*. Philadelphia: Temple University Press, 2020.

Cassidy, Sarah, Paul Bradley, Janine Robinson, Carrie Allison, Meghan McHugh, and Simon Baron-Cohen. "Suicidal Ideation and Suicide Plans or Attempts in Adults with Asperger's Syndrome Attending a Specialist Diagnostic Clinic: A Clinical Cohort Study." *Lancet Psychiatry* 1, no. 2 (July 2014): 142–47. https://doi.org/10.1016/s2215-0366(14)70248-2.

Centers for Disease Control and Prevention. "Facts About ASD." Last modified December 9, 2022. http://www.cdc.gov/ncbddd/autism/facts.html.

Centers for Disease Control and Prevention. "Timeline: Thimerosal in Vaccines (1999–2010)." Last modified August 19, 2020. https://www.cdc.gov/vaccinesafety/concerns/thimerosal/timeline.html.

Chapman, Robert. "Defining Neurodiversity for Research and Practice." In *Neurodiversity Studies: A New Critical Paradigm*, edited by Hanna Rosqvist, Nick Chown, and Anna Stenning, 218–20. London: Routledge, 2020.

Chen, June L., Geraldine Leader, Connie Sung, and Michael Leahy. "Trends in Employment for Individuals with Autism Spectrum Disorder: A Review of the Research Literature." *Review Journal of Autism and Developmental Disorders* 2, no. 2 (2015): 115–27. https://doi.org/10.1007/s40489-014-0041-6.

Cleaver, Joanne. "Combating Sensory Overload: How Zoos and Museums Are Redefining Inclusion." *New York Times*, April 22, 2022. https://www.nytimes.com/2022/04/22/travel/sensory-disabilities-travel.html.

Clements, C. John, Leslie K. Ball, Robert Ball, and R. Douglas Pratt. "Thiomersal in Vaccines: Is Removal Warranted?" *Drug Safety* 24, no. 8 (2001): 567–74. https://doi.org/10.2165/00002018-200124080-00001.

Collins, Sara R., Lauren A. Haynes, and Relebohile Masitha. "The State of US Health Insurance in 2022: Findings from the Commonwealth Fund Biennial Health Insurance Survey." Commonwealth Fund. September 2022. https://www.commonwealthfund.org/sites/default/files/2022-09/Collins_state_of_coverage_biennial_survey_2022_db.pdf.

Conrad, Peter, and Alison Angell. "Homosexuality and Remedicalization." *Society* 41, no. 5 (July 2004): 32–39. https://doi.org/10.1007/BF02688215.

Conrad, Peter, Julia Bandini, and Alexandria Vasquez. "Illness and the Internet: From Private to Public Experience." *Health* 20, no. 1 (2016): 22–32. https://doi.org/10.1177/1363459315611941.

Conrad, Peter, and Susan Markens. "Constructing the 'Gay Gene' in the News: Optimism and Skepticism in the US and British Press." *Health* 5, no. 3 (July 2001): 373–400. https://doi.org/10.1177/136345930100500306.

Cooper, John O., Timothy E. Heron, and William L. Heward. *Applied Behavior Analysis*. 2nd ed. Columbus, OH: Merrill Prentice Hall, 2007.

Croen, Lisa A., Judith K. Grether, and Steve Selvin. "Descriptive Epidemiology of Autism in a California Population: Who Is at Risk?" *Journal of Autism and Developmental Disorders* 32, no. 3 (June 2002): 217–24. https://doi.org/10.1023/a:1015405914950.

Cunningham, Allison B., and Laura Schreibman. "Stereotypy in Autism: The Importance of Function." *Research in Autism Spectrum Disorders* 2, no. 3 (July–September 2008): 469–79. https://doi.org/10.1016/j.rasd.2007 .09.006.

Davidson, Joyce. "Autistic Culture Online: Virtual Communication and Cultural Expression on the Spectrum." *Social & Cultural Geography* 9, no. 7 (2008): 791–806. https://doi.org/10.1080/14649360802382586.

Davis, Tonya N., Mark O'Reilly, Soyeon Kang, Russell Lang, Mandy Rispoli, Jeff Sigafoos, Giulio Lancioni, Daelynn Copeland, Shanna Attai, and Austin Mulloy. "Chelation Treatment for Autism Spectrum Disorders: A Systematic Review." *Research in Autism Spectrum Disorders* 7, no. 1 (January 2013): 49–55. https://doi.org/10.1016/j.rasd.2012.06.005.

de Bruin, Wändi Bruine, Htay-Wah Saw, and Dana P. Goldman. "Political Polarization in US Residents' COVID-19 Risk Perceptions, Policy Preferences, and Protective Behaviors." *Journal of Risk and Uncertainty* 61, no. 2 (2020): 177–94. https://doi.org/10.1007/s11166-020-09336-3.

Decoteau, Claire Laurier. "The 'Western Disease': Autism and Somali Parents' Embodied Health Movements." *Social Science & Medicine* 177 (March 2017): 169–76. https://doi.org/10.1016/j.socscimed.2017.01.064.

Decoteau, Claire Laurier. *The Western Disease: Contesting Autism in the Somali Diaspora.* Chicago: University of Chicago Press, 2021.

Decoteau, Claire Laurier, and Meghan Daniel. "Scientific Hegemony and the Field of Autism." *American Sociological Review* 85, no. 3 (May 2020): 451–76. https://doi.org/10.1177/0003122420922253.

Decoteau, Claire Laurier, and Kelly Underman. "Adjudicating Non-Knowledge in the Omnibus Autism Proceedings." *Social Studies of Science* 45, no. 4 (2015): 471–500. https://doi.org/10.1177/0306312715600278.

Deer, Brian. "How the Case Against the MMR Vaccine Was Fixed." *BMJ* 342 (January 2011): 77–82. https://doi.org/10.1136/bmj.c5347.

Deer, Brian. "How the Vaccine Crisis Was Meant to Make Money." *BMJ* 342 (January 2011): 136–42. https://doi.org/10.1136/bmj.c5258.

Depape, Anne-Marie R., Aoju Chen, Geoffrey B. C. Hall, and Laurel J. Trainor. "Use of Prosody and Information Structure in High Functioning Adults with Autism in Relation to Language Ability." *Frontiers in Psychology* 3 (March 2012): 72. https://doi.org/10.3389/fpsyg.2012.00072.

DeStefano, Frank, and Robert T. Chen. "Negative Association Between MMR and Autism." *Lancet* 353, no. 9169 (June 1999): 1987–88. https://doi .org/10.1016/S0140-6736(99)00160-9.

Dimitrova, Nevena, Şeyda Özçalışkan, and Lauren B. Adamson. "Parents' Translations of Child Gesture Facilitate Word Learning in Children with Autism, Down Syndrome and Typical Development." *Journal of Autism and Developmental Disorders* 46, no. 1 (January 2016): 221–31. https://doi.org/10.1007/s10803-015-2566-7.

Dixon, Dennis R., Talya Vogel, and Jonathan Tarbox. "A Brief History of Functional Analysis and Applied Behavior Analysis." In *Functional Assessment for Challenging Behaviors and Mental Health Disorders*, edited by Johnny L. Matson, 3–24. Cham, Switzerland: Springer, 2012. https://doi.org/10.1007/978-1-4614-3037-7_2.

Donvan, John, and Caren Zucker. *In a Different Key: The Story of Autism.* New York: Crown, 2016.

Dubin, Samuel, Megan Lane, Shane Morrison, Asa Radix, Uri Belkind, Christian Vercler, and David Inwards-Breland. "Medically Assisted Gender Affirmation: When Children and Parents Disagree." *Journal of Medical Ethics* 46, no. 5 (May 2020): 295–99. https://doi.org/10.1136/medethics-2019-105567.

Dudley, Matthew Z., Neal A. Halsey, Saad B. Omer, Walter A. Orenstein, Sean T. O'Leary, Rupali J. Limaye, and Daniel A. Salmon. "The State of Vaccine Safety Science: Systematic Reviews of the Evidence." *Lancet Infectious Diseases* 20, no. 5 (May 2020): E80–E89. https://doi.org/10.1016/S1473-3099(20)30130-4.

Dumit, Joseph. "Illnesses You Have to Fight to Get: Facts as Forces in Uncertain, Emergent Illnesses." *Social Science & Medicine* 62, no. 3 (February 2006): 577–90. https://doi.org/10.1016/j.socscimed.2005.06.018.

Durkin, Maureen S., Matthew J. Maenner, Craig J. Newschaffer, Li-Ching Lee, Christopher M. Cunniff, Julie L. Daniels, Russell S. Kirby, Lewis Leavitt, Lisa Miller, Walter Zahorodny, and Laura A. Schieve. "Advanced Parental Age and the Risk of Autism Spectrum Disorder." *American Journal of Epidemiology* 168, no. 11 (December 2008): 1268–76. https://doi.org/10.1093/aje/kwn250.

Dyer, Owen. "Andrew Wakefield Is Accused of Paying Children for Blood Samples." *BMJ* 335, no. 7611 (July 2007): 118–19. https://doi.org/10.1136/bmj.39280.513310.4E.

Einsiedel, Edna F., and Hannah Adamson. "Stem Cell Tourism and Future Stem Cell Tourists: Policy and Ethical Implications." *Developing World*

Bioethics 12, no. 1 (April 2012): 35–44. https://doi.org/10.1111/j.1471-8847
.2012.00319.x.

Elias, Rebecca, and Susan W. White. "Autism Goes to College: Understanding
the Needs of a Student Population on the Rise." *Journal of Autism and Developmental Disorders* 48, no. 3 (2018): 732–46. https://doi.org/10.1007/s10803
-017-3075-7.

Epstein, Steven. *Impure Science: AIDS, Activism, and the Politics of Knowledge.*
Oakland: University of California Press, 1996.

Evans, John H., and Eszter Hargittai. "Who Doesn't Trust Fauci? The
Public's Belief in the Expertise and Shared Values of Scientists in the
COVID-19 Pandemic." *Socius* 6 (2020): 2378023120947337. https://doi.org
/10.1177/2378023120947337.

Evans, Sara M., and Harry C. Boyte. *Free Spaces: The Sources of Democratic
Change in America.* Chicago: University of Chicago Press, 1986.

Eyal, Gil. *The Crisis of Expertise.* Hoboken, NJ: Wiley, 2019.

Eyal, Gil. "For a Sociology of Expertise: The Social Origins of the Autism
Epidemic." *American Journal of Sociology* 118, no. 4 (January 2013): 863–907.
https://doi.org/10.1086/668448.

Eyal, Gil, Brendan Hart, Emine Onculer, Neta Oren, and Natasha Rossi. *The
Autism Matrix.* Cambridge, UK: Polity, 2010.

Fantasia, Rick, and Eric L. Hirsch. "Culture in Rebellion: The Appropriation and Transformation of the Veil in the Algerian Revolution." In *Social
Movements and Culture,* edited by Hank Johnston and Bert Klandermans,
144–60. London: Routledge, 1995.

Fardella, Michelle A., Priscilla Burnham Riosa, and Jonathan A. Weiss. "A
Qualitative Investigation of Risk and Protective Factors for Interpersonal Violence in Adults on the Autism Spectrum." *Disability & Society*
33, no. 9 (October 2018): 1460–81. https://doi.org/10.1080/09687599.2018
.1498320.

Fenton, Anny T. "Abandoning Medical Authority: When Medical Professionals Confront Stigmatized Adolescent Sex and the Human Papillomavirus (HPV) Vaccine." *Journal of Health and Social Behavior* 60, no. 2
(2019): 240–56. https://doi.org/10.1177/0022146519849895.

Fleischer, Doris Zames, and Frieda Zames. *The Disability Rights Movement:
From Charity to Confrontation.* Philadelphia: Temple University Press,
2001.

Folstein, Susan, and Michael Rutter. "Infantile Autism: A Genetic Study of 21 Twin Pairs." *Journal of Child Psychology and Psychiatry* 18, no. 4 (September 1977): 297–321. https://doi.org/10.1111/j.1469-7610.1977.tb00443.x.

Fombonne, Eric, et al. "Beliefs in Vaccine as Causes of Autism Among SPARK Cohort Caregivers." *Vaccine* 38, no. 7 (February 2020): 1794–1803. https://doi.org/10.1016/j.vaccine.2019.12.026.

Foxx, Richard M. "Applied Behavior Analysis Treatment of Autism: The State of the Art." *Child and Adolescent Psychiatric Clinics* 17, no. 4 (October 2008): 821–34. https://doi.org/10.1016/j.chc.2008.06.007.

Fraguas, David, Covadonga M. Díaz-Caneja, Laura Pina-Camacho, Carmen Moreno, Manuel Durán-Cutilla, Miriam Ayora, Emiliano González-Vioque, Mario de Matteis, Robert L. Hendren, Celso Arango, and Mara Paralleda. "Dietary Interventions for Autism Spectrum Disorder: A Meta-Analysis." *Pediatrics* 144, no. 5 (November 2019): e20183218. https://doi.org/10.1542/peds.2018-3218.

Frickel, Scott, Sahra Gibbon, Jeff Howard, Joanna Kempner, Gwen Ottinger, and David J. Hess. "Undone Science: Charting Social Movement and Civil Society Challenges to Research Agenda Setting." *Science, Technology, & Human Values* 35, no. 4 (2010): 444–73. https://doi.org/10.1177/0162243909345836.

Fuller, Paul R. "Operant Conditioning of a Vegetative Human Organism." *American Journal of Psychology* 62, no. 4 (1949): 587–90. https://doi.org/10.2307/1418565.

Futrell, Robert, and Pete Simi. "Free Spaces, Collective Identity, and the Persistence of US White Power Activism." *Social Problems* 51, no. 1 (February 2004): 16–42. https://doi.org/10.1525/sp.2004.51.1.16.

Gabe, Jonathan, Gillian Olumide, and Michael Bury. "'It Takes Three to Tango': A Framework for Understanding Patient Partnership in Paediatric Clinics." *Social Science & Medicine* 59, no. 5 (September 2004): 1071–79. https://doi.org/10.1016/j.socscimed.2003.09.035.

Galvani, Alison P., Alyssa S. Parpia, Abhishek Pandey, Pratha Sah, Kenneth Colón, Gerald Friedman, Travis Campbell, James G. Kahn, Burton H. Singer, and Meagan C. Fitzpatrick. "Universal Healthcare as Pandemic Preparedness: The Lives and Costs That Could Have Been Saved During the COVID-19 Pandemic." *Proceedings of the National Academy of Sciences* 119, no. 25 (June 2022): e2200536119. https://doi.org/10.1073/pnas.2200536119.

Gardener, Hannah, Donna Spiegelman, and Stephen L. Buka. "Perinatal and Neonatal Risk Factors for Autism: A Comprehensive Meta-Analysis." *Pediatrics* 128, no. 2 (August 2011): 344–55. https://doi.org/10.1542/peds .2010-1036.

Gardener, Hannah, Donna Spiegelman, and Stephen L. Buka. "Prenatal Risk Factors for Autism: A Comprehensive Meta-Analysis." *British Journal of Psychiatry* 195, no. 1 (July 2009): 7–14. https://doi.org/10.1192/bjp.bp .108.051672.

Garske, Gregory G., and Jay R. Stewart. "Stigmatic and Mythical Thinking: Barriers to Vocational Rehabilitation Services for Persons with Severe Mental Illness." *Journal of Rehabilitation* 65, no. 4 (October–December 1999): 4–8.

Gengler, Amanda M. "'I Want You to Save My Kid!': Illness Management Strategies, Access, and Inequality at an Elite University Research Hospital." *Journal of Health and Social Behavior* 55, no. 3 (2014): 342–59. https:// doi.org/10.1177/0022146514544172.

Gibbs, Vicki, and Elizabeth Pellicano. "'Maybe We Just Seem Like Easy Targets': A Qualitative Analysis of Autistic Adults' Experiences of Interpersonal Violence." *Autism* (January 2023): 13623613221150375. https://doi .org/10.1177/13623613221150375.

Gieryn, Thomas F. *Cultural Boundaries of Science: Credibility on the Line.* Chicago: University of Chicago Press, 1999.

Godlee, Fiona, Jane Smith, and Harvey Marcovitch. "Wakefield's Article Linking MMR Vaccine and Autism Was Fraudulent." *BMJ* 342, no. 7788 (January 2011): 64–66. https://doi.org/10.1136/bmj.d1678.

Goffman, Erving. *Asylums: Essays on the Social Situation of Mental Patients and Other Inmates.* Piscataway, NJ: Aldine Transaction, 1961.

Goffman, Erving. "The Moral Career of the Mental Patient." *Psychiatry* 22, no. 2 (1959): 123–42.

Goin-Kochel, Robin P., and Barbara J. Myers. "Congenital Versus Regressive Onset of Autism Spectrum Disorders: Parents' Beliefs About Causes." *Focus on Autism and Other Developmental Disabilities* 20, no. 3 (Fall 2005): 169–79. https://doi.org/10.1177/10883576050200030501.

Gonnerman, Jennifer. "31 Shocks Later." *New York Magazine*, August 31, 2012. https://nymag.com/news/features/andre-mccollins-rotenberg-center -2012-9/.

Graetz, Janet E. "Autism Grows Up: Opportunities for Adults with Autism." *Disability & Society* 25, no. 1 (2010): 33–47. https://doi.org/10.1080/09687590903363324.

Granpeesheh, Doreen, Jonathan Tarbox, and Dennis R. Dixon. "Applied Behavior Analytic Interventions for Children with Autism: A Description and Review of Treatment Research." *Annals of Clinical Psychiatry* 21, no. 3 (July–September 2009): 162–73. https://pubmed.ncbi.nlm.nih.gov/19758537/.

Greenspan, Stanley I., and Serena Wieder. *Engaging Autism: Using the Floortime Approach to Help Children Relate, Communicate, and Think.* Boston: Da Capo Lifelong Books, 2006.

Grootens-Wiegers, Petronella, Irma M. Hein, Jos M. van den Broek, and Martine C. de Vries. "Medical Decision-Making in Children and Adolescents: Developmental and Neuroscientific Aspects." *BMC Pediatrics* 17, no. 1 (2017): 1–10. https://doi.org/10.1186/s12887-017-0869-x.

Gross, Zoe. "Foreword: Killing Words." In "Anti-Filicide Toolkit," Autistic Self Advocacy Network, 3–4. Last modified January 2022. http://autisticadvocacy.org/wp-content/uploads/2015/01/ASAN-Anti-Filicide-Toolkit-Complete.pdf.

Haas, Peter M. "Introduction: Epistemic Communities and International Policy Coordination." *International Organization* 46, no. 1 (Winter 1992): 1–35. https://doi.org/10.1017/S0020818300001442.

Haas, Stephen M., Meghan E. Irr, Nancy A. Jennings, and Lisa M. Wagner. "Communicating Thin: A Grounded Model of Online Negative Enabling Support Groups in the Pro-Anorexia Movement." *New Media & Society* 13, no. 1 (2011): 40–57. https://doi.org/10.1177/1461444810363910.

Hacking, Ian. *The Social Construction of What?* Cambridge, MA: Harvard University Press, 1999.

Haelle, Tara. "Dr. Bob Sears Could Lose License for Medical Negligence—Not Vaccine Choice." *Forbes.* Last modified September 11, 2016. https://www.forbes.com/sites/tarahaelle/2016/09/11/dr-bob-sears-could-lose-license-for-medical-negligence-not-vaccine-choice/#74962e4625f6.

Hallmayer, Joachim, Sue Cleveland, Andrea Torres, Jennifer Phillips, Brianne Cohen, Tiffany Torigoe, Janet Miller, Angie Fedele, Jack Collins, Karen Smith, Linda Lotspeich, Lisa A. Croen, Sally Ozonoff, Clara

Lajonchere, Judith K. Grether, and Neil Risch. "Genetic Heritability and Shared Environmental Factors Among Twin Pairs with Autism." *Archives of General Psychiatry* 68, no. 11 (November 2011): 1095–1102. https://doi .org/10.1001/archgenpsychiatry.2011.76.

Hamer, Dean, Stella Hu, Victoria L. Magnuson, Nan Hu, and Angela M. L. Pattatucci. "A Linkage Between DNA Markers on the X Chromosome and Male Sexual Orientation." *Science* 261, no. 5119 (1993): 321–27. https:// doi.org/10.1126/science.8332896.

Hannaford, Alex. "Andrew Wakefield: Autism Inc." *Guardian*, April 6, 2013. https://www.theguardian.com/society/2013/apr/06/what-happened-man -mmr-panic.

Hansen, Robin L., Sally Ozonoff, Paula Krakowiak, Kathleen Angkustsiri, Carrie Jones, Lesley J. Deprey, Dung-Nghi Le, Lisa A. Croen, and Irva Hertz-Picciotto. "Regression in Autism: Prevalence and Associated Factors in the CHARGE Study." *Ambulatory Pediatrics* 8, no. 1 (January–February 2008): 25–31. https://doi.org/10.1016/j.ambp.2007.08.006.

Happé, Francesca, Angelica Ronald, and Robert Plomin. "Time to Give Up on a Single Explanation for Autism." *Nature Neuroscience* 9 (2006): 1218–20. https://doi.org/10.1038/nn1770.

Happé, Francesca G., Hassan Mansour, Pippa Barrett, Tony Brown, Patricia Abbott, and Rebecca A. Charlton. "Demographic and Cognitive Profile of Individuals Seeking a Diagnosis of Autism Spectrum Disorder in Adulthood." *Journal of Autism and Developmental Disorders* 46, no. 11 (November 2016): 3469–80. https://doi.org/10.1007/s10803-016-2886-2.

Haraway, Donna. "Situated Knowledges: The Science Question in Feminism and the Privilege of Partial Perspective." *Feminist Studies* 14, no. 3 (Autumn 1988): 575–99. https://doi.org/10.2307/3178066.

Harrell, Erika. "Crime Against Persons with Disabilities, 2009–2019—Statistical Tables." Bureau of Justice Statistics. U.S. Department of Justice. November 2021. https://bjs.ojp.gov/library/publications/crime-against-persons -disabilities-2009-2019-statistical-tables.

Harris, James, and Joseph Piven. "Correcting the Record: Leo Kanner and the Broad Autism Phenotype." SpectrumNews.org, April 26, 2016. https:// www.spectrumnews.org/opinion/viewpoint/correcting-the-record-leo -kanner-and-the-broad-autism-phenotype/.

Hart, Brendan. "Autism Parents & Neurodiversity: Radical Translation, Joint Embodiment and the Prosthetic Environment." *BioSocieties* 9, no. 3 (September 2014): 284–303. https://doi.org/10.1057/biosoc.2014.20.

Hassrick, Elizabeth McGhee, Laura Graham Holmes, Collette Sosnowy, Jessica Walton, and Kathleen Carley. "Benefits and Risks: A Systematic Review of Information and Communication Technology Use by Autistic People." *Autism in Adulthood* 3, no. 1 (March 2021): 72–84. https://doi.org/10.1089/aut.2020.0048.

Hirsch, Eric L. *Urban Revolt: Ethnic Politics in the Nineteenth-Century Chicago Labor Movement.* Oakland: University of California Press, 1990.

Hodgetts, Sandra, Lonnie Zwaigenbaum, and David Nicholas. "Profile and Predictors of Service Needs for Families of Children with Autism Spectrum Disorders." *Autism* 19, no. 6 (August 2015): 673–83. https://doi.org/10.1177/1362361314543531.

Holbrook, Sarai, and Megan Israelsen. "Speech Prosody Interventions for Persons with Autism Spectrum Disorders: A Systematic Review." *American Journal of Speech-Language Pathology* 29, no. 4 (November 2020): 2189–205. https://doi.org/10.1044/2020_ajslp-19-00127.

Holzner, Burkart, and John Marx. *Knowledge Affiliation: The Knowledge System in Society.* Boston: Allyn and Bacon, 1979.

Hopf, Kathleen Pillsbury, Eric Madren, and Kirsten A. Santianni. "Use and Perceived Effectiveness of Complementary and Alternative Medicine to Treat and Manage the Symptoms of Autism in Children: A Survey of Parents in a Community Population." *Journal of Alternative and Complementary Medicine* 22, no. 2 (2015): 25–32. https://doi.org/10.1089/acm.2015.0163.

Huang, Yunhe, Samuel R. C. Arnold, Kitty-Rose Foley, and Julian N. Trollor. "Diagnosis of Autism in Adulthood: A Scoping Review." *Autism* 24, no. 6 (August 2020): 1311–27. https://doi.org/10.1177/1362361320903128.

Hughes, Karen, Mark A. Bellis, Lisa Jones, Sara Wood, Geoff Bates, Lindsay Eckley, Ellie McCoy, Christopher Mikton, Tom Shakespeare, and Alana Officer. "Prevalence and Risk of Violence Against Adults with Disabilities: A Systematic Review and Meta-Analysis of Observational Studies." *Lancet* 379, no. 9826 (April 2012): 1621–29. https://doi.org/10.1016/s0140-6736(11)61851-5.

Hultman, Christina M., Sven Sandin, Stephen Zvi Levine, Paul Lichtenstein, and Abraham Reichenberg. "Advancing Paternal Age and Risk of Autism:

New Evidence from a Population-Based Study and a Meta-Analysis of Epidemiological Studies." *Molecular Psychiatry* 16, no. 12 (December 2011): 1203–12. https://doi.org/10.1038/mp.2010.121.

Ibarra, Michelle. "Why Should You Travel to Cancun for SCT?" World Stem Cells Clinic. July 21, 2019. https://worldstemcellsclinic.com/blog/why-should-you-travel-to-cancun-for-sct/.

Institute of Medicine. *Immunization Safety Review: Vaccines and Autism.* Washington, DC: National Academies Press, 2004.

Institute of Medicine. "Methodological Approaches to Studying Health Outcomes Associated with the Current Immunization Schedule: Options, Feasibility, Ethical Issues, and Priorities." In *The Childhood Immunization Schedule and Safety: Stakeholder Concerns, Scientific Evidence, and Future Studies*, edited by Institute of Medicine. Washington, DC: National Academies Press, 2013.

Interagency Autism Coordinating Committee. "Autism Research Database." U.S. Department of Health and Human Services. https://iacc.hhs.gov/funding/data/.

Jaarsma, Pier, and Stellan Welin. "Autism as a Natural Human Variation: Reflections on the Claims of the Neurodiversity Movement." *Health Care Analysis* 20, no. 1 (March 2012): 20–30. https://doi.org/10.1007/s10728-011-0169-9.

James, Stephen, Paul Montgomery, and Katrina Williams. "Omega-3 Fatty Acids Supplementation for Autism Spectrum Disorders (ASD)." *Cochrane Database of Systematic Reviews* 11 (November 2011). https://doi.org/10.1002/14651858.cd007992.pub2.

James, Stephen, Shawn W. Stevenson, Natalie Silove, and Katrin Williams. "Chelation for Autism Spectrum Disorder (ASD)." *Cochrane Database of Systematic Reviews* 5, no. 5 (May 2015): CD010766. https://doi.org/10.1002/14651858.CD010766.pub2.

Jasanoff, Sheila. "Contested Boundaries in Policy-Relevant Science." *Social Studies of Science* 17, no. 2 (May 1987): 195–230. https://doi.org/10.1177/030631287017002001.

Jasanoff, Sheila. *The Fifth Branch: Science Advisers as Policymakers.* Cambridge, MA: Harvard University Press, 2009.

Jeremic, Vida, Karine Sénécal, Pascal Borry, Davit Chokoshvili, and Danya F. Vears. "Participation of Children in Medical Decision-Making: Challenges and Potential Solutions." *Journal of Bioethical Inquiry* 13, no. 4 (December 2016): 525–34. https://doi.org/10.1007/s11673-016-9747-8.

Jones, Bradley. "Increasing Share of Americans Favor a Single Government Program to Provide Health Care Coverage." Pew Research Center. September 29, 2020. https://www.pewresearch.org/fact-tank/2020/09/29/increasing-share-of-americans-favor-a-single-government-program-to-provide-health-care-coverage/.

Jones, Lisa, Mark A. Bellis, Sara Wood, Karen Hughes, Ellie McCoy, Lindsay Eckley, Geoff Bates, Christopher Mikton, Tom Shakespeare, and Alana Officer. "Prevalence and Risk of Violence Against Children with Disabilities: A Systematic Review and Meta-Analysis of Observational Studies." *Lancet* 380, no. 9845 (September 2012): 899–907. https://doi.org/10.1016/s0140-6736(12)60692-8.

Jordan, Chloe J. "Evolution of Autism Support and Understanding via the World Wide Web." *Intellectual and Developmental Disabilities* 48, no. 3 (June 2010): 220–27. https://doi.org/10.1352/1934-9556-48.3.220.

Jutel, Annemarie. *Putting a Name to It: Diagnosis in Contemporary Society*. Baltimore, MD: Johns Hopkins University Press, 2011.

Kanner, Leo. "Autistic Disturbances of Affective Contact." *Nervous Child* 2 (1943): 217–50.

Katusic, Maja Z., Scott M. Myers, Amy L. Weaver, and Robert G. Voigt. "IQ in Autism Spectrum Disorder: A Population-Based Birth Cohort Study." *Pediatrics* 148, no. 6 (2021): e2020049899. https://doi.org/10.1542/peds.2020-049899.

Kaufman, Joanne. "Ransom-Note Ads About Children's Health Are Canceled." *New York Times*, December 20, 2007. https://www.nytimes.com/2007/12/20/business/media/20child.html.

Kearns, Cristin E., Laura A. Schmidt, and Stanton A. Glantz. "Sugar Industry and Coronary Heart Disease Research: A Historical Analysis of Internal Industry Documents." *JAMA Internal Medicine* 176, no. 11 (November 2016): 1680–85. https://doi.org/10.1001/jamainternmed.2016.5394.

Kennedy, Deborah A., Kieran Cooley, Thomas R. Einarson, and Dugald Seely. "Objective Assessment of an Ionic Footbath (IonCleanse): Testing Its Ability to Remove Potentially Toxic Elements from the Body." *Journal of Environmental and Public Health* 2012: 258968. https://doi.org/10.1155/2012/258968.

Kern, Janet K., Madhukar H. Trivedi, Carolyn R. Garver, Bruce D. Grannemann, Alonzo A. Andrews, Jayshree S. Savla, Danny G. Johnson, Jyutika A. Mehta, and Jennifer L. Schroeder. "The Pattern of Sensory Processing Abnormalities in Autism." *Autism* 10, no. 5 (September 2006): 480–94. https://doi.org/10.1177/1362361306066564.

Kim, Hyun Uk. "Autism Across Cultures: Rethinking Autism." *Disability & Society* 27, no. 4 (2012): 535–45. https://doi.org/10.1080/09687599.2012.659463.

King, Marissa, and Peter Bearman. "Diagnostic Change and the Increased Prevalence of Autism." *International Journal of Epidemiology* 38, no. 5 (October 2009): 1224–34. https://doi.org/10.1093/ije/dyp261.

Kirkland, Anna. "The Legitimacy of Vaccine Critics: What Is Left After the Autism Hypothesis?" *Journal of Health Politics, Policy and Law* 37, no. 1 (February 2012): 69–97. https://doi.org/10.1215/03616878-1496020.

Klandermans, Bert. "Mobilization and Participation: Social-Psychological Expansions of Resource Mobilization Theory." *American Sociological Review* 59, no. 5 (1984): 583–600. https://doi.org/10.2307/2095417.

Klawiter, Maren. *The Biopolitics of Breast Cancer: Changing Cultures of Disease and Activism*. Minneapolis: University of Minnesota Press, 2008.

Klawiter, Maren. "Breast Cancer in Two Regimes: The Impact of Social Movements on Illness Experience." *Sociology of Health & Illness* 26, no. 6 (2004): 845–74. https://doi.org/10.1111/j.1467-9566.2004.421_1.x.

Kupferstein, Henny. "Evidence of Increased PTSD Symptoms in Autistics Exposed to Applied Behavior Analysis." *Advances in Autism* 4, no. 1 (2018): 19–29. https://doi.org/10.1108/AIA-08-2017-0016.

Kushak, Rafail I., Timothy M. Buie, Katherine F. Murray, David S. Newburg, Ceng Chen, Eirini Nestoridi, and Harland S. Winter. "Evaluation of Intestinal Function in Children with Autism and Gastrointestinal Symptoms." *Journal of Pediatric Gastroenterology and Nutrition* 62, no. 5 (2016): 687–91. https://doi.org/10.1097/mpg.0000000000001174.

Lai, Meng-Chuan, and Simon Baron-Cohen. "Identifying the Lost Generation of Adults with Autism Spectrum Conditions." *Lancet Psychiatry* 2, no. 11 (November 2015): 1013–27. https://doi.org/10.1016/s2215-0366(15)00277-1.

Lai, Meng-Chuan, Caroline Kassee, Richard Besney, Sarah Bonato, Laura Hull, William Mandy, Peter Szatmari, and Stephanie H. Ameis. "Prevalence of Co-occurring Mental Health Diagnoses in the Autism Population:

A Systematic Review and Meta-Analysis." *Lancet Psychiatry* 6, no. 10 (October 2019): 819–29. https://doi.org/10.1016/s2215-0366(19)30289-5.

Lai, Meng-Chuan, Michael V. Lombardo, Bonnie Auyeung, Bhismadev Chakrabarti, and Simon Baron-Cohen. "Sex/Gender Differences and Autism: Setting the Scene for Future Research." *Journal of the American Academy of Child & Adolescent Psychiatry* 54, no. 1 (January 2015): 11–24. https://doi.org/10.1016/j.jaac.2014.10.003.

Langan, Mary. "Parental Voices and Controversies in Autism." *Disability & Society* 26, no. 2 (February 2011): 193–205. https://doi.org/10.1080/0968759 9.2011.544059.

Lappé, Martine D. "The Maternal Body as Environment in Autism Science." *Social Studies of Science* 6, no. 4 (October 2016): 675–700. https://doi .org/10.1177/0306312716659372.

Lappé, Martine D. "Taking Care: Anticipation, Extraction and the Politics of Temporality in Autism Science." *BioSocieties* 9, no. 3 (September 2014): 304–28. https://doi.org/10.1057/biosoc.2014.14.

Larson, Heidi J., Louis Z. Cooper, Juhani Eskola, Samuel L. Katz, and Scott Ratzan. "Addressing the Vaccine Confidence Gap." *Lancet* 378, no. 9790 (August 2011): 526–35. https://doi.org/10.1016/s0140-6736(11)60678-8.

Lavelle, Tara A., Milton C. Weinstein, Joseph P. Newhouse, Kerim Munir, Karen A. Kuhlthau, and Lisa A. Prosser. "Economic Burden of Childhood Autism Spectrum Disorders." *Pediatrics* 133, no. 3 (March 2014): e520–e529. https://doi.org/10.1542/peds.2013-0763.

Laxman, Daniel J., Julie Lounds Taylor, Leann S. DaWalt, Jan S. Greenberg, and Marsha R. Mailick. "Loss in Services Precedes High School Exit for Teens with Autism Spectrum Disorder: A Longitudinal Study." *Autism Research* 12, no. 6 (June 2019): 911–21. https://doi.org/10.1002/aur.2113.

Lee, Aiden, Joel Ruhter, Christie Peters, Nancy De Lew, and Benjamin D. Sommers. "National Uninsured Rate Reaches All-Time Low in Early 2022." Office of the Assistant Secretary for Planning and Evaluation. U.S. Department of Health and Human Services. August 2, 2022. https://aspe .hhs.gov/reports/2022-uninsurance-at-all-time-low.

Legault, Mylène, Jean-Nicolas Bourdon, and Pierre Poirier. "From Neurodiversity to Neurodivergence: The Role of Epistemic and Cognitive Marginalization." *Synthese* 199, no. 5 (2021): 12843–868. https://doi.org/10.1007 /s11229-021-03356-5.

Leiter, Valerie. *Their Time Has Come: Youth with Disabilities on the Cusp of Adulthood.* New Brunswick, NJ: Rutgers University Press, 2012.

Levey, Noam. "Sick and Struggling to Pay, 100 Million People in the US Live with Medical Debt." National Public Radio. June 16, 2022. https://www.npr.org/sections/health-shots/2022/06/16/1104679219/medical-bills-debt-investigation.

Lewis, Laura Foran. "A Mixed Methods Study of Barriers to Formal Diagnosis of Autism Spectrum Disorder in Adults." *Journal of Autism and Developmental Disorders* 47, no. 8 (August 2017): 2410–24. https://doi.org/10.1007/s10803-017-3168-3.

Lipstein, Ellen A., William B. Brinkman, Alexander G. Fiks, Kristin S. Hendrix, Jennifer Kryworuchko, Victoria A. Miller, Lisa A. Prosser, Wendy J. Ungar, and David Fox. "An Emerging Field of Research: Challenges in Pediatric Decision Making." *Medical Decision Making* 35, no. 3 (April 2015): 403–8. https://doi.org/10.1177/0272989X14546901.

Liu, Ka-Yuet, Marissa King, and Peter Bearman. "Social Influence and the Autism Epidemic." *American Journal of Sociology* 115, no. 5 (March 2010): 1387–434. https://doi.org/10.1086/651448.

Locke, Jill, Anne Olsen, Rukiya Wideman, Margaret Mary Downey, Mark Kretzmann, Connie Kasari, and David S. Mandell. "A Tangled Web: The Challenges of Implementing an Evidence-Based Social Engagement Intervention for Children with Autism in Urban Public School Settings." *Behavior Therapy* 46, no. 1 (2015): 54–67. https://doi.org/10.1016/j.beth.2014.05.001.

Lord, Catherine, Cory Shulman, and Pamela DiLavore. "Regression and Word Loss in Autistic Spectrum Disorders." *Journal of Child Psychology and Psychiatry* 45, no. 5 (July 2004): 936–55. https://doi.org/10.1111/j.1469-7610.2004.t01-1-00287.x.

Lovaas, O. Ivar. "Behavioral Treatment and Normal Education and Intellectual Functioning in Young Autistic Children." *Journal of Consulting and Clinical Psychology* 55 (February 1987): 3–9. https://doi.org/10.1037//0022-006X.55.1.3.

Lovaas, O. Ivar, and Tristram Smith. "Early and Intensive Behavioral Intervention in Autism." In *Evidence-Based Psychotherapies for Children and Adolescents*, edited by John R. Weisz and Alan E. Kazdin, 325–40. New York: Guilford, 2003.

Lowe, Maria. "'Sowing the Seeds of Discontent': Tougaloo College's Social Science Forums as a Prefigurative Movement Free Space, 1952–1964." *Journal of Black Studies* 39, no. 6 (July 2009): 865–87. https://doi.org/10.1177/0021934707305401.

Luterman, Sara. "The Biggest Autism Advocacy Group Is Still Failing Too Many Autistic People." *Washington Post*, February 14, 2020. https://www.washingtonpost.com/outlook/2020/02/14/biggest-autism-advocacy-group-is-still-failing-too-many-autistic-people/.

Lyons, Samantha, Shival Salgaonkar, and Gerard T. Flaherty. "International Stem Cell Tourism: A Critical Literature Review and Evidence-Based Recommendations." *International Health* 14, no. 2 (March 2022): 132–41. https://doi.org/10.1093/inthealth/ihab050.

MacKendrick, Norah, and Kate Cairns. "The Polluted Child and Maternal Responsibility in the US Environmental Health Movement." *Signs* 44, no. 2 (Winter 2019): 307–32. https://doi.org/10.1086/699340.

MacKendrick, Norah, and Lindsay M. Stevens. "'Taking Back a Little Bit of Control': Managing the Contaminated Body Through Consumption." *Sociological Forum* 31, no. 2 (June 2016): 310–29. https://doi.org/10.1111/socf.12245.

Maenner, Matthew J., Kelly A. Shaw, Jon Baio, Anita Washington, Mary Patrick, Monica DiRienzo, Deborah L. Christensen, Lisa D. Wiggins, Sydney Pettygrove, Jennifer G. Andrews, Maya Lopez, Allison Hudson, Thaer Baroud, Yvette Schwenk, Tiffany White, Cordelia Robinson Rosenberg, Li-Ching Lee, Rebecca A. Harrington, Margaret Huston, Amy Hewitt, Amy Esler, Jennifer Hall-Lande, Jenny N. Poynter, Libby Hallas-Muchow, John N. Constantino, Robert T. Fitzgerald, Walter Zahorodny, Josephine Shenouda, Julie L. Daniels, Zachary Warren, Alison Vehorn, Angelica Salinas, Maureen S. Durkin, and Patricia M. Dietz. "Prevalence of Autism Spectrum Disorder Among Children Aged 8 Years—Autism and Developmental Disabilities Monitoring Network, 11 Sites, United States, 2016." *MMWR Surveillance Summaries* 69, no. 4 (March 2020): 1–12. https://doi.org/10.15585/mmwr.ss6904a1.

Maenner, Matthew J., Zachary Warren, Ashley Robinson Williams, Esther Amoakohene, Amanda V. Bakian, Deborah A. Bilder, Maureen S. Durkin, Robert T. Fitzgerald, Sarah M. Furnier, Michelle M. Hughes, Christine M. Ladd-Acosta, Dedria McArthur, Elise T. Pas, Angelica Salinas, Alison

Vehorn, Susan Williams, Amy Esler, Andrea Grzybowski, Jennifer Hall-Lande, Ruby H. N. Nguyen, Karen Pierce, Walter Zahorodny, Allison Hudson, Libby Hallas, Kristen Clancy Mancilla, Mary Patrick, Josephine Shenouda, Kate Sidwell, Monica DiRienzo, Johanna Gutierrez, Margaret H. Spivey, Maya Lopez, Sydney Pettygrove, Yvette D. Schwenk, Anita Washington, and Kelly A. Shaw. "Prevalence and Characteristics of Autism Spectrum Disorder Among Children Aged 8 Years—Autism and Developmental Disabilities Monitoring Network, 11 Sites, United States, 2020." *MMWR Surveillance Summaries* 72, no. 2 (March 2023): 1–14. https://doi.org/10.15585/mmwr.ss7011a1.

Makrygianni, Maria K., Angeliki Gena, Sofia Katoudi, and Petros Galanis. "The Effectiveness of Applied Behavior Analytic Interventions for Children with Autism Spectrum Disorder: A Meta-Analytic Study." *Research in Autism Spectrum Disorders* 51 (July 2018): 18–31. https://doi.org/10.1016/j.rasd.2018.03.006.

Malik-Soni, Natasha, Andrew Shaker, Helen Luck, Anne E. Mullin, Ryan E. Wiley, M. E. Suzanne Lewis, Joaquin Fuentes, and Thomas W. Frazier. "Tackling Healthcare Access Barriers for Individuals with Autism from Diagnosis to Adulthood." *Pediatric Research* 91, no. 5 (April 2022): 1028–35. https://doi.org/10.1038/s41390-021-01465-y.

Mandell, David S., Maytali M. Novak, and Cynthia D. Zubritsky. "Factors Associated with Age of Diagnosis Among Children with Autism Spectrum Disorders." *Pediatrics* 116, no. 6 (December 2005): 1480–86. https://doi.org/10.1542/peds.2005-0185.

Mannion, Arlene, and Geraldine Leader. "Comorbidity in Autism Spectrum Disorder: A Literature Review." *Research in Autism Spectrum Disorders* 7, no. 12 (December 2013): 1595–616. https://doi.org/10.1016/j.rasd.2013.09.006.

Markram, Kamila, and Henry Markram. "The Intense World Theory—A Unifying Theory of the Neurobiology of Autism." *Frontiers in Human Neuroscience* 4 (2010): 224. https://doi.org/10.3389/fnhum.2010.00224.

Matin, Behzad Karami, Sarah Byford, Shahin Soltani, Ali Kazemi-Karyani, Zahra Atafar, Ehsan Zereshki, Moslem Soofi, Satar Rezaei, Shiva Tolouei Rakhshan, and Parvin Jahangiri. "Contributing Factors to Healthcare Costs in Individuals with Autism Spectrum Disorder: A Systematic Review." *BMC Health Services Research* 22, no. 1 (May 2022): 1–20. https://doi.org/10.1186/s12913-022-07932-4.

Matson, Johnny L., Nicole C. Turygin, Jennifer Beighley, Robert Rieske, Kimberly Tureck, and Michael L. Matson. "Applied Behavior Analysis in Autism Spectrum Disorders: Recent Developments, Strengths, and Pitfalls." *Research in Autism Spectrum Disorders* 6, no. 1 (January–March 2012): 144–50. https://doi.org/10.1016/j.rasd.2011.03.014.

McAdam, Doug. "Recruitment to High-Risk Activism: The Case of Freedom Summer." *American Journal of Sociology* 92, no. 1 (July 1986): 64–90. http://www.jstor.org/stable/2779717.

McCann, Joanne, and Sue Peppé. "Prosody in Autism Spectrum Disorders: A Critical Review." *International Journal of Language & Communication Disorders* 38, no. 4 (October–December 2003): 325–50. https://doi.org/10.1080/1368282031000154204.

McCormick, Sabrina. "From 'Politico-Scientists' to Democratizing Science Movements: The Changing Climate of Citizens and Science." *Organization & Environment* 22, no. 1 (April 2009): 34–51. https://doi.org/10.1177/1086026609333419.

McCoy, Matthew S., Emily Y. Liu, Amy S. F. Lutz, and Dominic Sisti. "Ethical Advocacy across the Autism Spectrum: Beyond Partial Representation." *American Journal of Bioethics* 20, no. 4 (May 2020): 13–24. https://doi.org/10.1080/15265161.2020.1730482.

Melucci, Alberto. "The Process of Collective Identity." In *Social Movements and Culture*, edited by Hank Johnston and Bert Klandermans, 41–63. Minneapolis: University of Minnesota Press, 1995.

Miller, Michael E. "The Mysterious Death of a Doctor Who Peddled Autism 'Cures' to Thousands." *Washington Post*, July 16, 2015. https://www.washingtonpost.com/news/morning-mix/wp/2015/07/16/the-mysterious-death-of-a-doctor-who-peddled-autism-cures-to-thousands/.

Modabbernia, Amirhossein, Eva Velthorst, and Abraham Reichenberg. "Environmental Risk Factors for Autism: An Evidence-Based Review of Systematic Reviews and Meta-Analyses." *Molecular Autism* 8 (March 2017): 13. https://doi.org/10.1186/s13229-017-0121-4.

Mueller, Carlyn O., Anjali J. Forber-Pratt, and Julie Sriken. "Disability: Missing from the Conversation of Violence." *Journal of Social Issues* 75, no. 3 (September 2019): 707–25. https://doi.org/10.1111/josi.12339.

Murphy, Michelle. *Sick Building Syndrome and the Problem of Uncertainty: Environmental Politics, Technoscience, and Women Workers*. Durham, NC: Duke University Press, 2006.

Nadesan, Majia Holmer. *Constructing Autism: Unravelling the 'Truth' and Understanding the Social*. London: Routledge, 2005.

National Center for Education Statistics. *120 Years of American Education: A Statistical Portrait*. U.S. Department of Education. https://nces.ed.gov/pubs93/93442.pdf.

National Conference of State Legislatures. "Autism and Insurance Coverage State Laws." Last modified August 24, 2021. https://www.ncsl.org/research/health/autism-and-insurance-coverage-state-laws.aspx.

National Institute of Biomedical Imaging and Bioengineering. "Nuclear Medicine." U.S. Department of Health and Human Services. Last modified July 2016. https://www.nibib.nih.gov/science-education/science-topics/nuclear-medicine#1006.

National Library of Medicine. "MTHFR Gene." MedLine Plus. Last modified October 1, 2019. https://ghr.nlm.nih.gov/gene/MTHFR.

Navon, Daniel, and Gil Eyal. "Looping Genomes: Diagnostic Change and the Genetic Makeup of the Autism Population." *American Journal of Sociology* 121, no. 5 (March 2016): 1416–71. https://doi.org/10.1086/684201.

Ne'eman, Ari. "An Urgent Call to Action: Tell NYU Child Study Center to Abandon Stereotypes Against People with Disabilities." Autistic Self Advocacy Network. December 8, 2007. http://autisticadvocacy.org/2007/12/tell-nyu-child-study-center-to-abandon-stereotypes/.

Newman, Harmony D., and Laura M. Carpenter. "Embodiment Without Bodies? Analysis of Embodiment in US-based Pro-Breastfeeding and Anti-Male Circumcision Movements." *Sociology of Health and Illness* 36, no. 5 (June 2014): 639–54. https://doi.org/10.1111/1467-9566.12095.

Niño, Michael, Casey Harris, Grant Drawve, and Kevin M. Fitzpatrick. "Race and Ethnicity, Gender, and Age on Perceived Threats and Fear of COVID-19: Evidence from Two National Data Sources." *SSM-Population Health* 13 (March 2021): 100717. https://doi.org/10.1016/j.ssmph.2020.100717.

Nord, Derek K., Roger J. Stancliffe, Kelly Nye-Lengerman, and Amy S. Hewitt. "Employment in the Community for People with and Without Autism: A Comparative Analysis." *Research in Autism Spectrum Disorders* 24 (April 2016): 11–16. https://doi.org/10.1016/j.rasd.2015.12.013.

Norrelgen, Fritjof, Elisabeth Fernell, Mats Eriksson, Åsa Hedvall, Clara Persson, Maria Sjölin, Christopher Gillberg, and Liselotte Kjellmer. "Children with Autism Spectrum Disorders Who Do Not Develop Phrase

Speech in the Preschool Years." *Autism* 19, no. 8 (November 2015): 934–43. https://doi.org/10.1177/1362361314556782.

Offit, Paul. *Autism's False Prophets: Bad Science, Risky Medicine, and the Search for a Cure*. New York: Columbia University Press, 2010.

Okoro, Catherine A., NaTasha D. Hollis, Alissa C. Cyrus, and Shannon Griffin-Blake. "Prevalence of Disabilities and Health Care Access by Disability Status and Type Among Adults—United States, 2016." *Morbidity and Mortality Weekly Report* 67, no. 32 (August 2018): 882–87. https://doi.org/10.15585/mmwr.mm6732a3.

O'Reilly, Michelle, Tom Muskett, Khalid Karim, and Jessica N. Lester. "Parents' Constructions of Normality and Pathology in Child Mental Health Assessments." *Sociology of Health & Illness* 42, no. 3 (March 2020): 544–64. https://doi.org/10.1111/1467-9566.13030.

Oreskes, Naomi, and Erik Conway. *Merchants of Doubt: How a Handful of Scientists Obscured the Truth on Issues from Tobacco Smoke to Global Warming*. London: Bloomsbury, 2010.

Ortega, Francisco. "The Cerebral Subject and the Challenge of Neurodiversity." *BioSocieties* 4, no. 4 (December 2009): 425–45. https://doi.org/10.1017/S1745855209990287.

Oswald, Donald P., and Neil A. Sonenklar. "Medication Use Among Children with Autism Spectrum Disorders." *Journal of Child and Adolescent Psychopharmacology* 17, no. 3 (June 2007): 348–55. https://doi.org/10.1089/cap.2006.17303.

Owen-Smith, Ashli A., Stephen Bent, Frances L. Lynch, Karen J. Coleman, Vincent M. Yau, Kathryn A. Pearson, Maria L. Massolo, Virginia Quinn, and Lisa A. Croen. "Prevalence and Predictors of Complementary and Alternative Medicine Use in a Large Insured Sample of Children with Autism Spectrum Disorders." *Research in Autism Spectrum Disorders* 17 (September 2015): 40–51. https://doi.org/10.1016/j.rasd.2015.05.002.

Pangborn, Jon, and Sidney MacDonald Baker. *Autism: Effective Biomedical Treatments*. San Diego, CA: Autism Research Institute, 2005.

Parish, Susan L., Marsha Mailick Seltzer, Jan S. Greenberg, and Frank Floyd. "Economic Implications of Caregiving at Midlife: Comparing Parents with and Without Children Who Have Developmental Disabilities." *Mental Retardation* 42, no. 6 (December 2004): 413–26. https://pubmed.ncbi.nlm.nih.gov/15516174/.

Parish, Susan L., Roderick A. Rose, Michal Grinstein-Weiss, Erica L. Richman, and Megan E. Andrews. "Material Hardship in US Families Raising Children with Disabilities." *Exceptional Children* 75, no. 1 (2008): 71–92. https://doi.org/10.1177/001440290807500104.

Parish, Susan L., Kathleen C. Thomas, Christianna S. Williams, and Morgan K. Crossman. "Autism and Families' Financial Burden: The Association with Health Insurance Coverage." *American Journal on Intellectual and Developmental Disabilities* 120, no. 2 (2015): 166–75. https://doi.org/10.1352/1944-7558-120.2.166.

Park, Madison. "Medical Journal Retracts Study Linking Autism to Vaccine." CNN. Last modified February 2, 2010. http://www.cnn.com/2010/HEALTH/02/02/lancet.retraction.autism/index.html.

Pecchenino, Nicki. "Guest Opinion: Death by Legislature." *Santa Cruz Sentinel News*, March 9, 2012. http://www.santacruzsentinel.com/general-news/20120309/guest-opinion-death-by-legislature.

Perrin, James M., Daniel L. Coury, Susan L. Hyman, Lynn Cole, Ann M. Reynolds, and Traci Clemons. "Complementary and Alternative Medicine Use in a Large Pediatric Autism Sample." *Pediatrics* 130, suppl 2 (November 2012): S77–S82. https://doi.org/10.1542/peds.2012-0900E.

Peters-Scheffer, Nienke, Robert Didden, Hubert Korzilius, and Peter Sturmey. "A Meta-Analytic Study on the Effectiveness of Comprehensive ABA-Based Early Intervention Programs for Children with Autism Spectrum Disorders." *Research in Autism Spectrum Disorders* 5, no. 1 (January–March 2011): 60–69. https://doi.org/10.1016/j.rasd.2010.03.011.

Petryna, Adriana. "Biological Citizenship: The Science and Politics of Chernobyl-Exposed Populations." *Osiris* 19 (2004): 250–65. https://www.jstor.org/stable/3655243.

Pierson, Brendan. "D.C. Circuit Overturns FDA Ban on Shock Device for Disabled Students." Reuters, July 7, 2021. https://www.reuters.com/legal/litigation/dc-circuit-overturns-fda-ban-shock-device-disabled-students-2021-07-06/.

Pitts, Victoria. "Illness and Internet Empowerment: Writing and Reading Breast Cancer in Cyberspace." *Health (London)* 8, no. 1 (January 2004): 33–59. https://doi.org/10.1177/1363459304038794.

Plotkin, Stanley, Jeffrey S. Gerber, and Paul A. Offit. "Vaccines and Autism: A Tale of Shifting Hypotheses." *Clinical Infectious Diseases* 48, no. 4 (February 2009): 456–61. https://doi.org/10.1086/596476.

Polletta, Francesca. "'Free Spaces' in Collective Action." *Theory and Society* 28, no. 1 (February 1999): 1–38. https://www.jstor.org/stable/3108504.

Rabba, Aspasia Stacey, Cheryl Dissanayake, and Josephine Barbaro. "Parents' Experiences of an Early Autism Diagnosis: Insights Into Their Needs." *Research in Autism Spectrum Disorders* 66 (October 2019): 101415. https://doi.org/10.1016/j.rasd.2019.101415.

Randles, Jennifer. "'Willing to Do Anything for My Kids': Inventive Mothering, Diapers, and the Inequalities of Carework." *American Sociological Review* 86, no. 1 (2021): 35–59. https://doi.org/10.1177/0003122420977480.

Reich, Jennifer A. *Calling the Shots: Why Parents Reject Vaccines.* New York: New York University Press, 2016.

Reich, Jennifer A. "Neoliberal Mothering and Vaccine Refusal: Imagined Gated Communities and the Privilege of Choice." *Gender & Society* 28, no. 5 (October 2014): 679–704. https://doi.org/10.1177/0891243214532711.

Reich, Jennifer A. "Vaccine Refusal and Pharmaceutical Acquiescence: Parental Control and Ambivalence in Managing Children's Health." *American Sociological Review* 85, no. 1 (2020): 106–27. https://doi.org/10.1177/0003122419899604.

Reich, Jennifer A. "'We Are Fierce, Independent Thinkers and Intelligent': Social Capital and Stigma Management Among Mothers Who Refuse Vaccines." *Social Science & Medicine* 257 (July 2020): 112015. https://doi.org/10.1016/j.socscimed.2018.10.027.

Reventlow, Susanne Dalsgaard, Lotte Hvas, and Kirsti Malterud. "Making the Invisible Body Visible: Bone Scans, Osteoporosis and Women's Bodily Experiences." *Social Science & Medicine* 62, no. 11 (June 2006): 2720–31. https://doi.org/10.1016/j.socscimed.2005.11.009.

Rimland, Bernard. "The Autism Epidemic, Vaccinations, and Mercury." *Journal of Nutritional & Environmental Medicine* 10, no. 4 (2000): 261–66. https://doi.org/10.1080/13590840020013248.

Rimland, Bernard. "Controversies in the Treatment of Autistic Children: Vitamin and Drug Therapy." *Journal of Child Neurology* 3, no. 1_suppl (1988): S68–S72. https://doi.org/10.1177/0883073888003001S13.

Rimland, Bernard. "Do Children's Shots Invite Autism?" *Los Angeles Times*, April 26, 2000, A13. https://www.latimes.com/archives/la-xpm-2000-apr-26-me-23718-story.html.

Rimland, Bernard, and Stephen M. Edelson. "Autism Treatment Evaluation Checklist." Autism Research Institute. https://autism.org/autism-treatment-evaluation-checklist/.

Ritvo, Edward R., B. J. Freeman, Carmen Pingree, Anne Mason-Brothers, Lynn Jorde, William R. Jenson, William M. McMahon, Brent R. Peterson, Amy Mo, and Anne Ritvo. "The UCLA-University of Utah Epidemiological Survey of Autism: Prevalence." *American Journal of Psychiatry* 146, no. 2 (February 1989): 194–99. https://doi.org/10.1176/ajp.146.2.194.

Roberts, Dorothy. *Shattered Bonds: The Color of Child Welfare.* New York: Civitas, 2009.

Rodriguez, Joe, and Lisa Fernandez. "Parents of Autistic Children Speak Out on Sunnyvale Murder-Suicide." *Mercury News*, March 8, 2012. Last modified August 13, 2016. https://www.mercurynews.com/2012/03/08/parents -of-autistic-children-speak-out-on-sunnyvale-murder-suicide/.

Rogers, Sally J., and Laurie A. Vismara. "Evidence-Based Comprehensive Treatments for Early Autism." *Journal of Clinical Child & Adolescent Psychology* 37, no. 1 (January 2008): 8–38. https://doi.org/10.1080/15374410701817808.

Rose, Nikolas, and Carlos Novas. "Biological Citizenship." In *Global Assemblages: Technology, Politics, and Ethics as Anthropological Problems*, edited by Aihwa Ong and Stephen J. Collier, 439–63. Hoboken, NJ: Blackwell, 2005. https://doi.org/10.1002/9780470696569.ch23.

Ruggiero, Marco, Heinz Reinwald, and Stefania Pacini. "Is Chondroitin Sulfate Responsible for the Biological Effects Attributed to the GC Protein-Derived Macrophage Activating Factor (GcMAF)?" *Medical Hypotheses* 94 (September 2016): 126–31. https://doi.org/10.1016/j.mehy .2016.07.012.

Russell, Ginny, and Susan Kelly. "Looking Beyond Risk: A Study of Lay Epidemiology of Childhood Disorders." *Health, Risk & Society* 13, no. 2 (2011): 129–45. https://doi.org/10.1080/13698575.2010.515738.

Sacks, Oliver. "An Anthropologist on Mars." *New Yorker*, December 27, 1993.

Sampson, Zachary T. "After 16-Month Battle, Justina Pelletier Returns Home." *Boston Globe*, June 19, 2014. https://www.bostonglobe.com/metro /2014/06/18/justina-pelletier-returns-her-family-home-connecticut-ending -medical-and-legal-odyssey/ON7QhGURgprYZoVS7uuxeL/story.html.

Sathe, Nila, Jeffrey C. Andrews, Melissa L. McPheeters, and Zachary E. Warren. "Nutritional and Dietary Interventions for Autism Spectrum Disorder: A Systematic Review." *Pediatrics* 139, no. 6 (June 2017): e20170346. https://doi.org/10.1542/peds.2017-0346.

Schwartz, Jason L., and Arthur L. Caplan. "Vaccination Refusal: Ethics, Individual Rights, and the Common Good." *Primary Care: Clinics in*

Office Practice 38, no. 4 (December 2011): 717–28. https://doi.org/10.1016/j .pop.2011.07.009v.

Scotch, Richard K. "Politics and Policy in the History of the Disability Rights Movement." *Milbank Quarterly* 67, suppl 2 (1989): 380–400. https://doi.org /10.2307/3350150.

Scott, Ellen K. "'I Feel as If I Am the One Who Is Disabled': The Emotional Impact of Changed Employment Trajectories of Mothers Caring for Children with Disabilities." *Gender & Society* 24, no. 5 (September 2010): 672–96. https://doi.org/10.1177/0891243210382531.

Shapiro, Theodore. "Autism and the Psychoanalyst." *Psychoanalytic Inquiry* 20, no. 5 (2000): 648–59. https://doi.org/10.1080/07351692009348914.

Shattuck, Paul T., Anne M. Roux, Laura E. Hudson, Julie Lounds Taylor, Matthew J. Maenner, and Jean-François Trani. "Services for Adults with an Autism Spectrum Disorder." *Canadian Journal of Psychiatry* 57, no. 5 (2012): 284–91. https://doi.org/10.1177/070674371205700503.

Shelton, Deborah L. "Autism Doctor Loses License in Illinois, Missouri." *Chicago Tribune*, November 5, 2012. https://www.chicagotribune.com/news /ct-xpm-2012-11-05-ct-met-autism-doctor-20121106-story.html.

Shelton, Janie F., Estella M. Geraghty, Daniel J. Tancredi, Lora D. Delwiche, Rebecca J. Schmidt, Beate Ritz, Robin L. Hansen, and Irva Hertz-Picciotto. "Neurodevelopmental Disorders and Prenatal Residential Proximity to Agricultural Pesticides: The CHARGE Study." *Environmental Health Perspectives* 122, no. 10 (October 2014): 1103–9. https://doi.org/10.1289/ehp .1307044.

Shostak, Sara, Peter Conrad, and Allan V. Horwitz. "Sequencing and Its Consequences: Path Dependence and the Relationships Between Genetics and Medicalization." *American Journal of Sociology* 114, no. S1 (2008): S287–S316. https://doi.org/10.1086/595570.

Siddiqui, Mariam, Daniel A. Salmon, and Saad B. Omer. "Epidemiology of Vaccine Hesitancy in the United States." *Human Vaccines & Immunotherapeutics* 9, no. 12 (December 2013): 2643–48. https://doi.org/10.4161/hv.27243.

Sikich, Linmarie, Alexander Kolevzon, Bryan H. King, Christopher J. McDougle, Kevin B. Sanders, Soo-Jeong Kim, Marina Spanos, Tara Chandrasekhar, M. D. Pilar Trelles, Carol M. Rockhill, Michelle L. Palumbo, Allyson Witters Cundiff, Alicia Montgomery, Paige Siper, Mendy Minjarez, Lisa A. Nowinski, Sarah Marler, Lauren C. Shuffrey, Cheryl Alderman, Jordana

Weissman, Brooke Zappone, Jennifer E. Mullett, Hope Crosson, Natalie Hong, Stephen K. Siecinski, Stephanie N. Giamberardino, Sheng Luo, Lilin She, Manjushri Bhapkar, Russell Dean, Abby Scheer, Jacqueline L. Johnson, Simon G. Gregory, and Jeremy Veenstra-VanderWeele. "Intranasal Oxytocin in Children and Adolescents with Autism Spectrum Disorder." *New England Journal of Medicine* 385, no. 16 (2021): 1462–73. https://doi.org/10.1056/NEJMoa2103583.

Silberman, Steve. *NeuroTribes: The Legacy of Autism and the Future of Neurodiversity.* New York: Avery, 2015.

Silverman, Chloe. *Understanding Autism: Parents, Doctors, and the History of a Disorder.* Princeton, NJ: Princeton University Press, 2011.

Silverman, Chloe, and Jeffrey P. Brosco. "Understanding Autism: Parents and Pediatricians in Historical Perspective." *Archives of Pediatrics & Adolescent Medicine* 161, no. 4 (April 2007): 392–98. https://doi.org/10.1001/archpedi.161.4.392.

Simi, Pete, and Robert Futrell. "Cyberculture and the Endurance of White Power Activism." *Journal of Political and Military Sociology* 34, no. 1 (Summer 2006): 115–42. https://www.jstor.org/stable/45294188.

Simon, Bernd, and Bert Klandermans. "Politicized Collective Identity: A Social Psychological Analysis." *American Psychologist* 56, no. 4 (April 2001): 319–31. https://doi.org/10.1037/0003-066X.56.4.319.

Sinclair, Jim. "Don't Mourn for Us." *Our Voice* 1, no. 3 (1993).

Sinclair, Jim. "History of ANI." Autism Network International. January 2005. http://www.autreat.com/History_of_ANI.html.

Singh, Jennifer S. *Multiple Autisms: Spectrums of Advocacy and Genomic Science.* Minneapolis: University of Minnesota Press, 2016.

Singh, Jennifer S., and Garrett Bunyak. "Autism Disparities: A Systematic Review and Meta-Ethnography of Qualitative Research." *Qualitative Health Research* 29, no. 6 (May 2019): 796–808. https://doi.org/10.1177/1049732318808245.

Smith, Isaac C., Brian Reichow, and Fred R. Volkmar. "The Effects of DSM-5 Criteria on Number of Individuals Diagnosed with Autism Spectrum Disorder: A Systematic Review." *Journal of Autism and Developmental Disorders* 45, no. 8 (2015): 2541–52. https://doi.org/10.1007/s10803-015-2423-8.

Smith, Kathryn A., Jean-G. Gehricke, Suzannah Iadarola, Audrey Wolfe, and Karen A. Kuhlthau. "Disparities in Service Use Among Children with Autism: A Systematic Review." *Pediatrics* 145, suppl 1 (April 2020): S35–S46. https://doi.org/10.1542/peds.2019-1895g.

Smith, Tara C. "Vaccine Rejection and Hesitancy: A Review and Call to Action." *Open Forum Infectious Diseases* 4, no. 3 (Summer 2017). https://doi.org/10.1093/ofid/ofx146.

Social Security Administration. "Understanding Supplemental Security Income SSI Benefits—2023 Edition." Accessed March 27, 2023. https://www.ssa.gov/ssi/text-benefits-ussi.htm.

Sousa, Amy C. "From Refrigerator Mothers to Warrior-Heroes: The Cultural Identity Transformation of Mothers Raising Children with Intellectual Disabilities." *Symbolic Interaction* 34, no. 2 (Spring 2011): 220–43. https://doi.org/10.1525/si.2011.34.2.220.

Steinbrenner, Jessica R., Kara Hume, Samuel L. Odom, Kristi L. Morin, Sallie W. Nowell, Brianne Tomaszewski, Susan Szendrey, Nancy S. McIntyre, Serife Yücesoy-Özkan, and Melissa N. Savage. *Evidence-Based Practices for Children, Youth, and Young Adults with Autism.* Chapel Hill, NC: Frank Porter Graham Child Development Institute, 2020.

Stivers, Tanya. "Participating in Decisions About Treatment: Overt Parent Pressure for Antibiotic Medication in Pediatric Encounters." *Social Science & Medicine* 54, no. 7 (April 2002): 1111–30. https://doi.org/10.1016/S0277-9536(01)00085-5.

Strauss, Elissa. "Leading Vaccination Skeptic Dr. Bob Sears Is at Risk of Losing His Medical License." Slate, September 15, 2016. http://www.slate.com/blogs/xx_factor/2016/09/15/leading_vaccination_skeptic_dr_bob_sears_is_at_risk_of_losing_his_medical.html.

Strimbu, Kyle, and Jorge A. Tavel. "What Are Biomarkers?" *Current Opinion in HIV and AIDS* 5, no. 6 (November 2010): 463–66. https://doi.org/10.1097/COH.0b013e32833ed177.

Sweet, Paige L., and Danielle Giffort. "The Bad Expert." *Social Studies of Science* 51, no. 3 (2021): 313–38. https://doi.org/10.1177/0306312720970282.

Swidey, Neil, and Patricia Wen. "A Medical Collision with a Child in the Middle." *Boston Globe,* December 15, 2013. https://www.bostonglobe.com/metro/2013/12/15/justina/vnwzbbNdiodSD7WDTh6xZI/story.html.

Szasz, Andrew. *Shopping Our Way to Safety: How We Change from Protecting the Environment to Protecting Ourselves.* Minneapolis: University of Minnesota Press, 2007.

Tan, Catherine D. "Defending 'Snake Oil': The Preservation of Contentious Knowledge and Practices." *Social Studies of Science* 51, no. 4 (August 2021): 538–63. https://doi.org/10.1177/0306312721992543.

Tan, Catherine D. "'I'm a Normal Autistic Person, Not an Abnormal Neurotypical': Autism Spectrum Disorder Diagnosis as Biographical Illumination." *Social Science & Medicine* 197 (January 2018): 161–67. https://doi .org/10.1016/j.socscimed.2017.12.008.

Tan, Catherine D., and Gil Eyal. "'Two Opposite Ends of the World': The Management of Uncertainty in an Autism-Only School." *Journal of Contemporary Ethnography* 44, no. 1 (2015): 34–62. https://doi.org /10.1177/0891241613515000.

Tanne, Janice Hopkins. "US Needs Universal Access to Health Care, American College of Physicians Says." *BMJ* 335, no. 7632 (2007): 1228. https:// doi.org/10.1136/bmj.39423.499560.DB.

Taylor, Brent, Elizabeth Miller, CPaddy Farrington, Maria-Christina Petropoulos, Isabelle Favot-Mayaud, Jun Li, and Pauline A. Waight. "Autism and Measles, Mumps, and Rubella Vaccine: No Epidemiological Evidence for a Causal Association." *Lancet* 353, no. 9169 (June 1999): 2026–29. https://doi.org/10.1016/S0140-6736(99)01239-8.

Taylor, Verta. "Gender and Social Movements: Gender Processes in Women's Self-Help Movements." *Gender & Society* 13, no. 1 (February 1999): 8–33. https://doi.org/10.1177/089124399013001002.

Taylor, Verta, and Nancy E. Whittier. "Collective Identity in Social Movement Communities: Lesbian Feminist Mobilization." In *Frontiers in Social Movements Theory*, edited by Aldon D. Morris and Carol McClurg Mueller, 104–29. New Haven, CT: Yale University Press, 1992.

"Ten Hour Siege, a SWAT Team . . . and a TANK: How Police Dealt with Mother Who Refused to Give Her Child Medication." DailyMail.com. Last modified April 15, 2011. http://www.dailymail.co.uk/news/article-1377178 /SWAT-teams-10-hour-siege-mother-Maryanne-Godboldo-Detroit.html.

Thomas, Pauline, Walter Zahorodny, Bo Peng, Soyeon Kim, Nisha Jani, William Halperin, and Michael Brimacombe. "The Association of Autism Diagnosis with Socioeconomic Status." *Autism* 16, no. 2 (March 2012): 1–13. https://doi.org/10.1177/1362361311413397v.

Tomchek, Scott D., and Winnie Dunn. "Sensory Processing in Children with and Without Autism: A Comparative Study Using the Short Sensory

Profile." *American Journal of Occupational Therapy* 61, no. 2 (March–April 2007): 190–200. https://doi.org/10.5014/ajot.61.2.190.

Tsouderos, Trine. "'Miracle Drug' Called Junk Science." *Chicago Tribune*, May 21, 2009. https://www.chicagotribune.com/lifestyles/health/chi-autism -lupron-may21-story.html.

Tucker, Neely. "Daniel Amen Is the Most Popular Psychiatrist in America. To Most Researchers and Scientists, That's a Very Bad Thing." *Washington Post*, August 9, 2012. https://www.washingtonpost.com/lifestyle/magazine /daniel-amen-is-the-most-popular-psychiatrist-in-america-to-most -researchers-and-scientists-thats-a-very-bad-thing/2012/08/07/467ed52c -c540-11e1-8c16-5080b717c13e_story.html.

Tyson, Alec. "Republicans Remain Far Less Likely than Democrats to View COVID-19 as a Major Threat to Public Health." Pew Research Center. July 22, 2020. https://www.pewresearch.org/fact-tank/2020/07/22 /republicans-remain-far-less-likely-than-democrats-to-view-covid-19 -as-a-major-threat-to-public-health/.

Underman, Kelly, Paige L. Sweet, and Claire Laurier Decoteau. "Custodial Citizenship in the Omnibus Autism Proceeding." *Sociological Forum* 32, no. 3 (September 2017): 544–65. https://doi.org/10.1111/socf.12348.

U.S. Department of Labor. "Subminimum Wage." https://www.dol.gov/general /topic/wages/subminimumwage.

U.S. Environmental Protection Agency. "Biomonitoring—Lead." America's Children and the Environment (ACE). U.S. Environmental Protection Agency. Last modified June 29, 2022. https://www.epa.gov/americas childrenenvironment/biomonitoring-lead.

U.S. Food and Drug Administration. "Danger: Don't Drink Miracle Mineral Solution or Similar Products." Consumer Updates. Last modified August 12, 2019. https://www.fda.gov/consumers/consumer-updates/danger-dont -drink-miracle-mineral-solution-or-similar-products.

Vijaykumar, Santosh, Ricardo J. Wray, Trent Buskirk, Himakshi Piplani, Joya Banerjee, Michael Furdyk, and Reshma Pattni. "Youth, New Media, and HIV/AIDS: Determinants of Participation in an Online Health Social Movement." *Cyberpsychology, Behavior, and Social Networking* 17, no. 7 (July 2014): 488–95. https://doi.org/10.1089/cyber.2013.0124.

Viterna, Jocelyn S. "Pulled, Pushed, and Persuaded: Explaining Women's Mobilization Into the Salvadoran Guerrilla Army." *American Journal of Sociology* 112, no. 1 (July 2006): 1–45. https://doi.org/10.1086/502690.

Volk, Heather E., Tara Kerin, Fred Lurmann, Irva Hertz-Picciotto, Rob McConnell, and Daniel B. Campbell. "Autism Spectrum Disorder: Interaction of Air Pollution with the MET Receptor Tyrosine Kinase Gene." *Epidemiology* 25, no. 1 (January 2014): 44–47. https://doi.org/10.1097/ede .0000000000000030.

Volkmar, Fred R., Brian Reichow, and James McPartland. "Classification of Autism and Related Conditions: Progress, Challenges, and Opportunities." *Dialogues in Clinical Neuroscience* 14, no. 3 (2012): 229–37. https://doi .org/10.31887/DCNS.2012.14.3/fvolkmar.

Waggoner, Miranda R. "Motherhood Preconceived: The Emergence of the Preconception Health and Health Care Initiative." *Journal of Health Politics, Policy and Law* 38, no. 2 (2013): 345–71. https://doi.org/10.1215 /03616878-1966333.

Waggoner, Miranda R. *The Zero Trimester: Pre-Pregnancy Care and the Politics of Reproductive Risk.* Oakland: University of California Press, 2017.

Wakefield, A. J., S. H. Murch, A. Anthony, J. Linnell, D. M. Casson, M. Malik, M. Berelowitz, A. P. Dhillon, M. A. Thomson, P. Harvey, A. Valentine, S. E. Davies, and J. A. Walker-Smith. "Retracted: Ileal-Lymphoid-Nodular Hyperplasia, Non-Specific Colitis, and Pervasive Developmental Disorder in Children." *Lancet* 351, no. 9103 (February 1998): 637–41. https://doi .org/10.1016/S0140-6736(97)11096-0.

Walsh, Pat, Mayada Elsabbagh, Patrick Bolton, and Ilina Singh. "In Search of Biomarkers for Autism: Scientific, Social and Ethical Challenges." *Nature Reviews Neuroscience* 12, no. 10 (2011): 603–12. https://doi.org/10.1038/nrn3113.

Waltz, Mitzi. "Images and Narratives of Autism within Charity Discourses." *Disability & Society* 27, no. 2 (2012): 219–33. https://doi.org/10.1080/09687599 .2012.631796.

Weir, Elizabeth, Carrie Allison, and Simon Baron-Cohen. "Autistic Adults Have Poorer Quality Healthcare and Worse Health Based on Self-Report Data." *Molecular Autism* 13, no. 1 (2022): 23. https://doi.org/10.1186/s13229 -022-00501-w.

Whalley, Ben, and Michael E. Hyland. "Placebo by Proxy: The Effect of Parents' Beliefs on Therapy for Children's Temper Tantrums." *Journal of Behavioral Medicine* 36, no. 4 (2013): 341–46. https://doi.org/10.1007/s10865-012-9429-x.

White, Martha C. "Planning for Your Retirement, and for a Child's Special Needs, All at Once." *New York Times,* August 27, 2022. https://www .nytimes.com/2022/08/27/business/retirement-special-needs.html.

Whiteman, Honor. "Stem Cell Therapy: Is the US Missing a Trick?" Medical News Today. Last modified February 25, 2016. https://www.medicalnews today.com/articles/306974.

Wilkenfeld, Daniel A., and Allison M. McCarthy. "Ethical Concerns with Applied Behavior Analysis for Autism Spectrum Disorder." *Kennedy Institute of Ethics Journal* 30, no. 1 (2020): 31–69. https://doi.org/10.1353 /ken.2020.0000.

Willingham, Emily. "Conspiracy Fears Dominate Life and Death of Autism Doctor Bradstreet." *Forbes*, July 20, 2015. https://www.forbes.com/sites /emilywillingham/2015/07/20/conspiracy-fears-dominate-life-and-death -of-autism-doctor-bradstreet/#31af721e7f6f.

Willingham, Emily. "Here's Why Authorities Searched the Offices of Controversial Autism Doctor Bradstreet." *Forbes*, July 9, 2015. https://www .forbes.com/sites/emilywillingham/2015/07/09/government-search -of-autism-doctor-bradstreets-office-related-to-experimental-autism -treatment/?sh=65002b52b07e.

Winter, Jerry Alan. "The Development of the Disability Rights Movement as a Social Problem Solver." *Disability Studies Quarterly* 23, no. 1 (Winter 2003): 33–61. https://doi.org/10.18061/dsq.v23i1.399.

Wood, Robert A. "Allergic Reactions to Vaccines." *Pediatric Allergy and Immunology* 24, no. 6 (September 2013): 521–26. https://doi.org/10.1111/pai.12102.

World Health Organization. "Ten Threats to Global Health in 2019." https:// www.who.int/news-room/spotlight/ten-threats-to-global-health-in-2019.

Yergeau, Melanie. "Clinically Significant Disturbance: On Theorists Who Theorize Theory of Mind." *Disability Studies Quarterly* 33, no. 4 (2013). https://doi.org/10.18061/dsq.v33i4.3876.

Zola, Irving Kenneth. "Toward the Necessary Universalizing of a Disability Policy." *Milbank Quarterly* 67, suppl 2 pt 2 (1989): 401–28. https://doi .org/10.1111/j.1468-0009.2005.00436.x.

INDEX

primobiotics, 180

probation, 197

probiotics, 81, 102, 170

prognosis, 99

pronoun, *275–76, 277–78*

prosopagnosia, 121

prostate cancer, 26, 197

protests, 215

Prozac, 186

pseudoscience, 219

psychiatry, 168

psychoanalytical framework, 20

psychogenic hypothesis, 21

psychological evaluation, 130

psychotherapy, 168

puberty, 26, 186–87; early, 197

public: accommodations, 14; attention, 197; FAPE, 255; health, 8, 64; reactions of, xi; resistance, 30

punishment, treatment and, 76

pure sciences, 226

puzzle piece, 10

quality of life, 209

race, *273, 275–76, 277–78*; inequities, 110

racism, 153–54

Rainman, ix, 55

randomized controlled trials, 60

reciprocal altruism, 137

recovery: alternative biomedicine, 78–80; autism, 14; hope for, 88, 160, 222; as moral obligation, 80–81; progression, 195; prospect

of, 101; pursuit of, 194; search for, 85; solutions, reimagining of, 76–86; tools and strategies of, 156–96

referral, delayed, 110

"refrigerator mothers," 20–21, 63–70

regression, 59, 188

Reich, Jennifer, 239

relationships: interpersonal, 92; with parents, 206; social, 50, 111; vaccine-autism, 23, 45, 60, 163, 224

repetitive behavior, 8, 121, 156

representation, 11, 16; of autistic people, 42; criticism, resistance of, 215–17; disability, 198; of full autism spectrum, 212, 217; partial, 155, 210; scientific misrepresentation, 24

research, 58, 204; animal behavior, 44, 72; ARI, 22–23; articles, 133; by autistic people, 144; boundary work, 199; clinical, 40; collaborations, 22; for cure, 214; evidence-based, 78, 85, 160, 231; funding for, 153, 163, 254; genetic, 12, 22, 46; genomic, 22, 163; National Alliance for Autism Research, 22; peer-reviewed, 78, 223; on potential causes and interventions, 89; scientific, 14, 131; for treatments, 23; Wakefield, Andrew, 157

researchers, 198

responsibility: individual, 69; parental, 81

GPSR Authorized Representative: Easy Access System Europe, Mustamäe tee
50, 10621 Tallinn, Estonia, gpsr.requests@easproject.com

www.ingramcontent.com/pod-product-compliance
Lightning Source LLC
Chambersburg PA
CBHW021845020426
42334CB00013B/191